Liber

Liberalism
A Counter-History

DOMENICO LOSURDO
TRANSLATED BY GREGORY ELLIOTT

VERSO
London • New York

To Jean-Michel Goux, in friendship and gratitude

The translation of this work has been funded by SEPS
Segretariato Europeo per le Pubblicazioni Scientifiche

Via Val d'Aposa 7 – 40123 Bologna – Italy
seps@seps.it – www.seps.it

This paperback edition first published by Verso 2014
First published in English by Verso 2011
Translation © Gregory Elliott 2011, 2014
First published as *Controstoria del Liberalismo*
© Gius. Laterza & Figli 2006

Published by arrangement with Marco Vigevani Agenzia Letteraria

The moral rights of the author have been asserted

5 7 9 10 8 6

Verso
UK: 6 Meard Street, London W1F 0EG
US: 20 Jay Street, Suite 1010, Brooklyn, NY 11201
www.versobooks.com

Verso is the imprint of New Left Books

ISBN-13: 978-1-78168-166-4
eISBN-13: 978-78168-525-9 (UK)
eISBN-13: 978-78168-216-6 (US)

British Library Cataloguing in Publication Data
A catalogue record for this book is available from the British Library

Library of Congress Cataloging-in-Publication Data

Losurdo, Domenico.
[Controstoria del liberalismo. English]
Liberalism : a counter-history / Domenico Losurdo.
    pages cm.
 ISBN 978-1-78168-166-4 (pbk.) – ISBN 978-1-84467-693-4 (hard)
1. Liberalism. I. Title.
JC574.L6713 2014
320.51–dc23

2013033156

Typeset in Perpetua by MJ Gavan, Truro, Cornwall
Printed and bound by CPI Group (UK) Ltd, Croydon, CR0 4YY

Contents

A Short Methodological Introduction

How does this book differ from existing histories of liberalism, which continue to appear in growing numbers? Does it really succeed in making the innovation promised by the title? Once they have finished it, readers will be able to give their own answer. For now, the author can limit himself to a statement of intent. In formulating it, a great example can aid us. About to embark on the history of the collapse of the *ancien régime* in France, de Tocqueville observed of studies of the eighteenth century:

> [W]e imagine we know all about the French social order of that time, for the good reason that its surface glitter holds our gaze and we are familiar not only with the life stories of its outstanding figures but also, thanks to the many brilliant critical studies now available, with the works of the great writers who adorned that age. But we have only vague, often quite wrong conceptions of the manner in which public business was transacted and institutions functioned; of the exact relations between the various classes in the social hierarchy; of the situation and sentiments of that section of the population which as yet could neither make itself heard nor seen; and, by the same token, of the ideas and mores basic to the social structure of eighteenth-century France.[1]

There is no reason not to apply the methodology so brilliantly indicated by de Tocqueville to the movement and society of which he was an integral and influential part. Solely because he intends to draw attention to aspects that he believes have hitherto been largely and unjustly ignored, the author refers in the book's title to a 'counter-history'. Otherwise, it is a history, whose subject-matter alone remains to be specified: not liberal thought in its abstract purity, but liberalism, and hence the liberal movement and liberal society, in their

---

1 Alexis de Tocqueville, *The Ancien Régime and the French Revolution*, trans. Stuart Gilbert, London: Fontana, 1966, p. 24.

concrete reality. As with any other major historical movement, this involves investigating the conceptual developments, but also—and primarily—the political and social relations it found expression in, as well as the more or less contradictory link that was established between these two dimensions of social reality.

And so, in commencing the investigation, we are forced to pose a preliminary question concerning the subject whose history we intend to reconstruct: What is liberalism?

CHAPTER ONE

What Is Liberalism?

1. A series of embarrassing questions

The usual answer to this question admits of no doubt: liberalism is the tradition of thought whose central concern is the liberty of the individual, which is
ignored or ridden roughshod over by organicist philosophies of various kinds.
But if that is the case, how should we situate John C. Calhoun? This eminent
statesman, vice president of the United States in the mid-nineteenth century,
burst into an impassioned ode to individual liberty, which, appealing to Locke,
he vigorously defended against any abuse of power and any unwarranted interference by the state. And that is not all. Along with 'absolute governments'
and the 'concentration of power', he unstintingly criticized and condemned
fanaticism[1] and the spirit of 'crusade',[2] to which he opposed 'compromise' as
the guiding principle of genuine 'constitutional governments'.[3] With equal
eloquence Calhoun defended minority rights. It was not only a question of
guaranteeing the alternation of the various parties in government through suffrage: unduly extensive power was unacceptable in any event, even if limited
in duration and tempered by the promise or prospect of a periodic reversal of
roles in the relationship between governors and governed.[4] Unquestionably,
we seem to have all the characteristics of the most mature and attractive liberal
thought. On the other hand, however, disdaining the half-measures and timidity or fear of those who restricted themselves to accepting it as a necessary
'evil', Calhoun declared slavery to be 'a positive good' that civilization could
not possibly renounce. Calhoun repeatedly denounced intolerance and the

---

1 John C. Calhoun, *Union and Liberty*, ed. R.M. Lence, Indianapolis: Liberty Classics, 1992,
p. 529.
2 Ibid., pp. 528–31.
3 Ibid., pp. 30–1.
4 Ibid., pp. 30–3.

1

crusading spirit, not in order to challenge the enslavement of blacks or the ruthless hunting down of fugitive slaves, but exclusively to brand abolitionists as 'blind fanatics'[5] who 'consider themselves under the most sacred obligation to use every effort to destroy' slavery, a form of property legitimized and guaranteed by the Constitution.[6] Blacks were not among the minorities defended with such vigour and legal erudition. In fact, in their case, tolerance and the spirit of compromise seem to turn into their opposite: if fanaticism actually succeeded in its mad project of abolishing slavery, what would follow would be 'the extirpation of one or the other race'.[7] And, given the concrete balance of forces in the United States, it was not difficult to imagine which of the two would succumb: blacks could only survive on condition of being slaves.

So is Calhoun a liberal? No doubts on this score were harboured by Lord Acton, a prominent figure in liberalism in the second half of the nineteenth century, an advisor and friend of William Gladstone, one of the major figures in nineteenth-century England. In Acton's view, Calhoun was a champion of the cause of the struggle against any form of absolutism, including 'democratic absolutism'; the arguments he employed were 'the very perfection of political truth'. In short, we are dealing with one of the major authors and great minds in the liberal tradition and pantheon.[8]

Albeit in less emphatic language, the question has been answered in the affirmative by those who in our time celebrate Calhoun as 'a strong individualist',[9] as a champion of the 'defense of minority rights against the abuse of an overbearing majority',[10] or as a theorist of the sense of limits and the self-limitation that should characterize the majority.[11] In no doubt is one US publishing house, committed to republishing in a neo-liberal key 'Liberty Classics', among which the eminent statesman and ideologue of the slaveholding South features prominently.

The question we have posed does not only emerge from reconstructing the history of the United States. Prestigious scholars of the French Revolution, of firm liberal persuasion, have no hesitation in defining as 'liberal' those figures and

---

5   Ibid., p. 474.

6   Ibid., p. 582.

7   Ibid., pp. 529, 473.

8   Lord Acton, *Selected Writings*, 3 vols, ed. J. Rufus Fears, Indianapolis: Liberty Classics, vol. 1, pp. 240, 250; vol. 3, p. 593.

9   C. Gordon Post, Introduction to John C. Calhoun, *A Disquisition on Government*, New York: Liberal Arts Press, 1953, p. vii.

10   Ross M. Lence, Foreword to Calhoun, *Union and Liberty*, p. xxiii.

11   Giovanni Sartori, *Democrazia e definizioni*, Bologna: Il Mulino, 1976, p. 151; Sartori, *The Theory of Democracy Revisited*, Chatham (NJ): Chatham House Publishers, 1987, pp. 239, 252.

circles that had the merit of opposing the Jacobin diversion, but who were firmly committed to the defence of colonial slavery. The reference is to Pierre-Victor Malouet and members of the Massiac Club, who were 'all plantation-owners and slaveholders'.[12] Is it possible to be a liberal and slaveholder at the same time? Such was not the opinion of John Stuart Mill, judging at least from his polemic against the '*soi-disant*' British liberals (among them, perhaps, Acton and Gladstone), who, during the American Civil War, rallied en masse to 'a furious pro-Southern partisanship', or at any rate viewed the Union and Lincoln coolly and malevolently.[13]

We face a dilemma. If we answer the question formulated above (Is Calhoun a liberal?) in the affirmative, we can no longer maintain the traditional (and edifying) image of liberalism as the thought and volition of liberty. If, on the other hand, we answer in the negative, we find ourselves confronting a new problem and new question, which is no less embarrassing than the first: Why should we continue to dignify John Locke with the title of father of liberalism? Calhoun refers to black slavery as a 'positive good'. Yet without resorting to such brazen language, the English philosopher, to whom the US author explicitly appealed, regarded slavery in the colonies as self-evident and indisputable, and personally contributed to the legal formalization of the institution in Carolina. He took a hand in drafting the constitutional provision according to which '[e]very freeman of Carolina shall have absolute power and authority over his Negro slaves, of what opinion or religion soever.'[14] Locke was 'the last major philosopher to seek a justification for absolute and perpetual slavery'.[15] However, this did not prevent him from inveighing against the political 'slavery' that absolute monarchy sought to impose.[16] Similarly, in Calhoun the theorization of black slavery as a 'positive good' went hand in hand with warnings against a concentration of power that risked transforming 'the governed' into 'the slaves of the rulers'.[17] Of course, the American statesman was a slave-owner, but the

---

12 François Furet and Denis Richet, *La rivoluzione francese*, trans. Silvia Brilli Cattarini and Carla Patanè, Rome and Bari: Laterza, 1980, pp. 120–1, 160–1.

13 John Stuart Mill, *Collected Works*, 33 vols, ed. John M. Robson, Toronto and London: University of Toronto Press and Routledge and Kegan Paul, 1963–91, vol. 21, p. 157; vol. 1, p. 267.

14 John Locke, *Political Writings*, ed. David Wooton, London and New York: Penguin, 1993, p. 230.

15 David B. Davis, *The Problem of Slavery in the Age of Revolution, 1770–1823*, Ithaca: Cornell University Press, 1975, p. 45.

16 See John Locke, *Two Treatises of Government*, ed. William S. Carpenter, London and New York: Everyman's Library, 1924, bk 1, ch. 1.

17 Calhoun, *Union and Liberty*, p. 374.

English philosopher also had sound investments in the slave trade.[18] In fact, the latter's position proves even more compromising; for good or ill, in the slaveholding South of which Calhoun was the interpreter, there was no longer any place for the deportation of blacks from Africa, in a terrible voyage that condemned many of them to death before they landed in America.

Do we want to bring historical distance to bear in order to distinguish the positions of the two authors being compared here, and exclude from the liberal tradition only Calhoun, who continued to justify or celebrate the institution of slavery in the mid-nineteenth century? The southern statesman would have reacted indignantly to such inconsistency of treatment: as regards the English liberal philosopher, he would perhaps have repeated, in slightly different language, the thesis formulated by him in connection with George Washington: 'He was one of us—a slaveholder and a planter.'[19]

Contemporary with Calhoun was Francis Lieber, one of the most eminent intellectuals of his time. Sometimes saluted as a sort of Montesquieu redivivus, in correspondence and on respectful terms with de Tocqueville, he was doubtless a critic, if a cautious one, of the institution of slavery. He hoped it would wither away through its gradual transformation into a kind of servitude or semi-servitude on the autonomous initiative of the slaveholding states, whose right to self-government could not be questioned. That is why Lieber was also admired in the South, all the more so because he himself, albeit on a rather modest scale, owned and sometimes rented male and female slaves. When one of the latter died, following a mysterious pregnancy and subsequent abortion, he recorded in his diary the painful financial loss suffered: 'fully one thousand dollars—the hard labor of a year'.[20] New, painful economies were required to replace the deceased slave, because Lieber, unlike Calhoun, was not a planter and did not live off profits, but a university professor who essentially used slaves as domestic servants. Does this authorize us in including the first, rather than the second, in the liberal tradition? In any event, temporal distance plays no role here.

Let us now take a contemporary of Locke's. Andrew Fletcher was 'a champion of liberty' and, at the same time, 'a champion of slavery'.[21] Politically, he

---

18   Maurice Cranston, *John Locke*, London: Longmans, 1959, pp. 114–15; Hugh Thomas, *The Slave Trade*, New York: Simon & Schuster, 1997, pp. 199, 210.

19   Calhoun, *Union and Liberty*, p. 590.

20   Frank Freidel, *Francis Lieber*, Gloucester (MA): Peter Smith, 1968, pp. 278, 235–58.

21   Edmund S. Morgan, 'Slavery and Freedom: The American Paradox', *Journal of American History*, vol. LIX, no. 1, 1972, p. 11; cf. Karl Marx, *Capital: Volume One*, trans. Ben Fowkes, Harmondsworth: Penguin, 1976, p. 882 n. 9.

professed to be 'a republican on principle'[22] and culturally was 'a Scottish prophet of the Enlightenment'.[23] He too fled to Holland in the wake of the anti-Jacobite and anti-absolutist conspiracy, exactly like Locke, with whom he was in correspondence.[24] Fletcher's reputation crossed the Atlantic: Jefferson defined him as a 'patriot', whose merit was to have expressed the 'political principles' characteristic of 'the purest periods of the British Constitution'— those that subsequently caught on and prospered in free America.[25] Expressing positions rather similar to Fletcher's was his contemporary and fellow countryman James Burgh, who also enjoyed the respect of republican circles à la Jefferson,[26] and was mentioned favourably by Thomas Paine in the most celebrated opuscule of the American Revolution (*Common Sense*).[27]

Yet, in contrast to the other authors—though like them characterized by a peculiar tangle of love of liberty and legitimation or revindication of slavery— Fletcher and Burgh are virtually forgotten today, and no one seems to want to include them among exponents of the liberal tradition. The fact is that, in underlining the necessity of slavery, they were thinking primarily not of blacks in the colonies, but of the 'vagrants', the beggars, the odious, incorrigible rabble of the metropolis. Should they be regarded as illiberal for this reason? Were that to be the case, what would distinguish liberals from non-liberals would be not the condemnation of the institution of slavery, but only negative discrimination against peoples of colonial origin.

Liberal England presents us with another, different case. Francis Hutcheson, a moral philosopher of some significance (he was the 'never to be forgotten' master of Adam Smith),[28] on the one hand expressed criticisms and reservations about the slavery to which blacks were indiscriminately subjected. On the other hand, he stressed that, especially when dealing with the 'lower conditions' of society, slavery could be a 'useful punishment': it should be the 'ordinary

---

22 Marx, *Capital: Volume One*, p. 882 n. 9.

23 Edmund S. Morgan, *American Slavery, American Freedom*, New York: Norton, 1995, p. 325.

24 Henry R. Fox Bourne, *The Life of John Locke*, 2 vols, Aalen: Scientia, 1969, vol. 1, p. 481; John Locke, *The Correspondence*, 8 vols, ed. Esmond S. De Beer, Oxford: Clarendon Press, 1976–89, vols 5–7, *passim*.

25 Thomas Jefferson, *Writings*, ed. Merrill D. Peterson, New York: Library of America, 1984, p. 1134 (letter to the Earl of Buchan, 10 July 1803).

26 Morgan, *American Slavery, American Freedom*, p. 382; J. G. A. Pocock, *The Machiavellian Moment*, Princeton: Princeton University Press, 1975, p. 528.

27 Thomas Paine, *Collected Writings*, ed. Eric Foner, New York: Library of America, 1995, p. 45 n.

28 Adam Smith, *Correspondence*, ed. Ernest Campbell Mossner and Ian Simpson Ross, Indianapolis: Liberty Classics, 1987, p. 309 (letter to Archibald Davidson, 16 November 1787).

punishment of such idle vagrants as, after proper admonitions and tryals of temporary servitude, cannot be engaged to support themselves and their families by any useful labours'.[29] We are dealing with an author who, while evincing unease at hereditary, racial slavery, demanded a sort of penal slavery for those who, regardless of their skin colour, were guilty of vagrancy. Was Hutcheson a liberal?

Historically positioned between Locke and Calhoun, and with his focus precisely on the reality accepted by the two of them as obvious and indisputable, or even celebrated as a 'positive good', Adam Smith constructed an argument and expressed a position that warrants being cited at some length. Slavery could be more easily abolished under a 'despotic government' than a 'free government', with its representative bodies exclusively reserved in practice for white property-owners. In such circumstances, the condition of the black slaves was desperate: 'every law is made by their masters, who will never pass any thing prejudicial to themselves'. Hence '[t]he freedom of the free was the cause of the great oppression of the slaves … And as they are the most numerous part of mankind, no human person will wish for liberty in a country where this institution is established.'[30] Can an author who, in at least one concrete instance, expressed his preference for 'despotic government' be regarded as liberal? Or, differently put, is Smith more liberal or are Locke and Calhoun, who, along with slavery, defended the representative bodies condemned by Smith as the prop, in a slaveholding society, of an infamous institution contrary to any sense of humanity?

In fact, as the great economist had foreseen, slavery was abolished in the United States not thanks to local self-government, but by the iron fist of the Union's army and the temporary military dictatorship imposed by it. For this Lincoln was accused by his opponents of despotism and Jacobinism. He resorted to 'military government' and 'military commissions' and interpreted 'the word "law"' as '[t]he will of the President' and habeas corpus as the 'power of the President to imprison whom he pleases, as long as he pleases'.[31] Together with representatives of the secessionist Confederacy, the drafters of this indictment were those who aspired to a compromise peace, for the purposes of returning to constitutional normality. And once again we are obliged to ask the

---

29   David B. Davis, *The Problem of Slavery in Western Culture*, Ithaca and New York: Cornell University Press, 1966, pp. 374–9.

30   Adam Smith, *Lectures on Jurisprudence*, Indianapolis: Liberty Classics, 1982, pp. 452–3, 182.

31   Arthur M. Schlesinger Jr, ed., *History of US Political Parties*, New York and London: Chelsea House and Bawker, 1973, pp. 915–21.

question: Is it Lincoln who is more liberal, or his adversaries in the South, or his opponents in the North who came out in favour of compromise?

We have seen Mill adopt a position in favour of the Union and condemn the '*soi-disant*' liberals who cried scandal over the energy with which it conducted the war against the South and kept at bay those who, in the North itself, were inclined to tolerate the slaveholders' secession. However, we shall see that, when he turned his attention to the colonies, the English liberal justified the West's 'despotism' over 'races' that were still 'under age', and who were obliged to observe an 'absolute obedience' in order to be set on the path of progress. This is a formulation that would not have displeased Calhoun, who likewise legitimized slavery by reference to the backwardness and nonage of populations of African origin. It was only in America, and thanks to the paternal care of white masters, that the 'black race' succeeded in progressing and making the transition from its previous 'low, degraded and savage condition' to 'its present comparatively civilized condition'.[32] In Mill's view, 'any means' were licit for those who took on the task of educating 'savage tribes'; 'slavery' was sometimes a mandatory stage for inducing them to work and making them useful to civilization and progress (see below, Chapter 7, §3). But this was also the opinion of Calhoun, for whom slavery was an unavoidable means if one wished to achieve the end of civilizing blacks. Certainly, by contrast with the permanent slavery which, according to the US theorist and politician, blacks must be subjected to, the pedagogical dictatorship Mill refers to was destined to disappear in the distant, uncertain future. But the other side of the coin is that now explicitly subjected to this condition of unfreedom was not a particular ethnic group (the fragment of Africa located at the heart of the United States), but all the peoples invested by the West's colonial expansion and forced to endure political 'despotism' and servile or semi-servile forms of labour. Is demanding 'absolute obedience', for an indeterminate period of time, from the overwhelming majority of humanity compatible with the liberal profession of faith? Or is it synonymous with '*soi-disant*' liberalism?

2. The American Revolution and the revelation of an embarrassing truth

It is now clear that what primarily divides the authors mentioned up to this point is the problem of slavery. In one way or another, they all refer to the Britain deriving from the Glorious Revolution or the United States. These are

---

32   Calhoun, *Union and Liberty*, p. 473.

two countries that for around a century were a single state entity and formed, as it were, a single political party. Prior to the crisis that led to the American Revolution, the British on both sides of the Atlantic felt themselves to be proud subjects or citizens of '[a] land, perhaps the only one in the universe, in which political or civil liberty is the very end and scope of the constitution'.[33] Thus Blackstone. To confirm his thesis, he referred to Montesquieu, who spoke of England as the 'one nation in the world whose constitution has political liberty for its direct purpose'.[34] Not even the French liberal doubted the fact that 'England is currently the freest country in the world, not discounting any republic': the 'free nation', the 'free people' par excellence.[35]

At this time, no dark clouds seemed to threaten relations between the two shores of the Atlantic. There were no conflicts and, according to Montesquieu at least, there could not be, because even in its relationship with the colonies what characterized England was its love of liberty:

> If this nation sent colonies abroad, it would do so to extend its commerce more than its domination.
>
> As one likes to establish elsewhere what is established at home, it would give the form of its own government to the people of its colonies; and as this government would carry prosperity with it, one would see the formation of great peoples, even in the forests to which it had sent inhabitants.[36]

In these years, the English colonists in America proudly identified with Blackstone's thesis that 'our free constitution', which 'falls little short of perfection', differed markedly 'from the modern constitutions of other states', from the political order of 'the continent of Europe' as a whole.[37]

This was the ideology with which the Seven Years' War was fought by the British Empire. The English colonists in America were the most determined in interpreting it as a clash between the 'supporters of freedom in the world'— the British 'sons of noble liberty', or defenders of Protestantism—and a 'cruel and oppressive' France—despotic politically, and follower of 'Roman bigotry'

---

33 William Blackstone, *Commentaries on the Laws of England*, 4 vols, Chicago: University of Chicago Press, 1979, vol. 1, p. 6.

34 Charles-Louis Montesquieu, *The Spirit of the Laws*, trans. and ed. Anne M. Cohler, Basia Carolyn Miller and Harold Samuel Stone, Cambridge: Cambridge University Press, 1989, p. 156.

35 Charles-Louis Montesquieu, *Oeuvres complètes*, ed. Roger Caillois, Paris: Gallimard, 1949–51, vol. 1, p. 884; Montesquieu, *Spirit of the Laws*, pp. 243, 325.

36 Montesquieu, *Spirit of the Laws*, pp. 328–9.

37 Blackstone, *Commentaries*, vol. 1, pp. 122–3.

and Popery religiously. At the time, even the British Crown's transatlantic subjects liked to repeat with Locke that 'slavery' was 'directly opposite to the generous temper and courage of our nation'; it was utterly inconceivable for an 'Englishman'.[38] The French allegedly wanted to reduce the American colonists to a 'slavish subjection'. Fortunately, however, arriving to foil this attempt was Great Britain, '[t]he Mistress of the Nations—the grand Support of Liberty, the Scourge of Oppression and Tyranny!'[39]

It was an ideology that Edmund Burke sought to breathe new life into as late as 1775, in a desperate attempt to avoid the impending rupture. Presenting his motion of conciliation, he called upon people not to lose sight of, and not to sever, the ties that bound the American colonists to the mother country: what was at stake was a single 'nation' that shared 'the sacred temple consecrated to our common faith', the faith in 'liberty'. Largely unchallenged in countries like Spain or Prussia, slavery was 'a weed that grows in every soil' except the English. Accordingly, it was absurd to try to subdue the rebel colonists by force: 'An Englishman is the unfittest person on earth to argue another Englishman into slavery.'[40]

Obviously, the slavery referred to here is the one of which the absolute monarch is guilty. The other slavery, which shackles blacks, is passed over in silence. With the increasing inevitability of the revolution, or 'civil war' with all its 'horrors'[41]—as loyalists faithful to the Crown and British politicians in favour of compromise and preserving the unity of the English 'nation' and 'race'[42] preferred to call it—the picture changed markedly. The element of continuity is clear. Each of the two contending parties accused the other of wanting to reintroduce despotism, or political 'slavery'. The rebel colonists' charges are well known: they tirelessly denounced the tyranny of the British Crown and parliament, and their mad project of subjecting residents in America to a condition of 'perpetual bondage and slavery'.[43] But the response was not slow in coming. As early as 1773, a loyalist from New York had issued a warning: hitherto they had been 'watchful against *external* attacks on our freedom' (the

38   Locke, *Two Treatises*, p. 3.

39   Janice Potter-Mackinnon, *The Liberty We Seek*, Cambridge (MA): Harvard University Press, 1983, pp. 115–16.

40   Edmund Burke, *The Works: A New Edition*, 16 vols, London: Rivington, 1826, vol. 3, pp. 123–4, 66.

41   Boucher, quoted in Anne Y. Zimmer, *Jonathan Boucher*, Detroit: Wayne State University Press, 1978, p. 153.

42   Burke, *Works*, vol. 3, p. 135.

43   Barry Alan Shain, *The Myth of American Individualism*, Princeton: Princeton University Press, 1994, p. 290.

reference is to the Seven Years' War), but now a much more insidious danger had emerged—that of 'becom[ing] *enslaved* by tyrants within'. Again in New York, another loyalist repeated the point two years later: the rebels aspired 'to make us worse than slaves'.[44] In polemicizing against one another, the two branches the liberal party had divided into adopted the ideology and rhetoric that had presided over the self-celebration of the English nation in its entirety, as the sworn enemy of political slavery.

The novel factor was that, in the wake of the exchange of accusations, the other slavery—the one both branches had repressed as a disruptive element in their proud self-consciousness as members of the people and party of liberty—burst into the polemics alongside political slavery. In the rebel colonists' view, the London government, which in sovereign fashion imposed taxation on citizens or subjects not represented in the House of Commons, was behaving like a master towards his slaves. But—objected the others—if slavery is the issue, why not start to discuss the slavery that is manifested in brutal, unequivocal form precisely where liberty is so passionately lauded? As early as 1764, Benjamin Franklin, in London at the time to plead the colonists' cause, had to face the sarcastic comments of his interlocutors:

> You Americans make a great Clamour upon every little imaginary infringement of what you take to be your Liberties; and yet there are no People upon Earth such Enemies to Liberty, such absolute Tyrants, where you have the Opportunity, as you yourselves are.[45]

The self-styled champions of liberty branded taxation imposed without their explicit consent as synonymous with despotism and slavery. But they had no scruples about exercising the most absolute and arbitrary power over their slaves. This was a paradox: 'How is it', Samuel Johnson asked, 'that we hear the loudest yelps for liberty from the drivers of negroes?' Across the Atlantic, those who sought to contest the secession ironized in similar fashion. Thomas Hutchinson, royal governor of Massachusetts, rebuked the rebels for their inconsistency or hypocrisy: they denied Africans those rights that they claimed to be 'absolutely inalienable' in the most radical way imaginable.[46] Echoing him was an American loyalist (Jonathan Boucher), who, having taken refuge in England, revisited the events that forced him into exile and observed: 'the most

---

44   Potter-Mackinnon, *The Liberty We Seek*, p. 16.

45   Benjamin Franklin, *Writings*, ed. J. A. Leo Lemay, New York: Library of America, 1987, pp. 646–7.

46   Eric Foner, *The Story of American Freedom*, London: Picador, 1999, p. 32.

clamorous advocates for liberty were uniformly the harshest and worst masters of slaves'.[47]

It was not only the people most directly involved in the polemical and political struggle who expressed themselves so harshly. The intervention of John Millar, prominent exponent of the Scottish Enlightenment, was especially stinging:

> It affords a curious spectacle to observe, that the same people who talk in a high strain of political liberty, and who consider the privilege of imposing their own taxes as one of the inalienable rights of mankind, should make no scruple of reducing a great proportion of their fellow-creatures into circumstances by which they are not only deprived of property, but almost of every species of right. Fortune perhaps never produced a situation more calculated to ridicule a liberal hypothesis, or to show how little the conduct of men is at the bottom directed by any philosophical principles.[48]

Millar was a disciple of Adam Smith. The master seems to have seen things in the same way. When he declared that to a 'free government' controlled by slave-owners, he preferred a 'despotic government' capable of erasing the infamy of slavery, he made explicit reference to America. Translated into directly political terms, the great economist's words signify: the despotism the Crown is criticized for is preferable to the liberty demanded by the slave-owners, from which only a small class of planters and absolute masters benefits.

English abolitionists went even further, calling for the defence of British institutions threatened by 'arbitrary and inhuman uses, which prevail in a distant land'. So arbitrary and inhuman that, as indicated by an advert in the *New York Journal*, a black woman and her three-year-old daughter could be sold on the market separately, as if they were a cow and a calf. And hence (concluded Granville Sharp in 1769) one should not be led astray by 'theatrical bombast and ranting expressions in praise of liberty' employed by the slave-holding rebels; free English institutions must be vigorously defended against them.[49]

The accused reacted in their turn by upbraiding England for its hypocrisy: it boasted of its virtue and love of liberty, but who promoted and continued to promote the slave trade? And who was it that transported and sold slaves?

---

47 Boucher, quoted in Zimmer, *Jonathan Boucher*, p. 297.
48 John Millar, *The Origin of the Distinction of Ranks*, Aalen: Scientia, 1986, p. 294.
49 Sharp, quoted in Davis, *The Problem of Slavery in the Age of Revolution*, pp. 272–3, 386–7.

Thus argued Franklin,[50] advancing an argument that became central in the first draft of the Declaration of Independence elaborated by Jefferson. This is how, in the original version of that solemn document, the Britain derived from the Glorious Revolution and George III himself were charged. The latter

> has waged cruel war against human nature itself, violating the most sacred rights of life and liberty in the persons of a distant people who never offended him, captivating and carrying them into slavery in another hemisphere, or to incur miserable death in their transportation thither. This piratical war, the opprobrium of *infidel* powers, is the warfare of the CHRISTIAN king of Great Britain. Determined to keep open a market where MEN should be bought and sold, he has prostituted his negative for suppressing every legislative attempt to prohibit or restrain this execrable commerce ...[51]

3. The role of slavery between the two Atlantic shores

What should we make of this furious, unexpected polemic? There is no doubt that the accusations against the rebels struck a weak point. Virginia played a central role in the American Revolution. Forty per cent of the country's slaves were to be found there, but a majority of the authors of the rebellion unleashed in the name of liberty also came from there. For thirty-two of the United States' first thirty-six years of existence, slave-owners from Virginia occupied the post of president. This colony or state, founded on slavery, supplied the country with its most illustrious statesmen. It is enough to think of George Washington (great military and political protagonist of the anti-British revolt) and Thomas Jefferson and James Madison (authors, respectively, of the Declaration of Independence and the federal Constitution of 1787), all three of them slave-owners.[52] Regardless of this or that state, the influence slavery exercised on the country as a whole is clear. Sixty years after its foundation, we see that 'of the first sixteen presidential elections, between 1788 and 1848, all but four placed a southern slaveholder in the White House'.[53] Hence the persistence of the anti-American polemic on this point is understandable.

On the other side, we are familiar with Franklin's and Jefferson's ironic remarks about the moralizing anti-slavery lectures offered by a country deeply

---

50   Franklin, *Writings*, pp. 648–9.

51   Cf. Davis, *The Problem of Slavery in the Age of Revolution*, p. 273; Francis Jennings, *The Creation of America*, Cambridge and New York: Cambridge University Press, 2000, p. 169.

52   Morgan, *American Slavery, American Freedom*, pp. 5–6.

53   Foner, *The Story of American Freedom*, p. 36.

involved in the slave trade. Burke, theorist of 'conciliation with the colonies', likewise stressed this. In rejecting the proposal of those who urged 'a general enfranchisement of their slaves' to counter the rebellion of their masters and the colonists generally, he observed: 'Slaves as these unfortunate black people are, and dull as all men are from slavery, must they not a little suspect the offer of freedom from that very nation which has sold them to their present masters?' All the more so if this nation insisted on practising the slave trade, clashing with colonies that wished to restrict or abolish it. In the eyes of slaves landed in or deported to America, this would represent a peculiar spectacle:

> An offer of freedom from England, would come rather oddly, shipped to them in an African vessel, which is refused an entry into the ports of Virginia or Carolina, with a cargo of three hundred Angola negroes. It would be curious to see the Guinea captain attempting at the same instant to publish his proclamation of liberty, and to advertise his sale of slaves.[54]

Burke's irony hits home. In addition to Britain's role in the slave trade, slaves long continued to be present in the metropolis itself. It has been calculated that in the mid-eighteenth century there were around 100,000 of them.[55] Were British abolitionists horrified by the market in human flesh in the American colonies and New York? In Liverpool in 1766, eleven black slaves were put on sale and the market in 'black cattle' was still open in Dublin twelve years later, regularly advertised in the local press.[56]

The role played in the country's economy by the trade in slaves and their exploitation was sizeable: 'The *Liverpool Courier*, 22 August 1832, estimated that three-quarters of Britain's coffee, fifteen-sixteenths of its cotton, twenty-two twenty-thirds of its sugar, and thirty-four thirty-fifths of its tobacco were still produced by slaves.'[57] In sum, we should bear in mind the candid judgement of two eighteenth-century British witnesses. The first, Joshua Gee, acknowledged that '[a]ll this great increase in our treasure proceeds chiefly from the labour of negroes in the plantations'.[58] The second, Malachy Postlethwayt, engaged as he was in defending the role of the Royal African Company—the company that

---

54   Burke, *Works*, vol. 3, pp. 67–8.
55   Robin Blackburn, *The Overthrow of Colonial Slavery, 1776–1848*, London and New York: Verso, 1990, p. 80.
56   Seymour Drescher, *Capitalism and Antislavery*, Oxford and New York: Oxford University Press, 1987, p. 174 n. 34.
57   Ibid., p. 170 n. 19.
58   Gee, quoted in Christopher Hill, *Reformation to Industrial Revolution*, Harmondsworth: Penguin, 1969, p. 227.

controlled the slave trade—was even sharper: 'The *Negroe Trade* and the natural Consequences resulting from it, may be justly esteemed an inexhaustible Fund of Wealth and Naval Power to this Nation'; they were 'the first principle and foundation of all the rest, the main spring of the machine which sets every wheel in motion'.[59] The British Empire as a whole was merely 'a magnificent superstructure' upon this commerce.[60] Finally, there was the political influence of the institution of slavery. Although obviously inferior to what it was in the American colonies, it was certainly not nugatory in England: in the 1790 parliament, two or three dozen members sat who had interests in the West Indies.[61]

The exchange of accusations between rebel colonists and the mother country—that is, between two branches of the party that had hitherto proudly celebrated itself as the party of liberty—was a mutual, pitiless demystification. Not only did the England derived from the Glorious Revolution not challenge the slave trade, but on the contrary the latter experienced strong growth.[62] And one of the new liberal monarchy's first acts of international policy was wresting a monopoly on the slave trade from Spain. On the other side, the revolution that broke out across the Atlantic in the name of liberty involved official consecration of the institution of slavery, and the conquest and prolonged exercise of political hegemony by slave-owners.

Possibly the most articulate and pained intervention in this polemic was by Josiah Tucker, 'who, though a parson and a Tory, was, apart from that, an honourable man and a competent political economist'.[63] He denounced England's pre-eminent role in the slave trade: 'We ... the boasted Patrons of Liberty, and the professed Advocates for the natural Rights of Mankind, engage deeper in this murderous inhuman Traffic than any Nation whatever.' But even more hypocritical was the behaviour of the rebel colonists: 'the Advocates for Republicanism, and for the supposed Equality of Mankind, ought to have been foremost in suggesting some such humane System for abolishing the worst of all the Species of Slavery'.[64] But instead ...

---

59   Postlethwayt, quoted in Davis, *The Problem of Slavery in Western Culture*, p. 150; Eric R. Wolf, *Europe and the Peoples without History*, Berkeley: University of California Press, 1982, p. 198.

60   Postlethwayt, quoted in Jennings, *The Creation of America*, p. 206.

61   Blackburn, *The Overthrow of Colonial Slavery*, p. 143.

62   Richard S. Dunn, 'The Glorious Revolution and America', in Nicholas Canny, ed., *The Origins of Empire*, Oxford and New York: Oxford University Press, 1998, pp. 463–5.

63   Marx's characterization in Marx, *Capital: Volume One*, p. 926.

64   Josiah Tucker, *Collected Works*, London: Routledge and Thoemmes Press, 1993–96, vol. 5, pp. 21–2.

4. Holland, England, America

If, prior to constituting themselves as an independent state, the rebel colonies in America formed part of the British Empire, the latter assumed its liberal form with the ascent to the throne of William of Orange, who landed in England from Holland. On the other hand, while with his draft constitution for Carolina Locke referred to America, he wrote his first *Letter Concerning Toleration* in Holland, which was then 'the centre of conspiracy' against Stuart absolutism;[65] and Holland was also the birthplace of Bernard de Mandeville, unquestionably one of the more important figures in early liberalism.

We must not lose sight of the fact that the United Provinces, which emerged from the struggle against Philip II's Spain, equipped themselves with a liberal type of set-up a century before England. This was a country that from a socio-economic point of view as well had left the *ancien régime* behind. In the seventeenth century it had a per capita income one-and-a-half times that of England; whereas in the latter 60 per cent of the labour force was engaged in agriculture, the figure in Holland was 40 per cent. Moreover, the power structure was rather significant: in the country which emerged victorious from the clash with Philip II, 'a bourgeois oligarchy that had broken decisively with the aristocratic landholding ethos' was dominant.[66] It was these enlightened, tolerant, liberal bourgeois who embarked on colonial expansion; and in this historical period the slave trade was an integral part of it:

[T]he Dutch conducted the first serious slave trade in order to furnish the manpower for the sugar plantations; when they lost the plantations, they tried to remain in the field as slave traders, but by 1675, Dutch primacy ended, yielding place to the newly founded Royal African Company of the English.[67]

Locke was a shareholder in the Royal African Company. But the history of the United Provinces leads to America as well as Britain. It would seem that it was a Dutch peddler who introduced African slaves into Virginia.[68] New Amsterdam, which the Dutch were forced to cede to the British and which became New York, had a population 20 per cent of which was composed of

---

65   Bourne, *Life of John Locke*, vol. 1, p. 481.

66   Seymour Drescher, *From Slavery to Freedom*, London: Macmillan, 1999, pp. 203, 199.

67   Immanuel Wallerstein, *The Modern World System*, 3 vols, New York: Academic Press, 1974–89, vol. 2, p. 52.

68   Jennings, *Creation of America*, p. 26.

blacks, in large part slaves. In 1703 around 42 per cent of homeowners were also slave-owners.[69]

This represents the paradox already glimpsed in connection with Britain and the United States. Until the mid-seventeenth century, the country where the prologue to the successive liberal revolutions occurred—namely, Holland—had a 'hold' on the trade in slaves:[70] 'By the beginning of the eighteenth century, all of their [Dutch] possessions were slave or bound-labor societies.'[71] If, in one respect, it was synonymous with liberty at the time, in another, Holland was synonymous with slavery—and a particularly brutal form of it. In Voltaire's *Candide* a severe blow is dealt to the protagonist's naive optimism by the encounter in Surinam ('where the Dutch are') with a black slave, reduced to a 'dreadful state' by his Dutch master. The slave refers as follows to the working conditions to which he is forced to submit:

> When we're working at the sugar-mill and catch our finger in the grinding-wheel, they cut off our hand. When we try to run away, they cut off a leg. I have been in both these situations. This is the price you pay for the sugar you eat in Europe.[72]

In his turn, Condorcet, launching his abolitionist campaign in 1781, in particular targeted England and Holland, where the institution of slavery seemed especially deep-rooted on account of 'the general corruption of these nations'.[73] Finally, it is worth citing the American loyalist (Jonathan Boucher) whom we have seen ironizing about the passion for liberty displayed by slave-owners engaged in the rebellion. In his view, '[d]espotic nations treated their slaves better than those under republics; the Spanish were the best masters while the Dutch were the worst.'[74]

The first country to embark on the liberal road is one that exhibited an especially tenacious attachment to the institution of slavery. It appears that colonists of Dutch origin offered the most determined resistance to the first abolitionist measures, those introduced in the northern United States during the Revolution

---

69   David B. Davis, *Slavery and Human Progress*, Oxford and New York: Oxford University Press, 1986, p. 75.

70   Hill, *From Reformation to Industrial Revolution*, p. 156.

71   Drescher, *From Slavery to Freedom*, p. 215.

72   Voltaire, *Candide and Other Stories*, trans. and intro. Roger Pearson, London: Everyman's Library, 1992, p. 50.

73   Marie-Jean-Antoine Condorcet, *Oeuvres*, 12 vols, ed. Arthur Condorcet O'Connor and François Arago, Stuttgart and Bad Cannstatt: Fromman-Holzboog, 1968, vol. 7, p. 135.

74   Zimmer, *Jonathan Boucher*, p. 297.

and in its wake.[75] As regards Holland itself, in 1791 the States-General formally declared that the slave trade was essential to the development of the colonies' prosperity and commerce. Still in this period, clearly distinguishing itself from Britain, Holland recognized the right of slave-owners to transport and deposit their human chattels in the mother country before returning to the colonies. Finally, it is to be noted that Holland only abolished slavery in its colonies in 1863, when the secessionist and slaveholding Confederacy of the southern United States was going down to defeat.[76]

5. The Irish, the Indians and the inhabitants of Java

The English colonists' revolt in America was accompanied by another major controversy. For a long time, like that of the blacks, the Indians' fate had not in the slightest unsettled the deep conviction of the English on either side of the Atlantic that they were the chosen people of liberty. In both cases, they appealed to Locke, for whom (as we shall see) the natives of the New World approximated to 'wild beasts'. But with the eruption of the conflict between colonies and mother country, the exchange of accusations also encompassed the problem of the relationship with the Indians. England, Paine proclaimed in 1776, was 'that barbarous and hellish power, which hath stirred up the Indians and the Negroes to destroy us' or 'to cut the throats of the freemen of America'.[77] Similarly, the Declaration of Independence berated George III for having not only 'excited domestic insurrections amongst us' by black slaves, but also 'endeavoured to bring on the inhabitants of our frontiers, the merciless Indian Savages, whose known rule of warfare, is an undistinguished destruction of all ages, sexes and conditions'. In 1812, on the occasion of a new war between the two shores of the Atlantic, Madison condemned England for indiscriminately striking the civilian population with its fleet, not sparing women or children, and hence displaying a conduct similar to that of the red-skinned 'savages'.[78] Having been accomplices of the barbarians, the English became barbarians themselves.

In fact, the argument had begun much earlier, following the Crown procla-

---

75 Arthur Zilversmit, *The First Emancipation*, Chicago: University of Chicago Press, 1969, pp. 165, 182.

76 Drescher, *From Slavery to Freedom*, pp. 211, 218, 196.

77 Paine, *Collected Writings*, pp. 35, 137.

78 Henry S. Commager, ed., *Documents of American History*, 2 vols, New York: Appleton-Century-Crofts, 1963, vol. 1, pp. 208–9.

mation of 1763 that sought to halt or contain expansion west of the Allegany Mountains. This was a measure that did not please the colonists and George Washington, who regarded it as 'a temporary expedient', destined to be rapidly superseded, but which should not be respected even in the immediate present: those 'who neglect the present opportunity of hunting out good lands' were foolish.[79] The future president of the United States was not one of these 'fools'. In his new capacity, while declaring in official speeches that he wanted to bring the 'blessings of civilization' and 'happiness' to 'an unenlightened race of men',[80] in private correspondence he identified the Indians as 'savages' and 'wild beasts of the forest'. Given this, the British Crown's pretension to block further expansion by the colonists was absurd and ultimately immoral: they (Washington declared in a letter of 1783) would force 'the Savage [like] the Wolf to retire'.[81]

Even more extreme in this respect was Franklin, who in his *Autobiography* observed: 'if it be the Design of Providence to extirpate these Savages in order to make room for Cultivators of the Earth, it seems not improbable that Rum may be the appointed Means. It has already annihilated all the Tribes who formerly inhabited the Seacoast.'[82] The decimation or destruction of a people who worshipped 'the Devil' was part of a kind of divinely inspired eugenicist plan.[83] The de-humanization of the Indians was also subscribed to by those in Britain who supported reconciliation with the rebels. The Crown's attempt to block the colonists' expansionistic march seemed to Burke absurd and sacrilegious, for 'attempting to forbid as a crime, and to suppress as an evil, the command and blessing of Providence, "Increase and multiply."' Ultimately, it was an ill-fated 'endeavour to keep as a lair of wild beasts, that earth, which God, by an express charter, has given to the children of men'.[84]

Those on either side of the Atlantic who supported or justified the Crown's policy of 'conciliation' not of the colonists, but of the Indians, mounted some resistance to this process of de-humanization. In this context, a particular mention should be made of the figure of the likeable American loyalist whom

---

79   Nelcya Delanoë and Joelle Rostkowski, *Les Indiens dans l'histoire américaine*, Nancy: Presses Universitaires de Nancy, p. 39 (letter from Washington to his friend W. Crawford, 21 September 1767).

80   George Washington, *A Collection*, ed. William B. Allen, Indianapolis: Liberty Classics, 1988, pp. 475–6 (presidential message, 25 October 1791).

81   Delanoë and Rostkowski, *Les Indiens*, pp. 50–2 (letter from Washington to J. Duane, 7 September 1783).

82   Franklin, *Writings*, p. 1422.

83   Ibid., p. 98.

84   Burke, *Works*, vol. 3, pp. 63–4.

we have encountered several times, in his capacity as a critic of the peculiar libertarian zeal displayed by the 'harshest and wickedest slave masters'. To these same circles he attributed cruelty to the Indians. Sometimes they were killed and scalped with veritable religious fervour; they even became targets for shooting practice. They were branded savages and yet (objected Jonathan Boucher) they were no more savage 'than our progenitors appeared to Julius Caesar or to Agricola'.[85] We have seen Paine accuse the London government of seeking an alliance with Indian cut-throats. In reality, warned an English commander in 1783, it was precisely the now victorious colonists who 'were preparing to cut the throats of the Indians'. The victors' behaviour (added another officer) was 'shocking to humanity'.[86] This was an enduring controversy. In the later nineteenth century a historian descended from a family of loyalists who had taken refuge in Canada argued as follows: Did the rebels claim to be the descendants of those who had disembarked in America to escape intolerance and stay loyal to the cause of liberty? In fact, reversing the policy of the British Crown, which aimed at conversion, the Puritans had initiated a massacre of the Indians, assimilated to 'Canaanites and Amalekites'—that is, stocks marked out by the Old Testament for erasure from the face of the earth. This was 'one of the darkest pages in English colonial history', which was followed by the even more repugnant one written during the American Revolution, when the rebel colonists engaged in 'the entire destruction of the Six Indian Nations' that had remained loyal to England: 'by an order which, we believe, has no parallel in the annals of any civilized nation, [Congress] commands the complete destruction of those people as a nation ... including women and children'.[87]

In his private correspondence at least, Jefferson had no problem acknowledging the horror of the war against the Indians. But in his view responsibility for it resided with the London government, which had incited these savage, bloodthirsty 'tribes'. This was a situation that 'will oblige us now to pursue them to extermination, or drive them to new seats beyond our reach'. The 'confirmed brutalization, if not the extermination of this race in our America' was to be laid at Britain's door. As with the similar fate of 'the same colored man in Asia', as well as of the Irish—who for the English, whose skin 'colour' they shared, should be 'brethren'—it was attributable to a policy committed to

---

85 Boucher, quoted in Zimmer, *Jonathan Boucher*, p. 295.

86 Colin G. Calloway, *The American Revolution in Indian Country*, Cambridge: Cambridge University Press, 1995, pp. 278, 272.

87 Egerton Ryerson, *The Loyalists of America and Their Times*, 2 vols, New York: Haskell House, 1970, vol. 1, pp. 297–8 and n.; vol. 2, p. 100.

sowing death and destruction 'wherever ... Anglo-mercantile cupidity can find a two-penny interest in deluging the earth with human blood'.[88]

Jefferson was not wrong to compare the treatment suffered by the Indians with that reserved for the Irish. Just as, according to the loyalist accusation, Puritans and rebel colonists assimilated the Indians to 'Amalekites', so the Irish had already been compared to 'Amalekites' marked out for extermination, this time by the English conquerors.[89] The colonization of Ireland, with all its horrors, was the model for the subsequent colonization of North America.[90] If the British Empire as a whole mainly swept away Irish and blacks,[91] Indians and blacks were the principal victims of the territorial and commercial expansion first of the English colonies in America and then of the United States.

As with the black question, in the case of the Indians the exchange of accusations ended up taking the form of a mutual demystification. There is no doubt that, along with black enslavement and the black slave trade, the rise of the two liberal countries either side of the Atlantic involved a process of systematic expropriation and practical genocide first of the Irish and then of the Indians.

Similar observations can be made of Holland. A senior English civil servant, Sir Thomas Stamford Raffles, who during the Napoleonic Wars was deputy governor of Java for a time, stated that the previous administration was 'one of the extraordinary relations of treachery, bribery, massacre and meanness'. It is clear that colonial rivalry played a role in this judgement. Marx reports it, but pools 'Dutch colonial administration' and the English administration in his condemnation. As regards Holland more specifically:

Nothing is more characteristic than their system of stealing men in Celebes, in order to get slaves for Java ... The young people thus stolen were hidden in secret dungeons on Celebes, until they were ready for sending to the slave-ships. An official report says: 'This one town of Macassar, for example, is full of secret prisons, one more horrible than the other, crammed with unfortunates, victims of greed and tyranny fettered in chains, forcibly torn from their families.' ... Wherever [the Dutch] set foot, devastation and

---

88   Jefferson, *Writings*, pp. 1312–13 (letter to Alexander von Humboldt, 6 December 1813).

89   Karl Marx and Friedrich Engels, *Werke*, 38 vols, Berlin: Dietz, 1955–89, vol. 16, p. 447.

90   George M. Frederickson, *White Supremacy*, New York: Oxford University Press, 1982, pp. 14–16.

91   Hill, *From Reformation to Industrial Revolution*, p. 164.

depopulation followed. Banjuwangi, a province of Java, numbered over 80,000 inhabitants in 1750 and only 18,000 in 1811. That is peaceful commerce![92]

Once again, processes of enslavement and practical genocide were closely intertwined.

6. Grotius, Locke and the Founding Fathers: a comparative interpretation

At the start of the eighteenth century, Daniel Defoe underlined the ideological fraternity between the country that had emerged from the Glorious Revolution and the country which, a century earlier, had rebelled against Philip II and won 'freedom' and prosperity thanks to 'Heaven and the Assistance of England'.[93] In the mid-nineteenth century, liberal authors liked to contrast the ordered triumph of liberty that had occurred in Holland, England and the United States with a France in the grip of an interminable revolutionary cycle and Bonapartism.[94] It might therefore be useful to proceed to a brief comparative analysis of the texts and authors in which the liberal revolutions of these three countries found theoretical expression and consecration.

In the case of the Holland, we cannot but refer to Hugo Grotius, who dedicated two of his most important books (*Annales et Historiae de Rebus Belgicis* and *De Antiquitate Reipublicae Batavicae*) to the revolt against Philip II and the country that derived from it. Liberal Holland immediately engaged in overseas expansion and slave-trading, and it is interesting to observe the position Grotius adopted towards colonial peoples. Having condemned the superstitious and idolatrous character of the 'religious rites' peculiar to paganism, he added:

> when offered ... to an evil spirit, it is an act of falsehood and hypocrisy; nay, it is an act of absolute rebellion, whereby we not only deprive our legal sovereign of his just homage, but even transfer that homage to a base apostate and an open enemy!

---

92 Marx, *Capital: Volume One*, p. 916; cf. Werner Sombart, *Der moderne Kapitalismus*, 3 vols, Munich: DTV, 1987, vol. 1, pt II, p. 709.

93 Daniel Defoe, *Giving Alms No Charity, And Employing the Poor a Grievance to the Nation*, London, 1704, p. 6.

94 Édouard Laboulaye, *Le parti libéral*, Paris: Charpentier, 1863, p. viii; François Guizot, 'Discours sur l'histoire de la révolution d'Angleterre', in *Histoire d'Angleterre*, Brussels: Société Typographique Belge, 1850, pp. 41–2.

Targeted here were peoples with

> modes of worship ... of a nature little suited to a Being of goodness and of purity: Human sacrifices; naked races up and down the temples; games and dances replete with obscenity; instances whereof are seen even at this day among the savage natives of America and Africa, who are still lost in the thick clouds of Paganism.

It was peoples assailed by Europe's colonial expansion who were guilty of rebellion against God, and who must be punished for such a crime:

> Some ... are weak enough to imagine, that God, as a being of infinite goodness, will never be provoked to punish this rebellion; a spirit of revenge, say they, is wholly incompatible with the attribute of perfect goodness. A fatal and absurd idea this! The powers of Mercy must be limited, that her actions may be just; and when wickedness becomes excessive, punishment as it were unavoidably arises out of justice.[95]

Against peoples who, staining themselves with '[o]ffences that are committed against GOD' and violating the most basic norms of natural law, took the form of 'barbarians' or 'rather Beasts than men', war was 'natural', regardless of state borders and geographical distance. Indeed, 'the justest War is that which is undertaken against wild rapacious Beasts, and next to it is that against Men who are like Beasts [*homines belluis similes*].'[96]

This is the ideology that presided over the conquest of the New World. The sin of idolatry was the first of the arguments prompting Sepúlveda to regard war on the Indians and their enslavement as 'just'.[97] And in Grotius, along with the implicit legitimation of the genocidal practices underway in America, an explicit and insistent justification of slavery emerges. Sometimes it was punishment for criminal behaviour. Answerable for the latter were not only single individuals: 'a whole People may be brought into Subjection for a publick Crime'.[98] As well as in their capacity as 'rebels' against the Lord of the Universe, the inhabitants of America and Africa could also succumb to slavery

---

95   Hugo Grotius, *On the Truth of Christianity*, trans. Spencer Madan, London: J. Dodsby, 1782, pp. 195–6.

96   Hugo Grotius, *The Rights of War and Peace*, 3 vols, ed. Richard Tuck, Indianapolis: Liberty Fund, 2005, vol. 2, pp. 1027, 1024.

97   Lewis Hanke, *Aristotle and the American Indians*, London: Hollis and Carter, 1959, p. 41.

98   Grotius, *Rights of War and Peace*, vol. 2, p. 565.

as a result of a 'just war' (*bellum justum*), conducted by a European power. The prisoners captured during an armed conflict, formally declared in the requisite forms by the supreme authority of a state, were legitimately slaves.[99] And their descendants too were legitimate slaves: otherwise, what interest would the victor have in keeping the vanquished alive? As the slave of the one who had spared his life, the prisoner became part of the victor's property, and such property could be transmitted hereditarily or be an object of sale, just like 'the Property of Goods' (*rerum dominium*).[100]

Naturally, all this did not apply to 'those Nations where this Right of Bondage over Captives is not practised'; it did not apply to 'Christian' countries, which limited themselves to exchanging prisoners.[101] Banned in intra-European conflicts, slavery by right of war continued to be a reality as and when Christian, civilized Europe confronted colonial peoples, barbarians and pagans in what, by definition, was a 'just' war. On the other hand, regardless of their actual behaviour, the lesson of a great master should not be forgotten: 'as *Aristotle* said, some Men are naturally Slaves, that is, turned for Slavery. And some Nations also are of such a Temper, that they know better how to obey than to command'.[102] This was a truth also confirmed by Holy Scripture: 'the Apostle St Paul' called on individuals and peoples who had legitimately been reduced to slavery to put up with their lot and not escape it by rebellion or flight.[103]

On the one hand, Grotius paid homage to the 'free People' who in Holland had availed themselves of their right of resistance, legitimately shaking off the yoke of a despotic prince.[104] On the other, he had no difficulty justifying slavery and even the kind of 'wild beast' hunt against Indians underway in America.

Let us now pass on to the Glorious Revolution and Locke. The *Two Treatises of Government* may be regarded as key moments in the ideological preparation and consecration of the event that marks the birth of liberal England. We are dealing with texts deeply impregnated with the pathos of liberty, the condemnation of absolute power, the appeal to rise up against the wicked ones who seek to deprive man of his liberty and reduce him to slavery. But every now and then frightening passages open up in this ode to liberty, where slavery in the colonies is legitimized. As ultimate proof of the legitimacy of the institution, Grotius adduced the example of the Germans who, according to Tacitus'

---

99   See ibid., vol. 1, ch. iii, §4; vol. 3, ch. iii, §4.
100   See ibid., vol. 3, ch. vii, §§2, 5.
101   Ibid., vol. 3, pp. 1496, 1372.
102   Ibid., vol. 1, p. 264.
103   See ibid., vol. 2, ch. xxii, §11.
104   See ibid., vol. 2, ch. xvi, §16; vol. 1, ch. iv, §11.

testimony, 'ventured their very Liberty upon the Cast of a Die'.[105] In Locke's view, 'captives taken in a just war' (on the part of the victors) had 'forfeited their lives and, with it, their liberties'. They were slaves 'subjected to the absolute dominion and arbitrary power of their masters'.[106]

Up to now the thinking applies to blacks deported from Africa. But the fate reserved for Indians was not manifestly better. In addition to having an interest in the slave trade as a shareholder in the Royal African Company, the liberal English philosopher was concerned with the white colonists' expansionist march as secretary (in 1673–74) of the Council of Trade and Plantations. As has been justly observed:

> That so many of the examples Locke uses in his *Second Treatise* are American ones shows that his intention was to provide the settlers, for whom he had worked in so many other ways, with a powerful argument based in natural law rather than legislative decree to justify their depredations.[107]

The *Second Treatise* makes repeated reference to the 'wild Indian', who moved around 'insolent and injurious in the woods of America' or the 'vacant places of America'.[108] Ignorant of labour, which was the only thing that could confer property right, and occupying a land not 'improv[ed] by labour', or 'great tracts of unused' ground', the Indian inhabited 'unpossessed quarters', *in vacuis locis*.[109] In addition to labour and property, Indians were also ignorant of money. They thus not only proved alien to civilization, but were also 'not ... joined with the rest of mankind'.[110] As a result of their behaviour, they were not solely subject to human condemnation. Unquestionably, 'God commanded ... labour' and private property, and could certainly not want the world created by him to remain 'common and uncultivated'.[111]

When he sought to challenge the march of civilization, violently opposing exploitation through labour of the uncultivated land occupied by him, the Indian, along with any other criminal, could be equated with 'one of those wild savage beasts with whom men can have no society nor security', and who 'therefore may be destroyed as a lion or a tiger'. Locke never tired of

---

105   Ibid., vol. 2, p. 556.

106   Locke, *Two Treatises*, p. 158.

107   Anthony Pagden, 'The Struggle for Legitimacy and the Image of Empire in the Atlantic to c. 1700', in Canny, ed., *The Origins of Empire*, p. 43.

108   Locke, *Two Treatises*, pp. 129, 162, 134.

109   Ibid., pp. 136, 139, 152, 178.

110   Ibid., p. 139.

111   Ibid., pp. 133, 32.

insisting on the right possessed by any man to destroy those reduced to the level of 'beasts of prey', 'savage beasts'; to the level of 'a savage ravenous beast that is dangerous to his being'.[112]

These are phrases that remind us of those used by Grotius in connection with barbarous peoples and pagans in general, and by Washington in connection with the Indians. However, before coming to the Founding Fathers and the solemn documents that mark the birth of the United States, it is worth dwelling on another macroscopic exclusion clause that characterizes the celebration of liberty in Locke. 'Papists', declared the *Essay Concerning Toleration*, are 'like serpents never [to] be prevailed on by kind usage to lay by their venom'.[113] Even more than to English Catholics, this harsh declaration was formulated with a view to Ireland, where at the time unregistered priests were branded with a red-hot iron, when they were not punished with more severe penalties or death.[114] The Irish, in endemic, desperate revolt against spoliation and oppression by Anglican settlers, were contemptuously referred to by Locke as a population of 'brigands'. As for the rest, he reiterated the point the men are:

> forward to have compassion for sufferers and esteem for that religion as pure, and the professors of it as sincere, which can stand the test of persecution. But I think it is far otherwise with Catholics, who are less apt to be pitied than others because they receive no other usage than what they [by the] cruelty of their own principles and practices are known to deserve.[115]

The warning against feelings of 'compassion' makes it clear that we are dealing with Ireland primarily. Locke seems to have had no objections of any kind to the ruthless repression suffered by the Irish, whose fate calls to mind that reserved for Indians across the Atlantic.

We can now move on to examine the documents that informed the third liberal revolution and the foundation of the United States. At first sight, the Declaration of Independence and the 1787 Constitution seem inspired and pervaded by a universal pathos of liberty: 'all men are created equal'—such is the solemn preamble to the first document; it is necessary to 'secure the Blessings of Liberty to ourselves and our Posterity'—such is the no less solemn preamble

---

112   Ibid., pp. 122, 125, 212.

113   Locke, *Political Writings*, p. 202.

114   William Lecky, *A History of England in the Eighteenth Century*, 8 vols, London: Longmans, Green and Co., 1883–88, vol. 1, pp. 296–7.

115   Locke, *Political Writings*, p. 203.

to the second. But it requires a scarcely more attentive reading to encounter, already in Article 1 of the Constitution, a contrast between 'free Persons' and 'all other Persons'. The latter were, of course, slaves, whose number, reduced to three-fifths, had to be factored in and added to that of 'free persons' when it came to calculating the number of members in the House of Representatives to which slaveholding states were entitled.

With recourse to various euphemisms, a whole series of other Articles refer to this:

> No Person held to Service or Labour in One State, under the laws thereof, escaping into another, shall, in consequence of any Law or Regulation therein, be discharged from such Service or Labour, but shall be delivered up on claim of the Party to whom such Service or Labour may be due.

Where initially it was concealed among 'other persons' (the part of the population not made up of 'free persons'), now the relationship of slavery is modestly subsumed under the general category of persons 'held to Service or Labour'. On the basis of the principles of self-government, each individual state has the right to regulate it as it sees fit, while every state's obligation to return fugitive slaves is a moral obligation to guarantee a legitimate property-owner the services that 'may be due'. In a further linguistic expedient, tinged with the same discretion, the black slave trade becomes '[t]he migration or importation of such persons as any of the states now existing shall think proper to admit'. It was 'not [to] be prohibited by Congress prior to the year [1808]', and, pending that, could only be subjected to a fairly modest tax ('not exceeding ten dollars for each person' or slave). The articles requiring the Union to suppress insurrections or 'domestic violence'—primarily, a possible dreaded slave revolt in some particular state[116]—are formulated in similarly elliptical fashion.

Although repressed through a strict linguistic proscription, the institution of slavery proves to be a pervasive presence in the American Constitution. It is not even absent from the Declaration of Independence, where the accusation against George III of having appealed to black slaves takes the already noted form of having 'excited domestic insurrections amongst us'.

In the transition from Grotius to Locke, and from them to the founding documents of the American Revolution, we observe a phenomenon worth reflecting upon: although regarded as legitimate in all three cases, the institution of slavery was theorized and affirmed without the least reticence solely by

---

116   Cf. Paul Finkelman, *Slavery and the Founders*, Armonk (NY): Sharpe, 1996, pp. 3–5.

the Dutch author, whose life straddled the sixteenth and seventeenth centuries. In Locke, by contrast, at least in the case of the *Two Treatises of Government*, which were written and published on the eve and at the end of the Glorious Revolution, legitimation of slavery tends to occur exclusively between the lines of the discourse celebrating English liberty. The reticence reaches its peak in the documents that consecrate the foundation of the United States as the most glorious chapter in the history of liberty.

When it came to the relationship with the Indians, things were different: Grotius, Locke and Washington all referred to them as 'wild beasts'. A document like the Declaration of Independence, which was addressed to international public opinion and which (as we know) included among George III's most heinous crimes the fact that he had incited the 'merciless Indian savages' against the rebel colonists, was linguistically more cautious. But it remains the case that in all three liberal revolutions the demand for liberty and justification of the enslavement, as well as the decimation (or destruction), of barbarians, were closely intertwined.

7. Vulgar historicism and repression of the paradox of liberalism

In conclusion, the countries that were the protagonists of three major liberal revolutions were simultaneously the authors of two tragic chapters in modern (and contemporary) history. If that is so, however, can the habitual representation of the liberal tradition—namely, that it is characterized by the love of liberty as such—be regarded as valid? Let us return to our initial question: What is liberalism? As we register the disappearance of the old certainties, a great saying comes to mind: 'What is well-known, precisely because it is *well-*known, is not *known*. In the knowledge process, the commonest way to mislead oneself and others is to assume that something is well-known and to accept it as such'.[117]

Throwing a widespread apologia into crisis, the paradoxical tangle we have encountered while historically reconstructing the origins of liberalism is disturbing. We can therefore understand the tendency to repression. After all, that was the gesture, in their own day, of Locke and, especially, the rebel American colonists, who liked to draw a more or less thick veil of silence over the institution of slavery.

---

117   Georg W.F. Hegel, *Werke*, 20 vols, eds Eva Moldenhauer and Karl Markus Michel, Franfurt am Main: Suhrkamp, 1969–79, vol. 3, p. 35.

The same result can be arrived at in other ways. According to Hannah Arendt, what characterized the American Revolution was the project of realizing a political order based on liberty, while the persistence of black slavery referred to a cultural tradition homogeneously diffused either side of the Atlantic:

> [T]his indifference, difficult for us to understand, was not peculiar to Americans and hence must [not] be blamed ... on any perversion of the heart or upon the dominance of self-interest ... Slavery was no more part of the social question for Europeans than it was for Americans ... [118]

In fact, disquiet about slavery was so strongly felt in the Europe of the time that prominent authors not infrequently proceeded to a sharp contrast between the two shores of the Atlantic. Let us attend to Condorcet:

> The American forgets that negroes are men; he has no moral relationship with them; for him they are simply objects of profit ... and such is the excess of his stupid contempt for this unhappy species that, when back in Europe, he is indignant to see them dressed like men and placed alongside him. [119]

'The American' condemned here is the transatlantic colonist, whether French or English. In his turn, in 1771 Millar denounced 'the shocking barbarity to which the negroes in our colonies are frequently exposed'. Fortunately, 'the practice of slavery [has] been ... generally abolished in Europe'. Where it survived, across the Atlantic, the practice poisoned the whole society: cruelty and sadism were 'exhibited even by persons of the weaker sex, in an age distinguished for humanity and politeness'.[120] This was also the opinion of Condorcet, who pointed out how 'the young American woman witnesses', and sometimes even 'presides over', the brutal 'tortures' inflicted on black slaves.[121]

The thesis formulated by Arendt can even be inverted. In the late eighteenth century the institution of slavery began to be unacceptable in salons where the ideas of the *philosophes* circulated, and in churches influenced by the Quakers or other abolitionist sections of Christianity. Even as the Philadelphia Convention ratified the Constitution that sanctioned racial chattel slavery, a French defender of this institution bitterly noted his isolation:

---

118   Hannah Arendt, *On Revolution*, London: Faber & Faber, 1963, p. 66.

119   Condorcet, *Oeuvres*, vol. 3, pp. 647–8.

120   Millar, *Origin of the Distinction of Ranks*, pp. 258, 261.

121   Condorcet, *Oeuvres*, vol. 3, p. 648.

The extremely powerful empire of public opinion ... now offers its support to those in France and England who attack black slavery and pursue its abolition. The most odious interpretations are reserved for those who dare to hold a contrary opinion.[122]

Some years later, another French defender of slavery bemoaned the fact that 'negrophilia' had become a 'fashionable oddity', to the point of abolishing any sense of distance between the two races: 'African blood circulates much too abundantly in the veins of the Parisians themselves.'[123]

If we start out from the presupposition of a general 'indifference' to the lot of black slaves in these years, we shall understand nothing of the American Revolution. The 'last great philosopher' to justify slavery—Locke—was quite the reverse of unchallenged; and it is interesting to note that he was criticized together with the 'current American rebellion', which he was regarded as having inspired.[124] In both cases, celebration of a tendentially republican liberty was bound up with legitimation of the institution of slavery. After having cited various passages from the philosopher that leave no room for doubt in this regard, Josiah Tucker commented: '[s]uch is the language of the humane Mr Locke! The great and glorious Assertor of the natural Rights and Liberties of Mankind'; here were 'his real Sentiments concerning Slavery'.[125] Similarly, the American loyalist we have already encountered—Boucher—conjointly condemned the republican secession and Locke's claim to confer on 'every freeman of Carolina absolute power and property over his slaves'.[126]

While English patriots and loyalists opposed to secession ironized about the flag of liberty waved by slave-owners, the rebel colonists reacted not by invoking the legitimacy of enslaving blacks, but by highlighting the British Crown's massive involvement and principal responsibility in trafficking and trading human flesh. It is clear that the institution of slavery was now largely delegitimized. This explains the linguistic proscriptions that characterized the new state's Constitution. As a delegate to the Philadelphia Convention observed, his colleagues 'anxiously sought to avoid the admission of expressions which might be odious to the ears of Americans', but were 'willing to admit into their system those *things* which the *expressions signified*'.[127] The fact

---

122   Pierre-Victor Malouet, *Mémoire sur l'esclavage des nègres*, Neufchâtel, 1788, p. 152.

123   Louis-Narcisse Baudry des Lozières, *Les égarements du nigrophilisme*, Paris: Migneret, 1802, pp. 48, 156.

124   Tucker, *Collected Works*, vol. 1, p. 53.

125   Ibid., vol. 1, pp. 103–4.

126   Boucher, quoted in Zimmer, *Jonathan Boucher*, p. 296.

127   Foner, *The Story of American Freedom*, p. 36.

is that, from the start of the debate on the new constitutional order (pointed out another witness), people 'had been ashamed to use the term "Slaves" & had substituted a description'.[128] Less scrupulous (observed Condorcet in 1781) were the slaves' 'owners': they were 'guided by a false consciousness [*fausse conscience*]' that rendered them impervious to the 'protests of the defenders of humanity' and 'made them act not against their own interests, but to their own advantage'.[129]

As we can see, notwithstanding Arendt's contrary opinion, 'class interests'—principally of those who owned large plantations and a considerable number of slaves—played an important role, which did not escape contemporary observers. The fact is that Arendt ultimately ends up identifying with the viewpoint of the rebel colonists, who retained a clear conscience as champions of the cause of liberty, repressing the macroscopic fact of slavery by means of their ingenious euphemisms: what takes the place of such euphemisms is now the 'historicist' explanation.

8. Colonial expansions and the rebirth of slavery: the positions of Bodin, Grotius and Locke

Decidedly misleading as regards the American Revolution, might the 'historicist' approach be of some use in clarifying the reasons for the tangle of freedom and oppression that was already manifest in the two preceding liberal revolutions? Although contemporaries, in as much as both of them straddled the sixteenth and seventeenth centuries, Hugo Grotius and Jean Bodin expressed diametrically opposed positions on the issue of concern to us here. While the first justified slavery by appealing to the authority of the Bible and Aristotle, the second refuted both these arguments. Having observed that in the Hebrew world only gentiles could be subjected to perpetual slavery, and that Christians and Muslims observed similar norms and customs, Bodin concluded that 'those who profess all these three religions only partially observe the law of God with regard to slaves', as if the prohibition of this horrible institution only applied to blood relations, not humanity as a whole. If a distinction among the three monotheistic religions could be made, it was to the advantage of Islam, which had proved capable of expanding thanks to a courageous policy of emancipation.[130]

---

128 Finkelman, *Slavery and the Founders*, p. 3.

129 Condorcet, *Oeuvres*, vol. 7, p. 126.

130 Jean Bodin, *Six Books of the Commonwealth*, abridg. and trans. M. J. Tooley, Oxford: Basil Blackwell, n.d., pp. 18, 17.

Bodin also rejected Aristotle's thesis, adopted and even radicalized by Grotius, that some individuals and peoples are naturally slaves. As proof of this, the universal diffusion, temporal and spatial, of the institution of slavery was often cited. But (objected the French author) no less universally diffused were slave revolts:

> As for the argument that slavery could not have been so enduring if it had been contrary to nature, I would answer that the principle holds good for natural agents whose property it is to obey of necessity the unchanging laws of God. But man, being given the choice between good and evil, inclines for the most part to do that which is forbidden and chooses the evil, defying the laws of God and of nature. So much is such a one under the domination of his corrupt imagination, that he takes his own will for the law. There is no sort of impiety or wickedness which in this way has not come to be accounted virtuous and good.[131]

While it had long seemed obvious and been generally accepted, and still contin-ued to be, the institution of slavery pertained not to nature but to history—more precisely, to a deplorable and execrable chapter of history, which must rapidly be closed once and for all. It made no sense to try to justify it on the basis of right of war (as did Grotius): '[W]hat charity is there in sparing captives in order to derive some profit or pleasure from them as if they were cattle?'[132] In short, Grotius and Bodin were contemporaries. While the former was an expression of liberal Holland, the latter was a theorist of absolute monarchy. But it was he—not Grotius—who questioned the absolute power wielded by the master over his slaves.

We arrive at a similar result when, rather than with Grotius, we compare Bodin with Locke, whom he predated by some decades. Whereas the English liberal, also justifying slavery with his gaze on the past, pointed to Spartacus as culpable of an 'aggression' against 'property' and legitimate power, Bodin expressed himself quite differently: 'The Romans, who were so great and powerful ... however many laws they made, could not prevent the revolt of sixty thousand slaves led by Spartacus, who defeated the Roman army in open battle three times'.[133] In the English liberal the universalistic charge present in Bodin has disappeared, just as there is no longer any trace of the unconditional

---

131 Ibid., pp. 16, 17.

132 Ibid., p. 17.

133 Locke, *Two Treatises*, p. 216; Jean Bodin, *I sei libri dello Stato*, trans. Margherita Isnardi Parente, Turin: UTET, 1988, vol. 1, p. 247.

condemnation of slavery we can read in the French theorist of absolute monarchy. If we bear in mind 'the homicides, the cruelties and barbarities inflicted on slaves by their masters, it was an unmitigated catastrophe that the institution was ever introduced, and then, that once it had been declared abolished, it should ever have been allowed to persist.'[134]

The quotation above refers to persistence. In fact, Bodin traced a brief history of slavery in the world or, more precisely, the West (and the geographical area dominated by it). Certainly, the institution had been vital in Greco-Roman antiquity. As late as the American Civil War, the theorists and defenders of the southern cause appealed to the example and model of that splendid civilization in order to condemn abolitionism. By contrast, Bodin drew a rather realistic picture of classical antiquity. It was based on the enslavement of a number of human beings that was significantly greater than the number of free citizens. Consequently, it lived under the constant menace of slave revolts and, in order to solve the problem, did not hesitate to resort to the most barbaric measures, as proved by the massacre of 30,000 helots in Sparta 'in a single night'.[135] Subsequently, as a result also of the influence of Christianity, things seemed to change: 'Europe was freed of slavery after about 1250', but 'we see it today newly restored'. Following colonial expansion, it was 'in the process of being renewed throughout the world'. There had been a massive restoration of slavery, and already Portugal 'derives from it veritable herds as of beasts'.[136]

Hence, far from being affected by vulgar historicism's attempts at repression, the paradox that characterizes the American Revolution and early liberalism in general not only survives, but proves even more marked. We are in the presence of a political movement counter to the trend of authors who, centuries earlier, had pronounced an unequivocal condemnation of the institution of slavery. While Locke, champion of the struggle against absolute monarchy, justified the white master's absolute power over the black slave, a theorist of monarchical absolutism—Bodin—condemned such power.

In analyzing the relationship that the three liberal revolutions developed on the one hand with the blacks, and on the other with the Irish, Indians and natives, it is misleading to start out from the presupposition of a homogeneous historical time unmarked by fractures and flowing in unilinear fashion. Clearly predating Locke and Washington, and a contemporary of Grotius, was

---

134   Bodin, *Six Books*, p. 18.
135   Bodin, *I sei libri*, vol. 1, pp. 247–8.
136   Ibid., pp. 253, 238, 260.

Montaigne, in whom we find a memorable self-critical reflection on the West's colonial expansion that we would seek in vain in them. Such a reflection can even be read as a prefigurative but timely critique of the attitude of Grotius, Locke and Washington towards non-European populations. Among them there was 'nothing savage or barbarous'; the fact was that 'every man calls barbarous anything he is not accustomed to'. People took their own country as a model: 'There we always find the perfect religion, the perfect polity, the most developed and perfect way of doing anything!'[137] Going back further, we encounter Las Casas and his critique of the arguments employed to de-humanize the Indian 'barbarians'[138]—the arguments that are more or less widely echoed by Grotius, Locke and Washington.

It should be added that the 'historicist' explanation turns out to be unfounded not only as regards the relationship with colonial peoples. While Fletcher, a self-defined 'republican on principle', member of the Scottish parliament and supporter of the liberal political world derived from the Glorious Revolution, called for 'mak[ing] slaves of all those who are unable to provide for their own subsistence',[139] Bodin also condemned slavery for 'vagrants and idlers'.[140] According to the observation of a great historian, it was in 'the period between 1660 and 1760' (the decades of the rise of the liberal movement) that an attitude of unprecedented harshness spread in England towards wage-labourers and the unemployed, 'which has no modern parallel except in the behaviour of the less reputable of white colonists towards coloured labour'.[141]

To understand the radical character of the paradox we are examining, let us return to Bodin. He primarily attributed the return of slavery in the world to the 'greed of merchants', and then added: 'If the princes do not set things in good order, it will soon be full of slaves.'[142] Not only was slavery not a residue of the past and backwardness, but the remedy for it was to be sought not in the new political and social forces (liberal in orientation), but, on the contrary, in monarchical power. Thus argued Bodin, but thus likewise argued Smith two centuries later. On the other hand, in recommending the conversion of beggars

---

137   Michel de Montaigne, *The Complete Essays*, ed. and trans. M.A. Screech, London: Penguin, 2003, p. 231.

138   Bartolomé de las Casas, *La leggenda nera*, trans. Alberto Pincherle, Milan: Feltrinelli, 1981, ch. xii.

139   Marx, *Capital: Volume One*, pp. 882–3 n. 9.

140   Bodin, *I sei libri*, vol. 1, p. 262 (bk 1, ch. 5).

141   R.H. Tawney, *Religion and the Rise of Capitalism*, West Drayton: Pelican, 1948, p. 267. C.B. Macpherson, *The Political Theory of Possessive Individualism*, Oxford: Oxford University Press, 1962, pp. 227–8 and Morgan, *American Slavery, American Freedom*, p. 325 reach the same conclusion.

142   Bodin, *I sei libri*, vol. 1, p. 260 (bk 1, ch. 5).

into slaves, Fletcher polemicized against the Church, which he rebuked for having promoted the abolition of slavery in classical antiquity and for opposing its reintroduction in the modern world, thus encouraging the sloth and dissipation of vagrants.[143] In this case, too, the institution of slavery was felt to be in contradiction not with the new social and political forces, but with a power that was pre-modern in origin. Such considerations can also be applied to Grotius, who likewise developed an argument, if not against Christianity as such, then against interpretations of it in an abolitionist register:

> [W]hat the Apostles and antient Canons enjoin Slaves, of not leaving their Masters, is a general Maxim, and only opposed to the Error of those who rejected every Subjection, both private and publick, as a State inconsistent with the Liberty of Christians.[144]

The Virginian property-owners who prevented the baptism of slaves in the late seventeenth century, so as not to spoil the spirit of submission and to avoid the emergence of a sense of pride in them because they belonged to the same religious community as the masters, provoked complaints from Church and Crown alike.[145] Once again, we see that it was the forces of the *ancien régime* which acted to check and contain the novelty represented by racial slavery.

Recourse to vulgar historicism to 'explain' or repress the surprising tangle of freedom and oppression that characterizes the three liberal revolutions we have referred to is fruitless. The paradox persists and awaits a genuine, less comforting explanation.

---

143   Morgan, *American Slavery, American Freedom*, p. 325.
144   Grotius, *Rights of War and Peace*, vol. 2, p. 561.
145   Morgan, *American Slavery, American Freedom*, p. 332.

CHAPTER TWO

Liberalism and Racial Slavery: A Unique Twin Birth

1. The limitation of power and the emergence of an unprecedented absolute power

To render it explicable, the paradox must first be expounded in all its radicalism. Slavery is not something that persisted despite the success of the three liberal revolutions. On the contrary, it experienced its maximum development following that success: 'The total slave population in the Americas reached around 330,000 in 1700, nearly three million by 1800, and finally peaked at over six million in the 1850s'.[1] Contributing decisively to the rise of an institution synonymous with the absolute power of man over man was the liberal world. In the mid-eighteenth century, it was Great Britain that possessed the largest number of slaves (878,000). The fact is unexpected. Although its empire was far more extensive, Spain came well behind. Second position was held by Portugal, which possessed 700,000 slaves and was in fact a kind of semi-colony of Great Britain: much of the gold extracted by Brazilian slaves ended up in London.[2] Hence there is no doubt that absolutely pre-eminent in this field was the country at the head of the liberal movement, which had wrested primacy in the trading and ownership of black slaves precisely from the Glorious Revolution onwards. It was Pitt the Younger himself who, intervening in April 1792 in the House of Commons on the subject of slavery and the slave trade, acknowledged that '[n]o nation in Europe ... has ... plunged so deeply into this guilt as Great Britain.'[3]

---

1   Robin Blackburn, *The Making of New World Slavery*, London and New York: Verso, 1997, p. 3.

2   Robin Blackburn, *The Overthrow of Colonial Slavery, 1776–1848*, London and New York: Verso, 1990, p. 5.

3   Quoted in Hugh Thomas, *The Slave Trade*, New York: Simon & Schuster, 1997, p. 235.

That is not all. To a greater or lesser extent, there survived in the Spanish and Portuguese colonies '*ancillary* slavery', which is to be distinguished from '*systemic* slavery, linked to plantations and commodity production'. And it was the latter type of slavery, established above all in the eighteenth century (starting from the liberal revolution of 1688–89) and clearly predominant in the British colonies, which most consummately expressed the de-humanization of those who were now mere instruments of labour and chattels, subject to regular sale on the market.[4]

This did not even involve a return to the slavery peculiar to classical antiquity. Certainly, chattel slavery had been widespread in Rome. Yet the slave could reasonably hope that, if not he himself, then his children or grandchildren would be able to achieve freedom and even an eminent social position. Now, by contrast, his fate increasingly took the form of a cage from which it was impossible to escape. In the first half of the eighteenth century, numerous English colonies in America enacted laws that made the emancipation of slaves increasingly difficult.[5]

The Quakers lamented the advent of what seemed to them a new and repugnant system. Slavery for a determinate period of time, and the other forms of more or less servile labour hitherto in force, tended to give way to slavery in the strict sense, to a permanent, hereditary condemnation of a whole people, who were denied any prospect of change and improvement, any hope of freedom.[6] Again, in a statute of 1696, South Carolina declared that it could not prosper 'without the labor and service of negroes and other slaves'.[7] The barrier separating service and slavery was as yet not well defined, and the institution of slavery had not yet appeared in all its harshness. But the process that increasingly reduced slaves to chattels, and established the racial character of the condition they were subjected to, was already underway. An unbridgeable gulf separated blacks from the free population. Ever stricter laws prohibited interracial sexual and marital relations, making them a crime. We are now dealing with a hereditary caste of slaves, defined and recognizable by the colour of their skin. In this sense, in John Wesley's view, 'American slavery' was 'the vilest that ever saw the sun'.[8]

---

4 Blackburn, *The Overthrow of Colonial Slavery*, p. 9.

5 Winthrop D. Jordan, *White over Black*, New York: Norton, 1977, pp. 123, 399.

6 Arthur Zilversmit, *The First Emancipation*, Chicago: University of Chicago Press, 1969, p. 66.

7 Jordan, *White over Black*, p. 109.

8 Robert Isaac Wilberforce, *The Life of William Wilberforce*, 5 vols, London: Murray, 1838, vol. 1, p. 297 (letter from John Wesley to William Wilberforce, 24 February 1791).

The verdict of American Quakers and British abolitionists has been fully confirmed by contemporary historians. At the end of a 'cycle of degradation' of blacks, with the ignition of the white 'engine of oppression' and the conclusive soldering of 'slavery and racial discrimination', we see at work in the 'colonies of the British empire' in the late seventeenth century a 'chattel racial slavery' unknown in Elizabethan England (and also classical antiquity), but 'familiar to men living in the nineteenth century' and aware of the reality of the southern United States.[9] Hence slavery in its most radical form triumphed in the golden age of liberalism and at the heart of the liberal world. This was acknowledged by James Madison, slave-owner and liberal (like numerous protagonists of the American Revolution), who observed that 'the most oppressive dominion ever exercised by man over man'—power based on 'mere distinction of colour'—was imposed 'in the most enlightened period of time'.[10]

Correctly stated, in all its radicalism, the paradox we face consists in this: the rise of liberalism and the spread of racial chattel slavery are the product of a twin birth which, as we shall see, has rather unique characteristics.

2. The self-government of civil society and the triumph of large-scale property

On its emergence, the paradox we are attempting to explain did not escape the most attentive observers. We have just seen Madison's admission; and we are familiar with Samuel Johnson's irony on the passionate love of liberty displayed by slave-owners; and Adam Smith's observation on the nexus between the persistence and reinforcement of slavery, on the one hand, and the power of representative bodies hegemonized by slave-owners, on the other. In this connection, however, we must also record other, no less significant interventions. In fighting for conciliation of the rebel colonies, Burke recognized the influence of slavery within them. But this did not impair the 'spirit of freedom'. On the contrary, it was precisely here that freedom appeared 'more noble and liberal'. Indeed, 'these people of the southern colonies are more much more strongly ... attached to liberty, than those to the northward'.[11] This is a consideration that we also encounter, some decades later, from a Barbadian planter: 'you will ...

---

9   Jordan, *White over Black*, p. 98.

10   Max Farrand, ed., *The Records of the Federal Convention of 1787*, 4 vols, New Haven: Yale University Press, 1966, vol. 1, p. 135.

11   Edmund Burke, *The Works: A New Edition*, 16 vols, London: Rivington, 1826, vol. 3, p. 54.

find that no nations in the world have been more jealous of their liberties than those amongst whom the institution of slavery existed'.[12] On the other side, in England, countering Burke and his policy of conciliation of the rebel colonists, Josiah Tucker pointed out how 'the Champions for American Republicanism' were simultaneously the promoters of the 'absurd Tyranny' they exercised over their slaves: this was 'a *republican Tyranny*, the worst of all Tyrannies'.[13]

In the authors cited here, there is a more or less clear awareness, accompanied by different value judgements, of the paradox we are examining. And perhaps precisely now it begins to lose its aura of impenetrability. Why should we be surprised that those demanding, or in the forefront of the demand for, self-government and 'freedom' from central political power were the major slave-owners? In 1839 an eminent representative of Virginia observed that the position of the slave-owner stimulated in him 'a more liberal cast of character, more elevated principles, a wider expansion of thought, a deeper and more fervent love, and juster estimate of that liberty by which he is so highly distinguished'.[14]

The wealth and leisure it enjoyed, and the culture it thus managed to acquire, reinforced the proud self-consciousness of a class that became ever more intolerant of the abuses of power, the intrusions, the interference and the constraints of political power or religious authority. Shaking off these constraints, the planter and slave-owner developed a liberal spirit and a liberal mentality.

Confirming this phenomenon are the changes that occurred from the Middle Ages. Between 1263 and 1265, by means of the *Siete partidas*, Alfonso X of Castile regulated the institution of slavery, which he seemed to recognize reluctantly because it was always 'unnatural'. What limited the property right in the first instance was religion: an unbeliever was not permitted to own Christian slaves and, in any event, the slave had to be guaranteed the possibility of living in conformity with Christian principles—whence the recognition of his right to establish a family and have the chastity and honour of his wife and daughters respected. Later, there were even cases of masters denounced to the Inquisition for their failure to respect the rights of their slaves. Further limiting the power of the property-owner was the state, profoundly influenced by religion. It was committed to disciplining and limiting the punishment inflicted

---

12   Eric Williams, *Capitalism and Slavery*, London: Deutsch, 1990, pp. 199–200.

13   Josiah Tucker, *Collected Works*, London: Routledge and Thoemmes Press, 1993–96, vol. 5, pp. 21, 72.

14   Shearer Davis Bowman, *Masters and Lords*, New York: Oxford University Press, 1993, p. 21.

by masters on slaves and variously sought to promote their emancipation (we are dealing with Christian subjects). Emancipation occurred from above when the slave performed a meritorious deed for the country; in such cases, the master deprived of his property was compensated by the state.[15]

The advent of modern property entailed the master's ability to dispose of it as he saw fit. In the Virginia of the second half of the seventeenth century, a law was in force that sanctioned the effective impunity of a master even when he killed his slave. Such behaviour could not be considered a 'felony', since '[i]t cannot be presumed that prepense malice (which alone makes murder felony) should induce any man to destroy his own estate.'[16] First with the Glorious Revolution and then later, more completely, with the American Revolution, the assertion of self-government by civil society hegemonized by slaveholders involved the definitive liquidation of traditional forms of 'interference' by political and religious authority. Christian baptism and profession of faith were henceforth irrelevant. In Virginia at the end of the seventeenth century, one could proceed 'without the solemnities of jury' to the execution of a slave guilty of a capital crime; marriage between slaves was no longer a sacrament, and even funerals lost their solemnity. At the beginning of the nineteenth century, a Virginian jurist (George Tucker) could observe that the slave was positioned 'below the rank of human beings, not only politically, but physically and morally'.[17]

The conquest of self-government by civil society hegemonized by large-scale property involved an even more drastic deterioration in the condition of the indigenous population. The end of the control exercised by the London government swept away the last obstacles to the expansionistic march of the white colonists. Already harboured by Jefferson, and then explicitly and brutally formulated by the Monroe administration (the natives of the East must clear off the land, 'whether or not they agree, whether or not they become civilized'), the idea of deporting the Indians became a tragic reality with the Jackson Presidency:

---

15   Herbert S. Klein, *Slavery in the Americas*, Chicago: Dee, 1989, pp. 59–65; Blackburn, *The Overthrow of Colonial Slavery*, p. 39 and *The Making of New World Slavery*, pp. 50–2.

16   Klein, *Slavery in the Americas*, pp. 38–9; Stanley M. Elkins, *Slavery*, Chicago: University of Chicago Press, 1959, p. 59.

17   Klein, *Slavery in the Americas*, pp. 49, 39.

General Winfield Scott, with seven thousand troops and followed by 'civilian volunteers,' invaded the Cherokee domain, seized all the Indians they could find, and, in the middle of winter, sent them on the long trek to Arkansas and Oklahoma. The 'civilian volunteers' appropriated the Indians' livestock, household goods, and farm implements and burned their homes. Some fourteen thousand Indians were forced to travel the 'trail of tears,' as it came to be called, and about four thousand of them died on the way. An eyewitness to the exodus reported: 'Even aged females, apparently ready to drop into the grave, were travelling with heavy burdens attached to their backs, sometimes on frozen grounds and sometimes on muddy streets, with no covering for their feet.'[18]

3. The black slave and the white servant: from Grotius to Locke

While it stimulated the development of racial chattel slavery and created an unprecedented, unbridgeable gulf between whites and peoples of colour, the self-government of civil society triumphed, waving the flag of liberty and the struggle against despotism. Between these two elements, which emerged together during a unique twin birth, a relationship full of tensions and contradictions was established. Such a celebration of liberty, which was bound up with the reality of an unprecedented absolute power, can clearly be interpreted as an ideology. But however mystificatory it might be, ideology is never null. In fact, its mystificatory function cannot even be conceived without some incidence in concrete social reality. And still less can ideology be regarded as synonymous with conscious falsehood. Were that to be the case, it would not succeed in inspiring people and generating real social activity, and would be condemned to impotence. The theorists and agents of the liberal revolutions and movements were moved by a powerful, convinced pathos of liberty; and precisely for that reason, they displayed embarrassment at the reality of slavery. Obviously, in a majority of cases, such embarrassment did not push them to the point of questioning the 'property' on which the wealth and social influence of the class protagonist in the struggle for the self-government of civil society were based. As regards England, the course was taken that removed slavery in the strict sense to a geographical area remote from the metropolis, situated at the edge of the civilized world, where, precisely on account of the proximity and pressure of barbarous circumstances, the spirit of liberty was

---

18 Thomas F. Gossett, *Race*, New York: Schocken Books, 1965, p. 233.

not manifested in all its purity, unlike in England proper—the true homeland, the promised land of liberty.

However, this was a conclusion reached via a route marked by oscillations and contradictions of various kinds. In Grotius the colour barrier is not yet visible that separates the fate reserved for blacks from the condition to which the poorest layers of the white population can be subjected. We read: 'perfect and utter Slavery, is that which obliges a Man to serve his Master all his Life long, for Diet and other common Necessaries; which indeed, if it be thus understood, and confined within the Bounds of Nature, has nothing too hard and severe in it. However, slavery was not the only form of *servitus*, but only the 'most ignoble … Kind of Subjection' (*subjectionis species ignobilissima*).[19] There was also *servitus imperfecta*, peculiar, among others, to serfs and *mercenarii* or wage-labourers.[20] Thus, labour as such was subsumed under the category of 'service' (*servitus*) or 'subjection' (*subjectio*). Obviously, there is a difference between the two forms of 'service' and 'subjection'. While it violated 'natural reason' or 'the Rules of full and compleat Justice'—i.e. the norms of morality—on the basis of the legislation in force in some countries the master could kill his slave with impunity and hence exercise a right of life and death over him.[21] This was something not found in the sphere of *servitus imperfecta* and the labour relationship that employed *mercenarii* or wage-labourers. Nevertheless, we are dealing with a particular *species* of the single *genus* that is service or subjection. The boundary between the various species is fluid. For example, of the 'apprentices [*apprenticii*] in England', it was to be noted that they 'come nearest to the State of Slavery, during their Apprenticeship'—that is to say, to the condition of slaves proper.[22] On the other hand, by way of atoning for a crime one could be condemned to labour and to render one's services either as a slave or as an individual subjected to some form of 'imperfect slavery'.[23]

Compared with Grotius, Locke was concerned to distinguish more rigorously between the various kinds of service. Elements of continuity are certainly not lacking. Speaking of wage-labour and the contract that establishes it, the English philosopher wrote: 'a free man makes himself a servant to another'. As we can see, labour as such continues to be subsumed under the category of service. In fact, the contract introduces the wage-labourer 'into the family

---

19   Hugo Grotius, *The Rights of War and Peace*, 3 vols, ed. Richard Tuck, Indianapolis: Liberty Fund, 2005, vol. 2, pp. 557, 556.

20   See ibid., vol. 2, ch. v, §30.

21   See ibid., vol. 2, ch. v, §28; vol. 3, ch. xiv, §3.

22   Ibid., vol. 2, pp. 562–3 n. 7.

23   See ibid., vol. 2, ch. v, §32.

of his master, and under the ordinary discipline thereof'. This discipline was in fact very different from the unlimited power that characterized the relationship of slavery and defined the 'perfect condition of slavery'.[24] Grotius' distinction between *servitus perfecta* and *servitus imperfecta* reappears in broad outline.

But Locke urges us not to confuse servant and slave. Grotius compared the slave to a '*perpetual Hireling*', or a wage-labourer bound for the duration of his natural term to the same master.[25] By contrast, Locke stressed that we are dealing with two different statuses. In addition to being 'temporary', the power exercised by the master over a servant 'is no greater than what is contained in the contract between them'.[26] If, on the one hand, this made the condition of the servant better, on the other, it rendered that of the slave proper manifestly worse. Shaking off the moral inhibitions of Grotius, who called on the master to respect not only the life but also the specificity of his slave, Locke endlessly stressed that the master exercises over the slave an 'absolute dominion' and 'absolute power', a 'legislative power of life and death', an 'arbitrary power' encompassing 'life' itself.[27]

At this point, the slave tends to lose his human characteristics and become reduced to a thing and a chattel, as emerges in particular from the reference to the planters of the East Indies who possess 'slaves or horses' on the basis of a regular 'purchase', and this 'by bargain and money'.[28] Without any hint of criticism, Locke engaged in a conjunction that signifies a firm, indignant denunciation in abolitionist literature. This applies to Mirabeau, who (as we shall see) compared the condition of American slaves with 'our horses and our mules'; and to Marx, who observed in *Capital*: 'The slave-owner buys his worker in the same way as he buys his horse.'[29]

Locke marks a turning point theoretically. Sometimes freed by their masters, blacks slaves were long subjected to a condition not markedly dissimilar from that of indentured servants—that is, temporary white semi-slaves on a contractual basis. And it is this ambiguity that finds expression in the text of Grotius, who can hence also apply the category of contract to *servitus perfecta*. In Locke, by contrast, we can read the development which chattel slavery and racial

---

24   John Locke, *Two Treatises of Government*, ed. William S. Carpenter, London and New York: Everyman's Library, 1924, pp. 157–8, 128.

25   Grotius, *Rights of War and Peace*, vol. 3, p. 1483.

26   Locke, *Two Treatises*, p. 158.

27   See Grotius, *Rights of War and Peace*, vol. 3, ch. xiv, §6; Locke, *Two Treatises*, pp. 158, 128.

28   Ibid., p 90.

29   Karl Marx, *Capital: Volume One*, trans. Ben Fowkes, Harmondsworth: Penguin, 1976, p. 377.

slavery began to undergo from the late seventeenth century. A whole series of English colonies in America enacted laws intended to make it clear that the slave's conversion did not entail his emancipation.[30] Locke expressed himself thus in 1660 when, referring to Paul of Tarsus, he asserted that 'conversion did not dissolve any of those obligations they were tied in before ... the gospel continued them in the same condition and under the same civil obligations [under which] it found them. The married were not to leave their consorts, nor the servant freed from his master ...'[31] In complete conformity with this theoretical position, in the draft Carolina Constitution Locke reiterated the irrelevance of possible conversion to Christianity for the condition of the slave. And, once again, the element of novelty emerges. Although rejecting an abolitionist interpretation of Christianity, Grotius repeatedly appealed to Christian literature to underscore the common humanity of servant and master, both of them subject to the Father in Heaven, and hence in a relationship with each another that was in some sense one of fraternity.[32] The *Second Treatise of Government* is concerned, instead, to make it clear that the principle of equality applies exclusively to 'creatures of the same species and rank', only if 'the lord and master of them all should [not], by any manifest declaration of his will, set one above another, and confer on him, by an evident and clear appointment, an undoubted right to dominion and sovereignty'.[33] Blacks were burdened by the curse which, according to the Old Testament story, Noah had uttered against Ham and his descendants. This ideological motif, often invoked by defenders of the institution of slavery, seems also to find some echo in Locke.

There is no doubt: the English liberal philosopher legitimized the racial slavery that was being established in the politico-social reality of the time. Subject to ever more onerous conditions, the practice of emancipation tended to disappear; while, together with the neutralization of religion and baptism, laws prohibiting interracial sexual and marital relations sanctioned the insurmountable character of the boundary between whites and blacks. At this point the category of contract can serve to explain only the figure of the servant, while the slave is such as a result of right of war (more precisely, just war, of which Europeans engaged in colonial conquests are protagonists), or of a divine 'manifest declaration'.

---

30   Jordan, *White over Black*, pp. 84–93.
31   John Locke, *Two Tracts on Government*, ed. Philip Abrams, Cambridge: Cambridge University Press, 1967, p. 141.
32   See Grotius, *Rights of War and Peace*, vol. 3, ch. xiv, §2.
33   Locke, *Two Treatises*, pp. 118–19.

In order to clarify the difference between 'the perfect condition of slavery' and that of the indentured servant, Locke referred to the Old Testament, which provides for permanent, hereditary slavery only for gentiles, excluding from it servants who are blood relations of the Hebrew master.[34] The Old Testament line of demarcation between Hebrews and gentiles is configured in Locke as the line of demarcation between whites and blacks: servants of European origin are not subject to 'perfect slavery', which is intended for blacks and repressed to the colonies.

4. The pathos of liberty and unease about the institution of slavery: the case of Montesquieu

Liberal unease over slavery found what is perhaps its most acute expression in Montesquieu, who devoted some memorable pages to a critique of the institution. The reasons traditionally adduced by 'jurists' in justification of slavery were 'not sensible'.[35] And it was pointless trying to find others: 'If I had to defend the right we had of making Negroes slaves, here is what I would say: The peoples of Europe, having exterminated those of America, had to make slaves of those of Africa in order to use them to clear so much land.' Yet this condemnation, so ringing and seemingly unequivocal, soon gave way to a much more ambiguous discourse: 'There are countries where the heat enervates the body and weakens the courage so much that men come to perform an arduous duty only from fear of chastisement: slavery there runs less counter to reason'. In such cases, while not conforming to abstract reason, slavery was in accord with 'natural reason' (*raison naturelle*), which took account of climate and concrete circumstances.[36] True, Montesquieu observed that 'there is no climate on earth where one could not engage freemen to work'.[37] But if the tone is uncertain here, much clearer is the assertion that a distinction must be made between those countries where the climate can in some way be an element justifying slavery and those where 'even natural reasons reject it, as in the countries of Europe where it has so fortunately been abolished'.[38] Hence it is necessary to take cognizance of the 'uselessness of slavery among ourselves' and restrict

---

34 Ibid., p. 128.

35 Charles-Louis Montesquieu, *The Spirit of the Laws*, trans. and ed. Anne M. Cohler, Basia Carolyn Miller and Harold Samuel Stone, Cambridge: Cambridge University Press, 1989, p. 247.

36 Ibid., pp. 251–2.

37 Ibid., p. 253.

38 Ibid., p. 252.

'natural slavery [*servitude naturelle*] ... to certain particular countries of the world'.[39] On the one hand, Montesquieu endlessly stressed that freedom is an attribute—in fact, a way of living and being—of Nordic peoples, while, on the other, slavery had been 'naturalized ... among the southern peoples'.[40] A general law could be formulated: 'one must not be surprised that the coward-ice of the peoples of hot climates has almost always made them slaves and that the courage of the peoples of cold climates has kept them free. This is an effect that derives from its natural cause.'[41]

Prominent in Grotius and Locke, the contrast between metropolis and colonies also emerges in Montesquieu. It is not by chance that in *The Spirit of the Laws*, rather than being introduced in the books devoted to analysing freedom, the considerations on slavery make their appearance in the context of the discourse on the relationship between climate and laws and customs. The transition from Books XI–XIII, whose subjects are the 'Constitution', 'political freedom' and 'freedom' as such, to Books XIV-XVI, which deal with 'climate', despotism and 'domestic slavery' (slavery proper), is, at the same time, the transition from Europe—in particular, England—to the non-European world and the colonies. For that very reason, in asserting a climatic justification of slavery, its supporters would have no difficulty in appealing to Montesquieu.[42] With his argument the French philosopher targeted not the theorists of slavery as such, but those who held to the thesis that 'it would be good if there were slaves among us'.[43]

As regards the colonies, it was a question of seeing 'what the laws ought to do in relation to slavery'. Rather than abolition, Montesquieu's discourse focused on amending the institution: 'whatever the nature of slavery, civil laws must seek to remove, on the one hand, its abuses, and on the other, its dangers'.[44] Are those 'civil laws' the *Code noir* issued some years earlier by Louis XIV, which consecrated black slavery and, at the same time, proposed to regulate it? The language of that document suggests as much. While he reiterated his 'power', in the preamble the sovereign asserted his concern for black slaves, who lived in 'climates infinitely remote from our habitual sojourn'. They were to be guar-anteed food and adequate clothing (Articles 22 and 25). And such guarantees,

---

39   Ibid., p. 252.
40   Ibid., p. 355.
41   Ibid., p. 278.
42   David B. Davis, *The Problem of Slavery in Western Culture*, Ithaca and New York: Cornell University Press, 1966, pp. 394–5.
43   Montesquieu, *Spirit of the Laws*, p. 253.
44   Ibid., p. 254.

together with any treatment that was necessary, also applied to 'slaves who are infirm on account of old age, illness or other circumstances, regardless of whether the illness is curable' (Article 27).[45] These are concerns that also find expression in *The Spirit of the Laws*: 'The magistrate should see to it that the slave is nourished and clothed; this should be regulated by law.'[46] Montesquieu went on to assert that the slave must not be left completely at the mercy of the master's arbitrary power. The latter might impose a death penalty in his capacity as a 'judge', respecting legal 'formalities', not as a private person. The *Code noir* argued in analogous fashion, providing for sanctions for the master guilty of the arbitrary mutilation or killing of his slave (Articles 42–43).

The Spirit of the Laws counted the sexual exploitation of female slaves among the main 'abuses of slavery': 'Reason wants the power of the master not to extend beyond things that are of service to him; slavery must be for utility and not for voluptuousness. The laws of modesty are a part of natural right and should be felt by all the nations in the world.'[47]

In homage to the precepts of the 'Catholic, apostolic and Roman religion', the *Code noir* regarded as 'valid marriages' those contracted between slaves who professed this religion (Article 8). It banned the separate sale of individual members of the family thus constituted (Article 47) and sought to repress the sexual exploitation of female slaves. A free, single man who had had children by a slave was obliged to marry her and recognize the offspring, who were to be freed together with the mother (Article 9).

Further confirming that he intended to amend, rather than abolish, slavery is the fact that Montesquieu, as well as to its 'abuses', called attention to the 'dangers' it entailed and the 'precautions' required to confront them. Particular attention must be paid to the 'danger of a large number of slaves' and that represented by 'armed slaves'. This warranted a recommendation of a general kind: 'In the moderate state, the humanity one has for slaves will be able to prevent the dangers one could fear from there being too many of them. Men grow accustomed to anything, even to servitude, provided the master is not harsher than the servitude.'[48]

In his desire to temper colonial slavery, Montesquieu looked for inspiration to the norms promulgated by the *ancien régime*, which in fact had no influence in the English world admired by him. In any case, his condemnation of

---

45   The *Code noir* is reproduced and commented on in Louis Sala-Molins, *Le Code noir*, Paris: Presses Universitaires de France, 1988, pp. 89–203.

46   Montesquieu, *Spirit of the Laws*, p. 259.

47   Ibid., p. 255.

48   Ibid., p. 258.

slavery is sharp only when it also seeks to break in 'among ourselves', thereby throwing Europe's proud self-consciousness about being the exclusive locus of liberty into crisis. Along with despotism, slavery was present in Turkey and the Islamic world, and in Russia (in the form of abject serfdom), and prevailed unchallenged in Africa. But there was no room for it in Europe, or, rather, on metropolitan territory. The discourse relating to the colonies was different and more complex.

5. The Somersett case and the delineation of liberal identity

Blackstone's position is close to Montesquieu's. We are in the mid-eighteenth century: 'the law of England abhors, and can not endure the existence of, slavery within this nation'; not even its humblest, most base members, not even 'idle vagabonds' could be subjected to slavery.[49] The 'spirit of liberty' (argued the great jurist) 'is so deeply implanted in our constitution, and rooted even in our very soil' that it could not in any instance permit the presence or spectacle of a relationship that was the concentrated expression of absolute power.[50] '[S]trict slavery' existed in 'old Rome' and continued to flourish in 'modern Barbary', but was now incompatible with the 'spirit' of the English nation.[51]

On the other hand, among the rights enjoyed by free men was free, undisturbed enjoyment of property, including property in slaves, on condition that the latter remained banished to the colonial world. The relationship between master and slave—and this applied to all 'sorts of servants', including slaves—was one of the 'great relations in private life';[52] political authority had no right to intervene in it. And thus, celebration of England as the land of liberty was not perceived by Blackstone as being in contradiction with his reassertion of the black slave's duty to serve his master. That was a duty which, on the basis of the 'general principles' of the 'laws of England', did not come to an end even were the 'heathen negro' to be converted to Christianity. Not even in that case could the slave stake a claim to 'liberty'.[53]

Although recognized, the institution of slavery was, as it were, repressed from the 'soil' of England, confined to the border zone between the civilized

---

49   William Blackstone, *Commentaries on the Laws of England*, 4 vols, Chicago: University of Chicago Press, 1979, vol. 1, pp. 412–13.

50   Ibid., vol. 1, p. 123.

51   Ibid., vol. 1, p. 412.

52   Ibid., vol. 1, pp. 410–11.

53   Ibid., vol. 1, pp. 412–13.

world and barbarism. But what happened when a white master brought one of his slaves with him from the colonies as movable property? This was the problem raised by an impassioned debate in England in 1772. Turning to the courts, a slave—James Somersett—succeeded in extricating himself from the master who attempted to take him with him, in his capacity as movable property, on his return journey to Virginia. The Chief Justice's judgment did not challenge the institution of slavery; it limited itself to asserting that 'colonial laws' only applied 'in the colonies', and hence that slavery had no legal basis in England. Somersett's counsel eloquently proclaimed: 'The air of England is too pure for a slave to breathe.' But from this principle he deduced the conclusion that it was necessary to avoid an influx of blacks from Africa or America into England. Somersett's master was held responsible for an assault on the purity of the land of the free, who could not tolerate being confused and mixed up with slaves, rather than a violation of the liberty and dignity of a human being. Not by chance, the 1772 judgment provided the premises for the subsequent deportation to Sierra Leone of blacks who, as loyal subjects of the Crown, sought refuge in England after the victory of the rebel American colonists. [54]

The contours of liberal freedom are beginning to become clear. Authors like Burgh and Fletcher could still be regarded as champions of the cause of liberty by Jefferson, who lived in a situation where black slavery and widespread ownership of land (taken from the Indians) made the project of enslaving white vagrants purely academic. In Europe things were different, as emerges from the interventions of Montesquieu and Blackstone. Those who did not subscribe to the principle of the inadmissibility and 'uselessness of slavery among ourselves' began to be regarded as foreign to the emerging liberal party. Starting with Montesquieu and then, more clearly, Blackstone and the judgment in the Somersett case, what characterized the emergent liberal party were two essential points: (1) condemnation of despotic political power and the demand for self-government by civil society in the name of liberty and the rule of law; (2) assertion of the principle of the inadmissibility and 'uselessness of slavery among ourselves', or of the principle on whose basis England—and, prospectively, Europe—possessed 'too pure' an air to be able to tolerate the presence of slaves on its 'soil'. The second point is no less essential than the first. The legitimation of 'slavery among ourselves' would involve the dispersion of

---

54 Seymour Drescher, *Capitalism and Antislavery*, Oxford and New York: Oxford University Press, 1987, p. 37; David B. Davis, *The Problem of Slavery in the Age of Revolution*, Ithaca: Cornell University Press, 1975, pp. 231, 472, 495–6.

the pathos of liberty that played a key role in the liberal demand for self-government by civil society, or the self-government of the community of the free.

6. 'We won't be their Negroes': the colonists' rebellion

But the metropolis/colonies opposition, with its tendential exclusion of the latter from the sacred space of civilization and liberty, was bound to provoke a reaction from the colonists. Independently of particular concrete political and social demands, what was wounded was their self-consciousness. The metropolis seemed to be assimilating the American colonies to the 'modern Barbary' denounced by Blackstone; it seemed to be degrading them to a sort of dustbin, where the metropolitan rejects or prison population were dumped. The inmates of the mother country's prisons were deported across the Atlantic to supply, along with blacks from Africa, the more or less forced labour required by it. According to the observation of the English abolitionist David Ramsay, slavery continued to survive in the region of the confines of the civilized world—namely, the West—'where [its] proper religion and laws are not deemed to be in full force; and where individuals too often think themselves loosened from ties, which are binding in the mother country'.[55]

If it saved the metropolis's honour as the privileged site of liberty, despite the persistence of slavery on its extreme periphery, this view was wrong in the colonists' view, because it confounded and assimilated free Englishmen, prison rabble and people of colour. In this way, lamented James Otis, a prominent supporter of the liberal revolution underway, one forgot that the colonies had been founded not 'with a compound mixture of *English*, *Indian and Negro*, but with freeborn *British white* subjects'. Even more swingeing was Washington, who warned that the American colonists felt 'as miserably oppressed as our own blacks'.[56] Having repeated that the American colonists could boast a lineage not less noble and deserving of liberty than the metropolitan English, John Adams exclaimed with reference to the rulers in London: 'We won't be their Negroes'![57]

Quite apart even from the problem of representation, the spatial delimitation of the community of the free was perceived as an intolerable exclusion. On

---

55 Ramsay, quoted in Davis, *The Problem of Slavery in the Age of Revolution*, p. 387.

56 Blackburn, *The Overthrow of Colonial Slavery*, pp. 92, 14.

57 Adams, quoted in David B. Davis, 'A Big Business', *New York Review of Books*, 11 January 1998, p. 50 n. 3.

the other hand, the colonists, in demanding equality with the dominant British class, widened the gulf that separated them from blacks and Indians. While in London the zone of civilization was distinguished from the zone of barbarism, the sacred space from the profane, primarily by opposing the metropolis to the colonies, the American colonists were led to identify the boundary line principally in ethnic identity and skin colour. On the basis of the 1790 Naturalization Act, only whites could become citizens of the United States.[58]

The transition from a spatial delimitation of the community of the free to an ethnic and racial one brought with it combined, contradictory effects of inclusion and exclusion, emancipation and dis-emancipation. Whites, even the poorest among them, also came within the sacred space; they found themselves forming part of the community or race of the free, albeit situated at inferior levels. White slavery disappeared, condemned by New York polite society as 'contrary to ... the idea of liberty this country has so happily established'. But the tendential emancipation of poor whites was only the other side of the coin of further dis-emancipation of blacks. The condition of the black slave deteriorated by virtue of no longer being, as in colonial America, one of several systems of unfree labour.[59] In Virginia (and other states) land and black slaves were given to veterans of the War of Independence, in recognition of their contribution to the cause of the struggle against despotism;[60] the tendential social rise of poor whites coincided with the consummate de-humanization of black slaves.

7. Racial slavery and the further deterioration in the condition of the 'free' black

It was not only a question of slaves. The triumph of the ethnic delimitation of the community of the free was bound seriously to affect the condition of those blacks who were notionally free. They were now struck by a series of measures that tended to render the colour line, the demarcation between the race of the free and the race of slaves, inviolable. Blacks not subject to slavery began to be perceived as an anomaly that would sooner or later have to be rectified. Their condition at the end of the eighteenth century was summed up by one of them in Boston, referring both to strictly legal forms of oppression and to the insults

---

58 Eric Foner, *The Story of American Freedom*, London: Picador, 1999, p. 39.

59 Ibid., p. 19.

60 Ibid., pp. 19, 32; Blackburn, *The Overthrow of Colonial Slavery*, p. 116.

and threats which, while not legal, were widely tolerated by authority: 'we may truly be said to carry our lives in our hands, and the arrows of death are flying about our heads'.[61] It is a description that might seem unduly emotive. But we should attend to de Tocqueville:

> The electoral franchise has been conferred upon the Negroes in almost all the states in which slavery has been abolished, but if they come forward to vote, their lives are in danger. If oppressed, they may bring an action at law, but they will find none but whites among their judges.[62]

On close inspection, it can be said of 'emancipated Negroes' that 'their situation with regard to the Europeans is not unlike that of the Indians'. In fact, in some respects, they were 'still more to be pitied'. In any event, they were 'deprived of their rights' and 'exposed to the tyranny of the laws and the intolerance of the people'.[63] The condition of blacks not reduced to slavery was no different and no better as one moved from South to North. In fact (de Tocqueville pitilessly observed), 'the prejudice of race appears to be stronger in the states that have abolished slavery than in those where it still exists; and nowhere is it so intolerant as in those states where servitude has never been known.'[64]

The condition of the notionally free black was distinguished from that of the slave, but perhaps even more from that of the genuinely free white. Only thus can we explain the danger that constantly threatened him of being reduced to conditions of slavery, and the temptation that periodically emerged among whites—for example, in Virginia after the slave revolt or attempted revolt of 1831—to deport the entire population of free blacks to Africa or elsewhere. The latter were anyhow obliged to register, and could only change residence with the permission of the local authorities; they were presumed to be slaves and detained until they managed to prove otherwise. The despotism exercised over slaves was bound to affect, in one way or another, the population of colour as a whole. This was explained in 1801 by the postmaster general in the Jefferson administration, in a letter in which he recommended to a Georgian senator that blacks and men of colour be excluded from the postal service. 'Everything which tends to increase their knowledge of natural rights, of men and things, or

---

61 Leon F. Litwack, *North of Slavery*, Chicago: University of Chicago Press, 1961, pp. 16–17.

62 Alexis de Tocqueville, *Democracy in America*, London: Everyman's Library, 1994, vol. 1, p. 358.

63 Ibid., vol. 1, pp. 367–8.

64 Ibid., vol. 1, p. 359.

that affords them an opportunity of associating, acquiring and communicating sentiments, and of establishing a chain and line of intelligence' was extremely dangerous. Even the communication of feelings and ideas must be blocked or impeded by all possible means. In fact, the situation in Virginia immediately after the 1831 revolt was described as follows by a traveller: 'Military service [by white patrols] is performed night and day, Richmond resembles a town besieged ... the negroes ... will not venture to communicate with one another for fear of punishment.'[65]

8. Spatial and racial delimitation of the community of the free

The American Revolution threw into crisis the principle of the 'uselessness of slavery among ourselves', which seemed established within the liberal movement. Now, far from being confined to the colonies, slavery acquired a new visibility and centrality in a country with a culture, religion and language of European origin, which conversed with European countries as an equal and in fact claimed a kind of primacy in embodying the cause of liberty. Declared legally void in England in 1772, the institution of slavery received its juridical and even constitutional consecration, albeit with recourse to the euphemisms and circumlocutions we are familiar with, in the state born out of the revolt of colonists determined not to be treated like 'niggers'. There thus emerged a country characterized by 'a fixed and direct tie between slave ownership and political power',[66] as strikingly revealed both by the Constitution and the number of slave-owners who acceded to its highest institutional office.

But how did the platform of the liberal party shape up in a country which, like late-eighteenth-century England, could also boast of having air 'too pure' for it to be breathed by slaves? In fact, in the United States as well the ambition to retrieve the principle of the inadmissibility and 'uselessness of slavery among ourselves' continued to make itself heard. Albeit utterly fancifully, Jefferson harboured the idea of re-deporting the blacks to Africa. However, in the new situation that had been created, the project of transforming the North American republic into a land inhabited exclusively by freemen proved difficult to implement. It would be necessary seriously to infringe the right, possessed by genuinely free persons, to enjoy their property without external

---

65   Blackburn, *The Overthrow of Colonial Slavery*, p. 279.
66   David B. Davis, *The Slave Power Conspiracy and the Paranoid Style*, Baton Rouge: Louisiana State University Press, 1982, p. 33.

interference! So, in the first decades of the nineteenth century, a movement (the American Colonization Society) emerged that contrived a new way out: it was proposed to persuade the owners, by appealing to their religious feelings and also employing economic incentives, to free or sell their slaves, who, along with all the other blacks, would be sent to Africa to colonize it and convert it to Christianity.[67] In this way, without infringing the property rights guaranteed by law and the Constitution, it would have been possible to transform the United States into a land inhabited exclusively by free (and white) men.

It was a project doomed to fail from the outset. For a start, the acquisition of the slaves by the Union presupposed mobilizing enormous financial resources, and hence the imposition of high taxes. Expelled from the door in the shape of enforced expropriation, imposed from above, of the human cattle owned by the colonists, the spectre of despotic interference with private property by political power ended up arrogantly breaking in through the window as the taxation required to induce owners willingly to surrender their slaves, through a profitable sales contract. Moreover, taken as a whole, the class of planters had no intention of abandoning the source not only of its wealth, but also of its power.

The situation in the North was different. Here slaves were small in number and performed no essential economic function. Abolishing slavery, but at the same time adhering to the federal order that legitimized and guaranteed it in the South, the northern states seemed to want to give a new lease of life in the new situation to the compromise we have already encountered. Without being abolished, the institution whose presence constituted a kind of ironic counterpoint to the claim to be champions of the cause of liberty was banished to the deep South. In fact, four states (Indiana, Illinois, Iowa and Oregon) strictly prohibited access into their territories by blacks.[68] They thus avoided being contaminated by the presence not only of slaves, but also of blacks as such. This ban was the equivalent of the measure whereby, in the aftermath of the Somersett case, England deported to Sierra Leone blacks who not only were free, but also had the merit of having fought against the rebel colonists on behalf of the Empire. Nevertheless, even in the North of the United States, although it had been abolished, slavery had achieved the recognition it lacked in England, as demonstrated in particular by the constitutional provision that required the return of escaped slaves to their legitimate owners, in an indirect

---

67   George M. Frederickson, *The Black Image in the White Mind*, Hanover (NH): Wesleyan University Press, 1987, pp. 6ff.

68   Foner, *The Story of American Freedom*, p. 76.

sanction of the institution of slavery in states which were formally free. This was a point to which a representative of the South smugly drew attention: 'We have obtained a right to recover our slaves in whatever part of America they may take refuge, which is a right we had not before.'[69]

Clearly, in the United States as a whole the principle of the inadmissibility and 'uselessness of slavery among ourselves', which was more than ever reiterated across the Atlantic, had fallen into crisis. How had such a result been arrived at? Let us return to Burke. In asserting that the 'spirit of freedom' and the 'liberal' vision found their most consummate embodiment in the slave-owners of the southern colonies, he added that the colonists formed an integral part of the nation 'in whose veins the blood of freedom circulates', of 'the chosen race and sons of England': it was a question of 'pedigree', in the face of which 'human art' was powerless.[70] Here, as we can see, the spatial delimitation of the community of the free, which is the principle on which late-eighteenth-century liberal England was based, seems to be on the point of transmuting into a racial delimitation. And hence, in Calhoun and ideologists of the slaveholding South in general, a tendency already present in Burke comes to fruition. Having been spatial, the line of demarcation of the community of the free ends up becoming racial.

Moreover, there was no insurmountable barrier between the two types of delimitation. In 1845 John O'Sullivan, popular theorist of the providential 'manifest destiny' that put wind in the sails of US expansion, sought to assuage abolitionists' concerns about the introduction of slavery into Texas (wrested from Mexico and on the point of being annexed to the Union) with a significant argument. It was precisely its temporary extension that created the conditions for abolition of the 'the slavery of an inferior to a superior race', and hence 'furnished much probability of the ultimate disappearance of the negro race from our borders'. At the appropriate time, the ex-slaves would be driven further south, into the 'only receptacle' appropriate for them. In Latin America the population of mixed blood, which had formed following the fusion of the Spaniards with the natives, would easily be able to accommodate the blacks.[71] The racial delimitation of the community would then give way to a territorial delimitation. The end of slavery would, at the same time, entail the end of the presence of blacks in the land of liberty. Despite the abolitionists' cry of alarm,

---

69 Quoted in Paul Finkelman, *An Imperfect Union*, Chapel Hill: University of North Carolina Press, 1985, p. 28.

70 Burke, *Works*, vol. 3, pp. 66, 124.

71 John O'Sullivan, 'Annexation', *United States Magazine and Democratic Review*, vol. 4, July 1845, pp. 7–8.

the concentration of slaves in a zone immediately proximate to territories that were fundamentally foreign to the zone of civilization and liberty pushed in this direction.

For some time Lincoln harboured the idea of deporting the blacks, likewise regarded by him as ultimately alien to the community of the free, from the United States to Latin America after their emancipation.[72] In this sense, having confronted one another for decades, what clashed during the Civil War were the causes not of liberty and slavery, but precisely two different delimitations of the community of the free: the opposed parties accused one another of not knowing how, or not wanting, to delimit the community of the free effectively. To those who brandished the spectre of racial contamination as an inevitable consequence of the abolition of slavery, Lincoln replied by emphasizing that in the United States the overwhelming majority of 'mulattoes' were the result of sexual relations between white masters and their black slaves: 'slavery is the greatest source of amalgamation'. For the rest, he had 'no purpose to intro-duce political and social equality between the white and the black races', or to recognize the right of blacks to participate in political life or hold public office or perform the role of jury member. Lincoln declared himself well aware, like any other white man, of the radical difference between the two races and the supremacy of the whites.[73]

The crisis took a decisive step towards breaking-point following the Supreme Court's judgment in the Dred Scott case in summer 1857: 'like an ordinary article of merchandise and property', a black slave's legitimate owner had the right to take him with him in any part of the Union.[74] We can now understand Lincoln's reaction: the country could not remain permanently divided, 'half *slave* and half *free*'.[75] In contrast to the England of the Somersett case, the North of the United States could not pose as a land of the free whose air was 'too pure' to be breathed by a slave.

The transition from the spatial delimitation to the racial delimitation of the community of the free henceforth made it impossible to repress the reality of slavery. There was now no alternative to the condemnation of this institution except its explicit defence or celebration. As the conflict dividing the two sec-tions of the Union emerged more clearly, the South's ideologues all the more

---

72   Gossett, *Race*, pp. 254–5.

73   Abraham Lincoln, *Speeches and Writings*, 2 vols, ed. Don E. Fehrenbacher, New York: Library of America, 1989, vol. 1, pp. 401, 511–12, 636.

74   Richard Hofstadter, ed., *Great Issues in American History*, 3 vols, New York: Vintage Books, 1958–82, vol. 2, p. 369.

75   Lincoln, *Speeches and Writings*, vol. 1, p. 426.

provocatively mocked the circumlocutions and linguistic interdictions that had facilitated the Philadelphia compromise of 1787. 'Negro slavery', declared John Randolph, was a reality that 'the Constitution has vainly attempted to blink, by not using the term'.[76] With the lifting of this taboo, the legitimation of slavery lost the timidity that had previously characterized it, assuming a defiant tone. Having been a necessary evil, slavery became (in the words of Calhoun with which we are familiar) a 'positive good'. It made no sense to try to repress it as something to be ashamed of; in reality, it was the very foundation of civilization. Throwing into crisis the pathos of liberty that had presided over the foundation of the United States, and in a way de-legitimizing the very War of Independence, this new attitude helped make the clash between North and South inevitable.

9. The Civil War and the resumption of the controversy initiated with the American Revolution

In these circumstances, while the abolitionists adopted the arguments used during the American War of Independence by the British and the loyalists in their polemic against the South, the theorists of the South used arguments deployed by the rebel colonists. We have seen O'Sullivan, a New York lawyer and journalist, regard the South, bordering as it was on Mexico and Latin America, as the best place to deposit the blacks temporarily, pending their emancipation and deportation from the United States. Hence the South was a territory by no means uncontaminated by the barbarism of the blacks who lived there as slaves. Cohabitation with blacks, and sexual contamination, attested by a high number of mulattos—the abolitionist Theodore Parker piled it on—had also left profound traces on southern whites; it was precisely the influence of the 'African element' that explained attachment to an institution contrary to the principles of liberty.[77] And just as pre-revolutionary and revolutionary America had done, so too the South protested against the tendential exclusion, of which it felt itself the victim, from the authentic community of the free. It was now no longer the American colonies in their entirety, but the southern states that considered themselves assimilated to the 'modern Barbary' mentioned by Blackstone.

---

76 Randolph, quoted in Russell Kirk, *John Randolph of Roanoke*, Indianapolis: Liberty Press, 1978, p. 175.

77 Parker, quoted in Richard Slotkin, *The Fatal Environment*, New York: Harper Perennial, 1994, pp. 231–2.

Along with the one just noted, further aspects of the legal argument reappeared that had opposed the rebel colonists to England. In Calhoun's view,
the abolitionists of the North, who wanted to abolish slavery by a federal
law, were riding roughshod over the right of each individual state to self-
government, and seeking to found the Union on political slavery, on 'the bond
between master and slave'.[78] Naturally, the North reacted by ironizing about
this impassioned defence of liberty by the 'democratic', slaveholding South.
To understand the latter's subsequent response, we can return for a moment
to Franklin. Replying to his English interlocutors, who scoffed at the flag of
liberty waved by the rebel colonists and slave-owners, he did not limit himself
to recalling the Crown's interest and involvement in the slave trade. He also
employed a second argument, drawing attention to the fact that slavery and
servitude had not disappeared across the Atlantic. In particular, coalminers in
Scotland were 'absolute Slaves by your law'; they were 'bought and sold with
the Colliery, and have no more Liberty to leave it than our Negroes have to
leave their Master's Plantation'.[79] The authors of the denunciation of black
slavery were responsible for a white slavery that was certainly no better than
the one they condemned so vehemently.

Similarly, on the occasion of the conflict which had been brewing for decades
and reached breaking-point with the Civil War, the South retorted in two ways
to the accusations against it. It stressed that the North and abolitionist Britain
were not in a position to give lectures even on the way blacks (and peoples of
colour in general) were treated; and it pointed out how much slavery survived
in an industrial society notionally based on 'free' labour.

Let us focus for now on the first point. Already during the Philadelphia
Convention, the slave-owners rejected the lectures given them in the name
of morality, pointing out that the North derived major benefits from the institution of slavery, since its merchant shipping transported the slaves and the
commodities produced by them.[80] In 1808 the ban on the 'immigration or
introduction' of black slaves provided for by the federal Constitution had come
into effect. But it remained the case (observed the ideologues of the South)
that blacks in the North, in addition to suffering the poverty and oppression
that were the lot of the poor in general there, were exposed to maltreat-
ment and violence of every kind, as demonstrated by the periodic outbreak of

---

78   John C. Calhoun, *Union and Liberty*, ed. R. M. Lence, Indianapolis: Liberty Classics,
1992, p. 436.
79   Benjamin Franklin, *Writings*, ed. J. A. Leo Lemay, New York: Library of America,
1987, p. 651.
80   Paul Finkelman, *Slavery and the Founders*, Armonk (NY): Sharpe, 1996, pp. 23–4.

veritable pogroms. Even more repugnant (stressed Calhoun, in particular, in the years leading up to the Civil War) was the hypocrisy of Britain (the country which, having abolished slavery in its colonies, had become the model for the American abolitionists). '[T]he greatest slave dealer on earth', the country 'more responsible than any other … for the extent of that form of servitude' in the American continent, then engaged in waving the banner of abolitionism, with a view to attracting the lucrative production of tobacco, cotton, sugar and coffee to its colonies and ruining potential competitors.[81] In reality, what results had the putative emancipation of the slaves produced in the English colonies? The condition of the blacks was in no wise improved; in their case, freedom was more of a mirage than ever, while 'the supremacy of the European race' continued to be undisputed.[82] Inevitably, when 'two races of men, of different color', and markedly unequal in terms of culture and civilization, tried to live together, the inferior race was destined for subjection.[83] The very country that elevated itself into champion of the struggle against slavery distinguished itself in completely the opposite direction: not only did it use the labour of 'slaves' in India and other colonies, but it '[held] in unlimited subjection not less than one hundred and fifty million human beings, dispersed over every part of the globe'.[84] We find an even more explicit reference to the lot of the coolies in another eminent representative of the South, George Fitzhugh. Arraigned once again was Britain, which lauded itself for having abolished slavery in its colonies. In reality, the 'temporary slaves' from Asia who had taken the place of the blacks, 'if not worked to death before their terms of service expire', subsequently died of starvation.[85]

In its main lines, the controversy that developed on the eve and in the course of the Civil War reproduced and resumed the one that had occurred some decades earlier, during the clash between the two shores of the Atlantic.

10. 'Liberal system of policy', 'liberality of sentiment' and the institution of slavery

To understand the spread of the political use of the term 'liberal' in its various senses, we must remember two reference points. The first is the proud self-

---

81 Calhoun, quoted in Massimo L. Salvadori, *Potere e libertà nel mondo moderno*, Rome and Bari: Laterza, 1996, pp. 190–1.

82 Calhoun, *Union and Liberty*, p. 475.

83 Ibid., p. 467.

84 Calhoun, quoted in Salvadori, *Potere e libertà*, p. 193.

85 George Fitzhugh, *Sociology for the South*, Richmond: Morris, 1854, pp. 210–11.

consciousness that matured in the wake of the victory achieved during the Seven Years' War over the France of monarchical and religious absolutism, which was subsequently reinforced in England by the outcome of the Somersett case. The second is the struggles that developed within the community of the free. When the controversy provoked by the agitation of the rebel colonists erupted, the various positions confronting one another all tended to define themselves as in some sense 'liberal'. Burke sought to promote conciliation, calling upon 'the liberal government of this free nation' to evince a spirit of compromise.[86] Across the Atlantic, at the moment when the United States was founded, Washington emphasized 'the benefits of a wise and liberal Government', or a 'liberal system of policy', which asserted itself 'in such an enlightened, in such a liberal age', and which had as its basis 'the free cultivation of Letters, the unbounded extension of Commerce', or 'liberal and free commerce', 'the progressive refinement of Manners, the growing liberality of sentiment', with the prevalence of a 'liberal sentiment' of tolerance also regarding relations between 'every political and religious denomination of men in this country'.[87] Hitherto the term 'liberal' has occurred solely as an adjective. In other contexts, adjective and substantive are interchangeable: 'every Liberal Briton' (wrote the *London Gazette* in 1798) rejoiced at the problems facing revolutionary, tyrannical France, which had to confront the difficult situation created by the uprising of the black slaves in San Domingo.[88] Finally, the term in question made its appearance as a noun: signing himself 'A Liberal' was the author (possibly Paine) of an article in the *Pennsylvania Packet* of 25 March 1780, which came out for the abolition of slavery.[89]

Here we have four interventions, which share a liberal profession of faith, but with orientations that are fairly diverse as regards black slavery. In Europe, while stances in favour of it were not wanting, a critical orientation was prevalent: a more or less clear distance tended to be taken from the institution that had had to be repressed to the colonies, in order to confer credibility on the self-consciousness developed by the community of the free. *The Wealth of Nations*—Adam Smith's masterpiece, which appeared the same year as the Declaration of Independence drafted by Jefferson, a pre-eminent representative

---

86   Burke, *Works*, vol. 3, p. 153.

87   George Washington, *A Collection*, ed. William B. Allen, Indianapolis: Liberty Classics, 1988, pp. 242, 247, 242 ('Circular to the States', 4 June 1783), 326 (letter to La Fayette, 15 August 1786), 545 (letter to the Hebrew Congregation, January 1790).

88   Cf. David Geggus, 'British Opinion and the Emergence of Haiti, 1791–1805', in James Walvin, ed., *Slavery and British Society, 1776–1846*, London: Macmillan, 1982, p. 130.

89   Zilversmit, *The First Emancipation*, p. 132; Blackburn, *The Overthrow of Colonial Slavery*, p. 118.

of Virginia's planters and slave-owners—observed that the 'liberal reward of labour', with the payment of a wage that the 'free servant' and 'free man' could freely dispose of, was the only thing likely to stimulate individual industry; while economic stagnation was the result of servile labour, whether serfdom or slavery proper.[90] In his turn, Millar regarded the institution of slavery as in contradiction with 'the liberal sentiments entertained in the latter part of the eighteenth century', with the 'more liberal views' developed in the modern world.[91] Going still further, the great economist's disciple declared that credibility could be restored to the 'liberal hypothesis' only by avoiding its confusion with those who waved the flag of liberty while preserving and, in fact, developing the practice of slavery.

Across the Atlantic, by contrast, defence of that institution was much fiercer. Yet it would be mistaken to construct a clear-cut opposition. It is sufficient to reflect on the fact that the tutelary deity of the slaveholding South was, in the first instance, Burke. In 1832 an influential Virginian ideologue, Thomas R. Dew, lauded the advantages of slavery: 'the menial and low offices' were reserved for blacks, so that love of liberty and the 'republican spirit', peculiar to free, white citizens, flourished with a purity and vigour unknown in the rest of the United States, and had a precedent only in classical antiquity. But in saying this, Dew appealed to Burke and his thesis that, where slavery flourished, the spirit of liberty developed more abundantly.[92] In this way, the theorist of the slaveholding South indirectly adopted and subscribed to the British Whig's 'liberal' profession of faith.

In subsequent decades, during the struggle against the North, which was initially political and then military, the slaveholding South could count on many friends in liberal England. A few years before the Civil War, the arguments of the southern ideologues were explicitly echoed by Benjamin Disraeli. With the abolition of slavery in British and French colonies behind him, he characterized the abolition of slavery as 'a narrative of ignorance, injustice, blundering, waste, and havoc, not easily paralleled in the history of mankind'.[93] In America, if they mixed with the blacks, the whites 'would become so deteriorated that their states would probably be reconquered and regained by the aborigines'.[94] Would the abolition of slavery in the United States not encourage this

---

90   Adam Smith, *An Inquiry into the Nature and Causes of the Wealth of Nations*, Indianapolis: Liberty Classics, 1981, pp. 98–9.

91   John Millar, *The Origin of the Distinction of Ranks*, Aalen: Scientia, 1986, pp. 296, 250.

92   Hofstadter, *Great Issues in American History*, vol. II, pp. 319–20.

93   Benjamin Disraeli, *Lord George Bentinck*, London: Colburn, 1852, p. 325.

94   Ibid., p. 496.

admixture, imparting a novel dignity to it? Later, the secessionist Confederacy's desperate struggle met with a profoundly sympathetic echo from prominent cultural and political representatives of liberal England, provoking the indignation of John Stuart Mill.

On the occasion first of the Somersett case, then of the American Revolution and finally of the Civil War, the liberal world appeared profoundly divided over the problem of slavery. How are we to find our bearings in this seeming chaos?

11. From the assertion of the principle of the 'uselessness of slavery among ourselves' to the condemnation of slavery as such

We are trying to answer the question we posed at the beginning: Can authors like Fletcher and Calhoun be considered liberals? In the liberal England derived from the Glorious Revolution, Fletcher could calmly demand the introduction of slavery for vagrants without being in any way isolated, just as Hutcheson and Burgh, who expressed more or less similar positions, were not isolated. While Hutcheson was the master of Smith, Fletcher was in correspondence with Locke and enjoyed, along with Burgh, the respect of Jefferson and the circles close to him. These were the years when, as Hume put it, '[s]ome passionate admirers of the ancients, and zealous partizans of civil liberty ... cannot forbear regretting the loss of this institution [slavery]', which accounted for the grandeur of Athens and Rome.[95] However, with the establishment of the principle of the 'uselessness of slavery among ourselves', the positions expressed by Fletcher ceased to be, or ceased to be accepted as, liberal. It is true that they took a long time to die. As late as 1838, a German liberal reported the 'advice, certainly more hinted at than clearly stated, which would wish to find a remedy for the serious danger [represented by an unprecedented and acute social question] in the introduction of veritable slavery for factory workers'.[96] But it was a suggestion rejected with disdain: the line of demarcation of the liberal 'party' had been drawn for a while.

A similar argument can be advanced in connection with Calhoun. In his view, it was the North that was guilty of betraying the liberal principles which

---

95   David Hume, *Essays, Moral, Political, and Literary*, Indianapolis: Liberty Classics, 1987, p. 383.

96   Robert von Mohl, 'Gwerbe- und Fabrikwesen', in Lothar Gall and Rainer Koch, eds, *Der europäische Liberalismus im 19. Jahrhundert*, vol. 4, Frankfurt am Main: Ullstein, 1981, p. 91.

had inspired the American Revolution. In fact, 'the defence of human liberty against the aggressions of despotic power had always been most efficient in States where domestic slavery was found to prevail'. Within the Union, it was the South that had 'constantly inclined most strongly to the side of liberty, and been the first to see and first to resist the encroachments of power'.[97] And it was in the South that liberalism found its most authentic and mature expression. The term 'liberal' (warned John Randolph, sometimes defined as the 'American Burke'), which originally meant 'a man attached to enlarged and free principles—a votary of liberty', would see its true meaning twisted if it had to be used to refer to those who flirted with abolitionism.[98]

A contemporary liberal might be tempted to be shot of the unmanageable presence within the tradition of thought he refers to of an author like Burke, who celebrated the particular intensity of the liberal spirit and love of liberty among slave-owners; or of an author like Calhoun, who in the nineteenth century still hymned the 'positive good' that was slavery. And so both of them are officially included in the conservative party. However, such an operation immediately reveals its groundlessness. The category of conservatism is characterized by formalism, in the sense that it can subsume significantly different contents: it is a question of identifying what it is intended to conserve or guard. And there is no doubt that Burke and Calhoun aimed to be vigilant guardians of the social relations and political institutions which emerged, respectively, from the Glorious Revolution and the American Revolution—two eminently liberal revolutions. It would make no sense to regard Jefferson and Washington as liberals, but this is not the case with Burke—who, unlike them, was not a slave-owner and who, when he celebrated the 'liberal spirit' and 'liberal' emphasis of the slaveholding South, had in mind precisely figures like these two Virginian statesmen. As late as 1862 Lord Acton cited at length, and implicitly subscribed to, the passage by the British Whig who, far from excluding slave-owners, conferred on them a privileged position in the party of liberty.[99]

It would be just as illogical to exclude from that party Calhoun, who tirelessly reiterated his attachment to representative bodies and the principle of the limitation of power. If, then, going beyond the merely formal meaning of the term, conservatism is to be understood as an uncritical attachment to a pre-modern, pre-industrial society, characterized by the cult of clod of earth

---

97   Calhoun, *Union and Liberty*, pp. 468, 473.

98   Randolph, quoted in Kirk, *John Randolph of Roanoke*, pp. 63, 43 (for the characterization as 'the American Burke').

99   Lord Acton, *Selected Writings*, 3 vols, ed. J. Rufus Fears, Indianapolis: Liberty Classics, 1985–88, vol. 1, p. 329.

and bell tower, such a category could hardly account for Calhoun's positions. Once the rights of minorities had been guaranteed, he had no problem with extending the vote and even introducing male 'universal suffrage'; and, along with representative bodies, he celebrated the development of 'manufactures', industry and free trade.[100] If to anyone, the category of conservatism might be applied to Jefferson. He identified cultivators of the land as 'the chosen people of God', assimilated 'great cities' to the 'sores' of a 'human body',[101] and in 1812, during the war with Britain, accused the latter of being an instrument of 'Satan' because it had compelled America to abandon the 'paradise' of agriculture and engage in 'manufacturing', in order to meet the test of arms (see Chapter 8, §16). And the category of conservatism might also be applied to Washington. He too viewed with concern the prospect that the Americans might become 'a manufacturing people', rather than continuing to be 'Cultivators' of the land, thereby avoiding the scourge of the 'tumultuous populace of large cities'.[102] In particular, it is against Jefferson that Calhoun seems to be arguing when he rejects the thesis that manufacture 'destroy[s] the moral and physical power of the people'. In reality, this was a concern rendered ever more obsolete by 'the great perfection of machinery' introduced into industry.[103] Finally, if acceptance of free trade is an integral part of liberalism, it is clear that Calhoun can be included in such a tradition much more easily than his adversaries in the North, who were engaged in strict protectionist practices liable (according to the southern theorist's denunciation) to 'destroy the liberty of the country'.[104]

Construed in the broadest sense of the term, the liberal party encompassed both Whigs and Tories. The former did not even necessarily represent the more advanced wing. Josiah Tucker was a Tory, who reprehended Locke and Burke for being followers of a 'republicanism' based, precisely, upon slavery and serfdom. For the rest, arguing with 'Republican Zealots', he liked to position himself among the true interpreters of 'English constitutional Liberty'.[105] Disraeli was likewise a Tory, who, while on the one hand echoing the arguments of the slaveholding South, on the other significantly widened the social basis of British representative bodies, granting the vote to significant sections of the popular classes and anyway extending it much further than the Whigs had.

---

100 Calhoun, *Union and Liberty*, pp. 35–6, 315.

101 Thomas Jefferson, *Writings*, ed. Merrill D. Peterson, New York: Library of America, 1984, pp. 290–1.

102 Washington, *A Collection*, pp. 455 ('Fragments of the First Discarded Inaugural Address', April 1789), 554 (letter to La Fayette, 28 July 1791).

103 Calhoun, *Union and Liberty*, p. 308.

104 Ibid., p. 313.

105 Tucker, *Collected Works*, vol. 5, pp. ix, 12, 96.

On the other hand, outside the liberal party even before the Civil War were those who, in their concern to save the institution of slavery and indignation at the weapons supplied by representative bodies to an increasingly threatening abolitionist agitation, spoke with Fitzhugh in the southern United States of the 'collapse of liberal society', or ironized with Carlyle in Europe itself over ruinous 'anarchic–constitutional epochs'.[106] Although reiterating the absolute necessity of slavery as the foundation of civilization, both ended up challenging, at least on a theoretical level, the ethnic and spatial delimitations of the institution of slavery. For Fitzhugh, as was demonstrated by the examples of classical antiquity and confirmed by the reality of the modern world, work was inseparable from slavery, so that in one form or another 'slavery, *black or white*, was right and necessary'.[107] In justifying the slavery of the Afro-Americans across the Atlantic and branding the Irish 'black',[108] Carlyle, admired by Fitzhugh and other southerners, and in correspondence with some of them,[109] in his turn reached a general 'conclusion': 'whether established by law, or by law abrogated, [slavery] exists very extensively in this world, in and out of the West Indies; and … you cannot abolish slavery by act of parliament, but can only abolish the *name* of it, which is very little!'[110] Whether dealing with slaves, 'servants hired for life', or *adscripti glebae*, it was still slavery. On the other hand, if the slave was a 'servant hired for life', why should one prefer the servant hired for a month or a day?[111]

Spurred by the bitterness of the struggle underway, Fitzhugh and Carlyle ultimately returned to the positions of Fletcher, first marginalized and then regarded as alien to the liberal party. The transition from the liberal party's first turn to the second can be summarized thus: following the defeat of the South, the emancipation of black slaves and amendments to the US Constitution to that effect, a transition was made from asserting the principle of the 'uselessness of slavery among ourselves' in Europe and the 'free states' of the northern United States to general condemnation, on both sides of the Atlantic, of slavery as such. Starting from this second result, the positions expressed by Calhoun were also rejected by the liberal party. But that is not a reason to expel him

106 Thomas Carlyle, *Latter-Day Pamphlets*, ed. Michael K. Goldberg and Jules P. Seigel, Ottawa: Canadian Federation for the Humanities and Social Sciences, 1983, p. 439.

107 Fitzhugh, *Sociology for the South*, pp. 98, 225; cf. Domenico Losurdo, *Nietzsche, il ribelle aristocratico*, Turin: Bollati Boringhieri, 2002, ch. 12 *passim* and ch. 22, §1.

108 Carlyle, *Latter-Day Pamphlets*, pp. 463–5.

109 Fitzhugh, *Sociology for the South*, p. 286; Eugene D. Genovese, *A Consuming Fire*, Athens: University of Georgia Press, 1998, p. 107.

110 Carlyle, *Latter-Day Pamphlets*, p. 439.

111 Ibid., pp. 464–6.

retrospectively from the liberal tradition. Otherwise, the same fate would have to be meted out to Locke and a fair number of the protagonists of the American Revolution and the early decades of US history.

In any event, with the end of the Civil War a historical cycle came to a close. Having emerged together from a unique twin birth, which saw them entwined in a relationship not without its tensions, liberalism as a whole now broke with slavery in the strict sense—with hereditary, racial slavery. But before examining these new courses, it is appropriate to extend our analysis of the society that was established on the two Atlantic shores up to the Civil War. We have hitherto focused attention on the problem of black slavery. But what relations were developing within the white community?

CHAPTER THREE

White Servants between Metropolis and Colonies: Proto-Liberal Society

1. Franklin, Smith and 'vestiges of slavery' in the metropolis

First the rebel colonists during the American Revolution, and then the South of the United States during the conflict that pitted it against the North, accused their opponents of hypocrisy. The latter waxed indignant over black slavery, but shut its eyes to the fact that what were essentially slave relations persisted within the society it held up as a model. As we know, Franklin compared the miners of Scotland to the blacks of the American plantations, and thus challenged the London government's pretension to elevate itself into a champion of liberty.

Obviously, this was a polemical intervention, but one whose validity was confirmed by a rather authoritative witness. Although sharing the proud self-consciousness of his compatriots or the ruling class of his country, Adam Smith acknowledged the persistence in Great Britain of 'vestiges of slavery': a labour relationship not dissimilar from serfdom was in force in salt works and coal-mines. Just as the *adscripti glebae*, still very numerous in Eastern Europe, were forcibly bound to the land to be cultivated and sold at the same time as it, so in the country that had left behind the *ancien régime* some decades earlier, the *adscripti operi* were in a sense an integral part of the *opus* or works (the salt work or mine) and, when this was sold, passed together with their family into the service of the new master. Hence it was not a question of actual slavery, of chattel slavery, which allowed individual members of a family to be put on the market like any other commodity. The *adscripti operi* could marry and lead a genuine family life; they could own a minimum of property; and, naturally, they did not risk being killed with impunity: 'their lives are under the protection of the laws of the land'.[1] But it remained the case that in Scotland workers in coalmines and salt works were obliged to wear a collar on which the name of their master was inscribed.[2] In the wake of the great economist, Millar too could not but 'regret ... that any species of slavery should still remain in Great Britain'; and it was to be hoped that parliament would intervene to remedy the situation, finally sanctioning 'the freedom of the labouring people' in Scottish mines and salt works.[3]

Judging from Smith's *Lectures on Jurisprudence*, these were 'the only vestiges of slavery which remain amongst us'.[4] Does this mean that the other labour relations were based on freedom? Referring to England in the second half of the eighteenth century, Blackstone distinguished between three types of 'servant' in the strict sense (we ignore here personnel charged with overseeing and guarding the master's property): 'menial servants' or 'domestics', 'apprentices', and finally 'labourers', who worked outside the master's house. The most modern labour relation, least informed by feudal and servile echoes, would seem to be the last. In this connection, however, the great jurist indulged in celebrating 'very good regulations' on the basis of which, for example, 'all persons who have no visible effects may be compelled to work', while those who 'leave or desert their work' were punished. Over the domestic or apprentice, the master exercised a right of 'corporal punishment' that must not result in death or mutilation.[5]

But what happened if this limit was exceeded? We can infer Smith's answer: 'The master has a right to correct his servant moderately, and if he should die under his correction it is not murther, unless it was done with an offensive weapon or with forethought and without provocation.' It is difficult to regard such servants as free men even if, according to the great economist, they enjoyed 'almost the same privileges with their master, liberty, wages, etca'. In fact, what creates a radical difference is the power of correction exercised by the one over the other. The same Smith included menial servants, together with slaves proper, in the master's extended family.[6]

Masters did not confine themselves to monitoring their servant's industriousness. Let us attend to Hume's evidence: 'At present, all masters discourage

---

1   Adam Smith, *Lectures on Jurisprudence*, Indianapolis: Liberty Classics, 1982, p. 191.

2   David B. Davis, *The Problem of Slavery in Western Culture*, Ithaca and New York: Cornell University Press, 1966, p. 437.

3   John Millar, *The Origin of the Distinction of Ranks*, Aalen: Scientia, 1986, pp. 289–90.

4   Smith, *Lectures on Jurisprudence*, p. 191.

5   William Blackstone, *Commentaries on the Laws of England*, 4 vols, Chicago: University of Chicago Press, 1979, vol. 1, pp. 413–16.

6   Smith, *Lectures on Jurisprudence*, p. 456.

the marrying of their male servants, and admit not by any means the marriage of the females, who are then supposed altogether incapacitated for their service.'[7] The opportunity to have a family seems largely denied not only to the black slave, but also to the white domestic servant: the private lives of both were subject to the master's power or will.

Finally, it is to be noted that comparable to menial servants were 'apprentices',[8] whose condition, in England at any rate, had been regarded by Grotius as approximating closely enough to the slave's. And such, basically, was also Blackstone's opinion. He reiterated the slave's obligation to provide service 'for life' with a rather eloquent argument: fundamentally, it was the same relationship that the apprentice had with his master, except that in the latter case there was a time limit (seven years and sometimes more).[9]

As has justly been observed, '[f]or most of human history the expression "free labor" was an oxymoron.'[10]

2. The unemployed, beggars and workhouses

As the controversy between the two sides of the Union became increasingly bitter, Calhoun positively contrasted the condition of American slaves with that of inmates of workhouses or poorhouses in England. The former were lovingly treated and cared for by the master or mistress during illness or old age, while the latter were reduced to a 'forlorn and wretched condition'; the former continued to live among their family and friends, while the latter were uprooted from their environment and also separated from their loved ones.[11] The apologetic intention that governs the description or transfiguration of the institution of slavery is clear. Yet when it came to workhouses in England, Calhoun was not the only one to underscore the horror. In de Tocqueville's view, they afforded 'the most horrendous and repugnant [spectacle] of misery': on the one hand, the infirm incapable of work and waiting to die; on the other, women and children massed pell-mell 'like pigs in the mud of their sty; it is difficult not to trample over a semi-naked body'. Finally, there were the comparatively more

---

7   David Hume, *Essays, Moral, Political, and Literary*, Indianapolis: Liberty Classics, 1987, p. 386.

8   Smith, *Lectures*, p. 456.

9   Blackstone, *Commentaries*, vol. 1, pp. 412–13.

10   Seymour Drescher, *From Slavery to Freedom*, London: Macmillan, 1999, p. 401.

11   John C. Calhoun, *Union and Liberty*, ed. R. M. Lence, Indianapolis: Liberty Classics, 1992, p. 474.

'fortunate'—those in a position to work: they earned little or nothing and fed off the leftovers of stately homes.[12]

But however horrible, poverty and degradation were not the most significant aspect of workhouses. At the start of the eighteenth century, Defoe favourably mentioned the example of the workhouse in Bristol, which 'has been such a Terror to the Beggars that none of [them] will come near the City'.[13] In fact, the workhouse was subsequently described by Engels as a total institution: 'Paupers wear the uniform of the house and are subject to the will of the director without any protection whatsoever'; so that 'the "morally degenerate" parents cannot influence their children, families are separated; the man is sent to one wing, the woman to another, the children to a third'. Families were broken up, but for the rest all were amassed sometimes to the tune of twelve or sixteen in a single room. Any kind of violence was inflicted on them, not even sparing the elderly and children, and involving particular attention to women. In practice, the inmates of workhouses were treated as 'objects of disgust and horror placed outside the law and the human community'. Thus was explained the fact, underscored by Engels, that in order to escape the 'Poor Law Bastilles' (as they were popularly renamed), 'inmates of work houses often deliberately make themselves guilty of any crime whatsoever in order to go to prison'.[14] In fact (add contemporary historians), 'many indigents preferred to die of hunger and illness' rather than subject themselves to a workhouse.[15]

We are put in mind of the suicide that slaves often resorted to in order to escape their condition. Examined carefully, the 1834 law that shut up anyone requiring assistance in a workhouse in a sense vindicates Calhoun and those who pointed to slavery as the only possible solution to the problem of poverty. Fighting for the new legislation, its inspirer, Nassau William Senior, denounced the fatal contradiction in the rules hitherto in force, which allowed the poor person to enjoy a minimum of assistance for continuing a normal life: 'The labourer is to be a free agent, but without the hazards of free agency; to be free from the coercion, but to enjoy the assured existence of the slave.' But 'unit[ing] the irreconcilable advantages of freedom and servitude' was utterly absurd: a choice was required.[16] Arguing thus, the influential economist and liberal

---

12   Alexis de Tocqueville, *Oeuvres complètes*, ed. Jacob-Peter Mayer, Paris: Gallimard, 1951–, vol. 5, pt 2, p. 97.

13   Daniel Defoe, *Giving Alms no Charity, And Employing the Poor a Grievance to the Nation*, London, 1704, p. 15.

14   Karl Marx and Friedrich Engels, *Werke*, 38 vols, Berlin: Dietz, 1955–89, vol. 2, pp. 496–7.

15   Françoise Barret-Ducrocq, *Pauvreté, charité et morale à Londres au XIX siècle*, Paris: Presses Universitaires de France, 1991, p. 94.

16   Nassau William Senior, *Three Lectures on the Rate of Wages*, New York: Kelley, 1966, p. ix.

theorist, interlocutor and correspondent of Tocqueville, ended up recognizing the substantially slave-like character of the relations obtaining in workhouses.

Coming as it did in 1834, the new legislation coincided with the emancipation of blacks in the colonies. We can thus understand the irony, on the one hand, of the theorists of the slaveholding South in the United States and, on the other, of the English popular masses faced with a dominant class which, while it lauded itself for having abolished slavery in the colonies, reintroduced it in a different form in the metropolis itself.

3. Liberals, vagrants and workhouses

We have mentioned the role played by Senior in the passing of the 1834 law. But what position did the liberal tradition as a whole adopt towards workhouses and, more generally, the policy of disciplining poverty? According to Locke, it was necessary to intervene thoroughly and drastically in an infected area of society that was constantly expanding. From the age of three, the children of families not in a position to feed them should be sent out to work.[17] Moreover, it was necessary to intervene with their parents. To discourage the idleness and dissoluteness of vagrants, it was appropriate to proceed in areas frequented by them to 'the suppressing of superfluous brandy shops and unnecessary alehouses'.[18] Secondly, begging should be discouraged and restricted. Beggars were obliged to wear a 'badge'; to oversee them, and prevent them practising their activity outside the permitted area and hours, a special body was provided, the 'beadles of beggars', who in their turn were to be controlled by 'guardians' so that they performed their task with the requisite diligence and severity. But the whole community was called upon to participate in the beggar hunt, starting with the inhabitants of the house where the wretches had requested charity.[19]

Draconian penalties awaited vagrants who managed to escape this comprehensive control. It was right that those caught asking for alms outside their parish and near a sea port should be pressed into the navy: they were to be 'punished as deserters'—i.e. with the death penalty—'if they go on shore without leave; or, when sent on shore, if they either go further, or stay longer, than they have leave'. The other illegal beggars were to be interned in a normal

---

17 John Locke, *Political Writings*, ed. David Wootton, London and New York: Penguin, 1993, p. 454.
18 Ibid., p. 447.
19 Ibid., p. 460.

workhouse or house of correction. The master 'shall have no other consideration nor allowance but what their labour shall produce; whom therefore he
shall have power to employ according to his discretion'. Once again, this arbitrary power summons up the spectre of slavery. As is confirmed by a further
detail: that 'whoever shall counterfeit a pass shall lose his ears for the forgery
for the first time that he is found guilty thereof; and the second time, that he
shall be transported to the plantations, as in case of felony'.[20]

Certainly, in the nineteenth century the situation was different. With the
1834 reform, arriving in the workhouses were those who sought to escape
death from starvation in some way: the workhouses must be made as odious as
possible in order to reduce the number of those who sought refuge in them to
a minimum. In this philosophy, which began to take shape with Malthus,[21] de
Tocqueville likewise joined: 'It is obvious that we must make assistance unpleas-
ant, we must separate families, make the workhouse a prison and render our
charity repugnant.'[22]

In denouncing this institution, Calhoun referred exclusively to Europe. Yet
it was present, in one form or another, in the United States. De Tocqueville
referred to it, significantly, in the context of his analysis of the 'prison system'.
Who were the inmates? The answer was clear: 'The indigent who cannot earn
their living by honest work, and those who do not want to.'[23] It was therefore understandable that workhouses became particularly crowded at times of
crisis:

> The fluctuations in industry attract, when favourable, a large number of
> workers who find themselves without work in times of crisis. Thus we see
> that vagrancy, which is born of idleness, and stealing, which is invariably the
> result of vagrancy, are the two crimes that are experiencing the most rapid
> increase in the current state of society.[24]

The crime that led to internment was already identified with unemployment and poverty. Making the judicial decisions, for example in New York,
was a functionary who could readily deprive of their liberty those who in his

---

20   Ibid., p. 449.

21   See Thomas Robert Malthus, *An Essay on the Principle of Population*, 2 vols, ed. Patricia
Joyce, Cambridge: Cambridge University Press and Royal Economic Society, 1989, vol. 1, ch. 2.

22   Tocqueville, diary note of 4 February 1851, quoted in Hugh Brogan, Introduction to
Tocqueville, *Oeuvres complètes*, vol. 7, pt 2, p. 35.

23   Tocqueville, *Oeuvres complètes*, vol. 4, pt 1, p. 319.

24   Ibid., vol. 4, pt 1, pp. 50–1.

judgment 'have no means of subsistence'.[25] Protests were understandable: the poor person thus confined 'regards himself as unfortunate, not culpable; he challenges society's right violently to force him to do fruitless work and to deal with him against his will'.[26]

But let us return to England. John Stuart Mill was inclined to trivialize the horror of workhouses when he observed: 'Even the labourer who loses his employment by idleness or negligence, has nothing worse to suffer, in the most unfavourable case, than the discipline of a workhouse'.[27] But the liberal philosopher's opinion can be contrasted with that of modern scholars: once they had entered workhouses, the poor 'ceased to be citizens in any true sense of the word', because they lost 'the civil right of personal liberty'.[28] And this was a radical loss: the 'guardians' of the workhouses had the discretional power of inflicting the corporal punishment deemed most fitting on inmates.[29]

Bentham was decidedly enthusiastic. He tirelessly lauded the benefits of this institution, which he aimed further to perfect, locating the workhouse in a 'panoptical' building which allowed the director to exercise secret, total control—that is, to observe every single aspect of the behaviour of the unwitting inmates at any point in time:

> What hold can any other manufacturer have upon his workmen, equal to what my manufacturer would have upon his? What other master is there that can reduce his workmen, if idle, to a situation next to starving, without suffering them to go elsewhere? What other master is there, whose men can never get drunk unless he chooses that they should do so? and who, so far from being able to raise their wages by combination, are obliged to take whatever pittance he thinks it most for his interest to allow? ... and what other master or manufacturer is there, who to appearance constantly, and in reality as much as he thinks proper, has every look and motion of each workman under his eye?[30]

---

25   Ibid., vol. 5, pt 1, p. 71.

26   Ibid., vol. 5, pt 1, pp. 319–20.

27   John Stuart Mill, *Collected Works*, 33 vols, ed. John M. Robson, Toronto and London: University of Toronto Press and Routledge and Kegan Paul, 1963–91, vol. 2, p. 204.

28   T. H. Marshall, *Citizenship and Social Class and Other Essays*, Cambridge: Cambridge University Press, 1950, p. 24.

29   David B. Davis, *Slavery and Human Progress*, Oxford and New York: Oxford University Press, 1986, p. 122.

30   Jeremy Bentham, *The Works*, 11 vols, ed. John Bowring, Edinburgh: Tait, 1838–43, vol. 4, p. 56.

Hence the contribution to the development of national wealth by workhouses, intended to operate as 'industry-houses', would be enormous. They were to be spread over the whole national territory, confining up to 500,000 detainees, and in any event 'all persons, able-bodied or otherwise, having neither visible or assignable property, nor honest and sufficient means of livelihood'.[31] Thanks to this gigantic concentration-camp universe, where people would be interned without having committed any crime and without any control by the judiciary, it would be possible to perform the miracle of transforming the 'dross' that was the 'refuse of the population' into money.[32] And that was not all. Given the isolation it entailed, the workhouse made it possible to experiment, as we shall see, with producing a stock of especially industrious and conscientious labourers. Certainly, for such objectives to be achieved, rigorous discipline was required, which must be thoroughly internalized by the detainees in the workhouse:

> *Soldiers* wear *uniforms*, why not paupers?—those who save the country, why not those who are saved by it? Not the *permanent* hands only, but likewise the *coming-and-going* hands should wear the uniform while in the house, for order, distinction, and recognition, as well as for tidiness ...[33]

4. The servant as soldier

As we can see, it was Bentham who compared the condition of a workhouse inmate with that of the soldier. But it is appropriate to take a step back. During his residence in London, Franklin, discomfited by his English interlocutors mocking the flag of liberty waved by colonists who were often slave-owners, replied by highlighting, among other things, the persistence in England of slave-like relations even within the armed forces.[34] The reference was above all to the navy. Let us attend to historians of our day: 'the men of the fleet were so ill-paid, ill-fed, and ill-handled that it was impossible to obtain crews by free enlistment'. Many sought to escape this kind of sequestration, but Great Britain gave chase to them, without hesitating to search American ships and

---

31 Ibid., vol. 8, pp. 368–70.

32 Ibid., vol. 8, p. 398; Gertrude Himmelfarb, *The Idea of Poverty*, New York: Vintage Books, 1985, p. 80.

33 Bentham, *The Works*, vol. 8, p. 389.

34 Benjamin Franklin, *Writings*, ed. J. A. Leo Lemay, New York: Library of America, 1987, p. 652.

take by force deserters, including those who had become US citizens in the meantime. It was necessary to resort to drastic measures to ensure the functioning of 'more than 700 warships in commission, with nearly 150,000 sailors and marines'.[35] And so, like Franklin before him, we have Calhoun denouncing 'the slavery of impressed seamen'.[36]

This was a common theme in the journalism of the time. In Britain itself, defenders of slavery stressed the analogy between this institution and being pressed into the navy. Both practices were justified by exceptional circumstances—namely, the need to maintain the colonies and the navy, respectively. On the other side, the abolitionist Sharp condemned both practices.[37] By contrast, William Wilberforce sought to make distinctions, and was accused of hypocrisy by his opponents:[38] the pious pastor was moved by the condition of black slaves, but was indifferent to the no less grievous suffering of the kind of white slaves on whom the British Empire's military power and glory were based. The argument was far from trivial. Sailors were 'seized by press gangs from the streets of London and Liverpool'; and at a popular level no institution was more hated than the press gang.[39] The conditions to which men were then subjected can be readily be inferred from Locke's indirect comparison between the power of 'the captain of a galley' and that exercised by 'a lord over his slave'.[40] The capture of sailors in popular districts had something in common with the capture of blacks in Africa.

And it was not only the navy. A contemporary scholar summarizes the condition of those military 'captives in uniform' who were soldiers, called upon to defend a rapidly expanding empire in every corner of the world:

They were shipped abroad, often in foul conditions and sometimes against their will. They could be separated from their families, womenfolk and culture of origin for decades, often for ever. If judged disobedient or rebellious, they were likely to be flogged. If they tried to run away, they might

---

35   Allan Nevins and Henry S. Commager, *America: Story of a Free People*, Oxford: Oxford University Press, 1943, p. 138.

36   Calhoun, *Union and Liberty*, p. 291.

37   David B. Davis, *The Problem of Slavery in the Age of Revolution*, Ithaca: Cornell University Press, 1975, pp. 376, 394.

38   C. Duncan Rice, 'The Missionary Context of the British Anti-Slavery Movement', in James Walvin, ed., *Slavery and British Society, 1776–1846*, London: Macmillan, 1982, p. 151.

39   Foner, *The Story of American Freedom*, London: Picador, 1999, p. 6; E. P. Thompson, *The Making of the English Working Class*, London and New York: Penguin, 1988, p. 88.

40   John Locke, *Two Treatises of Government*, ed. William S. Carpenter, London and New York: Everyman's Library, 1924, p. 118.

be executed; and if they stayed and obeyed orders, they were apt to die prematurely anyway.[41]

For the rest, the way Locke described 'the common practice of martial discipline' is significant:

[T]he preservation of the army, and in it of the whole commonwealth, requires an absolute obedience to the command of every superior officer, and it is justly death to disobey or dispute the most dangerous or unreasonable of them; but yet we see that neither the sergeant that could command a soldier to march up to the mouth of a cannon, or stand in a breach where he is almost sure to perish, can command that soldier to give him one penny of his money; nor the general that can condemn him to death for deserting his post, or not obeying the most desperate orders, cannot yet with all his absolute power of life and death dispose of one farthing of that soldier's estate, or seize one jot of his goods; whom yet he can command anything, and hang for the least disobedience.[42]

This above all calls to mind the 'absolute power of life and death' wielded by officers over their subordinates. It is the phrase Locke habitually used to define the essence of slavery. Is it a rhetorical exaggeration? Already in Grotius we find the observation that the condition of the slave is not very different from that of the soldier.[43] But let us concentrate on liberal England. The mortality rate of soldiers en route to India was comparable to that affecting black slaves during their deportation from one side of the Atlantic to the other. Moreover, British soldiers were subject to the punishment traditionally reserved for slaves—flogging—and, paradoxically, continued to be even when this form of discipline had been abolished for Indian troops.[44]

Power relations in the army reproduced those existing in society. The figure of the soldier tended to coincide with that of the servant. At the start of the eighteenth century, Defoe observed: 'any Man would carry a Musket rather than starve ... 'tis Poverty makes Men Soldiers, and drives Crowds into the Armies'.[45] At the end of the century, Townsend reiterated that 'distress and

---

41   Linda Colley, *Captives*, London: Random House, 2002, p. 314.

42   Locke, *Two Treatises*, pp. 188–9.

43   See Hugo Grotius, *The Rights of War and Peace*, 3 vols, ed. Richard Tuck, Indianapolis: Liberty Fund, 2005, vol. 2, ch. v, §28.

44   Colley, *Captives*, pp. 314–16.

45   Defoe, *Giving Alms No Charity*, p. 24.

poverty' alone could impel 'the lower classes of the people to encounter all the horrors which await them on the tempestuous ocean, or in the field of battle'.[46] Or, to put the point this time with Mandeville, '[t]he Hardships and Fatigues of War that are personally suffer'd, fall upon them that bear the Brunt of every Thing'—namely, 'the working slaving People'.[47] On the other side, the figure of the officer tended to coincide with that of the master, and the contempt officers/masters had for troops was professed and even ostentatious. Troops of the line (lamented an ordinary soldier) were 'the lowest class of animals, and only fit to be ruled with the cat o' nine tails'[48]—that is, with the whip capable of inflicting the most sadistic punishments, those usually reserved for disobedient slaves.

5. The penal code, formation of a compulsory workforce, and the process of colonization

The problem of military recruitment is thus understandable: prisons were 'rumag'd for Malefactors'; the profession of soldier (observed Defoe) above all devolved on 'Men taken from the Gallows'.[49] Fortunately, there were plenty of them. From 1688 to 1820, the number of crimes carrying the death penalty increased from 50 to between 200 and 250, and they were almost always crimes against property. While attempted homicide was regarded as a petty crime until 1803, the theft of a shilling or handkerchief, or the illegal clipping of an ornamental bush, could entail hanging; and one could be consigned to the hangman even at the age of eleven.[50] In fact, in some cases, even young children ran this risk: in 1833 the death penalty was pronounced on a pickpocket of nine, although the sentence was subsequently commuted.[51]

Even more significant than the increase in penalties was the criminalization of behaviour that had hitherto been licit. The enclosure and private appropriation of common land underwent significant development; and the peasant or

---

46   Joseph Townsend, *A Dissertation on the Poor Laws by a Well-Wisher to Mankind*, Berkeley: University of California Press, 1971, p. 35.

47   Bernard de Mandeville, *The Fable of the Bees*, 2 vols, ed. Frederick B. Kaye, Indianapolis: Liberty Classics, 1988, vol. 1, p. 119.

48   Colley, *Captives*, p. 314.

49   Defoe, *Giving Alms No Charity*, p. 24.

50   E. P. Thompson, *Whigs and Hunters*, Harmondsworth: Penguin, 1977, pp. 22–3; Anthony Arblaster, *The Rise and Decline of Western Liberalism*, Oxford: Blackwell, 1987, p. 172; Robert Hughes, *The Fatal Shore*, London: Collins Harvill, 1987, p. 30.

51   Ronald W. Harris, *England in the Eighteenth Century*, London: Blandford Press, 1963, p. 211.

commoner who was late in appreciating the new situation became a thief, a criminal to be visited with all the force of the law. This might seem an arbitrary and brutal way to behave; but that is not what Locke thought. In legitimizing the colonists' appropriation of land left uncultivated by the Indians, the *Second Treatise of Government* simultaneously adopted a clear position in favour of enclosure in England. '[I]n the beginning, all the world was America';[52] and common land was a kind of vestige of this original, wild state, which work, private appropriation and money had subsequently overcome. It was a process that manifested itself on a large scale across the Atlantic, but which was not unknown in England: 'even amongst us, land that is left wholly to nature, that hath no improvement of pasturage, tillage, or planting, is called, as indeed it is, waste', until enclosure and private appropriation intervened positively.[53]

Along with the despoliation of the Indians and English peasants, Locke also justified terroristic legislation in defence of property: it was 'lawful for a man to kill a thief who has not in the least hurt him, nor declared any design upon his life, any farther than by the use of force, so to get him in his power as to take away his money, or what he pleases, from him'.[54] This was only a petty crime in appearance. In reality, the guilty party, if only momentarily, had deprived his victim of his 'right to liberty' and had made him a 'slave'. At this point, no one could exclude the possibility that theft would not be followed by homicide, since it was precisely the power of life and death that defined the relationship of slavery. This was synonymous with a state of war, and hence there was no reason why the thief should not be done to death, whatever the extent of the theft.[55] What Locke seems to be saying is that at stake is not only the shilling or handkerchief or whatever other rather minor stolen good: private property as such and, over and above it, liberty were in danger. Thus, what legitimized the pickpocket's killing or execution is the same liberal pathos that had presided over the condemnation of monarchical despotism as the source of political slavery.

In addition to common land, even birds and wild animals became objects of private appropriation by the landed aristocracy. In this instance, it was not possible to appeal to Locke. In fact, on the basis of his theory, not having been transformed by labour, birds and wild animals should have been regarded as common property. And yet, in accordance with legislation enacted after the Glorious Revolution, while the peasant slid into the condition of thief, the

---

52   Locke, *Two Treatises*, p. 140.

53   Ibid., p. 137.

54   Ibid., p. 126.

55   Ibid., pp. 125–6.

hunter was transformed into poacher; and here too the terrorism of the penal code was called on to compel respect for the incursion.[56]

As with the slavery and trading of blacks, the vulgar historicist explanation does not stand up when it comes to the expansion in crimes against property and the increased severity of the penalties provided for them. It is misleading to refer to the spirit of the times. 'It is very doubtful whether any other country possessed a criminal code with anything like so many capital provisions as there were in this single statute.'[57] The ruthless character of English legislation was already proverbial on its enactment. While Napoleon exercised his iron rule over France, a reformer like Sir Samuel Romilly felt compelled to offer a bitter observation: 'there is probably no other country in the world in which so many and so great a variety of human actions are punishable with loss of life as in England'.[58] Still at the beginning of the nineteenth century, Hegel denounced the 'draconian' severity whereby 'every thief in England [is] hanged', in an absurd equation of life and property, of the two 'qualitatively different' crimes that were homicide and theft. The class origins of such 'draconian' severity were even identified: for peasants guilty of illegal hunting 'the harshest and most disproportionate punishments' were provided, because 'those who made those laws and who are now sitting in the courts as magistrates and jurors' were the aristocracy, the very class that held a monopoly on hunting.[59]

The need to maintain law and order was only one aspect of the problem. Not infrequently, those sentenced to death (or even a long prison term) saw their sentence commuted to deportation to the colonies. Already in force for some time, from 1717 the practice of deportation assumed an official character and significant proportions.[60] So following the Glorious Revolution, we witness, on the one hand, the enactment of terroristic legislation and, on the other, the burgeoning phenomenon of deportation to remote colonies. Is there a link between the two events? It is difficult to deny that the formation of a large compulsory workforce through drastic harshening of the legal code ultimately made it possible to satisfy 'the labor needs of the plantations'.[61] On the other hand, underlying this practice was a specific theory. Locke repeatedly demanded penal slavery for those who made an attempt on another person's

---

56 Thompson, *Whigs and Hunters*.

57 Thus the legal historian Leon Radzinowicz, quoted in ibid., p. 23.

58 Harris, *England in the Eighteenth Century*, pp. 211, 214.

59 Domenico Losurdo, *Hegel and the Freedom of the Moderns*, trans. Marella and Jon Morris, Durham (NC) and London: Duke University Press, 2004, ch. 5, §8.

60 Hughes, *The Fatal Shore*, p. 41.

61 Eric Williams, *Capitalism and Slavery*, London: Deutsch, 1990, p. 12; cf. Hughes, *The Fatal Shore*, p. 40.

life or property. Already in the state of nature, '[t]he damnified person has this power of appropriating to himself the goods or service of the offender'.[62] Things were even clearer in the social state:

> Indeed, having by his fault forfeited his own life by some act that deserves death, he to whom he has forfeited it may, when he has him in his power, delay to take it, and make use of him to his own service; and he does him no injury by it. For, whenever he finds the hardship of his slavery outweigh the value of his life, it is in his power, by resisting the will of his master, to draw on himself the death he desires.[63]

The theory of the colonial war as just war (on the part of Europeans) and the theory of penal slavery legitimized and galvanized the deportation, respectively, of the black slaves and white semi-slaves required by colonial development. On the eve of the American Revolution, in Maryland alone there were 20,000 servants of criminal origin. To put the point with Samuel Johnson, they were 'a race of convicts, and ought to be content with anything we may allow them short of hanging'. And that is how an inexhaustible source of forced labour was fed.[64]

6. Indentured servants

This labour force proved precious for the purposes of populating and exploiting colonies as they were conquered. Initially, the flow of indentured servants went in the direction of America. Subsequently, supplanted and rendered superfluous by the massive introduction of black slaves, and in any event after the achievement of independence by the United States, white semi-slaves were diverted towards Australia, where they made an even more significant contribution to the process of exploiting the new colony. What were the characteristics of this labour relationship? Let us start with the journey of relocation or deportation from Britain. The horrors and mortality rate call to mind the famous 'middle passage' to which black slaves were subjected. Sometimes not even half the 'passengers' survived the voyage. Among them were to be found children between the ages of one and seven; they rarely escaped death. A witness related

---

62 Locke, *Two Treatises*, p. 122.

63 Ibid., p. 128.

64 Marcus W. Jernegan, *Laboring and Dependent Classes in Colonial America*, Westport (CI): Greenwood Press, 1980, pp. 77–9, and p. 48 (for the quotation from Dr Johnson).

having seen thirty-two children of tender years cast into the ocean in the course of a single voyage. Diseases continued to rage even after the crossing of the Atlantic; as a result, the new arrivals were often subjected to quarantine. There then intervened the moment of the market. In the papers commercial adverts of the following kind could be read: 'Just arrived at Leedstown, the Ship *Justitia* with about one Hundred Healthy Servants. Men, Women and Boys, among which are many Tradesmen ... The Sale will Commence on Tuesday, the 2nd of April' (*The Virginia Gazette*, 28 March 1771). Husband and wife were often separated, and might be separated from their children, permanently or for a long period; children under the age of five were obliged to render service until they were twenty-one. Flogged by their masters in the event of indiscipline or disobedience, servants sometimes fled, and then a manhunt was unleashed. The local press provided an accurate physical description of the fugitives who, once taken, were punished and branded with the letter R (standing for 'rogue') or subjected to the excision of ears. Thus rendered immediately recognizable, they no longer had any escape.[65]

What, then, was the difference compared with slaves proper? Sometimes white semi-slaves bemoaned their lot: 'Many blacks are treated better.' In fact, unlike real slaves, servants could turn to the judiciary and hope to be accepted into the community of the free, and were indeed admitted 'assuming they survived their period of labor'.[66] It is true that death often intervened first. But we are dealing with a social relation that is different from hereditary racial slavery.

Was it a social relation marked by freedom? We have seen Locke on the one hand stress the contractual, and hence free, genesis of the figure of servant, and on the other let slip the admission that he was not really free. But on this point we should also attend to Sieyès' opinion. Looking across the Atlantic, he argued thus:

> The final class, composed of men who have only their hands, can have need of regulated *slavery* in order to escape the *slavery of need*. Why restrict natural liberty? I want to sell my time and my services of whatever kind (I do not say my life) for a *year*, two *years*, etc., as occurs in English America. The law is silent in this connection, and it should only speak to prevent abuses of the institution that endanger liberty. Thus it will be possible to hire oneself or serve [*s'engager / s'asservir*] for a maximum of five years.[67]

---

65   Ibid., pp. 50–4.

66   Foner, *The Story of American Freedom*, p. 11.

67   Emmanuel-Joseph Sieyès, *Écrits politiques*, ed. Roberto Zapperi, Paris: Éditions des archives contemporaines, 1985, p. 76.

Sieyès did not disguise the fact that what characterized the figure of the indentured servant was subservience, 'servile engagement' (*engageance serve*), or 'legally regulated slavery'. However, especially after the outbreak of the French Revolution, apologetic concerns seem to have got the upper hand: in the new ideological and political climate, it was no longer possible to declare oneself in favour of an institution whose substantially slave-like character was acknowledged. And so we have Sieyès arguing against those for whom the indentured servant was a person who 'loses some of his freedom'. No:

> It is more accurate to say that, at the point when the contract is drawn up, far from being impeded in his liberty, he exercises it in the way most opportune to him. Any convention is an exchange in which each likes what he receives more than what he gives up.

It is true that for the duration of the contract the servant could not exercise the liberty ceded by him. But it was a general rule that the liberty of an individual 'never extends to the point of harming others'.[68]

On the other hand, from the outset Sieyès upheld contractual servitude in the name of 'natural liberty', of the right possessed by every individual to draw up the contract that seemed most opportune to him. In other words, the key category of liberal thought (the category of contract), invoked by Grotius to legitimize slavery proper, was applied by Sieyès solely to the labour relation that binds the indentured servant to his master. This was not dissimilar from Locke, the difference being that the French author, prior to the Revolution at least, stressed the fundamentally slave-like character of the relationship. That is why he was concerned to stress the vigilance the law should be called on to exercise: public officials should control the master's actions in order to prevent the 'person' of the servant 'being harmed through unduly prolonged hire or during the hire'.[69] Sieyès seems to propose a kind of code for regulating this white semi-slavery, on the model of the *Code noir* with which, in theory, the masters of black slaves should comply.

---

68 Ibid., pp. 89, 196.
69 Ibid., p. 76.

7. 'The extensive Herod-like kidnappings'

Among the compulsory labour force called on to ensure the development of the colonies were also youngsters of poor condition, deceived with honeyed words, abducted and deported across the Atlantic.[70] Alternatively, they arrived in America with their parents, who were often compelled to sell them, never seeing them again. The situation of children of popular extraction was not much better in England. Marx denounced 'the extensive Herod-like kidnappings perpetrated in the early days of the factory system, when children were stolen from the work houses and orphanages, and capital thereby incorporated a mass of unresisting human material'.[71] Going beyond the use of orphanages as a source of low-cost and more or less compulsory labour, we can make a general observation here. If, in the proto-liberal theory and practice of the time, the wage-labourer was (as we shall soon see) the *instrumentum vocale* Burke mentions, or the 'bipedal machine' referred to by Sieyès, his children were ultimately *res nullius*, destined to be used at the first opportunity precisely in their capacity as work tools and machines. Locke explicitly declared that poor children, who were to be sent to work from the age of three, must 'be taken off their [parents'] hands'.[72] Over a century later, Bentham's attitude was not dissimilar. He invited people to look for inspiration to 'manufactures where children, down to four years old, earn something, and where children a few years older earn a subsistence, and that a comfortable one'.[73] It was permissible and beneficial to 'tak[e] the children out of the hands of their parents as much as possible, and even, if possible, altogether'. There should be no hesitation:

> [Y]ou may even clap them up in an inspection-house, and then you make of them what you please. You need never grudge the parents *a peep behind the curtain* in the master's lodge ... you might keep up a sixteen or eighteen years separation between the male and female part of your young subjects ...[74]

The children of the poor were at the complete disposal of society. We are reminded of the fate reserved for slaves across the Atlantic. To end their presence on American soil, suggested Jefferson, one might at a moderate price, and

---

70 Williams, *Capitalism and Slavery*, p. 11.
71 Karl Marx, *Capital: Volume One*, trans. Ben Fowkes, Harmondsworth: Penguin, 1976, p. 527 n. 62.
72 Locke, *Political Writings*, p. 454.
73 Bentham, *Works*, vol. 4, p. 56.
74 Ibid., vol. 4, pp. 64–5.

perhaps even gratis, acquire newborn blacks, place them 'under the guardian-ship of the State', subject them to work as soon as possible, and thus largely recover the expenses required for their deportation to San Domingo, which should be set in train when convenient. Certainly, '[t]he separation of infants from their mothers ... would produce some scruples of humanity', but there was no need to be so fussy.[75] While he was motivated by economic calculations, rather than worries about racial purity, Bentham would have liked to proceed perhaps even more ruthlessly with the children of the poor in England: 'An inspection-house, to which a set of children had been consigned from their birth, might afford experiments enough ... What say you to a *foundling-hospital* upon this principle?'[76]

We shall see that Bentham also envisaged experiments of a eugenic character. But for now we can reach a conclusion by attending to an English economist (Edward G. Wakefield), who in 1834 published a successful book devoted to the contrast between America and England: 'it is the whole press of England, not I, that calls English children [of popular extraction] slaves'. The majority were compelled to work such long hours that they inadvertently fell asleep, only to be awoken and forced back to work with beatings and torments of every kind. As to foundlings, they were dispensed with rapidly enough: adverts were affixed to the doors of workhouses promoting their sale. In London the price of male and female children put on the market thus was significantly below that of black slaves in America; in rural regions, such commodities were even cheaper.[77]

8. Hundreds or thousands of wretches 'daily hanged for trifles'

Bearing down on this mass of wretches was legislation that was certainly not marked by the protection of civil liberties. One thinks of the blank warrants that allowed the police to arrest or search a person at will. Abolished by the Fourth Amendment to the US Constitution, this 'intolerable tool of oppression' (to adopt the description of it given by the French liberal Laboulaye in 1866)[78] long continued to survive in England. Smith himself tended if not

---

75   Jefferson, *Writings*, pp. 1450, 1485–7 (letters to Albert Gallatin, 26 December 1820, and Jared Sparks, 4 February 1824).

76   Bentham, *Works*, vol. 4, p. 64.

77   Edward Gibbon Wakefield, *The Collected Works of Edward Gibbon Wakefield*, ed. M. F. Lloyd Prichard, London and Glasgow: Collins, 1968, pp. 347–8.

78   Édouard Laboulaye, *Histoire des États-Unis*, 3 vols, Paris: Charpentier, 1866, vol. 3, pp. 541–2.

to justify it, in any case to trivialize it. He was astonished that the 'common people', rather than fighting for the free circulation and buying and selling of labour power, exhibited all its indignation 'against general warrants, an abusive practice undoubtedly, but such a one as was not likely to occasion any general oppression'.[79]

The death penalty was imposed with great facility but also with some discretion. With the passing in 1723 of the Black Act—the 'blacks' were alleged deer rustlers—in some cases it was not necessary to resort to a formal process to provide for the death sentence, which consigned to the hangman even those who had in some way aided a thief (or alleged thief) to escape justice.[80]

Without betraying any disquiet, Mandeville recognized that 'the Lives of Hundreds, if not Thousands, of Necessitous Wretches, that are daily hanged for Trifles' were being snuffed out;[81] execution often became a mass spectacle with pedagogical purposes.[82] The British liberal called upon magistrates not to be inhibited either by misplaced 'compassion' or by undue doubts and scruples. Certainly, thieves might have committed theft under the spur of necessity: 'what they can get Honestly is not sufficient to keep them'. Yet 'the Peace of the Society' required that the guilty be hanged. Yes, 'the Evidences perhaps want clearness or are otherwise insufficient'; and there was a risk that an innocent person might be put to death. But however 'terrible' that would be, the aim must be achieved that 'not one Guilty Person [be] suffered to escape with Impunity'. It would be a serious thing if overly scrupulous judges prioritized their 'Conscience' over the 'Advantage to a Nation'.[83] The courts of the property-owner judges were called upon to operate as a kind of committee of public safety.

We can then conclude that, setting aside the colonies in their entirety (including Ireland), in Britain itself full enjoyment of a private sphere of liberty guaranteed by the law—the 'modern' or 'negative' liberty that Constant and Berlin, respectively, refer to[84]—was the privilege of a small minority. The mass of people was subject to regulation and coercion that extended far beyond the workplace (or the place of punishment that was the prison, but also the

---

79   Adam Smith, *An Inquiry into the Nature and Causes of the Wealth of Nations*, Indianapolis: Liberty Classics, 1981, p. 157.

80   Thompson, *Whigs and Hunters*, pp. 23, 175.

81   Mandeville, *Fable of the Bees*, vol. 1, p. 273.

82   Hughes, *The Fatal Shore*, p. 31.

83   Mandeville, *Fable of the Bees*, vol. 1, pp. 272–3, 87.

84   Benajmin Constant, *Political Writings*, ed. and trans. Biancamaria Fontana, Cambridge: Cambridge University Press, 1988, pp. 309–28; Isaiah Berlin, *Four Essays on Liberty*, Oxford: Oxford University Press, 1969, pp. 118–72.

workhouse and the army). While Locke proposed regulating the consumption of alcohol by the popular classes, Mandeville believed that, at least on Sunday, 'every Amusement Abroad that might allure or draw them from' attending church should be 'prohibited'.[85] On the subject of alcohol, Burke argued differently: while it had no nutritional properties, it could alleviate hunger pangs in the poor person; moreover, 'at all times, and in all countries', alcohol, together with 'opium' and 'tobacco', had been turned to for the 'moral consolations' men sometimes needed.[86] Now, even more than the disciplining of workers and vagrants as in Locke and Mandeville, the problem was that of dulling the consciousness and suffering of the starving in general. What remained constant was the tendency to govern the existence of the popular classes even in its smallest details. The reference to opium added a touch of cynicism. Reports by government committees of inquiry would subsequently denounce the catastrophe: in the poorest districts, opium consumption was spreading, and was becoming a means of feeding or a substitute for it. It was sometimes given to infants, who '"shrank up into little old men", or "wizened like little monkeys" '.[87]

This detailed regulation obviously also included religious indoctrination. In Locke's view, for poor children to start work from the age of three was a beneficial measure not only economically, but also morally: 'Another advantage ... of bringing poor children ... to a working-school is that by this means they may be obliged to come constantly to church every Sunday along with their school-masters or dames, whereby they may be brought into some sense of religion'.[88] In his turn, Mandeville demanded that Sunday attendance of church become 'a Duty' for the poor and illiterate. Appealing to spontaneous religious feelings was insufficient: 'It is a Duty incumbent on all Magistrates to take particular Care' of what happened on Sundays. 'The Poor more especially and their Children should be made to go to Church on it both in the Fore and Afternoon'. Positive results would not be wanting: 'Where this Care is taken by the Magistrates as far as it lies in their Power, Ministers of the Gospel may instill into the smallest Capacities' devotion and the virtue of obedience.[89]

Controlled in their private life, the popular classes were even more so in the public existence which, amid a host of difficulties, they sought: 'Between 1793

---

85   Mandeville, *Fable of the Bees*, vol. 1, p. 307.

86   Edmund Burke, *The Works: A New Edition*, 16 vols, London: Rivington, 1826, vol. 7, pp. 413–14.

87   Marx, *Capital: Volume One*, p. 522 and n. 51.

88   Locke, *Political Writings*, p. 454.

89   Mandeville, *Fable of the Bees*, vol. 1, pp. 307–8.

& 1820, more than 60 acts directed at repression of working-class collective action were passed by Parliament.'[90] More even than trade-union activity in the strict sense—that is, action aimed at raising wages and improving working conditions—the very attempt by servants to escape their isolation and communicate with one another was viewed with dismay. They (thundered Mandeville in alarm) 'assemble when they please with Impunity'. They even developed relations of mutual solidarity; they sought to aid a colleague dismissed or flogged by his master. Simply by virtue of not confining themselves to the vertical, subaltern relationship with their superiors, but seeking to develop horizontal relations with one another, servants were to be considered culpable of unacceptable subversion: they were 'daily incroaching upon Masters and Mistresses, and endeavouring to be more upon the Level with them'; they had already raised 'the low Dignity of their Condition ... from the Original Meanness which the publick Welfare requires it should always remain in'. Exceeding every limit, the servant posed as a gentleman; this was the 'comedy' of the 'Gentleman Footman', a comedy which in fact, in the absence of timely intervention, might turn into a 'tragedy' for the whole nation.[91]

Particularly significant in this context was the position taken by Adam Smith. He acknowledged that '[w]e have no acts of parliament against combining to lower the price of work; but many against combining to raise it.' Besides, '[t]he masters, being fewer in number, can combine much more easily ... Masters are always and everywhere in a sort of tacit, but constant and uniform combination, not to raise the wages of labour above their actual rate', or 'to sink the wages of labour even below this rate'.[92] Hence even were masters and workers to be treated identically in legislative terms, the former would always enjoy an advantageous situation. But they were also favoured by the precarious living conditions of the opposing party:

> In order to bring the point to a speedy decision, they [the workers] have always recourse to the loudest clamour, and sometimes to the most shocking violence and outrage. They are desperate, and act with the folly and extravagance of desperate men, who must either starve, or frighten their masters into an immediate compliance with their demands.[93]

---

90 Karl Polanyi, quoted in Immanuel Wallerstein, *The Modern World System*, 3 vols, New York: Academic Press, 1974–89, vol. 3, p. 121 n. 333.

91 Mandeville, *Fable of the Bees*, vol. 1, p. 306.

92 Smith, *The Wealth of Nations*, pp. 83–4.

93 Ibid., pp. 84–5.

All this did not prevent Smith from recommending that the government act severely against working-class combinations. Certainly, '[p]eople of the same trade seldom meet together, even for merriment and diversion, but the conversation ends in a conspiracy against the public, or in some contrivance to raise prices'. However, it was 'impossible to prevent such meetings, by any law which … would be consistent with liberty and justice'. But the government must forestall any working-class gathering, even the most casual and seemingly innocuous. For example, the requirement of bureaucratic registration for those who practice a specific profession ended up 'connect[ing] individuals who might never otherwise be known to one another'. Utterly intolerable was any 'regulation which enables those of the same trade to tax themselves in order to provide for their poor, their sick, their widows and orphans, by giving them a common interest to manage'.[94] Consequently, not only trade-union activity, but even a mutual aid society was to be considered illegal. Smith recognized that he was dealing with 'desperate men', who risked dying of starvation. And yet this consideration took second place to the need to avoid meetings, 'conversations' or gatherings that tended to be synonymous with a 'conspiracy against the public'.

In order to criminalize at birth any popular association, the dominant class in England resorted to yet more summary methods, which can be described in Constant's words: 'the horrendous expedient of sending spies to incite ignorant minds and suggest rebellion to them, so as then to be able to denounce them'. Results were not wanting: 'The wretches captivated those who had the misfortune to listen to them and probably also accused those they did not succeed in captivating.' And justice came crashing down on both.[95]

9. A whole with singular characteristics

We have seen Mandeville call on judges to be summary in condemning to death those guilty or suspected of theft and pilferage, even at the cost of striking down some innocents. The priority was the need to safeguard 'the peace of the society' or 'advantage to a nation'. Blackstone acknowledged that press-ganging men into the navy seemed dubious and detrimental to liberty. It was 'only defensible for public necessity, to which all private considerations must

---

94   Ibid., p. 145.
95   Benjamin Constant, *Mélanges de littérature et de politique*, 2 vols, Louvain: Michel, 1830, vol. 1, p. 28 and *passim*.

give way'.[96] In his turn, Locke repeatedly called on people not to lose sight of 'the public good', 'the good of the nation', 'the public weal', or 'the preservation of the whole', 'the whole commonwealth'.[97]

What is so passionately invoked here is a Whole demanding the sacrifice, permanent not temporary, of the overwhelming majority of the population, whose condition was all the more tragic because any prospect of improvement seemed pretty remote. In fact, even to entertain projects tending towards such improvement was synonymous not only with abstract utopianism, but also and above all with dangerous subversion. According to Townsend, the 'stock of human happiness is ... much increased' by the presence of 'the poor', who were compelled to perform the most arduous and painful work. The poor fully deserved their fate, were by definition wastrels and vagrants. But it would be a disaster for society if, by some chance, they were to mend their ways: 'The fleets and armies of a state would soon be in want of soldiers and of sailors, if sobriety and diligence universally prevailed';[98] and the country's economy would find itself in difficulties. Mandeville reached the same conclusion: 'To make the society ... happy ... it is requisite that great numbers ... should be ignorant as well as poor'; 'the surest wealth consists in a multitude of laborious poor'.[99] And let us now read Arthur Young: 'every one but an idiot knows that the lower classes must be kept poor, or they will never be industrious',[100] and would not produce the 'wealth of nations' referred to by Smith. Later, in France, Destutt de Tracy arrived at the same conclusion: 'In poor nations the people are comfortable, in rich nations they are generally poor.'[101] Why was the proposition, in its various forms, that society's happiness and wealth depended on the hardship and deprivation of the poor, who formed a large majority of the population, not perceived as contradictory? It is Locke who explains the logic of this Whole with special characteristics: slaves 'cannot ... be considered as any part of civil society, the chief end whereof is the preservation of property'.[102] And this was also Algernon Sidney's opinion: 'a kingdom or city ... is composed of freemen and equals: Servants may be in it, but are not members of it.' Indeed, 'no man, whilst he is a servant, can be a member of a commonwealth'; he is not even a member of the people, because 'the people' comprises

---

96   Blackstone, *Commentaries*, vol. 1, p. 407.

97   Locke, *Two Treatises*, pp. 202–3, 196–7, 205, 188.

98   Townsend, *A Dissertation on the Poor Laws*, p. 35.

99   Quoted in Marx, *Capital: Volume One*, p. 765.

100   Young, quoted in R. H. Tawney, *Religion and the Rise of Capitalism*, West Drayton: Pelican, 1948, p. 268.

101   Destutt de Tracy, quoted in Marx, *Capital: Volume One*, p. 802.

102   Locke, *Two Treatises*, p. 158.

'all the freemen'.[103] The poor were the servile caste required by society; they were the subterranean foundation of the social edifice, those whom Nietzsche defined as 'the blind moles of culture'. With society and civilization, the poor and the moles continued to have a relationship of estrangement.[104]

10. Wage-labour and the categories of slavery

Some decades after Franklin, in transition from the first to the second great controversy in the liberal party, the governor of South Carolina, James Henry Hammond, likewise applied himself to emphasizing how much quasi-slavery persisted in Britain. He sent an open letter to Thomas Clarkson, the venerable patriarch of English abolitionism, putting his finger on the sore point of the workers' condition in the country that boasted of having abolished slavery in its colonies:

> When you look around you, how dare you talk to us before the world of Slavery? … If you are really humane, philanthropic, and charitable, here are objects for you. Relieve them. Emancipate them. Raise them from the condition of brutes, to the level of human beings—of American slaves, at least.[105]

Obviously, reactions in Britain were indignant, insisting on the characteristic feature of the freeman that applied to even the most wretched wage-labourer. However, in defining him, the liberal tradition frequently had recourse to the same categories as were used in classical antiquity and across the Atlantic in relation to the black slave.

In Locke's view, not genuinely capable of intellectual and moral life was 'the greatest part of Mankind, who are given up to Labour, and enslaved to the necessity of their mean Condition; whose Lives are worn out, only in the Provisions for Living'. Wholly absorbed in 'still[ing] the Croaking of their own Bellies, or the Cries of their Children', such people had no possibility of thinking about other things:

---

103 Algernon Sidney, *Discourses Concerning Government*, ed. Thomas G. West, Indianapolis: Liberty Classics, 1990, pp. 89, 103.

104 Cf. Domenico Losurdo, *Nietzsche, il ribelle aristocratico*, Turin: Bollati Boringhieri, 2002, ch. 12, §4.

105 Clarkson, quote in Davis, *Slavery and Human Progress*, pp. 233–4.

'Tis not to be expected, that a Man, who drudges on, all his Life, in a laborious Trade, should be more knowing in the variety of Things done in the World, than a Pack-horse, who is driven constantly forwards and backwards, in a narrow Lane, and dirty Road, only to Market, should be skilled in the Geography of the Country.

Locke had no hesitation in asserting that 'there is a greater distance between some Men, and others, in this respect, than between some Men and some Beasts'. To appreciate this, it was enough to contrast 'Westminster-hall' and the 'Exchange' with 'Alms-Houses' and 'Bedlam'.[106] The boundary separating the human world from the animal world was imperceptible and evanescent: 'if we compare the Understanding and Abilities of some Men, and some Brutes, we shall find so little difference, that 'twill be hard to say, that that of the Man is either clearer or larger.'[107]

Similarly, Mandeville, condemning the spread of education to popular strata, compared the wage-labourer to a 'horse': 'No Creatures submit contentedly to their Equals, and should a Horse know as much as a Man, I should not desire to be his Rider.'[108] This was a metaphor that reappeared on the occasion of his polemic against the excessive generosity displayed by the rich master to the servant in England: 'A Man may have Five and Twenty Horses in his Stables without being guilty of Folly, if it suits with the rest of his Circumstances, but if he keeps but one, and overfeeds it to shew his Wealth, he is a Fool for his Pains.'[109]

It was not only English liberalism that argued in these terms. In fact, the process of de-humanization possibly reached its peak in Sieyès:

The unfortunates devoted to arduous work, producers of other people's enjoyments, who receive scarcely enough to sustain their suffering, needy bodies; this enormous crowd of bipedal tools, without liberty, without morality, without intellectual faculties, equipped solely with hands that earn little and a mind burdened with a thousand worries that serves them only to suffer ... are these what you call men? They are deemed civilized [*policés*], but have we seen a single one of them who was capable of entering into society?[110]

---

106   John Locke, *An Essay Concerning Human Understanding*, ed. Peter H. Nidditch, Oxford: Oxford University Press, 1975, pp. 707, 709.

107   Ibid., p. 666.

108   Mandeville, *Fable of the Bees*, vol. 1, p. 290.

109   Ibid., vol. 1, p. 305.

110   Sieyès, *Écrits politiques*, pp. 236, 75, 81.

On other occasions, the process of de-humanization occurred in a different fashion. Adopting the distinction, peculiar to classical antiquity, between the various instruments of labour, Burke subsumed the wage-labourer under the category of *instrumentum vocale*.[111] Similarly, Sieyès referred to the 'majority of men' defined, above all in private notes predating 1789, as 'work machines' (*machines de travail*), 'instruments of labour' (*instruments de labeur*), 'human instruments of production' (*instruments humains de la production*), or 'bipedal tools' (*instruments bipèdes*).[112]

Traces of this process of de-humanization can even be found in Smith. By dint of the duress and monotony of his work, a wage-labourer 'generally becomes as stupid and ignorant as it is possible for a human creature to become', incapable of participating 'in any rational conversation' or 'conceiving any generous ... sentiment'.[113]

As across the Atlantic with black slaves and slaves in general, so in Europe the dominant class was separated from white servants by a gulf that had ethnic and racial connotations. In Locke's view, 'a day-labourer [is] no more capable of reasoning than almost a perfect natural [i.e., an ignorant aborigine]': neither had yet reached the level of 'rational creatures and Christians'.[114] In his turn, Sieyès was of the opinion that the 'human instruments of production' pertained to a 'people' different from (and inferior to) that comprising 'the heads of production' or 'intelligent persons', 'respectable folk'.[115]

A further reason intervened to render the gulf separating the community of the free from servants and slaves unbridgeable. The latter were considered incapable of fully appreciating the humiliations, the frustrations, the sufferings, the pain, as well as all the other feelings characteristic of man's spiritual exist-ence. We have seen how Mandeville argued in relation to the mass of wretches in Europe. They were forced to suffer hardship and privations and often ended up on the gallows 'for trifles', which they made themselves guilty of in an attempt to escape hunger. However,

> To be happy is to be pleas'd, and the less Notion a Man has of a better way of Living, the more content he'll be with his own ... when a Man enjoys

---

111   Burke, *Works*, vol. 7, p. 383.

112   Sieyès, *Écrits politiques*, pp. 236, 75, 81.

113   Smith, *The Wealth of Nations*, p. 782.

114   John Locke, *The Conduct of the Understanding*, Edinburgh: William and Robert Chambers, 1839, pp. 10, 12.

115   Sieyès, *Écrits politiques*, pp. 89, 75.

himself, Laughs and Sings, and in his Gesture and Behaviour shews me all the tokens of Content and Satisfaction, I pronounce him happy ...

On careful examination, the 'greatest King' could envy 'the Peace of Mind' of 'the meanest and most unciviliz'd Peasant' and his 'Tranquillity of ... Soul'.[116] In no less emphatic terms, the Virginian theorist we have already encountered, Thomas R. Dew, expressed himself on the subject of slaves: 'we have no doubts that they form the happiest portion of our society. A merrier being does not exist on the face of the globe, than the negro slave of the United States'.[117]

Not only is it very difficult to define the condition of white servants in Europe as free, but the image of them transmitted by the liberal thought of the time is not much different from the image of the black slave in the southern United States. So was the governor of South Carolina right to mock the abolitionists' hypocrisy and credulity? That would be a hasty conclusion. In any event, we are obliged to reflect further on the characteristics of the society that was being formed either side of the Atlantic and on the categories best suited to understanding it.

---

116   Mandeville, *Fable of the Bees*, vol. 1, pp. 311–16.
117   Dew, quoted in Richard Hofstadter, ed., *Great Issues in American History*, 3 vols, New York: Vintage Books, 1958–82, vol. 2, p. 318.

CHAPTER FOUR

Were Eighteenth- and Nineteenth-Century England and America Liberal?

1. The elusive liberalism of de Tocqueville's America

How should we define the political regime which, following the Dutch prologue and starting from the liberal revolutions, was established first in Britain and then in the United States? As regards the latter, Washington was in no doubt. We have seen him immediately after the achievement of independence celebrating the 'wise and liberal government' his country had given itself. Some years later, on the eve of the ratification of the federal Constitution, which consecrated a strong executive power, the general-president coined a kind of advertising slogan, declaring himself in favour of a 'liberal & energetic' government.[1] Yet if by liberalism is meant every individual's equal enjoyment of a private sphere of liberty guaranteed by law—'modern liberty' or 'negative liberty'—it is not difficult to perceive the rather problematic character of employing such a category. Even if we discount the problem of slavery, we know the condition of semi-slavery to which notionally free blacks were subjected.

We can ignore the population of colour in its entirety and still not thereby arrive at a different result. Those in the United States who were untainted by any crime, but interned in workhouses that were (as de Tocqueville himself acknowledged) an integral part of the 'prison system', did not exactly enjoy civil equality or modern liberty. And that is not all: such was the condition of the poor that, even in their capacity as witnesses, they were locked up in prison until the legal proceedings were over. And thus, 'in the same country that the plaintiff is put in prison, the thief remains at liberty if he can pay a bail bond'. Of 'three thousand examples' which might be given, there was that of two

---

1 Cf. Domenico Losurdo, *Democrazia o bonopartismo*, Turin: Bollati Boringhieri, 1993, ch. 3, §3.

young Irishmen 'detained for a whole year while waiting for the judges to deign to hear their deposition'. We can now come to de Tocqueville's unanticipated conclusion: we are dealing with laws consolidated by 'customs' and which yet can seem 'monstrous'; they 'have provided everything for the convenience of the wealthy and virtually nothing for the protection of the poor', of whose liberty 'they dispose cheaply'.[2]

But let us now pass over both populations of colonial origin and the poorest strata of the white community, who were denied not only political rights, but also 'modern liberty'. Let us focus exclusively on the dominant class—i.e. on white, male property-owners. Did full civil and political equality obtain in this milieu? There are reasons to doubt it. One thinks of the 'three-fifths' constitutional provision on the basis of which, in calculating the number of seats due to the southern states, partial account was also taken of the number of slaves. Far from being a negligible detail, this clause played a significant role in the history of the United States: 'four southern voters' ended up exercising 'more political power than ten northern voters'. Thus is explained the 'Virginia dynasty' that long succeeded in holding the country's presidency.[3] This was why Jefferson was branded the 'black president' by his opponents:[4] he arrived in power thanks to the inclusion in the electoral result of blacks who remained his slaves. On the eve of the Civil War, Lincoln proclaimed polemically: 'It is a truth that cannot be denied, that in all the free States no white man is the equal of the white man of the slave States.'[5] This was a thesis repeated in 1864 by a French liberal (Édouard Laboulaye). With the 'three-fifths' clause, it was as if the US Constitution was addressed to 'the folks of the South':

Because you have slaves, you will be allowed to elect a representative with ten thousand votes, while the Yankees [of the North], who live off their own labour, will require thirty thousand votes. The conclusion for the folks of the South is that they constitute a particular, superior race, that they are great lords. The aristocratic spirit has been developed and strengthened by the Constitution.[6]

2   Alexis de Tocqueville, *Oeuvres complètes*, ed. Jacob-Peter Mayer, Paris: Gallimard, 1951–, vol. 4, pt 1, pp. 323–6.

3   Francis Jennings, *The Creation of America*, Cambridge and New York: Cambridge University Press, 2000, p. 301.

4   Garry Wills, *'Negro President'*, Boston: Houghton Mifflin, 2003.

5   Abraham Lincoln, *Speeches and Writings*, 2 vols, ed. Don E. Fehrenbacher, New York: Library of America, 1989, vol. 2, p. 378.

6   Édouard Laboulaye, *Histoire des États-Unis*, 3 vols, Paris: Charpentier, 1866, vol. 3, p. 359.

Accused of breaching the principle of political equality within the dominant elite itself, the southern planters replied by declaring that, in actual fact, the principle of civil equality was infringed to their detriment. They regarded themselves as suffering negative discrimination, in as much as they were deprived of the freedom to transfer their human cattle to any part of the Union. They considered it inadmissible that owners of the *instrumentum vocale* should be treated worse than the owners of any other movable goods. As Jefferson Davis, president of the secessionist Confederacy, declared at the moment of abandoning the Union, the North was wrong to hamper in any way 'property in slaves', to act 'to the prejudice, detriment or discouragement of the owners of that species of property', which was 'recognized in the Constitution' and which, on that basis, should enjoy complete equality of treatment with other types of property.[7] This exchange of accusations played a far from subsidiary role in the conflict that issued in the Civil War.

2. Absolute power and the community obligations of the slave-owners

From Constant onwards, modern or liberal liberty has been described and celebrated as the undisturbed enjoyment of private property. But slave-owners were in fact subject to a whole series of public obligations. There can be no doubt that the Glorious Revolution and then the American Revolution consecrated the self-government of a civil society composed of, and hegemonized by, slave-owners, who were more determined than ever not to tolerate interference by central political power and the Church. But it would be mistaken to equate the self-government of civil society, now freed from these fetters, with the free movement of the individual members composing it. Certainly, they could reduce the slaves they legitimately owned to chattels. In the New England of 1732, a master put up for sale a nineteen-year-old female slave along with her son of six months: they could be acquired (the advert announced) 'together or separately'. There were no obstacles to bringing to market even adulterous offspring; a New Jersey master did this with the offspring of his relations with three black women whom he owned. Not by chance, slaves were frequently given names usually reserved for dogs and horses.[8]

---

7 Jefferson Davis, quoted in Richard Hofstadter, ed., *Great Issues in American History*, 3 vols, New York: Vintage Books, 1958–82, vol. 2, pp. 399–400.

8 Arthur Zilversmit, *The First Emancipation*, Chicago: University of Chicago Press, 1969, pp. 10–11, 7.

There can be no doubt that the slave-master wielded absolute power over his legitimate 'property', but not to the extent of being able freely to challenge the process of reification and commodification that had occurred. In this case, the community requirement prevailed of keeping the barrier between the race of masters and the race of servants clear and fixed. Let us attend to de Tocqueville: blacks had been 'forbidden ... under severe penalties, to be taught to read or write'.[9] The prohibition aimed to exclude the race of servants from any form of education, which was regarded as a serious source of danger not only because it was liable to fuel unacceptable hopes and claims, but also because it risked facilitating the communication of ideas and sentiments between blacks that was to be frustrated by any means. And yet, in the case of violation of such rules, to be struck in the first instance were white property-owners, who thus saw their negative liberty seriously restricted. The bans affecting slaves did not leave their masters unaffected. After Nat Turner's rebellion, it became a crime in Georgia even to provide a slave with paper and writing materials.[10]

Particularly significant was the legislation that banned interracial sexual relations and marriages. Later, in 1896, when upholding the constitutional legitimacy of provisions for racial segregation as a whole, the US Supreme Court conceded that the ban on 'the intermarriage of the two races' might, 'in a technical sense', breach freedom of contract, but extricated itself from an awkward situation by adding that the right of any individual state to legislate in this area was 'universally recognized'.[11] In fact, opposition was not lacking. The provision made in Virginia at the start of the eighteenth century, according to which not only those directly responsible for the sexual or marital relation were to be punished, was significant: 'extremely severe penalties' were prescribed for the priest guilty of having consecrated the interracial family bond.[12] And hence, along with 'freedom of contract', religious freedom itself was in some sense affected.

The absolute power exercised over black slaves ended up having negative and even dramatic consequences for whites. Take Pennsylvania in the early decades of the eighteenth century. The free black caught violating the ban on miscegenation (as it later came to be called)[13] risked being sold as a slave. This

---

9   Tocqueville, *Oeuvres complètes*, vol. 1, p. 380.

10   Eugene D. Genovese, *A Consuming Fire*, Athens: University of Georgia Press, 1998, p. 24.

11   Plessy versus Ferguson, quoted in Hofstadter, *Great Isssues in American History*, vol. 3, p. 56.

12   Herbert S. Klein, *Slavery in the Americas*, Chicago: Dee, 1989, pp. 51, 234–5.

13   The term was coined in late 1863: cf. Forrest G. Wood, *Black Scare*, Berkeley: University of California Press, 1968, pp. 53ff.

involved serious consequences for the white woman, who had to suffer forced separation from her partner and the terrible punishment inflicted on him. Let us now see what happened in colonial Virginia immediately after the Glorious Revolution. On the basis of a law of 1691, a free white woman who had had a child by a black man or mulatto could be sentenced to five years of servitude and, above all, be forced to surrender the child to the parish, which then sold him or her as a servant for a term of thirty years.[14] But there is more. Well-nigh insurmountable obstacles were placed in the way of recognition of the offspring of a relationship between an owner and one of his slaves. The father faced a tragic alternative: either to suffer exile from Virginia with his de facto family; or to agree to the child being a slave together with the mother.[15] More summary was New York's legislation, which automatically converted all children born of a slave mother into slaves.[16] We thus find ourselves in the presence of a society that in fact exercised such severe duress over its privileged members, partly legal and partly social, as to choke even the most natural feelings. As has justly been noted, in enslaving 'their children and their children's children', white people were in fact 'enslaving themselves'.[17]

Further to clarify the entanglement between the individual property-owner's absolute power over his human livestock and his subservience to the 'master race' of which he was a member, we can offer a final consideration. We have already noted the law in force in Virginia whereby it was meaningless to define and treat the killing of a slave by his owner as a 'felony'. Yet in not a few states, on the basis of legislation that survived even after the Second World War (see below, chapter 10, §5), a white man who had sexual relations with a black woman was guilty of a 'felony'. Thus, it was permissible for an owner to flog and beat his female slave to the point of killing her—property right was sacred; but so strong was the control exercised by the class of property-owners and the community of the free over their individual members that only by exposing himself to risks of various kinds could he have sexual relations with her. Other than by legal provisions, the ban on miscegenation was enforced by the intervention in the 1850s here and there of vigilante gangs, engaged in spying on, intimidating and attacking whites tempted by the fascination of their female slaves and women of colour in general.[18]

---

14   Klein, *Slavery in the Americas*, pp. 50–1.
15   Ibid., pp. 242–3.
16   Zilversmit, *The First Emancipation*, p. 13.
17   Joel Williamson, *New People*, New York: Free Press, 1980, p. 63.
18   Ibid., p. 66.

While, in one respect, they were a form of property and a chattel completely at the disposal of their legitimate master, in another slaves represented the enemy within, against whom it was necessary to be constantly on guard. Certainly, to avert the threat recourse could be had to terror, ruthlessly and even sadistically striking at guilty individuals and transforming execution into a kind of terrifying educative spectacle for all the rest: the slaves in a particular area were obliged to witness the torment of two of their fellows, guilty of murder and condemned to be burnt alive.[19] But that was not sufficient. Once again, preservation of the institution of slavery required heavy sacrifices even on the part of the dominant class. In 1741, in New York, mysterious fires fanned fears of a slave revolt: condemned to death and burnt alive were two blacks whose lives the master had in vain sought to save, testifying that at the time of the fire they were at home. Some years later, in the environs of the same city, a black, having confessed to setting fire to a barn, suffered the same torment. There was only one difference: the crowd of white spectators contrived to ensure that the flames were not extinguished too quickly, so that the spectacle and sufferings of the rebel black lasted as long as possible; his cries were heard three miles away. In any case, the master heard them very clearly: he sobbed loudly, because his slave was dear to him. But he was powerless, and the most he could do was to see to it that the torture was not prolonged any further.[20] Faced with the security requirements of the community they belonged to, individual slave-owners could not demand free disposal over their property.

Given the circumstances, these security requirements were a permanent given. We can make a general observation:

> While the colonial slave codes seem at first sight to have been intended to discipline Negroes, to deny them freedoms available to other Americans, a very slight shift in perspective shows the codes in a different light; they aimed, paradoxically, at disciplining white men. Principally, the law told the white man, not the Negro, what he must do; the codes were for the eyes and ears of slaveowners (sometimes the law required publication of the code in the newspaper and that clergymen read it to their congregations). It was the white man who was *required* to punish his runaways, prevent assemblages of slaves, enforce the curfews, sit on the special courts, and ride the patrols.[21]

---

19   Zilversmit, *The First Emancipation*, p. 21.

20   Ibid., pp. 19–22.

21   Winthrop D. Jordan, *White over Black*, New York: Norton, 1977, p. 108.

Specific penalties were provided for slave-owners who failed to inflict the punishments prescribed by law. According to a law in force in South Carolina, on her fourth attempt at flight a female slave was to be 'severely whipped ... branded on the left cheek with the letter R, and [have] her left ear cut off'. Until 1722, it was the slave-owners themselves who, directly or indirectly, had to provide for the execution of these operations.[22]

In crisis situations the duty of vigilance made itself strongly felt. We have seen a 'military service' of whites patrolling day and night in Richmond in 1831. In such cases, observed Gustave de Beaumont during his journey in de Tocqueville's company, 'society arms itself with all its rigours' and mobilizes 'all social forces', seeking in every possible way to encourage 'informing' and control; in South Carolina, along with the fugitive slave the death penalty awaited 'any person who has helped him in his escape'.[23] Significant too were the results of the passage of laws on fugitive slaves in 1850. Subject to punishment was not only the citizen who sought to hide or help the black pursued or sought by his legitimate owners, but also those who did not collaborate in his capture. This was a legal provision which (as its critics put it) sought to compel 'every freeborn American to become a manhunter'.[24]

As well as slave-owners, slave society ended up affecting the white community as a whole. Precisely because, in addition to being chattels, black slaves were also the enemy within, abolitionists were immediately suspected of treason, thus becoming the target of a series of more or less harsh repressive measures depending on the gravity of the impending danger. Severe restrictions were placed on the press: in 1800 the slave revolt in Virginia was often ignored by southern newspapers; there was the danger of spreading the contagion of subversion further.[25] In 1836 the president of the United States (Andrew Jackson) permitted the postmaster general to block the circulation of all publications critical of the institution of slavery. Rounding off the gag placed on abolitionists, the House of Representatives adopted a resolution banning the examination of anti-slavery petitions.[26]

Repression could take much more drastic forms. In 1805, denouncing writings liable to have an incendiary impact on slaves, South Carolina passed laws that provided for executing as traitors those who were in some way stained with the guilt of having stirred up a slave revolt or supported it. Georgia

---

22   Ibid., p. 112.
23   Gustave de Beaumont, *Marie, ou L'esclavage aux États Unis*, Paris: Gosselin, 1840, p. 230.
24   Robert William Fogel, *Without Consent or Contract*, New York: Norton, 1991, p. 342.
25   Jordan, *White over Black*, p. 108.
26   Eric Foner, *The Story of American Freedom*, London: Picador, 1999, p. 85.

proceeded similarly.[27] Bound up with terror from above was terror from below. While it took less ruthless forms in the North (it aimed at preventing meetings and destroying the means of propaganda or the property of 'agitators'), in the South violence against abolitionists took the form of a pogrom that did not hesitate to torture and physically eliminate traitors and their supporters, with complete impunity.[28] The situation in the South in the years preceding the Civil War was described as follows by Joel R. Poinsett, an important political figure in the Union, in a letter written by him at the end of 1850:

> We are both [i.e., Poinsett and his correspondent] heartily sick of this atmosphere redolent of insane violence ... There is a strong party averse to violent men and violent measures, but they are frightened into submission—afraid even to exchange opinions with others who think like them, lest they should be betrayed.[29]

In fact, the contemporary historian who cites this testimony concludes that, through recourse to lynching, violence and threats of every kind, the South succeeded in silencing not only any opposition, but also any mild dissent. In addition to abolitionists, those who wanted to distance themselves from this pitiless witch-hunt felt threatened, and were threatened. They were impelled by terror into 'holding one's tongue, killing one's doubts, burying one's reservations'.[30] There is no doubt about it: the terroristic power wielded by slave-owners over their blacks also ended up affecting, on a lasting basis, members and fractions of the dominant race and class.

3. Three legislations, three castes, one 'master-race democracy'

So how are we to define the political regime of the society we are examining? Are we dealing with a liberal society? The problem posed in connection with a figure like Calhoun is now presented in more general terms. At least until the Civil War, there were three different sets of legislation in the United States. In relation to slaves, things are immediately clear. In the mid-nineteenth century, the black abolitionist Frederick Douglass calculated that there were

---

27   Jordan, *White over Black*, p. 399.
28   David Grimsted, *American Mobbing, 1828–1861*, New York: Oxford University Press, 1988, pp. 85–6.
29   Ibid., p. 114.
30   Ibid., p. 124.

seventy-two crimes in Virginia which, when committed by a slave, carried the death penalty, whereas only two of them involved the same penalty for a white man.[31]

But special laws also affected men of colour who were notionally free—and not only because, in different ways depending on diverse local realities and in different historical periods, they were excluded from certain professions, from the right to own land, from the possibility of testifying in courts against whites or forming part of the judicial panel. There was a still more revealing circumstance: even ignoring slaves, the same crime continued to have very different consequences depending on the skin colour of the person responsible for it. Obviously, only free people of colour ran the risk of being reduced to slavery. This was the fate that befell those in Pennsylvania, who, in the early decades of the eighteenth century, were caught breaking the ban on miscegenation, or if they were not able to pay the fine issued to them for having traded with other blacks without permission.[32] Certainly, the situation in the North changed with the abolition of slavery that followed the Revolution. But the complete control whites had over the magistracy remained in place. This was something highlighted by de Tocqueville, and its consequences were spelt out in the North as follows by a particularly courageous judge from Ohio: 'The white man may now plunder the Negro, he may abuse his person; he may take his life: He may do this in open daylight … and he must be acquitted, unless [there be] some white man present [prepared to give evidence against the culprit]'.[33]

Clear and insuperable was the barrier separating whites, the dominant race, from people of colour as such. In the words of Beaumont, '[w]hether slaves or freemen, negroes everywhere form a different people from the whites.'[34] This was an observation confirmed by de Tocqueville: 'In Philadelphia blacks are not buried in the same cemetery as whites'. Segregation also obtained in prisons: 'blacks were also separated from whites for meals'. And again: 'in Maryland [a slaveholding state] free blacks pay taxes for schools just like whites, but cannot send their children to them'.[35] And (we might add) in mid-nineteenth-century Virginia, the law denied notionally free blacks 'the right to learn how to read and write'.[36]

---

31   Frederick Douglass, 'What to the Slave Is the Fourth of July', in Alice Moore Dunbar, ed., *Masterpieces of Negro Eloquence, 1818–1913*, Mineola (NY): Dover Publications, 2000, pp. 23–4.

32   Zilversmit, *The First Emancipation*, p. 19.

33   Leon F. Litwack, *North of Slavery*, Chicago: University of Chicago Press, 1961, p. 94.

34   Beaumont, *Marie*, p. 3.

35   Tocqueville, *Oeuvres complètes*, vol. 5, pt 1, p. 247.

36   Brenda Stevenson, *Life in Black and White*, New York: Oxford University Press, 1996, p. 275; David B. Davis, 'White Wives and Slave Mothers', *New York Review of Books*, 20 February 1997, p. 35.

We are in the presence of a racial state, articulated (according to the explicit declaration of its theorists and apologists in the South), into 'three *castes*— ... free whites, free colored, and slave colored population'.[37] Still in the early decades of the nineteenth century, the caste model was also evoked by some observers of the North. Referring to their own society, where slavery had been abolished, they spoke of a division into 'Brahmins and pariahs', as demonstrated by the racial segregation that operated at every level, from public transport to theatres and from churches to cemeteries, and which allowed blacks to enter hotels, restaurants and meeting-places for the most part solely in the capacity of servants. Yes, acknowledged another observer, who proposed to banish blacks from Indiana in order to spare them a yet worse fate, they were treated like 'a race legally and socially excommunicated, as the Helots of Sparta— as the Pariahs of India—disfranchised outcasts; a separate and degraded caste'.[38]

When we identify three castes in the post-bellum United States, we are obviously ignoring the Indians, who were regarded until the Dawes Act of 1887 as 'domestic dependent nations'—that is, as a set of nations with their own particular identity, under the protectorate of Washington, and whose members did not form part of American society in the strict sense.[39] It should be added that the discourse of the three castes is not without a dubious ideological component: it tends to neglect the differences that remained within the white community, which could impact heavily not only on the material living conditions, but also on the civil rights, of the poorest strata. The Articles of the Confederacy, designed to regulate the new state that was being formed, explicitly excluded 'paupers' and 'vagrants' from the group of 'free inhabitants' (Article IV). But it is true that, when we examine the society as a whole, the main demarcations were colour lines and, within the black community, the line separating slaves proper from the rest—from 'free' blacks, who in fact lived the nightmare of being deported or enslaved in their turn. On the other side, the absolute centrality of the colour line galvanized (as the southern ideologue of the three castes pointed out) the 'spirit of equality' within the white community, with a fairly rapid disappearance of the most odious forms of discrimination.[40]

---

37 Dew quoted in Hofstadter, *Great Issues in American History*, vol. 2, p. 319.

38 Litwack, *North of Slavery*, pp. 97, 67.

39 Nelcya Delanoë and Joëlle Rostkowski, *Les Indiens dans l'histoire américaine*, Nancy: Presses Universitaires de Nancy, 1991, pp. 74–5, 124.

40 Dew, quoted in Hofstadter, *Great Issues in American History*, vol. 2, p. 320.

In this sense we can speak of 'castes', as do distinguished historians of the institution of slavery.[41] But registration of the naturalistic and racial rigidity of the relations between social classes tells us little about the nature of the political regime in the society under examination. On the basis of the history of South Africa, reference has sometimes been made to 'segregationist liberalism'[42] in order to explain the tangle of freedom (for whites) and oppression (of colonial populations). It is a category that completely excludes from the focus of attention the practices of expropriation, deportation and annihilation implemented against the native populations of southern Africa or the Amerindians. Even as regards blacks and other ethnic groups, such a category seems to refer only to the period subsequent to the abolition of slavery. Like the adjective, the substantive is misleading. On the one hand, the white community soon shook off censitary discrimination, long recommended and in fact regarded as insuperable by exponents of classical liberalism. On the other, the property-owner-citizens were subject to a series of obligations that it would be very difficult to integrate into the modern liberty theorized by Constant.

On other occasions, rather than to 'segregationist liberalism', reference has been made to 'aristocratic republicanism',[43] explicitly in connection with the pre–Civil War United States. Such a definition completely obscures the character both of the dominant aristocracy and of the plebs oppressed by it, and the entanglement between social classes and ethnic groups. Nevertheless, the substantive makes it possible to take a step forward: we are not dealing with property-owners interested solely in the enjoyment of their private sphere; they also led a rich political life. While far from being generally enjoyed, 'modern liberty' was scarcely the sole objective of the protagonists of the Revolution and the Founding Fathers of the United States. For Hamilton, the 'distinction between freedom and slavery' was clear: in the first case, 'a man is governed by the laws to which he has given his consent'; in the second, 'he is governed by the will of another'.[44] Or, in Franklin's words, submitting to taxation from a legislative body where one is not represented signifies being considered and treated as 'a conquer'd People'.[45] To be excluded from political decisions, to

---

41   Pierre L. Van den Berghe, *Race and Racism*, New York: Wiley, 1967, pp. 6, 10; Robin Blackburn, *The Overthrow of Colonial Slavery, 1776–1848*, London and New York: Verso, 1990, pp. 62, 205, 425.

42   Hosea Jaffe, *Sudafrica*, trans. Alda Carrer and Davide Danti, Milan: Jaca Book, 1997, p. 150.

43   Fogel, *Without Contract or Consent*, p. 413.

44   Alexander Hamilton, *Writings*, ed. Joanne B. Freeman, New York: Library of America, 2001, p. 11.

45   Benjamin Franklin, *Writings*, ed. J. A. Leo Lemay, New York: Library of America, 1987, p. 405.

be subject to laws imposed from without, however reasonable and liberal, was synonymous with political slavery or, at any rate, represented the onset of it.

In fact, Calhoun, the author with whom we began when we posed the crucial question—what is liberalism?—professed democracy even more than liberalism; he was an eminent member of the Democratic Party of the United States. The category of liberalism should unify the two Anglo-Saxon countries. But Calhoun defined the Constitution of his country as 'democratic, in contradistinction to aristocracy and monarchy', and hence in contradistinction to Great Britain, where 'title[s] of nobility' and other 'artificial distinctions' that had been abolished in the North American republic survived.[46] Certainly, it was not an unqualified democracy, as might appear from the title of de Tocqueville's book, which (as we shall see), in expressing itself thus, thought it possible to ignore the condition of Indians and blacks. Still less was it the 'frontier democracy' to which an eminent US historian, inclined to hagiography, pays homage.[47] Apart from anything else, the definition suggested by him evokes, in reticent, uncritical fashion, only the gradual expansion of the white colonists to the West, and hence only the relationship between two of the 'three races' referred to (as we shall see) by *Democracy in America*.

Calhoun was concerned to distinguish the democracy whose theorist he aspired to be from 'absolute democracy', guilty of wanting to ride roughshod over the rights of states and slave-owners.[48] Hence we are at the antipodes of the 'abolitionist democracy' dear to an eminent US historian and passionate Afro-American activist.[49] But then how are we to define a democracy which, far from wanting to abolish or even simply repress or hide slavery, celebrated it as a 'positive good'? Reference has sometimes been made to 'Hellenic democracy, based on the work of non-European slaves'.[50] But this definition too is inadequate. It overlooks, or does not accurately describe, the fate reserved for Indians. And it does not take account of another crucial element: absent from ancient Greece was the racial chattel slavery which, in the American case, was conjoined not with direct democracy but representative democracy.

---

46 John C. Calhoun, *Union and Liberty*, ed. R. M. Lence, Indianapolis: Liberty Classics, 1992, pp. 81–2.

47 Frederick Jackson Turner, 'The Significance of the Frontier in American History', in *The Significance of the Frontier in American History and Other Essays*, ed. John Mack Faragher, New York: Holt, 1994, p. 54.

48 Calhoun, *Union and Liberty*, pp. 120, 61.

49 William E. B. Du Bois, *Black Reconstruction in America*, ed. David L. Lewis, New York: Athenaeum, 1992, p. 185.

50 Jaffe, *Sudafrica*, p. 177.

Corresponding to the modernity of the mode of production was the modernity of the political regime.

With reference in particular to the English colonies, another distinguished black theorist and activist speaks interchangeably of 'white plantocracy' or 'planter democracy'.[51] However, calling attention to but one narrow social caste, this definition commits the error of concentrating exclusively on the South, which was not in fact separated by any barrier from the North. This applies at an economic level: after land, slaves were the country's largest property; in 1860 their value was three times greater than the share capital in manufacturing and the railway industry. The cotton grown in the South was far and away the most sizeable US export, and made a decisive contribution to financing the country's imports and industrial development.[52] At a political–constitutional level, the obligation to take part in hunting down escaped slaves and returning them obviously also extended to the citizens of the North. Finally, on an ideological level, we must not forget the racial apartheid in force in the free states. If the process of expropriating and deporting Indians is added to this, it is clear that, albeit with obvious differences between its two parts, the racial discrimination practised in the United States played a decisive role at a national level. Finally, although more adequate than those cited above, even the category of 'white democracy'[53] has a limitation—that of not stressing the proud seigneurial self-consciousness of the community of the free and the explosive violence such a community could unleash against the excluded.

Following, then, the suggestion of distinguished US historians and sociologists, we should speak of a '*Herrenvolk* democracy'—that is, a democracy which applied exclusively to the 'master race'.[54] The clear line of demarcation between whites, on the one hand, and blacks and Indians, on the other, was conducive to the development of relations of equality within the white community. The members of an aristocracy of class or race tended to celebrate themselves as 'peers'; the manifest inequality imposed on the excluded was the other aspect of the relationship of parity established between those who enjoyed the power to exclude 'inferiors'. It must be added that the equality in question was primarily a clear line of demarcation from the excluded. This is

---

51   Eric Williams, *British Historians and the West Indies*, New York: Africana Publishing Corporation, 1972, p. 95 and *From Columbus to Castro*, New York and Evanston: Harper & Row, 1970, pp. 394, 397.

52   George M. Frederickson, 'America's Original Sin', *New York Review of Books*, 25 March 2004, p. 34.

53   Jaffe, *Sudafrica*, p. 150.

54   Van den Berghe, *Race and Racism, passim*; George M. Frederickson, *White Supremacy*, New York: Oxford University Press, 1982, *passim*; Jennings, *The Creation of America, passim*.

what was expressed by the slogan that presided over the American Revolution: 'We won't be their Negroes'! For the rest, conflicts and mutual charges of abuses of power and violations of the principle of equality were (as we know) not lacking within the community of freemen and masters.

After all, it was Josiah Tucker who had already come close to understanding the true nature of the republicanism for which he reprehended Locke and the rebellious American colonists: 'all Republicans ancient and modern ... suggest no other Schemes but those of pulling down and leveling all Distinctions above them, and of tyrannizing over those miserable Beings, who are unfortunately placed below them.'[55] And again: 'he that is a Tyrant over his Inferiors is, of Course, a Patriot, and a Leveller in respect to his Superiors.'[56]

4. Freemen, servants and slaves

However, if they can serve to analyse the society that emerged from the American Revolution, what help is the discourse of the three castes and the category of 'master-race democracy' when it comes to understanding the politico-social relations that obtained in England? At least until the abolition of slavery in the colonies, the situations on both sides of the Atlantic had not a few points in common—and not only because slaves and the slave market were far from absent from the metropolis itself. More important is the consideration that the British Empire should be analysed as a whole, without repressing the reality of the colonies. Its economic development and political and military rise owed much to the *asiento*—that is, to a monopoly on the slave trade. At the same time, those who derived their wealth from trade and property in human cattle were well represented in the British parliament. Hence we see the caste of white freemen and that of slaves operative here as well. Certainly, viewed from the London observatory, the third caste—notionally free blacks—was completely irrelevant. An initial difference between the two shores of the Atlantic thus emerges.

There is another, more significant one, which concerns the bulk of the metropolitan population. Within the American white community itself, there were small sections to which legal equality and even negative liberty were denied. This emerges from the description of de Tocqueville, who comments that it was the legacy of the 'civil laws' of England, clearly weighted in favour of the

---

55   Josiah Tucker, *Collected Works*, London: Routledge and Thoemmes Press, 1993–96, vol. 5, p. 22.

56   Ibid., vol. 5, p. 20.

rich.[57] In the United States the group of whites denied these privileges was a rather small sector, which fairly rapidly disappeared. The very presence of blacks, whether slaves or semi-slaves, encouraged the spread of a sense of relative equality between members of the higher 'caste'. The situation of the white community in England was very different. Here exclusion from the enjoyment of legal equality and negative liberty was much more widespread. Let us ignore Ireland, which even after the formation of the United Kingdom in fact continued to be a colony. Let us focus on England proper, starting with Locke.

He made a sharp distinction between three groups: men 'by the right of Nature, subjected to the absolute dominion and arbitrary power of their masters', or subject to a 'perfect condition of slavery',[58] who were the black slaves from Africa; then freemen; and finally, white servants who were blood relations of the freemen. A key paragraph of the *Second Treatise of Government* clarifies this:

> [W]e find among the Jews, as well as other nations, that men did sell themselves; but it is plain this was only to drudgery, not to slavery; for it is evident the person sold was not under an absolute, arbitrary, despotical power, for the master could not have power to kill him at any time, whom at a certain time he was obliged to let go free out of his service; and the master of such a servant was so far from having an arbitrary power over his life that he could not at pleasure so much as maim him, but the loss of an eye or tooth set him free (Exod. xxi).[59]

Here Locke primarily had in mind the two figures of the black slave and the indentured white servant. As we know, even the second was subject to buying and selling, was in large measure a commodity, exported to America and regularly traded on the market where possible purchasers arrived alerted by adverts in the local press. It goes without saying that the master possessed an extensive right of punishment, even if not as unlimited as that wielded over the black slave. We can understand then the comparison with the servant in the Old Testament, who, although not subject to a 'perfect condition of slavery', experiences a condition that might by contrast be defined as 'imperfect slavery'. This imperfect slavery was defined by Locke by the term of servitude or drudgery.

---

57   Tocqueville, *Oeuvres complètes*, vol. 4, pt 1, p. 326.
58   John Locke, *Two Treatises of Government*, ed. William S. Carpenter, London and New York: Everyman's Library, 1924, pp. 158, 128.
59   Ibid., p. 128.

Within the British Empire three different legal situations coexisted—the first marked by liberty, the second by servitude, and the third by slavery in the strict sense. Notwithstanding the racial abyss that was now open, and which separated black slave from white servant, in England the latter did not form part of the community of the free in the strict sense. Even if different from that wielded by 'a lord over his slave', the power of 'a master over his servant', who was subject to the 'ordinary discipline' applied by the master within his family, was indisputable.[60] Significantly, although he was concerned to distinguish between slave and servant, Locke sometimes also used the second term to refer to the figure of the slave proper. In the *First Treatise of Government*, we can read: 'those who were rich in the patriarch's days, as in the West Indies now, bought men and maid-servants, and by their increase as well as purchasing of new, came to have large and numerous families'.[61] As demonstrated by the reference to the property-owners of the West Indies and the property right they exercised over the offspring of 'servants', it is clear that the discourse here concerns hereditary slavery.

The tripartite division formulated by Locke also appears in Mandeville. In the first place, we have 'the great Number of Slaves, that are yearly fetch'd from Africa' to America.[62] In England, on the other hand, 'Slaves are not allow'd', but free men can avail themselves of 'the Children of the Poor', of 'willing Hands for all the Drudgery and hard and dirty Labour'.[63] Once again we encounter the three figures of the freeman, the servant and the slave. It is so difficult to confuse the second with the first that the similarities with the third leap to the eye: 'the meanest Indigent part of the Nation' is 'the working slaving People', which is eternally destined to perform 'dirty slavish Work'.[64]

Finally, let us turn to Blackstone. In celebrating England as the land of liberty, he stressed that there was no place in it for 'proper slavery', 'strict slavery', 'absolute slavery', wherein the master was endowed with absolute, unlimited power over the life and fate of the slave. This insistent clarification left room for forms of compulsory labour different from that to which blacks in the colonies were subjected. In the great jurist's writings too an intermediate condition between liberty and slavery ends up emerging, a sort of non-'absolute' slavery, slavery not understood in the 'strict' sense. Along with slaves,

---

60   Ibid., p. 158.
61   Ibid., p. 90.
62   Bernard de Mandeville, *The Fable of the Bees*, 2 vols, ed. Frederick B. Kaye, Indianapolis: Liberty Classics, 1988, vol. 2, p. 199.
63   Ibid., vol. 2, p. 259.
64   Ibid., vol. 1, pp. 119, 302.

'domestics', 'apprentices' and 'labourers' were servants. We are dealing with 'different types of servant', each with its specific characteristics, but all brought together by the fact of being subject to servitude.[65] Active once again is the legacy of Grotius, for whom *servitus* was the general category for understanding and defining the character of work. In Locke, Mandeville and Blackstone what is new is the stress on the distinction between two types of *servitus*—that in force in the metropolis and that operative in the colonies. Thus, we pass from Grotius' bipartite division to a tripartite division.

5. England and the three 'castes'

But now, setting aside major authors, let us take a look at the social reality and ideology that characterized Britain during the eighteenth and nineteenth centuries. Far from the 'vestiges of slavery' referred to by Smith, the persistence of servile relations is very clear from the treatment of the poor and the possibility of disposing of their children as a *res nullius* in workhouses, in the army, in prisons, and in the recruitment of servants sent to settle the colonies. An economist we have already encountered, Wakefield, drew attention to 'English slavery' and 'white slaves' in 1834.[66] At this time authors of the most varied political persuasion compared slaves across the Atlantic with suffering workers in England: anti-abolitionists who echoed Calhoun-type statements; more or less radical currents that aimed at a more general emancipation of labour; more detached observers who confined themselves to registering the fact, like the economist we have just cited. And the comparison was established not simply by focusing on the spectre of death from starvation that constantly haunted the English worker. Certainly, this is an aspect that cannot be ignored: the number of poor people who, in order to avoid starvation, committed some crime in the hope of being able to survive as deportees or 'galley slaves', was not negligible.[67] But considerable attention was also paid to encroachments on a more specifically liberal freedom—namely, 'modern liberty'. For this to emerge with greater clarity, let us leave behind the cities and industrial centres and move to the countryside to hear the rural labourers' grievances:

---

65   William Blackstone, *Commentaries on the Laws of England*, 4 vols, Chicago: University of Chicago Press, 1979, vol. 1, pp. 411–12.

66   Edward Gibbon Wakefield, *The Collected Works of Edward Gibbon Wakefield*, ed. M. F. Lloyd Prichard, London and Glasgow: Collins, 1968, pp. 339, 343.

67   Ibid., p. 344.

Speaking generally, since all laws have their exceptions, the privileged classes of our rural districts take infinite pains to be abhorred by their poorest neighbours. They enclose commons. They stop footpaths. They wall in their parks. They set spring-guns and man-traps ... They build jails, and fill them. They make new crimes and new punishments for the poor. They interfere with the marriages of the poor, compelling some, and forbidding others to come together. They shut up paupers in workhouses, separating husband and wife, in pounds by day and wards by night. They harness poor men to carts. They superintend alehouses, decry skittles, deprecate beer-shops, meddle with fairs, and otherwise curtail the already narrow amusements of the poor.[68]

Around twenty years later, the popular and radical *Reynold's Newspaper*, condemning the 'slavery' that existed in England, listed the flogging of soldiers and sailors, the separation of husbands and wives in workhouses, the obligation of rural servants to request permission from their masters before they could marry, and the systematic sexual abuse to which 'the wives and daughters of the poorer orders' were subject.[69]

Wakefield reported the *cahier de doléances* deriving from the countryside and considered them incontrovertible. Writing on the immediate eve of the abolition of slavery in British colonies, he believed it possible to distinguish three figures—'freeman', 'slave' and 'pauper'—within the empire as a whole.[70] We are put in mind of the discourse of the three castes we have encountered in a theorist from the American South. In fact, in 1864 the *Saturday Review* (a periodical that circulated among the middle and upper classes) observed that the poor in England formed 'a caste apart, a race', placed in a social condition that underwent no alteration 'from the cradle to the grave', and which was divided from the rest of society by a barrier similar to that existing in America between whites and blacks. The respectable English periodical proceeded as follows:

The English poor man or child is expected always to remember the condition in which God has placed him, exactly as the negro is expected to remember the skin which God has given him. The relation in both instances is that of perpetual superior to perpetual inferior, of chief to dependant, and no amount of kindness or goodness is suffered to alter this relation.[71]

---

68   Ibid., p. 342.
69   Douglas A. Lorimer, *Colour, Class and the Victorians*, Leicester: Leicester University Press, 1978, p. 94.
70   Wakefield, *Collected Works*, p. 339.
71   Lorimer, *Colour, Class and the Victorians*, pp. 101–2.

We are—it is important not to forget it—in 1864. Many decades had passed since the Glorious Revolution and the birth of liberal England. And yet, if the situation was unstable and tending to change as a result of popular struggles, the reality of a caste society continued to make itself felt. Already abolished thirty years earlier in the English colonies, the caste of slaves was on the point of disappearing in the United States as well. Having been three, the castes were becoming two in number on both sides of the Atlantic: corresponding to the black semi-slaves of the United States were the white servants of England. A more or less rigid barrier continued to separate both from the caste of genuine freemen.

A sort of social apartheid seems to correspond to the racial apartheid. In eighteenth-century England we find Charles Seymour, Duke of Somerset, having his coach preceded by outriders who were charged with clearing the road in order to spare the nobleman the annoyance of meeting with plebeian persons and glances.[72] Even a century later, a kind of segregation existed between the different social classes in English churches.[73] And the already noted *cahier de doléances* drawn up by rural labourers bemoaned the fact that even then the aristocracy resorted to a curtain to shield itself from any 'vulgar gaze'.[74] When Senior visited Naples, what made him angry was the mixing of ranks: 'In cold countries the debased classes keep at home; here they live in the streets'. Worse, they were so little removed from the upper classes that they lived in the cellars of seigneurial palaces. The result? '[Y]ou never are free from the sight, or, indeed, from the contact of loathsome degeneration.'[75]

6. The reproduction of the servile caste and the beginnings of eugenics

How to 'continue the race of journeymen and servants'?[76] Smith's phrase reveals that social mobility was limited or non-existent. The heaviest, worst-paid work was entrusted to a stratum that tended to be reproduced from one generation to the next, and hence to a kind of hereditary servile caste.

---

72   John Cannon, *Aristocratic Century*, Cambridge: Cambridge University Press, 1984, p. 172.

73   Lorimer, *Colour, Class and the Victorians*, p. 104.

74   Wakefield, *Collected Works*, p. 342.

75   Nassau William Senior, *Journals Kept in France and Italy from 1848 to 1852*, 2 vols, ed. M. C. M. Simpson, London: Henry S. King and Co., 1871, vol. 2, p. 7.

76   Adam Smith, *An Inquiry into the Nature and Causes of the Wealth of Nations*, Indianapolis: Liberty Classics, 1981, p. 98.

The reproduction of this caste or race was absolutely necessary. According to Mandeville, a decidedly beneficial role was played by war. If, with its periodic massacres, it did not provide a remedy for excess male births, women, sought after by too many aspiring, competitive males, would become a kind of rare commodity accessible only to the rich. Society would then lose its re-supply of 'the Children of the Poor; the greatest and most extensive of all temporal Blessings'. The hereditary reproduction of the poor destined to perform 'the Drudgery of hard and dirty Labour' would prove difficult or impossible.[77]

The natural order, of which war was a part, spontaneously generated the race of semi-slaves that society could never do without. However, this supposedly spontaneous process must be encouraged by timely political interventions from above. According to Mandeville, access to education on the part of the 'Labouring Poor' was to be avoided at all costs: the 'Proportion of the Society' would be compromised by it.[78] The requisite cheap, docile and obedient labour force would risk disappearing. Other representatives of the liberal tradition invoked much more extensive intervention. For the purposes of generating a potentially perfect race of docile workers and instruments of labour, the concentration-camp universe of the 'workhouses' could prove useful. Locking up the children of delinquents and 'suspects' therein, one could (observed Bentham) produce an 'indigenous class' that would be distinguished for its industriousness and sense of discipline. If early marriage was promoted within this class, treating the offspring as apprentices until they attained their majority, the workhouses and society would dispose of an inexhaustible reserve of manpower of the highest quality. In other words, through the 'gentlest of all revolutions'—a sexual revolution[79]—the 'indigenous class', propagating itself in hereditary fashion from one generation to the next, would be transformed into a kind of indigenous race.

Sieyès envisaged a similarly 'gentle' revolution, and likewise for the purposes of producing a class or race of labourers as docile as possible. Like Bentham, the French liberal indulged in a eugenicist utopia (or dystopia). He imagined a 'cross' (*croisement*) between monkeys and 'blacks' for creating domesticated beings adapted to servile work: 'the new race of anthropomorphic monkeys'. In this way, whites, who remained at the top of the social hierarchy as directors of production, could dispose of blacks as auxiliary instruments of production, or slaves proper, who would precisely be the anthropomorphic monkeys:

---

77   Mandeville, *Fable of the Bees*, vol. 2, pp. 258–9, 261–2.

78   Ibid., vol. 1, p. 302.

79   Bentham, quoted in Gertrude Himmelfarb, *The Idea of Poverty*, New York: Vintage Books, 1985, pp. 78–83.

However extraordinary, however immoral this idea might seem at first sight, I have reflected on it at length, and can find no other way in a great nation, especially in countries that are very hot or very cold, to reconcile the directors of works with the simple instruments of labour.[80]

While, on the one hand, it was necessary to encourage the production and reproduction of a race of servants or actual slaves, on the other, it was necessary to limit, so far as possible, the unproductive, parasitic surplus population, the mass of poor who, far from creating wealth, devoured it like locusts. To maintain the demographic balance, Malthus called for a policy that postponed marriage and procreation among the popular classes; otherwise, nature would dispose of them with wars, famines and epidemics. In this respect the role of medicine was problematic. In 1764 Franklin wrote to a doctor: 'Half the Lives you save are not worth saving, as being useless; and almost the other Half ought not to be sav'd, as being mischievous. Does your Conscience never hint to you the Impiety of being in constant Warfare against the Plans of Providence?'[81] Some decades later, de Tocqueville hoped that one could finally be shot of the 'prison rabble' like rats, maybe thanks to a massive fire.[82] Did the French liberal 'dream of genocide'?[83] The claim is exaggerated. But there remains his harsh polemic against a 'bastard charity' that threatened order: 'It is the philanthropy of Paris that is killing us.'[84]

A general conclusion is indicated. The eugenic temptation runs deep in the liberal tradition. Not by chance, the discipline that took this name had its baptism in Great Britain and experienced extraordinary success in the United States.[85]

7. The elusive liberalism of the United Kingdom of Great Britain and Ireland

As in the case of the United States, we are compelled to pose a crucial question in connection with Great Britain: Was it a liberal society? Even after the

80   Emmanuel-Joseph Sieyès, *Écrits politiques*, ed. Roberto Zapperi, Paris: Éditions des archives contemporaines, 1985, p. 75.

81   Franklin, *Writings*, p. 803 (letter to John Fothergill, 14 March 1764).

82   Tocqueville, *Oeuvres complètes*, vol. 8, pt 1, pp. 173–4 (letter to Gustave de Beaumont, 22 November 1836).

83   Michelle Perrot, Introduction to ibid., vol. 4, pt 1, p. 38.

84   Tocqueville, *Oeuvres complètes*, vol. 4, pt 1, p. 38.

85   Cf. Domenico Losurdo, *Nietzsche, il ribelle aristocratico*, Turin: Bollati Boringhieri, 2002, ch. 19, §1; ch. 23, §2.

abolition of slavery in the colonies proper, we certainly cannot speak of generalized enjoyment of the quintessential liberal freedom—modern liberty—by the United Kingdom's inhabitants.

The Irish certainly did not enjoy it, being as they were (acknowledged de Tocqueville) constantly subjected to 'emergency measures' and at the mercy of 'military tribunals' and a numerous, hateful gendarmerie. In Castlebar, on the basis of the Insurrection Act, 'any man caught without a passport outdoors after sunset is deported'.[86] In the press of the time, the condition of the Irish was often compared with that of blacks across the Atlantic. According to the judgement in 1824 of a rich English merchant, who was a disciple of Smith and an ardent Quaker and abolitionist (James Cropper), the Irish found themselves in a worse situation than black slaves.[87] In any event, the Irish represented for Britain what the blacks were for the United States; they were 'two phenomena of the same kind'.[88] De Beaumont's opinion found indirect confirmation from de Tocqueville. From *Democracy in America* we know of the complete deafness of the judiciary, monopolized by whites, to the legitimate complaints of blacks. A conclusion suggests itself, also indicated by evidence gathered in Maryland: 'The white population and the black population are in a state of war. They never mix. One of them must give way to the other.'[89] The French liberal heard a similar observation in the island subjugated and colonized by Britain: 'To tell the truth, there is no justice in Ireland. Virtually all the country's magistrates are in open warfare with the population. So the population does not even have the idea of public justice.'[90] In both cases a cornerstone of the *Rechtsstaat*—the judiciary—was at war with a substantial part of the population.

On both sides of the Atlantic, laws that prevented or hampered access to education and outlawed marriage with members of the higher caste served to prolong the oppression of the blacks and the Irish. In Ireland, too, miscegenation was a crime punished with great severity; on the basis of a law of 1725, a priest guilty of secretly celebrating a mixed marriage could even be condemned to death.[91] And in Ireland as well, attempts were made to obstruct

---

86 Tocqueville, *Oeuvres complètes*, vol. 4, pt 1, p. 38.

87 David B. Davis, *Slavery and Human Progress*, Oxford and New York: Oxford University Press, 1986, pp. 180, 184.

88 Gustave de Beaumont, *L'irlande sociale, politique et religieuse*, 2 vols, ed. Goderlaine Charpentier, Villeneuve d'Ascq: CERIUL-Université Charles-de-Gaulle Lille III, 1990, vol. 2, p. 307.

89 Tocqueville, *Oeuvres complètes*, vol. 5, pt 1, p. 247.

90 Ibid., vol. 5, pt 2, pp. 94–5. De Tocqueville is reporting a conversation between two influential representatives of the English political world, Nassau William Senior and John Revans.

91 William Lecky, *A History of England in the Eighteenth Century*, 8 vols, London: Longmans, Green and Co., 1883–88, vol. 2, pp. 371–3; cf. also vol. 1, p. 289.

the native population's access to education. We can conclude on this point by attending to the words of a nineteenth-century liberal Anglo-Irish historian: British legislation aimed to deprive the Irish of their 'property' and 'industry'; it 'was intended to make them poor and to keep them poor, to crush in them every germ of enterprise, to degrade them into a servile caste who could never hope to rise to the level of their oppressors'.[92]

In 1798, three years prior to the formation of the United Kingdom of Great Britain and Ireland, the Irish numbered 'about four and a half million—a third of the population of the British Isles'.[93] Accordingly, a higher percentage of people were to be deprived of their negative liberty than in the United States, where, at the time of independence, blacks made up one-fifth of the population. It must be added that, before and after the Glorious Revolution, Britain's rulers treated the Irish, on the one hand, like Indians, to be deprived of their land and thinned out through more or less drastic measures; and on the other, like blacks whose forced labour might conveniently be used. Hence the oscillation between practices of enslavement and genocidal practices.

In Britain itself the popular classes saw their negative liberty seriously infringed, to the extent that they were assimilated in the culture and press of the time to an inferior 'caste' or 'race'. But now it is appropriate to concentrate on relations within the upper 'caste'. As we know, the American colonists' rebellion developed out of protests against the negative discrimination they suffered by dint of their exclusion from the legislative body. At the same time, we must not forget that in eighteenth-century Britain the right to representation was a privilege granted by the Crown, so that even large industrial towns were excluded from the House of Commons, where, by contrast, boroughs which had virtually been abandoned, but which had the right to be 'represented' in London mainly by local nobles, were present. Bearing in mind that the House of Lords was the hereditary preserve of the landed aristocracy, a conclusion is dictated: in the case of Britain itself, not even relations within the property-owning classes were stamped by equality.

Equality was further compromised by another circumstance: only the second electoral Reform Act, put through by Disraeli in 1867, 'effected the full political emancipation of Non-conformists'. Until then, significant forms of religious discrimination were in force:

---

92   Ibid., vol. 1, p. 288.
93   Thomas Pakenham, *The Year of Liberty*, New York: Random House, 1969, p. 30.

Persons, whether Protestant or Catholic, who would not take the Communion according to the rites of the Church of England, were still debarred from holding office either under the Crown or in the municipalities; the doors of Parliament were still closed to Roman Catholics, and the doors of the Universities to dissenters of every kind. [94]

Hence, on closer inspection, the non-conformists (among whom must obviously be included the Jews)[95] were deprived not only of political equality, but also of full legal equality. Only in 1871 did all universities, including Oxford and Cambridge, 'throw open College Fellowships and University posts to persons of every, or of no, religious denomination'.[96]

The argument with which Macaulay criticized the exclusion of Jews from political rights in 1831 is significant:

> It would be impious to let a Jew sit in Parliament. But a Jew may make money; and money may make members of Parliament ... That a Jew should be privy-councilor to a Christian king would be an eternal disgrace to the nation. But the Jew may govern the money-market, and the money-market may govern the world.[97]

In a paradoxical argument against the forms of discrimination of which Jews were victims, Macaulay seems to echo anti-Jewish stereotypes, but in reality the meaning of his discourse is clear: it was absurd and inadmissible to seek to deny political and even civil equality to those who, economically at any rate, were already members of the dominant elite.

Finally, it should be borne in mind that, like the class that was the protagonist of the American Revolution and the establishment of a racial state, the English aristocracy in no way restricted itself to aspiring to a merely negative liberty. Some decades before Hamilton (and the American revolutionaries), in England Sidney had already declared that 'nothing denotes a slave but a dependence upon the will of another', or upon a law to which he had not given his consent.[98]

---

94 George M. Trevelyan, *History of England*, London: Longmans, Green and Co., 1945, pp. 631, 474.

95 Michael C. N. Salbstein, *The Emancipation of the Jews in Britain*, London and Toronto: Associated University Presses, 1982.

96 Trevelyan, *History of England*, p. 681.

97 Thomas Babington Macaulay, *Critical and Historical Essays*, 5 vols, Leipzig: Tauchnitz, 1850, vol. 1, p. 295.

98 Algernon Sidney, *Discourses Concerning Government*, ed. Thomas G. West, Indianapolis: Liberty Classics, 1990, p. 402.

Locke did not formulate things very differently, when with political 'slavery' he contrasted 'liberty' understood as 'be[ing] under no other legislative power but that established by consent in the commonwealth'.[99] Again it was Locke who stressed the equivalence between the English and Latin terms;[100] and the latter clearly implied the participation of the *cives* in public life. The English philosopher argued along similar lines to the American revolutionaries, who not by chance appealed to him: he who wants to decide on his own, excluding me from the process of forming laws, may legitimately be suspected of 'hav[ing] a design to take away everything else', not just political 'liberty'; he ultimately aims to 'make me a slave'.[101]

Regardless of the position adopted by this or that theorist, the English aristocracy aimed to play, and really did play, a political role of the first order. In addition to the upper house, 'the lower house of Parliament was essentially a landowners' club' until almost the end of the nineteenth century. The aristocracy exercised political power directly: 'it was the landed elite, not a separate service elite, that was in control of public affairs'.[102] It was a control that encompassed the judiciary and local government and which, above all in the countryside, was seamless. Virtually until the end of the nineteenth century, 'the grandees and gentry were still the unchallenged authorities, responsible to no one but themselves.'[103]

As in the South of the United States, the uncontested power of a social class in England did not preclude the imposition of restrictions on its individual members. The titled property-owner was required to respect a series of obligations, sanctioned partly by law and partly by custom. One thinks of primogeniture and the inalienability of property, as well as the endogamy that was fairly widespread within the aristocracy—a practice that once again calls to mind the ban on miscegenation in the United States. The members of the nobility 'were concerned with voluntary service to the state, both locally and nationally, as civilians and as military men'. While they enjoyed their property and their wealth, patrician officers adopted the pose of 'chivalric heroes' required, when the nation was in danger, to exhibit 'spartan and stoical bravery'.[104]

---

99   Locke, *Two Treatises of Government*, p. 127.
100   See ibid., p. 183.
101   Ibid., pp. 125–6.
102   David Cannadine, *The Decline and Fall of the British Aristocracy*, New Haven and London: Yale University Press, 1990, pp. 14, 21.
103   Ibid., p. 14
104   Ibid., pp. 13, 74.

How should we define the society we have been analysing? Once again, we encounter the problem that has dogged us since the beginning of this book: Can we speak of liberalism in connection with Calhoun's thinking and the reality of the United States where he lived and worked? And can we speak of it in relation to the United Kingdom of Great Britain and Ireland? Given the dominant representation of liberalism today, what sense would it make to define as liberal a society where a considerable part of the population was subject to military dictatorship, where the popular metropolitan classes were at least partially excluded from negative liberty, where this type of liberty was by no means the ideal of the possessing classes, and where the principle of civil and political equality was limited among the latter in various ways?

A constitutive element of a liberal regime should be competition between various candidates. But what actually happened?

> Many elections saw no contest at all. In seven general elections from 1760 to 1800, less than a tenth of the country seats were contested. Of the boroughs, some were purely inert in that their owners sold the seats or appointed the members without question; some seats were as much a property as seats in the French *parlements*.[105]

8. Liberalism, 'property-owning individualism' and 'aristocratic society'

In an attempt to overcome the difficulty encountered in defining eighteenth- and nineteenth-century British society, reference has sometimes been made to 'individualism' rather than liberalism; and the history of the intellectual tradition being examined now seems profoundly stamped with a 'property-owning individualism' or 'possessive individualism'.[106] This definition has some legitimacy. In Locke, political power begins to be configured as tyranny, and hence violence, when it attacks private property (belonging to the dominant class); and it is then licit to resist such violence. The citizen, in fact the individual, takes back the power he already possessed in the state of nature, which consists in 'us[ing] such means for the preserving of his own property as he thinks good and Nature allows him'.[107] The sphere of legality is the sphere of respect

---

105   Robert R. Palmer, *The Age of Democratic Revolution*, 2 vols, Princeton: Princeton University Press, 1959–64, vol. 1, p. 46.

106   C. B. Macpherson, *The Political Theory of Possessive Individualism*, Oxford: Oxford University Press, 1962.

107   Locke, *Two Treatises*, p. 205.

for private property, while violence is defined in the first instance by its violation.

On closer examination, however, the category of 'property-owning individualism' proves completely inadequate. We are confronted with a society and intellectual tradition which, far from being inspired by a superstitious respect for property and property right in general, in fact promoted and legitimized massive expropriations of the Irish and Indians. It is true that a central chapter in the second of Locke's *Two Treatises of Government* bears the title 'Of Property'. But 'Expropriation' might have been more fitting, given that it aims to justify white colonists' appropriation of land from idle Indians incapable of cultivating it. Ignoring the colonies and colonial populations, or populations of colonial origin, the category of 'property-owning individualism' seems to focus attention exclusively on the white community in the capitalist metropolis, and on the conflict between property-owners and non-property-owners.

Even if we confine our attention to the metropolis, we see that the *Second Treatise* justifies and demands the enclosure of common land in England, and hence the massive expropriation of peasants. Like the transatlantic territories occupied by the Indians, common land was not properly fertilized by labour; and hence in both cases there was as yet no legitimate owner. In classic authors of the liberal tradition, we find the assertion and detailed demonstration that the property claimed by natives, and by social groups in the metropolis assimilated to natives, was in reality *res nullius*.

Paradoxically, despite its critical intentions, the category of 'property-owning individualism' ends up crediting the ideological self-consciousness of the classes that arrived in power in England and America advancing the slogan of liberty and property. Marx argued quite differently. *Capital* denounced the 'stoical peace of mind [of] the political economist' and of liberal thinkers in the face of 'the most shameless violation of the "sacred rights of property"', and 'the forcible expropriation of the people', carried out in England. In the early decades of the nineteenth century, in order to speed up the enclosure process, brutal methods were sometimes employed without hesitation: entire villages were destroyed and razed to the ground, so as to force the peasants to flee and transform common land into private property and pasture in the service of the textile industry.[108]

In examining the category of 'property-owning individualism', we have hitherto concentrated on the adjective. If we now turn our attention to the

---

108 Karl Marx, *Capital: Volume One*, trans. Ben Fowkes, Harmondsworth: Penguin, 1976, pp. 889, 891.

noun, we shall find that it too proves rather problematic. The excluded were likened by the dominant class to instruments of labour, bipedal machines. In other words, they saw their quality as human beings and individuals denied. Certainly, the privileged insisted strongly on this quality, which they attributed exclusively to themselves. But is this individualism? Here, too, we find the modern historian aligning himself with the ideological self-consciousness of a social class and political movement he intends to criticize.

Rather than 'property-owning individualism', the categories applied to England by some leading liberal authors of the nineteenth century seem more apt. In Constant's view, 'England is, at bottom, simply a vast, opulent and vigorous aristocracy.'[109] The judgement formulated by de Tocqueville in the 1830s was no different: 'Not only does the aristocracy seem more solidly stable than ever, but the nation leaves the government, seemingly without any signs of disapproval, to a very small number of families', an 'aristocracy' primarily based on 'birth'.[110] Hence we are dealing with an 'aristocratic community' characterized by the domination of 'a small number of powerful and wealthy citizens'.[111] Besides, it was Disraeli himself who criticized the Whig Party, which long dominated the country that emerged from the Glorious Revolution, for having aimed to establish an aristocracy and oligarchy on the Venetian model.[112]

9. 'Master-race democracy' between the United States and England

A question remains unanswered: Albeit intrinsically aristocratic, was England nevertheless a liberal society? Constant was in no doubt: it was the country where 'social differences are most respected' (wholly to the advantage of the aristocracy), but where, at the same time, 'the rights of each man are most guaranteed'.[113] This was also de Tocqueville's opinion, but only after 1848, once anxiety about the socialist and Bonapartist drift of France had eclipsed

---

109 Benjamin Constant, *Mélanges de littérature et de politique*, 2 vols, Louvain: Michel, 1830, vol. 1, p. 23.

110 Tocqueville, *Oeuvres complètes*, vol. 13, pt 2, p. 327 (letter to L. de Kergorlay, 4 August 1857).

111 Alexis de Tocqueville, *Democracy in America*, London: Everyman's Library, 1994, vol. 2, p. 107.

112 Benjamin Disraeli, *Coningsby*, ed. Sheila M. Smith, Oxford and New York: Oxford University Press, 1982, pp. 323–4.

113 Benjamin Constant, *Oeuvres*, ed. Alfred Roulin, Paris: Gallimard, 1957, pp. 155, 150–1.

any other consideration. '[T]he aristocratic constitution of English society' was incontestable, and yet it was still the 'wealthiest and freest country'.[114]

Prior to the fall of the July Monarchy, by contrast, de Tocqueville had his doubts and reservations. It was necessary to distinguish between 'two different forms of liberty'. One should not confuse 'the democratic and, dare I say it, correct conception of liberty' with the 'aristocratic conception of liberty', understood not as 'common right' but as 'privilege'. The latter prevailed in England, as in 'aristocratic societies' in general, with the result that there was no place for 'general liberty'.[115] *Democracy in America* referred and subscribed to the observation of a US citizen who had journeyed extensively in Europe: 'The English treat their servants with a stiffness and imperiousness of manner which surprises us.'[116] Not that the pathos of liberty was absent among those who adopted the stance of absolute masters. On the contrary: 'It can happen that the love of liberty is all the more alive among some the less one encounters guarantees of liberty for all. The rarer it is, the exception in such cases is all the more precious.' This aristocratic conception of liberty produces, among those who have been thus educated, an exalted sense of their individual value and a passionate taste for independence.[117]

Regardless of the value judgement, which is the converse, we are put in mind of Burke's well-known observation: freedom appears even 'more noble and more liberal' to slave-masters. Should we equate England with slaveholding Virginia? In fact, points in common were not wanting, as emerges from a reading of de Tocqueville. He observed that in the United States whites refused to recognize 'the common features of humanity' in blacks.[118] But in England, too, inequalities were so marked and insuperable that 'each class assumes the aspect of a distinct race'; 'general ideas' were lacking, starting precisely with the idea of humanity.[119]

At this point, de Tocqueville was concerned to distinguish American democracy from the aristocracy predominant in England. However, on several occasions his analysis ended up drawing attention to the similarities between the two societies. What took the form of class relations on one side of the Atlantic presented itself as race relations on the other. In the case of England,

---

114 Tocqueville, *Oeuvres complètes*, vol. 13, pt 2, p. 333 (letter to L. de Kergorlay, 27 February 1857).

115 Ibid., vol. 2, pt 1, p. 62.

116 Tocqueville, *Democracy in America*, vol. 2, p. 177.

117 Tocqueville, *Oeuvres complètes*, vol. 2, pt 1, p. 62.

118 Tocqueville, *Democracy in America*, vol. 1, p. 358.

119 Ibid., vol. 2, p. 14.

we can speak of liberal society in the same way that Burke spoke of liberal society in connection with the Virginia and Poland of his time. An essential point remains: often excluded from the enjoyment of civil rights and negative liberty in England itself, the popular classes, by de Tocqueville's indirect but all the more significant admission, continued to be separated from the upper class or caste by a gulf that calls to mind the one obtaining in a racial state.

In this sense, it can be said that for some time even the society which emerged in England from the Glorious Revolution was configured as a sort of 'master-race democracy', on condition that this category is not understood in a purely ethnic sense. On this side of the Atlantic, too, an insurmountable barrier separated the community of the free and masters from the mass of servants, not fortuitously compared by Locke to 'natives'. And far from being satisfied with negative liberty, the dominant aristocracy cultivated the ideal of active participation in political life, cultivating 'republican' ideals. Several influential contemporary interpreters base their arguments on this, when referring to a 'neo-Roman' vision or 'Machiavellian moment'.[120] And again we face the danger of inadvertent transfiguration: these two categories highlight the pathos of free, egalitarian participation in public life, but end up passing in silence over the macroscopic exclusion clauses presupposed by such pathos. The ideal of a rich public life, of 'neo-Roman' or 'Machiavellian' character, is indeed present in an author like Fletcher, who on the one hand declared himself 'republican in principle', while on the other he advocated slavery for vagrants. Locke can be assimilated to such a milieu. He declared in favour of black slavery in the colonies and 'drudgery' for wage-labourers in the metropolis. At the same time, with his focus on the aristocracy he developed a pathos of the Commonwealth and the *civitas*, which echoes the republican models of antiquity. This, at least, was the opinion of Josiah Tucker, who identified and denounced Locke as a 'republican Whig' and supporter of slavery.[121]

But perhaps the author who in England best expressed the ideal of 'master-race democracy' was Sidney. His insistence on the equality of free men was very marked: 'the equality in which men are born is so perfect, that no man will suffer his natural liberty to be abridged, except others do the like'. Definitive is his condemnation of political slavery, inherent not only in absolute monarchy, but also in any political regime that claimed to subject the freeman to laws decided without his consent. But this pathos of liberty implied the demand for

---

120   Quentin Skinner, *Liberty Before Liberalism*, Cambridge: Cambridge University Press, 1998, pp. 1ff.; J. G. A. Pocock, *The Machiavellian Moment*, Princeton: Princeton University Press, 1975.

121   Tucker, quoted in J. G. A. Pocock, *Virtue, Commerce, and History*, Cambridge: Cambridge University Press, 1988, pp. 119, 187.

the master's right to be 'judge' of his own servant without outside interference.[122] One should not lose sight of the fact that 'in many places (even by the law of God) the master hath a power of life and death over his servant'.[123] It was understood that 'the base and effeminate Asiaticks and Africans', incapable of understanding the value of 'liberty', were rightly regarded by Aristotle as '*slaves by nature*' and 'little different from beasts'.[124] Not by chance—together with Locke, Fletcher and Burgh—Sidney was indicated by Jefferson as a leading authority for understanding 'the general principles of liberty' that inspired the United States.[125]

Tucker also conjoined Locke and Sidney, but this time critically. He further pointed out that Sidney was an admirer of 'Polish liberty'[126] (and of a country where serfdom in its harshest form, to which peasants were subjected, was intertwined with the rich political life of the aristocracy that dominated the Diet), and paid homage to 'republican liberty' (see below, Chapter 5, §2). Also expressing himself in flattering terms about Poland, as well as the 'southern colonies' of America, was Burke, who not by chance became the tutelary deity of the slaveholding South. Admiration for a regime of republican liberty founded on the slavery or servitude of a considerable proportion of the population, for a 'master-race democracy', was well represented in English liberalism. The authors expressing such positions could in their turn count on widespread sympathy across the Atlantic.

---

122   Sidney, *Discourses Concerning Government*, pp. 548–9.
123   Ibid., p. 312.
124   Ibid., p. 9.
125   Thomas Jefferson, *Writings*, ed. Merrill D. Peterson, New York: Library of America, 1984, p. 479.
126   Tucker, quoted in Pocock, *Virtue, Commerce, and History*, p. 178.

CHAPTER FIVE

The Revolution in France and San Domingo, the Crisis of the English and American Models, and the Formation of Radicalism either Side of the Atlantic

1. The liberal inception of the French Revolution

We have hitherto been concerned almost exclusively with England and the United States. The truth is that the liberal party in France betrayed its weakness fairly early on. And yet, several years before the appearance of *The Spirit of the Laws*, Voltaire likewise proceeded to celebrate the country that embodied the cause of liberalism at the time: 'Commerce, which has brought wealth to the citizenry of England, has helped to make them free, and freedom has developed commerce in its turn. By means of it the nation has grown great'.[1] Indeed, '[t]he English are the only people on earth who have managed to prescribe limits to the power of kings'; they alone were genuinely free.[2] More generally, given the difficulty they faced in dealing with comprehensive censorship, the *philosophes* hoped to escape this kind of cage and hence looked with sympathy across the Channel. Even Helvétius, whom Diderot rebuked for his indulgence towards enlightened despotism, was compelled to make a significant concession: 'It is said that this century is the century of philosophy ... Today, everyone seems occupied with the search for truth. But there is only one country where it can be published with impunity—and that is England.'[3] The island happily

---

1   Voltaire, *Philosophical Letters*, trans. Ernest Dilworth, New York: Mineola, 2003, p. 39.
2   Ibid., p. 31.
3   Claude-Adrien Helvétius, *De l'homme*, in *Oeuvres complètes*, vols 7–12, Hildesheim: Olms, 1967–69, vol. 8, p. 86. For the criticism of Helvétius, cf. Denis Diderot, 'Réfutation suivie de l'ouvrage d'Helvétius intitulé 'L'homme'', in *Oeuvres*, ed. Laurent Versini, vol. 1, Paris: Laffont, 1994, p. 862.

rid of absolute monarchy exercised a powerful attraction. In the columns of the *Encyclopédie*, Diderot held up England as an example of 'temperate monarchy', where 'the sovereign is repository solely of executive power'.[4] A little less than ten years later, proposing to restrict representative bodies to 'major property-owners',[5] he still viewed cross-Channel political institutions with great interest. In Condorcet's view, too, they had the merit of having realized, albeit to an inadequate extent, the principles of the limitation of royal power, freedom of the press, habeas corpus and judicial independence.[6]

In fact, two years prior to the storming of the Bastille and the intervention of the popular masses on the political scene, the English model seemed to have triumphed in France as well. Supported by a wide popular consensus, the noble *parlements* challenged royal absolutism: 'the anti-absolutism of the parlements', or 'aristocratic liberalism', became the vehicle for widespread 'liberal demands'.[7] Preserve of a nobility which, as a result also of the sale of offices, was open to the bourgeoisie, the French *parlements* for a while seemed destined to play godfather to the advent of a constitutional monarchy and to perform a role similar to that of the House of Lords and the House of Commons in England. Not by chance they appealed to Montesquieu, president of the Bordeaux *Parlement* and a great admirer of the country that had emerged from the Glorious Revolution.

Burke viewed this sensationally missed opportunity with regret, when he delivered his harsh indictment of a revolution that had degenerated rapidly and wickedly. Had it ended at the stage when the struggle was led by the *parlements*, the French

> would have shamed despotism from the earth [and] rendered the cause of liberty venerable in the eyes of every worthy mind in every nation … You would have had a free constitution … a liberal order of commons to emulate and recruit that nobility …[8]

---

4   Denis Diderot, *Oeuvres politiques*, ed. Paul Vernière, Paris: Garnier, 1963, p. 41 (article on *Représentants*).

5   Ibid., p. 369.

6   Cf. Gabriel Bonno, *La Constitution britannique devant l'opinion française de Montesquieu à Bonaparte*, Paris: Champion, 1931, p. 156.

7   François Furet and Denis Richet, *La rivoluzione francese*, trans. Silvia Brilli Cattarini and Carla Patanè, Rome and Bari: Laterza, 1980, pp. 47, 49, 55.

8   Edmund Burke, *The Works: A New Edition*, 16 vols, London: Rivington, 1826, vol. 5, p. 84.

Unfortunately, this happy, auspicious moment had been short-lived; and people had started chasing after 'a pure democracy' that in fact secreted a tendency to a 'party tyranny' and 'a mischievous and ignoble oligarchy'.[9]

Reflections on the Revolution in France was published on 1 November 1790, but its basic arguments had already been set out with great clarity in a speech by Burke in the Commons on 9 February of that year. Jacobinism lay in the future. Rather than transforming the British Whig into the prophet of a catastrophe no one was in a position to predict at the time, we should examine the events that had occurred when he levelled his serious charges against the French Revolution. Revealing is the observation that, rather than striving to create a 'bad constitution' *ex nihilo*, the French should have engaged in further improving the 'good one', of which '[t]hey were in possession … the day the states met in separate orders'. The ruinous turn occurred when, in the course of the meeting of the Estates-General summoned by the King—at which the 'good' Constitution finally emerged or, rather, re-emerged—the tradition whereby the orders sat in separate chambers was abandoned and the transition to voting by head was decided, with the consequent transformation on 9 July of the Estates-General into a constituent National Assembly wherein the former Third Estate now possessed a majority. Thus burst onto the scene the 'bad constitution', which 'melted down the whole into one incongruous, ill-connected mass'. Everything else flowed from this: the attack on 'the root of all property' and 'confiscat[ion] [of] all the possessions of the church'—the reference is to the night of 4 August 1789 and the abolition of feudal privileges (hunting rights, tithes, and so on)—and the promulgation on 26 August of the 'mad declaration' of the Rights of Man, that 'sort of *institute* and *digest* of anarchy'.[10]

But everything began on 9 July. The French Revolution proved fatally degenerate even before the capture of the Bastille and the intervention of the popular masses—in a sense, even before its inception. And in fact Burke was concerned to stress that 'the glorious event commonly called the Revolution in England' was in fact 'a revolution, not made, but prevented': William of Orange 'was called in by the flower of the English aristocracy to defend its antient constitution, and not to level all distinctions',[11] as, alas, had happened in France. The latter had now gone beyond its fleeting liberal phase, which extended from the agitation of the *parlements* to the summoning of the Estates-General.

---

9   Ibid., vol. 5, pp. 230–2.
10   Ibid., vol. 5, pp. 13–14.
11   Ibid., vol. 5, pp. 18–20.

The subsequent liberal tradition is inclined to extend the felicitous phase of the French Revolution somewhat, and identify the turning point in the tumultuous intervention of the popular masses, initially rural and then urban; thus de Tocqueville. But it is interesting to note that he, too, after 1848 at any rate, extolled the period when the movement was directed by the *parlements*, all of them striving to reverse 'the old absolute power' and 'the old arbitrary system', and win 'political liberty', in a struggle promoted and led not by the 'low classes' but by the 'higher'.[12] Certainly, contrary to Burke, who tended to conceive the parliamentary agitation on the model of the so-called Glorious Revolution, de Tocqueville was prepared to stress that in this phase, appearances to the contrary notwithstanding, an authentic revolution was underway:

> It should not be thought that the *Parlement* presented these principles as novelties. On the contrary, it derived them very industriously from the depths of the antiquity of the monarchy ... It is a strange sight to see ideas that had hardly been born thus wrapped in ancient swaddling clothes.[13]

It was 'a very great revolution, but one that should rapidly have faded into the immensity of what happened and thus disappeared from the view of history'.[14] Only in a subsequent phase 'was the *Parlement* no longer praised' in the revolutionary movement, but 'reviled, turning its liberalism against it'.[15] The ruinous parabola of the French Revolution could be synthesized thus: 'At the outset it was Montesquieu who was quoted and expounded; at the end people spoke exclusively of Rousseau.' The turning point was described in terms similar to those we have noted in Burke: the rot set in when people rushed towards 'pure democracy' and laid claim to change 'the very structure of society'.[16]

Even closer to Burke was Guizot, who pointed to the eruption of the 'Third Estate's struggle against the nobility and the clergy' as the moment when the French Revolution ceased to have 'liberty' as its goal and aimed exclusively at 'power', paving the way for the subsequent, interminable struggles—'those of the poor against the rich, of the common people against the bourgeoisie, of the rabble against respectable folk [*honnêtes gens*]'.[17]

---

12 Alexis de Tocqueville, *Oeuvres complètes*, ed. Jacob-Peter Mayer, Paris: Gallimard, 1951–, vol. 2, pt 2, pp. 47–8.

13 Ibid., vol. 2, pt 2, pp. 55–6.

14 Ibid., vol. 2, pt 2, p. 76.

15 Ibid., vol. 2, pt 2, p. 100.

16 Ibid., vol. 2, pt 2, p. 107.

17 François Guizot, *Mélanges politiques et historiques*, Paris: Lévy, 1869, pp. 2–3.

2. Parliaments, diets, the liberal aristocracy and serfdom

For Burke, the revolution in France should ultimately have confined itself to liberalizing the *ancien régime*. This was not an isolated, polemical idea. In stressing the particular attachment to liberty displayed by slave-owners, the discourse of reconciliation with the rebel colonists offered a general consideration:

> [T]hese people of the southern colonies are much more strongly, and with an higher and more stubborn spirit, attached to liberty, than those to the northward. Such were all the ancient commonwealths; such were our Gothick ancestors; such in our days were the Poles; and such will be all masters of slaves, who are not slaves themselves. In such a people, the haughtiness of domination combines with the spirit of freedom, fortifies it, and renders it invincible.[18]

No distinction is made here between slavery in the strict sense and the serfdom prevalent, in its harshest forms, in eastern Europe. In any event, the servile subjection of blacks or peasants, far from contradicting it, rendered the love of liberty by property-owners and freemen stronger and more credible.

Sidney too was an admirer of Poland. Along with other 'northern nations', it was inspired by a love of liberty. What demonstrated this was, among other things, the fact that the king derived from 'popular elections'—in other words, appointment by the Diet of nobles.[19] Certainly, proudly asserting their condition as free, equal men in the face of the monarch were magnates who wielded absolute power over their serfs. But Sidney argued along the lines we have already encountered: as with slavery, liberalism was also compatible with serfdom. In fact, both institutions rendered the appreciation of liberty more profound and more jealous.

In Burke there is complete consistency between the recognition granted Poland and that granted the French *parlements*. The latters' agitation was quite the reverse of an isolated phenomenon: 'In Sweden the years from 1719 to 1772 are known as the Age of Freedom, because at this time the Diet or Riksdag ruled without interference by the King. Indeed, these Swedish Whigs, after their revolution of 1719, had the works of John Locke translated into Swedish.' In Hungary the nobles instead appealed above all to Montesquieu,[20] while, in

---

18 Burke, *Works*, vol. 3, p. 54.

19 Algernon Sidney, *Discourses Concerning Government*, ed. Thomas G. West, Indianapolis: Liberty Classics, 1990, pp. 167, 101.

20 Robert R. Palmer, *The Age of Democratic Revolution*, 2 vols, Princeton: Princeton University Press, 1959–64, vol. 1, pp. 31, 106.

even more ringing language, the Polish aristocracy paid homage to 'republican liberty'.[21] In conclusion, '[t]he diets, estates, parlements, and councils all stoutly defended liberty, and indeed stood for many genuine liberal ideas; but at the same time they palpably insisted on the maintenance or enlargement of their own privileges.'[22] In this context we can also situate Bismarck's celebration some decades later of the 'liberal caste sentiments' (*ständisch-liberale Stimmung*) of the class he belonged to,[23] which was interested in extending the jurisdiction and powers of representative bodies also in order to reinforce control over servants.

A similar observation can be made in connection with the agitation set off by the French *parlements*: guiding the 'assault' on royal absolutism was 'one of the *ancien régime*'s most traditional institutions'.[24] And, in addition to the English model, it was to this initial phase of the French Revolution—the one admired by Burke and de Tocqueville post-1848—that the liberal nobility of the Hapsburg Empire appealed to condemn Joseph II's anti-feudal reforms, to reassert the role of diets and intermediate bodies, and hence 'regain ... control over their peasants' and the 'other political liberties' they had lost.[25] Sidney had already specified that a common feature of 'northern nations', which embodied the principle of liberty, was assignment of a decisive role to 'lords, commons, diets, assemblies of estates, cortes, and parliaments'.[26]

The aristocratic liberalism represented in France by the *parlements* was thus widely diffused in Europe, especially central and eastern Europe. Certainly, unlike Burke, Montesquieu expressed a negative opinion of Poland, 'where the peasants are slaves of the nobility'.[27] The British Whig was well aware of these social relations. In fact, he started out from them to underscore the emphatic love of liberty displayed by slave-owners in Poland, as across the Atlantic. By contrast, Montesquieu saw liberty at work in the English colonies in America, but not in Poland. Does Burke demonstrate greater logical rigour? In reality, in accordance with his principle of the 'uselessness of slavery among ourselves', Montesquieu did not identify with Poland, which could not invoke the

21   Karl Marx, *Manuskripte über die polnische Frage*, ed. Werner Conze and Dieter Hertz-Eichenrode, 's-Gravenhage: Mouton, 1961, p. 110.

22   Palmer, *Age of Democratic Revolution*, vol. 1, p. 108.

23   Otto von Bismarck, *Gedanken und Erinnerungen*, Stuttgart and Berlin: Cotta, 1928, pp. 51–2.

24   Furet and Richet, *La rivoluzione francese*, p. 48.

25   Palmer, *Age of Democratic Revolution*, vol. 1, pp. 384–5.

26   Sidney, *Discourses Concerning Government*, p. 167.

27   Charles-Louis Montesquieu, *The Spirit of the Laws*, trans. and ed. Anne M. Cohler, Basia Carolyn Miller and Harold Samuel Stone, Cambridge: Cambridge University Press, 1989, p. 17.

justification or extenuation of a hot climate and where the zone of unfreedom lacked spatial as well as racial delimitation.

It remains the case that Burke's attitude had deep roots in the philosophy of history of the liberal tradition, which from Montesquieu onwards tended to date the inception of the history of freedom and free, representative government from the ancient Germans. Among them, as we know from Grotius, the institution of slavery was very much present and yet (according to the author of *The Spirit of the Laws*), 'the English have taken their idea of political government from the Germans'.[28] On the basis of such presuppositions, Madame de Staël celebrated the liberty enjoyed by old France, despite the heavy presence of serfdom,[29] and Constant 'the intermediate bodies' and '*Parlements*' wrongly weakened by royal despotism,[30] which played an important role in the initial phase of the revolution.

3. The American Revolution and the crisis of the English model

Despite the seemingly favourable initial prospects, the English model met with rapid defeat in Paris. In reality, it was already deeply tarnished when the crisis of the *ancien régime* reached maturity in France. In the 1760s, while the colonists' rebellion was brewing across the Atlantic, John Wilkes attacked 'the whole organization of the British oligarchy' in London and initiated a crisis of such gravity as to make the Italian Pietro Verri believe in the imminence of 'civil war'. Persecuted at home, Wilkes for a time found refuge in Paris, where he formed relations with the group of *philosophes*.[31]

However, the turning point in the process that threw the English model into crisis in France was represented by the American Revolution. The British Constitution now ceased to be celebrated, and criticisms of Montesquieu for having transfigured it were not lacking.[32] The increasingly bitter condemnation of the *ancien régime* derived comfort from transatlantic political and social developments. Although not refusing England acknowledgement of the merits earned with the liquidation of royal absolutism, Condorcet looked primarily to America, with its magnificent 'spectacle of equality', without any trace of the

---

28 Ibid., p. 166.

29 Germaine de Staël-Holstein, *Considérations sur la Révolution française*, ed. Jacques Godechot, Paris: Tallandier, 1983, pp. 85–6.

30 Benjamin Constant, *Oeuvres*, ed. Alfred Roulin, Paris: Gallimard, 1957, p. 1078.

31 Franco Venturi, *Settecento riformatore*, 5 vols, Turin: Einaudi, 1969–90, vol. 3, pp. 383, 398–400.

32 Bonno, *La Constitution britannique*, pp. 133ff.

belief diffused, albeit to different degrees, on both sides of the Channel that nature had 'divided the human race into three or four orders', condemning only one of them to 'work much and eat little'.[33] Now appeal was no longer made to the Glorious Revolution, from which a liberal but also aristocratic England had emerged, but to the 'happy revolution' across the Atlantic,[34] which had given birth to a markedly superior politico-social reality: 'there is no distinction of orders' and 'there is nothing that confines one part of the human species to an abjectness consigning it to idiocy as well as misery'.[35]

Diderot was even more swingeing. The new country, which offered 'all the inhabitants of Europe an asylum from fanaticism and tyranny', was an alternative model to the *ancien régime* that continued to be all the rage in the old continent as a whole, and where 'the inept, the corrupt rich and the pernicious [are promoted] to the most important offices'. Adherence to the cause of the rebel colonists was, at the same time, a ruthless critique of the behaviour of British troops and against Britain as such. This emerges from celebration of the 'brave Americans, who have preferred to see their women outraged, their children slain, their homes destroyed, their fields ruined, their cities burnt, and who have preferred to shed their blood and die, rather than lose the least part of their liberty'.[36] Thanks also to the support furnished to the American revolutionaries by France, their arguments were bound to find a favourable echo in Paris, and they involved an unequivocal condemnation of the country that Paine in *Common Sense* (substantially translated immediately after its publication) branded as 'British barbarity', 'the Royal Brute of Britain', whose aristocratic character was already evident from 'what is called the Magna Charta'.[37] Nor should we lose sight of the presence in Paris, in the decisive years of the revolutionary crisis, of Jefferson, who, a few weeks after the storming of the Bastille, advised France to keep its distance from England's worst aspects (a form of representation that was quite the reverse of equal—in fact, 'abominably partial'—as well as the 'absolute' power which the monarch continued to possess in reality thanks to the venality of parliamentarians).[38]

---

33 Marie-Jean-Antoine Condorcet, *Oeuvres*, 12 vols, ed. Arthur Condorcet O'Connor and François Arago, Stuttgart and Bad Cannstatt: Frommann-Holzboog, 1968, vol. 8, p. 19.

34 Ibid., vol. 8, p. 3.

35 Ibid., vol. 8, pp. 28–9.

36 Denis Diderot, *Saggio sui regni di Claudio e di Nerone e sui costume e gli scritti di Seneca*, trans. Secondo Carpanetto and Luciano Guerci, Palermo: Sellerio, 1987, pp. 327–8.

37 Thomas Paine, *Collected Writings*, ed. Eric Foner, New York: Library of America, 1995, pp. 31, 34, 33; Bernard Faÿ, *L'esprit révolutionnaire en France et aux États-Unis à la fin du XVIII siècle*, Paris: Champion, 1925, p. 62 (for the translation of substantial extracts in France).

38 Thomas Jefferson, *Writings*, ed. Merrill D. Peterson, New York: Library of America, 1984,

This was the intellectual climate in which Brissot and Clavière, two figures destined to play a central role in the French Revolution, published a book in 1787 dedicated 'to the American Congress and the friends of the United States in the two worlds', and marked throughout by admiration for 'free Americans' and 'free America', for its 'free' and 'excellent' Constitution and noble 'republican customs'.[39] The counterpoint to such celebration was, of course, condemnation of 'London's ministerial despotism' and the 'ferocity' of its troops. The 'English nation' was now vainly seeking to remedy the 'devastation of its cruel dementia' and renew relations with the country born in the wake of the struggle against it.[40] This division must be followed by an intellectual and political alliance between those who had struggled together against England—namely, the United States and France, which 'with its arms helped assert the independence of free America', and which was now summoned to take inspiration from the great new model embodied by the country thrown up by the revolution.[41] On this basis, Brissot and Clavière set up the French–American Society.

When, two years later, the debate began that issued in the Declaration of the Rights of Man and of the Citizen, not a few interventions appealed to the American example and the sort of synthetic proclamation of the rights of man contained in the Declaration of Independence. In an attempt to counter the revolution's radicalization, Malouet, who became the spokesman for the interests of slave-owners in the colonies, drew attention to the radical differences between the United States and France. In the first case, there was a society 'entirely composed of property-owners already accustomed to equality'. In the second, one witnessed the agitation of 'an immense multitude of men without property' in a daily struggle for survival and 'placed by fate in a condition of dependency': a gulf separated 'the fortunate and the unfortunate classes of society'. This was where appeals to 'democracy' and the rights of man could have devastating consequences for the social order.[42] Stripped of its ideological caution and reticence, the meaning of the speech was clear. In America, thanks to expansion into territories occupied by the Indians and their expropriation, it was possible significantly to expand the ranks of property-owners who were European in origin. On the other hand, the 'unfortunate classes' were not in a

---

pp. 957–8 (letter to Diodati, 3 August 1789).

39   Étienne Clavière and Jacques-Pierre Brissot de Warville, *De la France et des États-Unis*, Paris: Éditions du CTHS, 1996, pp. 64, 95 and *passim*.

40   Ibid., pp. iii–iv.

41   Ibid., p. 340.

42   Malouet, quoted in Antoine de Baecque, Wolfgang Schmale and Michel Vovelle, eds, *L'An des droits de l'homme*, Paris: CNRS Press, 1988, pp. 105–6.

position to do harm: they mainly comprised blacks reduced to slavery or relegated to a subaltern caste and subject to iron social control. Waved exclusively within the white community and the superior race, the flag of democracy and the rights of man had nothing subversive about it. But in France ...

Malouet's reasoning was not flawless. However, it was no longer possible to revert to the situation prior to the American Revolution. After the formation of significantly more democratic representative bodies at federal and state levels in the United States, little credibility could attach to the British parliament, which on the basis of a law of 1716 that remained in force for nearly two centuries (until 1911) was elected every seven years,[43] and monopolized by the landed aristocracy. Moreover, it was undermined by a corruption that had become proverbial in Europe and across the Atlantic, which seemed in France to be a repeat of the sale of offices—an essential element of the *ancien régime* that was to be got rid of.

In the course of their argument with London, the American revolutionaries had equated citizens deprived of the right of representation with slaves. But now this argument came to be applied in France by those who were opposed to censitary discrimination in the suffrage. This, thundered Robespierre, criticizing those inspired by the 'example of England', reduced the excluded to a condition similar to the slave: 'liberty consists in obeying the laws one has given oneself and slavery in being forced to submit to an alien will'.[44] Some years later, Babeuf argued in similar fashion: 'citizens whose will is inactive—such men are slaves'.[45] These were declarations that could have come from the mouth of an American revolutionary; only now, pronounced in favour not of a narrow elite of gentlemen and property-owners, but of the mass of the dispossessed, they assumed a very different political and social value.

4. The transfiguration of American 'master-race democracy' in a universalistic key

Focusing attention on the problem of slavery, the argument that developed on both sides of the Atlantic initially discredited England, protagonist of the slave trade, more than it did the rebel colonists: 'staining the reputation of that

43 Cf. Joel H. Wiener, *Great Britain: The Lion at Home*, New York: Chelsea House, 1983, vol. 1, p. 56.

44 Maximilien de Robespierre, *Oeuvres*, 10 vols, Paris: Presses Universitaires de France, 1912–67, vol. 7, pp. 162–3.

45 François-Noël Babeuf, *Écrits*, ed. Claude Mazauric, 1988, p. 189.

nation' (observed Diderot in 1774) 'is the fact that its blacks are the unhappiest of blacks'. Indeed, 'the Englishman, enemy of tyranny at home, is the most ferocious despot abroad'.[46] The *Philosophical and Political History of the Two Indias* reiterated the point: 'The English, this people so jealous of their own liberty, have contempt for that of other men'. They did not hesitate to employ the most bestial methods and the most refined forms of torture to smother any hint of rebellion and any aspiration to freedom by their slaves; 'it is to this excess of barbarism that the trading and slavery of blacks have necessarily led the usurpers'.[47]

Later, when it allied with the powers of the *ancien régime* to fight revolutionary France, and refused to follow the latter's example in abolishing slavery (decreed by the Jacobin Convention in February 1794, in the wake of the revolution by the black slaves led by Toussaint L'Ouverture), England was widely discredited in Europe. Robespierre was not alone in declaring that the island across the Channel could seem like a model of liberty only at a time when France groaned under monarchical absolutism. This was also Kant's opinion: 'England, which at one time could count on the sympathy of the best men in the world ... has now completely lost that sympathy.'[48]

While it provoked the crisis of the English model, the American Revolution prompted portrayals and hopes that were destined to prove completely unrealistic. At work was the illusion that the institution of slavery was destined rapidly to disappear in the republic produced by a great struggle for freedom. The founders of the French–American Society explicitly expressed themselves in such terms: 'The most beautiful feature for which one honours the public spirit in the United States' was 'the emancipation of the blacks'. Thanks to the Quakers' abolitionist campaigning, it 'will soon be universal in all this part of the world', so that only the Europeans, still committed to the slave trade and the oppression of blacks, would remain to blush at 'their barbarism'.[49]

Condorcet adopted a similar position: the rebel colonists were the 'friends of universal liberty'.[50] Consequently, one could start from the presupposition that the stain of slavery would soon be washed away:

---

46 Diderot, 'Réfutation suivie de l'ouvrage d'Helvétius', p. 895.

47 Guillaume-Thomas Raynal, *Histoire philosophique et politique des Deux Indes*, ed. Yves Benot, Paris: Maspero, 1981, p. 257.

48 Cf. Domenico Losurdo, *Autocensura e compromesso nel pensiero politico di Kant*, Naples: Bibliopolis, 1983, pp. 90–1.

49 Clavière and Brissot, *De la France et des États-Unis*, pp. 324–5.

50 Condorcet, *Oeuvres*, vol. 8, p. 51.

Slavery is universally regarded in the thirteen states as a crime of *lèse-humanité* ... Now, given this opinion, it will be hard for the private interests of the slave-owners to prevail for long in a country where the press is free and where all measures of public authority, all the deliberations of the legislative body ... are necessarily public acts.[51]

This illusion is readily explicable: it involved a confusion between the abolition of the slave trade (effectively provided for by the US Constitution, which sanctioned its termination in 1808) and the abolition of slavery (which continued to flourish); and there was a sense that the process set in train in the North would shortly encompass the Union as a whole. More generally, the rebel colonists' passionate denunciation of despotism and political slavery sounded like a declaration of war on any form of enslavement, and hence like the inception of black emancipation.

The process of transfiguring events across the Atlantic sometimes became a total misunderstanding. Enthusiastically saluting the rebel colonists, Raynal advertised a prize for answers to the question whether 'the discovery of America has been useful or harmful to the human race'. The four responses submitted concurred in denouncing the event as a harbinger of intolerance and slavery and pointing to the American Revolution as the remedy for such ills.[52] The rebellion that broke out in the name also of the right to untrammelled expansion into lands inhabited by savages was thus construed in the completely opposite sense!

5. The colonists of San Domingo, the American model and the second liberal inception of the French Revolution

At the outset, it was not understood in France that the independence secured by the white colonists strengthened their control over the Indians and blacks; and it was not realized that a similar dialectic was tending to develop in the French colonies. In the 1781 edition of the *History of the Two Indias*, Diderot on the one hand evoked the figure of a 'black Spartacus', summoned to rise up against the slave-owners, but on the other, harking back to the example of the American Revolution, declared for the concession of self-government to San Domingo too, which would precisely have entailed the triumph of the

---

51   Ibid., vol. 7, p. 139.
52   Fay, *L'esprit révolutionnaire*, pp. 132–3.

slave-owners. The philosopher did not perceive the contradiction, and nor did Brissot, who took a similar position.[53]

With the outbreak of the French Revolution, self-government became the watchword of colonists interested in preserving the institution of slavery and shielding their property from the interference, whims and despotism attributed to central government. Among the first to make himself spokesman for these ideas and interests was Malouet, who in 1788 had already engaged in a sharp polemic against the abolitionists. Certainly, the institution of slavery was out of the question for a 'free and proud nation' like France. To tolerate it on metropolitan territory would risk erasing the boundary between liberty and slavery and inducing a 'general enslavement'. Malouet was a liberal and admired England, where he took refuge following the failure of projects for establishing a monarchy on the English model in France. He appealed to the 'wise Locke' and his *Treatises of Government* to argue that slavery for 'barbarous peoples ... does not offend the right of nature'.[54] Hence Malouet took care not to challenge the spatial and racial delimitation of slavery, as had his contemporary and fellow countryman Melon (against whom Montesquieu argued): slavery was inconceivable in the metropolis and, within the colonies, for the white race.

In relation to blacks, however, the discourse was very different: transported to America, they were providentially released from the 'most absurd despotism', which raged in Africa. It was true that they continued to suffer slavery, albeit of a decidedly milder variety than that prevalent in their countries of origin. However, much more so than the American slave, whose subsistence was guaranteed and who was protected by a series of laws, it was the European 'worker' (*journalier*) who was 'subject to the *absolute will*', the power of life and death, of his master, who, denying or ejecting him from work, could calmly condemn him to death. People cried scandal at the punishments inflicted on slaves, but what happened in Europe? A peasant who stole was hanged, a poacher was condemned to 'forced labour'—a slavery much more pitiless than that typically existing across the Atlantic.[55] Thus, we encounter the arguments that would later receive more developed theoretical systematization particularly in Calhoun.

---

53   Yves Benot, *La révolution française et la fin des colonies*, Paris: La Découverte, 1988, pp. 189–90.

54   Pierre-Victor Malouet, *Mémoire sur l'esclavage des nègres*, Neufchâtel, 1788, p. 10.

55   Ibid., pp. 27, 33–4. Cf. Carminella Biondi, *Mon frère, tu es mon esclave*, Pisa: Libreria Goliardica, 1973, pp. 23–8.

Once the French Revolution had broken out, supporting the colonists' inter-ests and arguments was the Massiac Club, founded in Paris in August 1789, of which Malouet was a prominent member. Likewise aligned in defence of the colonists' right to self-government and the undisturbed enjoyment of their property (plantations and slaves) was Antoine Barnave. We are dealing with an important author who expressed his liberal convictions not only in immedi-ately political terms, but also at the level of the philosophy of history. In him too we find the dialectic we are already familiar with: ringing condemnation of political 'slavery'[56] did not prevent him from forcefully and skilfully defend-ing the cause of the slaveholding colonists. The 'spirit of liberty' (he observed) increased and strengthened with the expansion of 'industry', 'wealth' and, above all, 'movable wealth'. That was why, even prior to England with its splendid 'Constitution', it emerged in Holland, 'the country where movable wealth has accumulated most'.[57] Slaves were an integral part of this 'movable property', and had already been classified among the 'movable' goods in Louis XIV's *Code noir*.[58]

The Massiac Club and Barnave were generally considered 'Anglomanes' and genuinely were, in the sense that they opposed the radicalization of the French Revolution and admired and envied the country across the Channel for its orderly rule of law and strict censitary discrimination, which consecrated the untrammelled, exclusive domination of the property-owning classes. However, in another respect they were led to appeal predominantly to the American model, with its pathos of the inviolable autonomy of representative bodies and states from central power and the guarantee that derived from it of the inviolability of the institution of slavery. In the face of central government, the colonies adopted the stance of the southern states. In March 1790 the colo-nists won a temporary victory:

The National Assembly declared that it had not the slightest intention of updating any branch of its trade with the colonies. It placed the colonists and their property under the special protection of the nation. It declared anyone who plotted to incite uprisings against them a criminal to the nation.

---

56   Antoine-P.-J. M. Barnave, *Introduction à la révolution française*, ed. Fernand Rude, Paris: Colin, 1960, pp. 13, 18, 35.

57   Ibid., pp. 28–9.

58   See articles 44–46 of the *Code noir* in Louis Sala-Molins, *Le Code noir*, Paris: Presses Universitaires de France, 1988, pp. 178–83.

It was a success that was repeated about a year later: 'The National Assembly made it a constitutional rule that no law on the condition of unfree persons in the colonies could be made except at the formal, unsolicited request of the colonial Assemblies.'[59] Even if the whole discourse revolved around the problem of slavery, the relevant term did not appear: the articles of the US Constitution were imitated in substance and form alike. This was the French Revolution's second liberal inception. Just as the *parlements* expressed the desire for self-government by the liberal nobility in the metropolis, so the colonial Assemblies gave voice to the slave-owners' desire for self-government in the colonies.

Yet this second liberal inception was even more precarious than the first. Following the defeat suffered during the Seven Years' War, France had lost virtually all its colonial empire in 1763. This had imparted to the critique of colonialism and the institution of slavery a diffusion and radicalism hampered, by contrast, in the English and American world by substantial material interests and a national, chauvinistic spirit understandably reinforced by victory. We can thus understand the split that immediately occurred in the French liberal party. Aspiring to a constitutional monarchy with the right to make war and peace reserved to the king, Mirabeau, like Malouet and Barnave, looked to England. Unlike them, however, he ended up rejecting the American model when it came to regulating the relations between central power, on the one hand, and colonies and colonists, on the other. In the Constituent Assembly the latter demanded that they be represented in proportion not only to their numbers, but also to the number of their slaves, in accordance with a criterion identical or similar to that adopted by the US Constitution. Here is Mirabeau's stinging reply:

> If the colonists want the blacks and people of colour to be men, well then, emancipate them, so that all are electors and all can be elected. Otherwise, we beg them to note that, in proportioning the number of deputies to the population of France, we have not taken into consideration the number of our horses and mules. The colonists' claim to have twenty representatives is therefore utterly ridiculous.[60]

It was an argument that also applied in the United States, as is confirmed by a subsequent position of Mirabeau's:

---

59   Jean-Pierre Biondi and François Zuccarelli, *16 pluviôse an II*, Paris: Denoël, 1989, pp. 48, 75.

60   Mirabeau, quoted in Pierre Dockès, 'Condorcet et l'esclavage des nègres', in Jean-Michel Servet, ed., *Les idées économiques sous la Révolution*, Lyon: Presses Universitaires de Lyon, 1989, p. 86 n. 4 (speech in National Assembly, 3 July 1789).

I shall not debase either this assembly or myself by seeking to prove that the blacks have a right to liberty. You decided this question when you declared that all men are born and remain equal and free. And it is not on this side of the Atlantic that corrupt fallacies will dare to maintain that blacks are not men.[61]

The condemnation of ideologies of slavery targeted both French colonists and the English colonists who had now constituted themselves as an independent state: the polemic against the former could not but encompass the latter; the initial ambiguity, which had led French abolitionists to attribute a completely imaginary universalistic impetus to the authors of the American Revolution, was dispelled—all the more so in that it was the very ideologues of slavery who drew attention to the vitality of that institution in the United States. Brissot had believed that the example of the Quakers of Pennsylvania would act as a model; in a sense adopting an observation already present in Smith, Malouet had pointed out in 1788 that the abolition of slavery decided by it affected a fairly limited number of people and certainly did not extend to the southern states, where the presence of slaves and blacks was much more pronounced.[62] In 1802 Baudry des Lozières' sarcasm was stinging. Precisely where 'Brissot locates perfection', slavery not only flourished undisturbed, but manifested itself in particularly rigid form: 'The North Americans, those lovers of liberty, those ardent republicans, who in their books celebrate their independence so much, buy and sell slaves.' Moreover, 'this country of liberty is very miserly in granting freedom' and 'those who are freed' were treated 'extremely harshly'.[63]

6. The crisis of the English and American models and the formation of French radicalism

Certainly, figures were not lacking in the abolitionist camp who continued to harbour illusions about a possible restoration of the American model to its former splendour. The abolition of an institution whose stubborn survival was incomprehensible in a country so strongly attached to the cause of liberty

---

61   Mirabeau, quoted in Benot, *La révolution française*, p. 115.

62   Malouet, *Mémoire*, pp. 43–4; Adam Smith, *An Inquiry into the Nature and Causes of the Wealth of Nations*, Indianapolis: Liberty Classics, 1981, p. 388.

63   Louis-Narcisse Baudry des Lozières, *Les égarements du nigrophilisme*, Paris: Migneret, 1802, pp. 82–3, 76.

would suffice. When in 1824 Lafayette visited the United States, where nearly fifty years earlier he had fought in the War of Independence, he cautiously tried to point out 'the disadvantages of slavery' in Ohio. However, his speech met with no success; in fact, his good intentions had an ironic objective accompaniment, since in various southern cities public notices warned 'people of color' to stay away from the ceremonies in honour of the illustrious guest.[64]

Residual illusions were also evident in Grégoire. Demonstrating political naivety, in an attempt to convince Jefferson to abandon his racial prejudices, he referred to the figure of Toussaint L'Ouverture to prove the ability of blacks to achieve a level of excellence![65] The French abbot was unaware of his interlocutor's efforts, in his capacity as US president, to reduce the republic born in the wake of the black slave revolution led by Toussaint L'Ouverture to hunger and force it to surrender (see below, Chapter 5, §8). Similarly, he did not know that in 1801 the latter was lamenting in his correspondence the fact that citizens of San Domingo were abducted by American corsairs and sold as slaves.[66] Leading the United States in 1801 was precisely Jefferson who, some years later, wrote to a friend in ironic terms about the French abolitionist abbot.[67]

As the predicted and desired emancipation of black slaves became an ever more problematic and remote prospect, bitter disappointment set in, as demonstrated in particular by Condorcet's evolution. On the immediate eve of the French Revolution, when the Constitution consecrating slavery was in force across the Atlantic, he still continued to draw a rather optimistic picture. The various states of the new republic and the 'common Senate that represents them' were unanimous in desiring the abolition of slavery; it was an 'act of justice' dictated by 'humanity', but also by 'honour'. A severe warning was already implicit in this final observation: 'How, without blushing, can one dare to demand these declarations of rights, these inviolable bulwarks of the liberty and security of citizens, if every day one permits oneself to violate the most sacred articles?'[68]

Some years later, where once it had been implicit, the distancing became explicit, even if it continued to be cautiously phrased. Compared with the French Revolution, the American presented itself as 'more peaceful', but also as 'slower' and 'more incomplete'. Sooner or later, it too would end up apply-

---

64   Eric Foner, *The Story of American Freedom*, London: Picador, 1999, p. 47.

65   See Henri Grégoire, *An Enquiry Concerning the Intellectual and Moral Faculties, and Literature of Negroes*, trans. David Bailie Warden, Armonk (NY): Sharpe, 1997, pp. 42–3.

66   Yves Benot, *La démence coloniale sous Napoléon*, Paris: La Découverte, 1992, p. 28.

67   Winthrop D. Jordan, *White over Black*, New York: Norton, 1977, pp. 454–5.

68   Condorcet, *Oeuvres*, vol. 9, p. 471.

ing the principle of liberty and equality in its universality. But for the time being there continued the 'crimes whose avarice soils the shores of America, Africa or Asia', the 'bloody contempt for men of another colour', the slave trade between the two shores of the Atlantic, the tragedy of Africa and the 'shameful brigandage that has corrupted and depopulated it for two centuries'. By contrast, it was a merit of the more advanced French culture to treat as '*friends* ... those blacks whom their stupid tyrants disdain to rank among men'.[69]

We have seen Condorcet denounce the 'general corruption' of Holland and England as slaveholding societies. This denunciation increasingly tended also to encompass the country that emerged from the third liberal revolution. The Terror was already hanging over Condorcet himself, who nevertheless identified revolutionary France as the country called upon to put an end to

the cunning and false policy which, forgetting that all men have equal rights by virtue of their very nature, wanted on the one hand to measure the extent of the rights to be granted by the size of the territory, the climate, national character, the wealth of the people, the degree of perfection of trade and industry; and on the other to sub-divide these same rights unequally between different classes of men, assigning them to birth, wealth and profession, thus creating contrary interests and opposed powers, to then establish a balance between them that is rendered necessary solely by these institutions and which does not even correct their dangerous influences.[70]

The United States no longer represented the genuine antithesis of the *ancien régime*, construed by Condorcet as a complex system of forms of discrimination and privilege that lacerated the unity of the human race. It was necessary to overcome once and for all a political order in which, intertwined with the hierarchization of peoples on the basis of climate, geographical location or differential economic development, there was a hierarchization within any individual people on the basis of birth or membership of an estate. While the first type of discrimination found concentrated expression across the Atlantic, the second had certainly not disappeared in England. The critical or scornful reference to the argument of 'climate' (a position prominent in Montesquieu and often used to justify the slavery of colonial peoples), and to the argument of the 'balance' of powers (often invoked in England to justify the privileges of the House of Lords and the landed aristocracy), demonstrates that Condorcet

---

69   Ibid., vol. 6, pp. 194–202 and *passim*, 239–40.
70   Ibid., vol. 6, p. 178.

had become critical of the American and English models alike, and had ultimately broken with both fractions of the liberal party.

Fully to understand Condorcet's mature view, it is important to take account of a peculiarity of the French Revolution. In the course of its development, the popular uprising in the metropolis against the *ancien régime* was soon followed by the clash in the colonies between freemen and slaves and between blacks and whites. The two conflicts were all the more closely intertwined because sections of the bourgeoisie and liberal nobility, engaged against the process of radicalization underway in Paris, were sometimes simultaneously interested, as the owners of slaves in the colonies, in preventing their emancipation. Those on the opposite side were thus led to assimilate noble privilege and racial privilege, branding them conjointly as two different expressions of aristocratic arrogance. In 1791 the Jacobin Sonthonax pointed to the liberal and spokesman for the slaveholding colonies, Barnave, as the 'protector of the aristocracy of the epidermis'.[71] A few years before the outbreak of the July Revolution, although now ferociously critical of Jacobinism, Abbé Grégoire issued a firm denunciation, already encapsulated in the title of his little book, of the 'nobility of the skin'. The analogy was now developed in all its aspects. The ban on interracial marriages in the United States was compared to the social obligation which, under the *ancien régime*, required the aristocracy not to contaminate itself with elements alien to it, with commoners: at work in both cases was an insane concern to safeguard 'the purity of the blood'.[72] It was understood that 'the nobility of the skin will suffer the same fate as the nobility of the scroll'.[73] In short, the absolute power possessed by the slave-owner was certainly no more tolerable than that exercised by the monarch, and hence the 'colonists' were 'similar to all despots'.[74]

In this comparative perspective, the negative judgement on the United States was manifest: 'Civilization is only dawning: five million Africans transported to America are still in chains there.'[75] And if there was an encouraging example in the New World, it was not afforded by the 'colonists' and the country they had founded in North America:

Simply by virtue of its existence, the republic of Haiti will be able to have a major influence on the destiny of Africans in the new world ... A black

---

71   Sonthonax, quoted in Benot, *La révolution française*, p. 82.
72   Henri Grégoire, *De la noblesse de la peau*, Grenoble: Jérôme Millon, 1996, pp. 50–1, 61.
73   Ibid., p. 83.
74   Ibid., p. 75.
75   Ibid., p. 113.

republic in the mid-Atlantic is a raised beacon to which the blushing oppressors and the sighing oppressed look. Seeing it, hope smiles on five million slaves scattered over the Antilles and the American continent.[76]

Criticism of the American model became even more explicit and bitter as those who wished to preserve slavery in the colonies appealed to it. Against the abolitionist projects or ambitions of Paris, the colonists invoked the spectre of a repeat of the American Revolution. They too would be forced into independence if they did not succeed in securing self-government, so as to be able to freely dispose of their slaves, without a 'despotic' power interfering with their legitimate property from without and above. Again, after the July Revolution, the French colonists declared themselves ready 'to hand themselves over to the American Union if the metropolis did not permit them slaves'.[77] Making this observation in 1842 was Victor Schoelcher who, six years later, played a key role in the definitive abolition of slavery in the French colonies, which had been reintroduced by Napoleon in 1802. And we can then understand the bitterness of the polemic against the transatlantic republic. 'Skin prejudices' remained particularly 'inveterate among the Americans'; they could be considered 'the most ferocious masters on the earth',[78] authors of 'one of the most upsetting spectacles the world has ever offered'. Not only blacks, but also white abolitionists, were hit by the most savage violence. Lynching threatened anyone who dared to challenge the 'iniquitous property' and 'demand freedom for all members of the human race'. 'There is no cruelty of the most barbarous age that has not been committed by the slave states of North America.' Hence the hope for a revolution from below: 'I hope that these brusque lynchers will one day all be hung by rebellious slaves'.[79] Not by chance, Schoelcher, in condemning the crimes committed by 'us other barbarians of the West',[80] expressed his admiration for the 'colossal revolution of S. Domingo'[81] and for the figure of Toussaint L'Ouverture, to whom he devoted a sympathetic biography.

The gulf separating the new political current forming in France from the two fractions of the liberal party is clear. Like Schoelcher, Brissot, who had played a significant part in founding the French–American Society, did not

---

76   Ibid., pp. 81–2.

77   Victor Schoelcher, *Des colonies françaises*, Paris: Éditions du CTHS, 1998, p. 242 n.

78   Ibid., pp. 166, 172.

79   Ibid., pp. 312–13.

80   Victor Schoelcher, *Esclavage et colonisation*, ed. Émile Tersen, Paris: Presses Universitaires de France, 1948, p. 75.

81   Ibid., p. 97.

hesitate to justify armed rebellion by black slaves and their right to revolution.[82] At this point the French–American Society was dead and buried. Between the July Revolution and the 1848 Revolution, manifestly in debate with French radicalism, de Tocqueville could once again present the United States as a model or source of inspiration only on condition of dropping the analogy between noble aristocracy and racial aristocracy, between monarchical despotism and slave despotism—the analogy on whose basis the North American republic was configured not as a model of liberty and democracy, but as a variant (and then not even the best) of the *ancien régime*.

7. The liberal inception of the revolution in Latin America and its radical outcome

In the metropolis and colonies alike, the French Revolution was transformed in a radical direction. To clarify this process further, we must begin with the definition which, in the course of the struggle against Stuart absolutism, at the start of the English liberal movement, one of its exponents gave of the 'true liberty' dear to him: 'we know by a certain law that our wives, our children, our servants, our goods, are our own, that we build, we plough, we sow, we reap, for ourselves'.[83] In the event, 'our servants' did not passively endure assimilation to 'our goods' and, in opposition to the 'true liberty' cherished by the exponent of English proto-liberalism, demanded a quite different liberty, which required the intervention of political power to abolish servitude in its various forms and promote the emancipation of the subaltern classes. This is what occurred in France, thanks to the historically auspicious context already analysed. In the metropolis, the first liberal inception of the French Revolution was immediately followed by the revolt of the peasants (with the end, sealed on the night of 4 August 1789, of the feudal system), and then the agitation of the urban popular masses. The second liberal inception, which was to have consecrated self-government by slave-owners, ended up inciting the revolution of the slaves themselves. The latter achieved emancipation and later managed to frustrate the terrible war machine of Napoleonic France.

A similar dialectic manifested itself in Latin America. Initially, the independence movement and revolution took the form of reactions against reform by the Spanish crown, which 'reversed the old policy of segregating the Indians and

---

82   Benot, *La révolution francaise*, p. 40.

83   Sir Thomas Aston, quoted in Christopher Hill, *The Century of Revolution*, New York: Norton, 1961, p. 188.

urged them to assimilate by speaking Spanish and dressing in European style'. Such integrationist measures soon provoked the hostility of the Creole elite. The latter professed liberalism, and was liberal: it read Locke, Montesquieu and Adam Smith; it sometimes sought to enter into relations with Jefferson; it protested against central government interference and the obstacles it placed in the way of developing local industry; it aspired to emulate the example of the American Revolution.[84] As for the English colonists in the North, so for the Latin American Creoles in the South, the slave, as the planter's private property, did not pertain to the public sphere. In the various manifestos that signalled the start of the war of independence against Spain, no positions in favour of abolishing slavery were adopted.[85]

Where the English colonists had indignantly rejected London's attempt to block their expansion beyond the Allegany Mountains, and proudly declared that they did not want to be treated 'like negroes, the Latin American Creoles claimed equality with the peninsula's ruling class and superiority to the Indians and, obviously, slaves deported from Africa. To this end they reminded Madrid that they were descendants of the conquistadores and, ultimately, artisans of the grandeur of the Spanish Empire. We are reminded of Franklin who, in the course of the controversy with the London government, had stressed the merits earned by the American colonists, 'hazarding their Lives and Fortunes in subduing and settling new Countries, extending the Dominion and encreasing the Commerce of their Mother Nation', enhancing the glory, 'the Grandeur and Stability of the British Empire'.[86]

But it was not long before the two roads diverged sharply. The fact is that in Spanish America, together with the Creole revolution but counter to it, an Indian revolution developed. In fact, the latter had announced itself decades earlier, as demonstrated by the series of revolts culminating in 1780–81 in the Túpac Amaru rebellion, which sought to win the blacks to its cause, liberating them too from the shackles of slavery. By contrast, the Creoles initially rose up with liberal slogans, demanding self-government, challenging interference by central power, aiming, like the North American colonists, to strengthen their control over the native populations and blacks. It was precisely this

---

84 Lester D. Langley, *The Americas in the Age of Revolution*, New Haven: Yale University Press, 1996, pp. 161–4.

85 Richard Hocquellet, 'Crise de la monarchie hispanique et question coloniale', in Yves Benot and Marcel Dorigny, eds, *Rétablissement de l'esclavage dans les colonies françaises*, Paris: Maisonneuve et Larose, 2003, p. 432.

86 Benjamin Franklin, *Writings*, ed. J. A. Leo Lemay, New York: Library of America, 1987, pp. 407, 760.

political project that formed the main target of the struggle by the Latin American Indians. Their revolution brings to mind the one that later erupted in San Domingo, and which issued in the formation of a new country: Haiti.

There is no doubt: it was San Domingo–Haiti that gave the Creole independence movement a decisive turn. To overcome the fierce resistance of the Spanish troops, Simón Bolívar sought to secure the support of the rebel ex-slaves of the Caribbean state, which he personally visited. The president at the time was Alexandre Pétion, who immediately received the Latin American revolutionary. He promised him the aid he requested on condition that he freed the slaves in areas as they were wrested from Spanish control. Transcending the class and caste limits of the social group he belonged to, and demonstrating intellectual and political courage, Bolívar accepted. Seven ships, 6,000 men with arms and munitions, a printing press and numerous advisors set out from the island.[87] This was the beginning of the abolition of slavery in much of Latin America.

Bolívar started out as a liberal, appealing to Montesquieu,[88] underlining the need for 'a liberal Constitution'[89] with 'eminently liberal provisions', which were to sanction 'the rights of man, the freedom to act, think, speak and write',[90] as well as 'the division and balance of powers, civil liberty, freedom of conscience, a free press'—in short, 'everything sublime that there is in politics'. He celebrated the 'British Constitution' and, above all, the American, the 'most perfect of Constitutions'.[91] However, when he demanded not only liberty, but the 'absolute freedom of the slaves', Bolívar in fact took his distance from the United States, where, even in the North, blacks were confined to a caste which was not that of genuinely free men. And this distancing from the North American republic was confirmed by a further observation that 'it is impossible to be free and slaves at the same time'. But especially significant was another element: the slave revolution from below, which in the United States represented a general nightmare, now became an object of explicit celebration. Bolívar not only appealed to the 'history of the helots, Spartacus and Haiti',[92] but in so doing defined Venezuelan and Latin American identity in a way that is worth reflecting on:

---

87   Robin Blackburn, *The Overthrow of Colonial Slavery*, London and New York: Verso, 1990, pp. 345–7; Langley, *The Americas in the Age of Revolution*, p. 194.

88   Simón Bolívar, *Obras completas*, ed. Vicente Lecuna, Caracas: Ministerio de Educación nacional de los Estados Unidos de Venezuela, n.d., vol. 1, p. 168; vol. 3, p. 680.

89   Ibid., vol. 1, p. 170.

90   Ibid., vol. 3, p. 679.

91   Ibid., vol. 3, pp. 685, 680.

92   Ibid., vol. 3, p. 694.

Let us bear in mind that our people is neither European nor North American. Rather than an emanation of Europe, it is a mixture of Africa and America because Spain itself ceased to be Europe on account of its African blood, its institutions and its character. It is impossible to determine exactly which human family we belong to. The majority of the indigenous population has been destroyed, the Europeans have mixed with Americans and Africans, and the latter with Indians and Europeans. All born from the breast of one and the same Mother, our fathers, different by origin and blood, are foreigners to one another and all visibly differ in their skin. Such diversity entails a consequence of the greatest importance. Thanks to the Constitution, interpreter of Nature, all citizens of Venezuela enjoy complete political equality.[93]

The countries formed out of the independence struggle against the Madrid government thus acquired a political, social and ethnic identity characterized by an admixture of black and Indian, and hence very different from US identity. While the North American colonists identified with the chosen people who sailed across the Atlantic to conquer the promised land, to be wrested from its unauthorized inhabitants and cleansed of their presence (see below, Chapter 7, §5), the Latin American revolutionaries, in the wake of their argument with Spain, tended to denounce the genocidal practices of the conquistadores, Spanish in particular and European in general. Here too the road had been indicated by the black slaves of San Domingo who, after having broken with Napoleonic France and defeated its attempts to re-conquer it and reintroduce slavery, had assumed the Indian name of Haiti. For Bolívar miscegenation—the mixing denounced in the United States, and sometimes with particular fervour by abolitionist circles—became a political project, which rejected any racial discrimination, and an essential element in a new, proud identity. However, precisely on account of its radicalism, this project found itself confronting almost insurmountable difficulties. Thanks to the politico-social homogeneity (strengthened by the availability of land and westward expansion) of its dominant class, and thanks also to the confinement of much of the 'dangerous classes' in slavery, the North American republic soon succeeded in achieving a stable structure. It took the form of a 'master-race democracy' and a racial state, based on the rule of law within the white community and among the chosen people. The situation in Latin America was very different: between liberal beginnings and radical outcomes, the revolution had mobilized a front stamped with profound social and ethnic contradictions. Thus two contrasting

---

93   Ibid., vol. 3, p. 682.

ideas of liberty confronted one another: one calls to mind the English gentleman determined to dispose freely of his servants; the other ultimately refers to the struggle that had put an end to black slavery in San Domingo—Haiti.

8. The United States and San Domingo—Haiti: two antagonistic poles

Around 1830 the American continent presented a rather telling picture. While it had disappeared in a considerable part of Latin America, slavery remained in force in the European colonies, including British and Dutch ones, and above all in the United States. We can say that from the slave revolution onwards there developed a pent-up confrontation, a kind of cold war, between San Domingo and the United States. On one side, we have a country that saw ex-slaves in power, authors of a revolution that was possibly unique in world history; on the other, a country almost always led in the early decades of its existence by slave-owning presidents. On one side, we have a country that sanctioned the principle of racial equality to the point where, at least when it was ruled by Toussaint L'Ouverture, whites could play a leading role in the plantations; on the other, a country that constituted the first historical example of a racial state.

Hence the tension between those two poles is understandable. When, in 1826, Abbé Grégoire pointed to Haiti as the 'beacon' looked to by slaves, he clearly had in mind the island's contribution to the abolition of slavery in Latin America. On the other side, with the emergence and advance of the slave revolution, the French colonists of San Domingo responded by entertaining the idea, and brandishing the threat, of secession from France and adhesion to the North American Union. Once the new revolutionary power had consolidated itself, it was a constant concern of the United States, where not a few ex-colonists took refuge, to overthrow or at least isolate it through a cordon sanitaire. It would be dangerous, observed Jefferson in 1799, to enter into commercial relations with San Domingo. That would result in 'black crews' disembarking in the United States, and these emancipated slaves could represent 'combustion' for the slaveholding South.[94] On the basis of such concerns, South Carolina banned the entry into its territory of any 'man of colour' from San Domingo or any of the other French islands, which might in some way have been infected by the new, dangerous ideas of liberty and racial equality.[95]

---

94 Jefferson, quoted in Jordan, *White over Black*, p. 381.
95 Michael Zuckerman, *Almost Chosen People*, Berkeley: University of California Press, 1993, p. 182.

Regardless of commercial exchanges, stressed influential political figures in the North American republic, by its very example the island risked challenging the institution of slavery far beyond its borders. Its inhabitants would in fact be 'dangerous neighbors to the Southern States, and an asylum for renegades from these parts'.[96] In conclusion, 'the peace of eleven states will not permit the fruits of a successful negro revolution to be exhibited among them'.[97] We can now understand Jefferson's support for Napoleon's attempt to re-conquer the island and reintroduce slavery. The US president assured the representative of France that 'nothing will be easier than to furnish your army and fleet with everything and to reduce Toussaint to starvation'.[98] Having succeeded Jefferson, Madison was likewise in no doubt as to the position to adopt: France was 'the sole sovereign of Saint Domingue'.[99]

With the consolidation of black power and the emergence of Haiti, the conflict did not come to an end. It also extended to the Caribbean islands under British control. Unrest spread among the black slaves and the governor of Barbados was well aware of 'the dangers of insurrection'. For this reason, projects to reform and moderate the institution of slavery were entertained in London. This was a prospect immediately opposed by the colonists of Jamaica, who, sheltering behind defence of 'their undoubted and acknowledged rights' to self-government, threatened revolt against royal despotism and secession and adhesion to the North American republic.[100]

But the example of San Domingo–Haiti had its most profound influence on Latin America. In 1822 the president, Jean-Pierre Boyer, proceeded to the annexation (which proved short-lived) of the Spanish part of the island, with the consequent emancipation of several thousand blacks, who along with freedom experienced notable social ascent, becoming small landowners. Slaves and free blacks in Cuba, who secretly kept the image of the Haitian leader, hoped for something similar. On the opposite side, sensing the danger, slave-owners of a liberal persuasion had already made contact with the US consul in Havana a decade earlier and outlined a project for joining the United States, which elicited the interest of Madison and Jefferson. In Calhoun's view the annexation desired by him was a sort of pre-emptive counter-revolution: it would put paid for ever to the danger of a Cuba 'revolutionized by Negroes', which would have increased or doubled the threat already posed by Haiti.[101]

---

96 Albert Gallatin, quoted in Langley, *The Americas in the Age of Revolution*, p. 129.
97 Thomas Hart Benton, quoted in ibid., p. 85.
98 Jefferson, quoted in Zuckerman, *Almost Chosen People*, p. 205.
99 Madison, quoted in ibid., p. 213.
100 Eric Williams, *Capitalism and Slavery*, London: Deutsch, 1990, pp. 202, 200.
101 Blackburn, *Overthrow of Colonial Slavery*, pp. 388, 395–6.

Later, while the island of black power helped spread black emancipation in much of Latin America, the United States reintroduced slavery in Texas, which had previously been taken from Mexico. In the years immediately preceding the Civil War, an attempt was made to expand the territory of the North American republic and, with it, the institution of slavery into other parts of Mexico and, above all, Nicaragua. One participant in this adventure, which after initial successes ended in dramatic failure, was William Walker. He considered himself—and in his own way was—a liberal, who enjoyed significant support in the United States. He proposed to fight the despotic legacy of Spanish power and extend his country's free institutions, but exclusively for the benefit of the authentic white community. For those alien to the 'strong, haughty race, bred to liberty' who were the custodians of 'a mission to place Americans under the rule of free laws', slavery was indicated. The decree of abolition promulgated in the wake of a movement that had found inspiration and support in Haiti was therefore cancelled.[102]

Only after the end of the Civil War did the United States agree to open diplomatic relations with Haiti. But it was a move bereft of any warmth, and in fact functional for a project of ethnic cleansing. The idea, also entertained by Lincoln, of depositing on the island of black power the ex-slaves, who were to be deported from the republic that continued to be inspired by the principle of white supremacy and purity, had not yet been abandoned.[103]

9. Liberalism and the critique of abolitionist radicalism

Hence a distinguished historian of slavery has appropriately warned against the tendency 'to confuse liberal principles with antislavery commitment'.[104] Let us examine the reaction of various authors and sections of the liberal movement to the conflict that issued in the Civil War. We shall set aside Calhoun and the other theorists of the slaveholding South. And we already know Disraeli's denunciation of the catastrophe of abolishing slavery in English colonies. On the point of the Confederacy's military collapse, Lord Acton wrote to the general who had commanded its army:

---

102   Richard Slotkin, *The Fatal Environment*, New York: Harper Perennial, 1994, pp. 245–61, in particular p. 257 (for the quotation from Walker).

103   Langley, *The Americas in the Age of Revolution*, p. 270.

104   David B. Davis, *The Problem of Slavery in the Age of Revolution*, Ithaca: Cornell University Press, 1975, p. 255.

I saw in States Rights the only availing check upon the absolutism of the sovereign will, and secession filled me with hope, not as the destruction but as the redemption of Democracy ... Therefore I deemed that you were fighting the battles of our liberty, our progress, and our civilization; and I mourn for the stake which was lost at Richmond more deeply than I rejoice over that which was saved at Waterloo.[105]

The defeat of the liberalism embodied in the Confederacy weighed more than the victory won some decades earlier by liberal England over Napoleonic despotism. Why? On the outbreak of the Civil War, although acknowledging 'all the horrors of American slavery', Lord Acton had unhesitatingly rejected 'the categorical prohibition of slavery' demanded by the abolitionists, as informed by an 'abstract, ideal absolutism' quite contrary to 'the English spirit',[106] and to the liberal spirit as such, characterized as it was by flexibility and practical common sense.

Some years earlier, Lieber had expressed himself in similar terms. He condemned the abolitionists as 'jacobins', followers of the 'fifth monarchy', incorrigible visionaries and fanatics: 'if people must have slaves it is their affair to keep them'.[107] Were such a declaration to be interpreted literally, not only would the right of states to self-government be inviolable, but also the right of each individual citizen to choose the type of property he preferred: let us not forget that at the time Lieber was himself a slave-owner! And hence while Disraeli ironized about the naive, misinformed 'philanthropy' of 'the pure abolitionists',[108] the American liberal took his distance from such circles even more clearly: 'I am not an abolitionist.'[109]

Lieber was on excellent terms with de Tocqueville, who in his turn declared: 'I have never been an abolitionist in the ordinary sense of the term'; 'I have always been strongly opposed to the abolitionist party'. What was meant by these declarations, contained in two letters from 1857? 'I have never believed it possible to destroy slavery in old states': the abolitionists' error was to seek 'to effect a premature, dangerous abolition of slavery in countries where this abominable institution has always existed'. We are dealing with a firm

---

105   Lord Acton, *Selected Writings*, 3 vols, ed. J. Rufus Fears, Indianapolis: Liberty Classics, 1985–88, vol. 1, pp. xx–xxi (letter to Robert E. Lee).

106   Ibid., vol. 1, pp. 257–8.

107   Lieber, quoted in Frank Freidel, *Francis Lieber*, Gloucester (MA): Peter Smith, 1968, p. 255.

108   Benjamin Disraeli, *Lord George Bentinck*, London: Colburn, 1852, pp. 324, 327.

109   Lieber, quoted in Freidel, *Francis Lieber*, p. 125.

condemnation of slavery at a theoretical level, but one without results on the practical level. The situation in the South could only be altered through an initiative from above and from the centre, thereby throwing 'the great experiment of Self-Government' into crisis. And so? Preservation of the status quo was appropriate. However regrettable, people must resign themselves to the continuation of slavery in the South for a long time. However,

> to introduce it into new states, to spread this horrible plague over a large area of the earth that has hitherto been immune to it, to impose all the crimes and all the miseries that accompany slavery on millions of men of future generations (masters or slaves), who could avoid this, is a crime against the human race, and this seems to me horrendous and inexcusable.[110]

In fact, an expansion of the zone of slavery had already occurred at the time of the annexation to the Union of Texas, seized from Mexico. De Tocqueville seemed to be ready to accept a compromise even more favourable to the slave-holding South, as emerges from a letter of 13 April 1857, once again sent to a transatlantic interlocutor:

> I agree with you about the fact that the greatest internal threat to the northern states today is not so much slavery as the corruption of democratic institutions … As for the policy permitting slavery to develop in a whole portion of the territory where it was hitherto unknown, I will concede, as you argue, that one can do nothing but tolerate this extension in the special, current interests of the Union.

Yet this could not go on indefinitely. It was inadmissible that there 'can be contained in the clauses of any contract the destruction of the right and duty of the present generation to prevent the spread of the most horrible of all social evils to millions and millions of men of future generations'.[111] The condemnation of slavery was passionate, but it was possibly necessary to tolerate the preservation and even the extension of the institution for some time. The reason emerges from a letter sent to the English economist Senior: dismemberment of the country which, more than any other, embodied the cause of liberty, 'would inflict a serious wound on the whole human race, stoking up war in the heart of a great continent from which it has been banished for more than a century'.[112]

---

110   Tocqueville, *Oeuvres complètes*, vol. 7, pp. 189–90 (letter to T. Sedgwick, 10 January 1857), p. 193 (letter to E. V. Childe, 2 April 1857).

111   Ibid., vol. 7, pp. 195–6 (letter to T. Sedgwick, 13 April 1857).

112   Ibid., vol. 6, pt 2, p. 190 (letter to Nassau William Senior, 4 September 1856).

De Tocqueville was ready to sacrifice the cause of abolishing slavery to the objective of preserving the unity and stability of the United States.

Although powerfully encouraged first by French defeat in the Seven Years' War and the loss of many of its colonies, and then by the revolution in San Domingo, radical abolitionism was a short-lived affair in France itself. Immediately after Thermidor, and in fact even at the moment of its preparation, the colonists' agitation in defence of the liberal principle of self-government (and white supremacy) resumed: it must be local assemblies that determined people's status and hence the condition of the blacks in the colonies. As we know, this was the position of the liberal Massiac Club. Those who resisted the Thermidorian turn were immediately branded traitors and renegades to the white race (see below, Chapter 8, §12). The 'Anglomane' and pro-slaveholding Malouet returned to hold positions of power under Napoleon,[113] who reintroduced colonial slavery and the black slave trade.

The liberal movement certainly did not respond to this restoration, terminated only by the revolution of February 1848, with united, decisive opposition. There were some (including Granier de Cassagnac) who defended the institution of slavery in the name of liberalism, who in fact (polemically observed an ardent abolitionist) even claimed 'a monopoly on liberalism'.[114] To be precise, along with 'liberalism', Cassagnac also professed himself a follower of 'democracy': positions no different from those maintained across the Atlantic by Calhoun, with the difference that the former regarded slavery as 'a provisional and empirical means of creating order' and 'maintaining the blacks in the apprenticeship of Christianity, work and the family'.[115] On the other side of the scale it is to be noted that, at least in his opponents' view, the French author was mistaken in having developed in justification of slavery a philosophy of history that did not maintain the spatial or racial delimitation of the institution, with a tendency hence to regress to positions à la Fletcher, who was now alien to the liberal movement. By contrast, an integral part of it was Thiers, who, drawing up a catastrophic balance sheet of the abolition of slavery in Britain's colonies, pointed to the 'base and barbarous idleness [of] Negroes left to their own devices'.[116]

---

113 Florence Gauthier, *Triomphe et mort du droit naturel en Révolution*, Paris: Presses Universitaires de France, 1992, pp. 260–3, 288.

114 Henri-Alexandre Wallon, Introduction to *Histoire de l'esclavage dans l'antiquité*, vol. 1, Aalen: Scientia, 1974, p. v.

115 See the letter from Granier de Cassagnac published in *Journal des Débats*, 23 July 1841.

116 Thiers, quoted in Seymour Drescher, *From Slavery to Freedom*, London: Macmillan, 1999, p. 167.

Guizot seemed more susceptible to abolitionist ideas. Nevertheless, he stressed their impracticality with an argument that is already familiar from US history: it would be necessary to compensate the owners of a legitimate form of property, but there were insufficient funds for this operation.[117] *Le Courier de la Gironde* came out in favour of a gradual abolitionism which, avoiding the 'savage liberty' of 'brutalized beings', would take the form of an extended phase of 'liberal slavery' (*esclavage libéral*)—i.e. a somewhat mitigated slavery.[118] Likewise opposed to hasty measures was de Tocqueville. In May 1847, noting that the 'Bey of Tunisia' had already abolished the 'odious institution'—which in Muslim countries, by the French liberal's admission, took a 'milder' form— de Tocqueville expressed the opinion that 'we should doubtless only proceed to the abolition of slavery with care and moderation'.[119]

We can conclude with a general consideration relating to the France of the July Monarchy: 'Immediate and complete emancipation was not even considered as an abolitionist program until less than a year before the Revolution of 1848.' In fact, the golden age of French liberalism, far from involving the abolition of slavery, saw its expansion: 'as a result of the expanding French conquest of Algeria, there was far more territory with slaves under French sovereignty by the mid-1840s than there had been at the time of the July Revolution in 1830.'[120]

10. The enduring effectiveness of the black revolution from below

But if things stood thus, how was the abolition of slavery achieved? Although firmly opposed by a formidable international coalition and the liberal movement as a whole, the San Domingo revolution had a lasting influence, which proved all the stronger when conflicts within the community of the free and the white community as a whole intensified. We already know the decisive role played by the country governed by ex-slaves in propelling the independence movement in Latin America towards abolitionist positions.

Outside the southern United States, slavery continued to be very much present in the European colonies in the Caribbean. However, here too Haiti's

---

117   Cf. ibid., pp. 167–8.
118   André-Jean Tudesq, *Les grands notables en France*, Paris: Presses Universitaires de France, 1964, p. 842.
119   Tocqueville, *Oeuvres complètes*, vol. 3, pt 1, p. 330.
120   Drescher, *From Slavery to Freedom*, pp. 163, 167.

presence made itself felt. Proceeding in 1822 to annexation of the Spanish part of the island, the ex-slaves now in power delivered a further serious blow to the institution of slavery. The following year, the revolt of the black slaves in Demerara (today's Guyana) erupted. This was a colony that had been affected by the upheavals which had reverberated in San Domingo from France. In 1794–95 a revolution exported and imposed by French forces had transformed Holland into the Batavian Republic and forced the Prince of Orange to flee to England. In the wake of events in Demerara, at the time under Dutch control, liberal agitation had developed, promoted by slave-owners who, witnessing the emergence of the prospect of black emancipation on the San Domingo model, had rapidly abandoned any sympathy for France and sought Britain's intervention and protection.[121]

But the incorporation of Demerara into the British Empire did not extinguish the fire, which smouldered under the ashes. A black revolt broke out in 1823 and led to the death of three whites; martial law was proclaimed and 250 slaves were killed or executed. And yet, repressed in one place, revolts exploded again some years later and only a short distance away—this time in Jamaica, in 1831. In both cases Methodist and Baptist missionaries played a significant role. By converting the slaves to Christianity, they furnished them with a culture, consciousness and the possibility of meeting and communicating that clashed irreconcilably with the de-humanization and commodification of human livestock upon which the institution of slavery was based. The first revolt saw the death sentence for the Reverend John Smith, and his death in prison shortly before execution of the sentence and the arrival from London of a notice of pardon. The second became known as the 'war of the Baptists'. In both cases, in addition to rebellious slaves, the repression by the white dominant class struck the Baptist and Methodist community. In Jamaica hundreds of black Christians were flogged, tortured or shot; and English missionaries also suffered arrest and humiliation of every kind. In fact, in neighbouring Barbados churches were sacked and destroyed and there were riots and attempted pogroms against the Methodist community. The colonists' hatred of the non-conformist churches, accused of encouraging the slave revolt, could not be contained.[122] It was a danger that seemed all the more real and immediate because of Haiti's proximity and the processes of emancipation underway in Latin America. Thanks to this geographical proximity, there now intervened in the struggle (wrote

---

121   Emília Viotti da Costa, *Crowns of Glory, Tears of Blood*, New York: Oxford University Press, 1994, p. 20.

122   David B. Davis, *Slavery and Human Progress*, Oxford and New York: Oxford University Press, 1986, pp. 195–8.

a white Jamaican to his governor) a 'third party' (in addition to the Crown, prompted in a reformist direction by Christian abolitionism, and the colonists, engaged in defence of self-government and their property). And this 'third party' comprised the slave, who 'knows his strength, and will assert his claim to freedom'.[123]

At this point, the abolition of slavery in the colonies presented itself to the dominant class of liberal England as the requisite way out in the face of two challenges: the first consisted in the black slaves' revolution from below; the second in the indignation that was widespread in the British Christian community which, with growing impatience, demanded decisive measures against the colonists, guilty of enslaving blacks and persecuting Christians.

11. The role of Christian fundamentalism

This second challenge brings us to a movement we have not hitherto been concerned with, and which cannot be confused with either the liberal tradition or French-style radicalism. While the crisis that soon led to the black revolution in San Domingo was deepening, at a time when the campaign to suppress the slave trade seemed to be at an impasse, the dying John Wesley wrote a heartfelt letter to William Wilberforce:

> Unless the Divine power has raised you up to be an Athanasius contra mundum, I see not how you can go through your glorious enterprise, in opposing that execrable villainy which is the scandal of religion, of England, and of human nature. Unless God has raised you up for this very thing, you will be worn out by the opposition of men and devils; but if God be for you who can be against you? Are all of them together stronger than God? Oh be not weary of well-doing. Go in the name of God, and in the power of His might, till even American slavery, the vilest that ever saw the sun, shall vanish away before it.[124]

The recipient of this letter was unquestionably one of the major actors in the struggle that led to the abolition first of the slave trade and then of slavery as such. A fervent Christian, member of the House of Commons and on close

---

123 Williams, *Capitalism and Slavery*, p. 207.
124 Robert Isaac Wilberforce, *The Life of William Wilberforce*, 5 vols, London: Murray, 1838, vol. 1, p. 297 (letter from Wesley to Wilberforce, 24 February 1791).

terms with Pitt the Younger, while he received honorary French citizenship in 1792 for his anti-slavery campaign, he had nothing to do with the revolution of 1789 or, a fortiori, with radicalism. Far from welcoming the black slave revolt in San Domingo, he continued in his unwavering support for the British government, which, during the war against France, was the guarantor in the West Indies of the repression of slave revolts and the preservation of slavery.

But if he identified with the England of the time and its dominant class, Wilberforce can scarcely be regarded as a liberal. Prior to directing his efforts against slavery, his religious zeal was engaged in the 'reform of public manners', to be advanced through the foundation of a new society intended as the 'guardian of the religion and morals of the people', which proposed to struggle 'against Vice and Immorality' and even aspired to the 'suppression of Vice'. Hence the crusade launched against publications branded blasphemous and indecent, against rural feasts considered licentious, against the non-observance of the Sabbath among the popular classes.[125] Only subsequently did Christian fervour target the particular sin that was slavery—an institution completely unacceptable not only because of the obstacles it often put in the way of the spread of Christianity among slaves, but also because of the sexual libertinism in which it permitted their masters to indulge. Thus, another prominent supporter of English abolitionism (James Ramsay), along with slavery, called for an attack on 'arbitrary divorces and bigamy'. Similarly, Granville Sharp combined abolitionist campaigning with a struggle against divorce legislation which, in flagrant violation of divine law, allowed the guilty couple to proceed to new weddings; and from this he moved on to announce that, together with those responsible for the slave trade and their accomplices, adulterers and those guilty of immorality would not escape divine punishment.[126]

In Sharp's view, defenders of the institution of slavery were 'refined modern Sadducees'. The Sadducees of Biblical fame had not hesitated to come to terms with Hellenistic and Roman culture, thereby contaminating Judaism and the word of God, and depriving them of their purity. Caught up in the enjoyment of wealth and the material world, they had forgotten or denied spiritual, otherworldly values. According to the English abolitionist, the modern Sadducees were no different. Ultimately, they were susceptible to the blandishments of the Demon, or the 'Demon of Demons'. But the Bible must not be venerated in church, while remaining a dead letter in real life. On the contrary, it must serve as a guide in all political questions and the smallest problems of everyday

---

125 Blackburn, *Overthrow of Colonial Slavery*, p. 142.
126 Davis, *The Problem of Slavery in the Age of Revolution*, pp. 387, 394.

life. All the more so in that the turning point was at hand: the times in which slavery continued to survive were the 'latter days of Infidelity & Deism', representing the agony of the apocalyptic 'Beast'.[127]

There is no doubt that here we have an attitude which, in contemporary terms, we would define as fundamentalist. It is a trait that was even more clearly exhibited in the United States. Here too Christian abolitionism had a programme which, along with slavery, wanted to attack vice and immorality as such. Theodore Parker denounced as contrary to the Scriptures and divine law (the only truly valid law) the 'usury' by which 'banking capital' was stained, the 'brothels' and bars that sold rum, and which the police not only did not target, but in fact frequented more assiduously than the 'house of God'.[128]

Compared with Britain, there was in fact a novel element. In the United States, where the law on the return of fugitive slaves required all citizens to be complicit with an institution that became ever more odious, a delicate dilemma of conscience emerged. The 'higher laws' of Holy Scripture must not be forgotten. For a true Christian, admonished the English abolitionist Sharp in an indignant letter to Franklin, the other laws were 'so clearly null and void by their iniquity, that it would be even a *crime* to regard them as law'.[129]

Along with its fundamentalist character, the radicalism of Christian abolitionism was strengthened in the United States. 'When rulers have inverted their function and enacted wickedness into a law that treads down the inalienable rights of man', declared Parker, the Christian must know how to go to the limit: 'I know no ruler but God, no law but natural Justice ... I am not afraid of men. I can offend them. I care nothing for their hate or their esteem. But I should not dare to violate His laws, come what may come ...'[130] Sanctioned by Holy Scripture, divine, eternal, natural law was, in any event, inviolable: 'To say that there is no law higher than what the State can make is practical atheism ... If there is no God to make a law for me, then there is no God for me.' The challenge to constituted authority was open and declared: 'REBELLION TO TYRANTS IS OBEDIENCE TO GOD'.[131]

The federal Constitution, which obliged the Union as a whole to defend the slaveholding states against any potential slave revolution, seemed to William Garrison 'An Agreement with Hell' and a 'Covenant with Death'. In 1845

---

127 Sharp, quoted in Davis, Ibid., pp. 387–90, 395.
128 Parker, quoted in Henry S. Commager, *Theodore Parker*, Gloucester (MA): Peter Smith, 1978, p. 212.
129 Sharp, quoted in Davis, *The Problem of Slavery in the Age of Revolution*, p. 401.
130 Parker, quoted in Commager, *Theodore Parker*, p. 207.
131 Parker, quoted in ibid., pp. 208, 210–11.

another abolitionist, Wendell Phillips, drew attention to slave-owners' purchase of the most important public offices and the tripling of slavery that had occurred since the ratification of the federal Constitution, which came to be branded as a 'pro-Slavery Compact'. The coexistence of slaveholding states and free states was no longer licit, unless the latter wanted to become 'partners in the guilt and responsible for the sin of slavery'.[132] Street demonstrations in which the American Constitution was burnt were understandable. In the years preceding the Civil War, when he briefly harboured the illusion that the South was on the point of giving in, Parker exulted in these terms: 'The Devil is in great wrath because he knoweth that his time is short.'[133]

On the basis of this view, no compromise was possible. And Garrison explicitly stated as much. His polemic against defenders of the institution of slavery and their accomplices assumed openly threatening tones. But also unequivocal was his condemnation of theorists of '*gradual* abolition' and 'moderation', and even of those in the North who displayed 'apathy' or limited enthusiasm for the 'standard of emancipation'[134] and the struggle against slavery, that 'heinous crime in the sight of God'.[135] Abolitionist radicalism and Christian fundamentalism were closely interwoven, as emerges from the summons to a crusade against 'the governments of this world', which 'in their essential elements, and as present administered ... are all Anti-Christ'. This involved achieving

> the emancipation of our whole race from the dominion of man, from the thraldom of self, from the government of brute force, from the bondage of sin—and bringing them under the dominion of God, the control of an inward spirit, the government of the law of love, and into the obedience and liberty of Christ ...[136]

The fundamentalist character of such positions did not escape Calhoun. He thundered against 'the rabid fanatics, who regard slavery as a sin, and thus regarding it, deem it their highest duty to destroy it, even should it involve the destruction of the constitution and the Union'. For them abolition was a conscientious obligation; only thus did they conceive it possible to liberate

---

132   Phillips, quoted in Paul Finkelman, *Slavery and the Founders*, Armonk (NY): Sharpe, 1996, pp. 1–5.

133   Parker, quoted in Commager, *Theodore Parker*, p. 254.

134   Garrison, quoted in Richard Hofstadter, ed., *Great Issues in American History*, 3 vols, New York: Vintage Books, 1958–82, vol. 2, pp. 321–2.

135   Garrison, quoted in Aileen S. Kraditor, *Means and Ends in American Abolitionism*, Chicago: Dee, 1989, p. 5.

136   Garrison, quoted in ibid., p. 86.

themselves from the agonizing sense of being accomplices of the unforgivable 'sin' allegedly represented by slavery, against which they then proclaimed a full-scale 'crusade', 'a general crusade'.[137] In the view of southern theorists, these Christians blinded by abolitionist fury were alien to the liberal world and substantially akin to Jacobins. In fact, a movement similar to French radicalism tended to emerge in the United States, at various times and in various modes, but always on the basis of the crisis of the English and American models. The crisis of the first coincided with the rebellion against the London government. What provoked or intensified the crisis of the second was the progressive isolation of the North American republic as a slaveholding state, engaged not only in the defence of slavery but also its expansion, and which resisted unperturbed, despite the disappearance of that institution first in much of Latin America and subsequently in British and French colonies. At this point, the country that at its birth had celebrated itself as the land of liberty appeared as the champion of slavery.

There thus developed in the United States as well a radicalism that drew on Christianity. Such a 'party' no longer identified with either the English or the American model. It rejected both the spatial and the racial delimitation of the community of the free, and thus regarded the exclusion clauses that characterized the English and American models as unacceptable. And in order to change things, it did not preclude appeals to the revolutionary initiative of the excluded. This was the religious and political climate in which John Brown's armed raid into Virginia in 1859 matured, intent on inciting a slave uprising and convinced that, without the shedding of blood, there was no remission of sins. The attempt failed miserably and ended with the protagonist being hanged, but Parker reiterated the slaves' right to armed rebellion: sooner or later, 'the Fire of Vengeance may be waked up even in an African's heart'.[138]

12. What is radicalism? The contrast with liberalism

Formed in the wake of disappointment in the English and American models, how did 'radicalism' differ from liberalism? The answer is obvious, if we refer to authors like Locke and Calhoun, profoundly liberal and yet at the same time without any doubts as to the legitimacy of black slavery. The answer is not

---

137   John C. Calhoun, *Union and Liberty*, ed. R. M. Lence, Indianapolis: Liberty Classics, 1992, pp. 528–31, 261–2, 469.

138   Parker, quoted in Commager, *Theodore Parker*, p. 254.

even difficult if we draw a comparison with authors such as Burke, Jefferson and Acton who, notwithstanding reservations and criticisms of the institution, on various grounds represented ideological and political reference points for the slaveholding South, or even continued to defend it to the end. The line of demarcation also proves sufficiently clear if we compare authors like Blackstone and Montesquieu, who tended to contest 'slavery among ourselves' rather than slavery as such, with a radicalism committed to rejecting both the spatial delimitation (the English model until 1833) and the racial delimitation (the American model until 1865) of the community of the free. But how is de Tocqueville clearly distinguished from authors like Diderot, Condorcet and Schoelcher, whom I have included in the process of French radicalism's formation and development? What sense does it make to situate in two different, even opposed formations de Tocqueville and Condorcet, who were, respectively, one of the great critics of the Terror and one of its most illustrious victims? Is it right to include in the same party French and American radicals who adopted such a different attitude towards Christianity?

Before answering these questions, it is worth lingering over something that characterized the liberal tradition from its outset. Let us take authors like Montesquieu, Smith and Millar. Although condemning slavery more or less sharply, all three continued to regard England—a country in the front rank in the slave trade—as a model. In no instance did criticism or condemnation of slavery involve exclusion of the beneficiaries or theorists of the institution from the community of the free and the liberal party. On more than one occasion, Burke distanced himself from the institution of slavery, but when the conflict between the two Atlantic shores erupted he not only celebrated the love of liberty which particularly animated southern colonies, but disdainfully rejected the idea that, in an attempt to suppress the rebellion, appeal might be made to 'servile hands'.[139] In other words, the British Whig continued to include slave-owners in the community of the free while excluding a priori their victims.

Criticism of the institution of slavery was clear and firm in Hume. But this did not prevent him from asserting that 'European nations' represented 'that part of the globe [which] maintain[s] sentiments of liberty, honour, equity and valour superior to the rest of mankind'.[140] By contrast, there was reason to believe that blacks were 'naturally inferior to the whites' and inferior to

---

139   Burke, *Works*, vol. 3, p. 67.
140   David Hume, *The History of England*, 6 vols, Indianapolis: Liberty Classics, 1983–85, vol. 1, p. 161.

the point of lacking any 'symptoms' of 'ingenuity' and free spirit.[141] So once again, despite the condemnation of slavery, it was its beneficiaries—not its victims—who formed an integral part of the community of the free and the liberal party.

The boundaries of the community of the free could lose something of their naturalistic rigidity; but the rituals of self-celebration, and the enormous repression it was based on, persisted. In 1772 Arthur Young calculated that, out of 775 million global inhabitants, only 33 million enjoyed liberty; and they were concentrated in a fairly restricted zone of the planet, excluding Asia, Africa and virtually all of America, as well as the southern and eastern parts of Europe itself.[142] This was a theme subsequently taken up and eloquently developed by Adam Smith:

> We are apt to imagine that slavery is quite extirpated because we know nothing of it in this part of the world, but even at present it is almost universal. A small part of the west of Europe is the only portion of the globe that is free from it, and is nothing in comparison with the vast continents where it still prevails.[143]

In similar vein, Millar contrasted 'Great Britain, in which liberty is generally so well understood, and so highly valued', with 'all those tribes of barbarians, in different parts of the world, with which we have any correspondence' and among whom 'the practice of domestic slavery' continued to rage.[144] Europe and the West were complacently depicted as a tiny island of liberty and civilization in a tempestuous ocean of tyranny, slavery and barbarism. In order to indulge in such self-celebration, Young, Smith and Millar were in fact obliged to overlook a far from trivial detail: the slave trade, which involved the most brutal form of slavery—chattel slavery—and in which western Europe, starting precisely with liberal England, was engaged for centuries.

De Tocqueville's attitude was not very different. When he published *Democracy in America*, there were few countries or colonies in the western hemisphere where slavery persisted, since it had been abolished in much of Latin America and the British colonies. In the interval between the publication of the

---

141   David Hume, *Essays, Moral, Political, and Literary*, Liberty Classics: Indianapolis, 1987, p. 208 n.

142   Cf. Seymour Drescher, *Capitalism and Antislavery*, Oxford and New York: Oxford University Press, 1987, p. 17.

143   Adam Smith, *Lectures on Jurisprudence*, Indianapolis: Liberty Classics, 1982, pp. 451–2.

144   John Millar, *The Origin of the Distinction of Ranks*, Aalen: Scientia, 1986, pp. 289, 247.

first and second volumes of the work, the United States introduced into Texas the institution that should have been synonymous with the absolute power of man over man. But this prompted no uncertainty in the French liberal when it came to identifying the American continent as the locus of liberty. Volume One of *Democracy in America* appeared shortly after the abolition of slavery in the British colonies. But that would appear to have been an irrelevant event in the opinion of de Tocqueville, who, when it came to comparing England and the United States, had no doubt that the latter country most fully embodied the cause of liberty. And Jefferson, the president slave-owner and unyielding opponent of the country born out of a revolution by black slaves, seemed to the French liberal to be 'the greatest democrat whom the democracy of America has as yet produced'.[145]

Lincoln himself initially conducted the Civil War as a crusade against rebellion and separatism, not for the abolition of slavery, which could continue to survive in states loyal to central government. It was only later, with the recruitment of blacks into the Union army and hence with the direct intervention of slaves and ex-slaves in the conflict, that the civil war between whites was transformed into a revolution, conducted partly from above and partly from below, making the abolition of slavery inevitable. But in the first phase of the war the Union did not a priori exclude slave states from its bosom, just as liberal critics of the institution of slavery did not expel those who had a different and even contrary position on the problem from the liberal party.

The tendency we are examining finds fullest expression in Lieber. Cautious criticisms of the institution of slavery did not prevent him, even on the immediate eve of the Civil War, from attributing to the United States—the country that even more than England embodied the great cause of 'liberal institutions' and 'self-government'—the 'great mission' of spreading liberty throughout the world. '[E]very American' must always bear in mind the grandeur of the constitutional principles and texts of his country. Otherwise, they would resemble 'the missionary that should proceed to convert the world without bible or prayer-book'.[146]

While it was the sacred text of liberty for the liberal author, for the radicals Garrison and Phillips the US Constitution, which sanctioned slavery and the racial state, was an instrument of Satan. Over and above the very different significance assigned to the problem of slavery, here we have two opposed

---

145 Alexis de Tocqueville, *Democracy in America*, London: Everyman's Library, 1994, vol. 1, p. 206.

146 Francis Lieber, *Civil Liberty and Self-Government*, Philadelphia: Lippincott, 1859, pp. 264, 21.

delimitations of political geography, of the camp of friends and enemies. Notwithstanding the argument and conflict over slavery, liberalism's various exponents continued to recognize themselves as members of the same party and the same community of the free. By contrast, excluded from it were blacks, whom at an interval of decades Jefferson and Lincoln intended to deport from the Union and who, not by chance, after emancipation first in the North and then in the South did not come to enjoy either political or civil equality. Montesquieu and de Tocqueville, not to mention Lieber and Acton, could indeed criticize slavery, but it was understood that that their interlocutors were not black slaves but their masters. The latter were called upon to demonstrate moral sensitivity and political consistency and hence agree to expunge a stain that affected the credibility of the community of the free as such.

Condorcet's attitude was very different. Here is how he addressed the black slaves in 1781:

> Dear friends, although I am not the same colour as you, I have always regarded you as my brothers. Nature has fashioned you to have the same spirit, the same reason and the same virtues as whites. I am only speaking here of whites in Europe, for when it comes to whites in the colonies, I shall not insult you by comparing them to you ... Should one set off in search of a man in the islands of America, one would certainly not find him among the populations of white flesh.[147]

The French philosopher was not yet aware of it, but the ruling group in the North American republic was on the point of being situated outside not only the party of liberty, but even the human race. What we have here is a political and ideological current different from liberalism—the radicalism that had been formed or was in the process of being formed. It might seem debatable to apply this category to an author who recommended extreme gradualism in the process of abolishing slavery. But that is not the main point. Marat himself, in 1791, proposed 'gradually to prepare the transition from slavery to liberty'. And yet, already unequivocally condemning 'the barbarism of the colonists', it was not to them that he looked to make the desired change, and not even to the National Assembly which, coming to terms with the slaveholders, rode roughshod over the rights of man and 'the sacred foundations of the Constitution'.[148] The actual interlocutors tended to be the black slaves themselves, as would

---

147 Condorcet, *Oeuvres*, vol. 7, p. 63.
148 Cf. *L'Ami du peuple*, 18 May 1791, quoted in Benot, *La révolution française*, pp. 120–1.

become clear in the course of Marat's subsequent evolution. As for Condorcet, despite the gradualist character of his abolitionism, he deflected back onto slave-holding whites the de-humanizing drive they had mobilized against blacks.

This was an attitude that could also develop on the basis of a profoundly Christian consciousness. Here is how Garrison expressed himself in 1841 on the subject of slave-owners:

> No political, no religious copartnership should be had with them, for they are the meanest of thieves and the worst of robbers. We should as soon think of entering into a compact with the convicts at Botany Bay and New Zealand ... We do not acknowledge them to be within the pale of Christianity, of republicanism, of humanity.[149]

But some decades earlier the English abolitionist Percival Stockdale had already declared: '*We* are the savages; the Africans act like *men*; like beings endowed with rational and immortal minds'.[150] Once again, indignation at the treatment inflicted on the black slaves could even conduce to a de-humanization of the de-humanizers.

In regarding slaves as their interlocutors, radicals did not hesitate to appeal to a revolution from below by victims of the institution it was intended to abolish. Even prior to the revolution by San Domingo's slaves, Raynal and Diderot's *History of the Two Indias* evoked a massive uprising, led by a black Spartacus, which might involve replacing the *Code noir* in force by a '*Code blanc*' that repaid the slaveholders for the injustices they had committed.[151] Within the liberal tradition, in Smith we can come across evocation of a dictatorship from above putting an end to the scandal of an institution that sullied the community of the free, but certainly not hopes for a revolution from below. We know the sympathy or admiration with which Grégoire and Schoelcher viewed Toussaint L'Ouverture and Haiti. These are two names that do not appear in de Tocqueville. In connection with San Domingo, he limited himself to mentioning the 'bloody catastrophe that has put an end to its existence'.[152] Paradoxically, the island ceased to exist the moment it put an end, for the first time in the Americas, to the institution of slavery!

---

149 Garrison, quoted in Charles Edward Merriam, *A History of American Political Theories*, New York: Kelley, 1969, p. 209.

150 Stockdale, quoted in David Geggus, 'British Opinion and the Emergence of Haiti', in James Walvin, ed., *Slavery and British Society*, London: Macmillan, 1982, p. 127.

151 Raynal, *Histoire philosophique et politique des Deux Indes*, pp. 202–3.

152 Tocqueville, *Oeuvres complètes*, vol. 4, pt 1, p. 278.

Finally, Diderot reported an observation by Helvétius: 'What is the cause of England's extreme power? Its government.' He followed up this assessment with a polemical question: 'But what is the cause of the extreme poverty of Scotland and Ireland?'[153] Judgement of the metropolis could not be separated from judgement of the colonies and semi-colonies. From the standpoint of authors like Diderot and Schoelcher, England and the United States, the holy sites of liberty in de Tocqueville's view, were responsible for the most ferocious and barbarous despotism. Even when it criticized slavery, the liberal tradition did not question the identification of the West with civilization and of the colonial world with barbarism. Radicalism's position was different: in the first instance, it identified and denounced barbarism in those responsible for, and complicit with, the most macroscopic violation of the rights and dignity of man.

Marx and Engels may be regarded as critical inheritors of radicalism. For the first in particular, not only was it epistemologically and politically arbitrary to ignore the politico-social reality of the colonies, but (as we shall see) those colonies were the requisite starting-point for understanding the 'barbarism' of bourgeois society.

13. Liberalism, the self-celebration of the community of the free and repression of the lot imposed on colonial peoples

The discourse developed by liberalism is profoundly marked by repression of the lot imposed on colonial peoples. The self-celebration of the land of the free or the people of the free proved all the more persuasive in that it overlooked the slavery inflicted on colonial populations or populations of colonial origin. Only on this condition could Montesquieu, Blackstone and the American revolutionaries point to England or the United States as a model of liberty.

This also applies to de Tocqueville. He lucidly and unsparingly described the inhuman treatment meted out to Indians and blacks. The former were forced to endure the 'frightful sufferings' attendant upon 'forced migrations' (the successive deportations imposed by the whites), and were even close to being wiped off the face of the earth.[154] As to the blacks, let us leave to one side the specifically slaveholding states of the South: What was the situation in the rest? Over and above harsh material living conditions, 'a wretched and precarious

---

153 Diderot, 'Réfutation suivie de l'ouvrage d'Helvétius', p. 895.
154 Tocqueville, *Democracy in America*, vol. 1, pp. 339, 354–5.

existence', desperate poverty and a higher mortality rate than among slaves,[155] on the notionally free black also weighed exclusion from the enjoyment of civil rights (as well as political rights): he was subjected to the 'tyranny of the law' and the 'intolerance of customs' (see above, Chapter 2, §7). And so, discounting the Far West and the South, even in the case of the free states we cannot speak of democracy or even strictly of the rule of law. But that was not the conclusion reached by de Tocqueville, who celebrated the democracy, 'alive, active, triumphant', he saw operative in the United States:

> You will see there a people among whom conditions are more equal than they have ever been among us; among whom the social structure, the customs, the laws, everything is democratic; among whom everything comes from the people and returns to it, and where, nevertheless, each individual enjoys an independence that is fuller, and a liberty that is greater, than in any other time or place on earth.[156]

While he felt sympathy for the tragedy of the Indians and blacks, their fate had no epistemological relevance and in no way altered his overall political judgement. The programmatic declaration made by de Tocqueville at the start of the chapter devoted to the problem of 'the three races that inhabit the territory of the United States' is unequivocal: 'The principal task that I had imposed upon myself is now performed: I have shown, as far as I was able, the laws and the customs of the American democracy. Here I might stop'. It was only in order to avoid possible disappointment on the reader's part that de Tocqueville spoke of relations between the three 'races': 'These topics are collaterally connected with my subject without forming a part of it; they are American without being democratic, and to portray democracy has been my principal aim.'[157] Democracy could be defined and liberty lauded focusing exclusively on the white community. If, instead, we regard this abstraction as arbitrary, and bear in mind the entanglement of slavery and liberty revealed by authoritative US scholars, we cannot but be even more surprised by de Tocqueville's epistemological than his political naivety. He celebrated as the locus of liberty one of the few countries in the New World where racial chattel slavery reigned and flourished and which, at the time of the French liberal's journey, had as its president Andrew Jackson, slave-owner and protagonist of a policy of deporting and

---

155   Ibid., vol. 1, p. 368 and n. 41.

156   Tocqueville, *Oeuvres complètes*, vol. 3, pt 3, p. 174 (speech to the Constituent Assembly, 12 September 1848).

157   Tocqueville, *Democracy in America*, vol. 1, p. 331.

decimating the Indian; a president, moreover, who, blocking the circulation of abolitionist material by post, also struck at the freedom of expression of significant sections of the white community.

Such naivety reached its culmination in a French follower of de Tocqueville—namely, Édouard Laboulaye. He too contrasted the United States with a France plagued by constant revolutionary upheavals. In the former, he observed in 1849 in the inaugural lecture (published separately the following year) of a course devoted to US history, a Constitution characterized by extraordinary 'wisdom' and rejection of any 'demagogic' element made it possible to enjoy peace and, at the same time, the greatest liberty and 'the most absolute political equality'—an equality that was 'complete, absolute, in laws and customs alike'.[158] As to the problem of the relations between the three races referred to by de Tocqueville, nothing remains in the text we are examining but the celebration of the remarkable successes achieved by 'a nation of European race', by this 'strong race of emigrants' or this 'people of Puritans'—in other words, the 'American race'. Even if it was a story that had unfolded across the Atlantic, it covered 'our race' (European and white) as a whole in glory.[159] This was a view reiterated ten years later, in an emotional essay published on the occasion of de Tocqueville's death: the homage paid to the author of *Democracy in America* ended with homage to the 'beautiful federal Constitution that has protected the liberty of the United States for seventy years'.[160] We are on the eve of the Civil War. But even its outbreak does not seem to have prompted any second thoughts in Laboulaye: it was understood that 'complete, candid, sincere liberty' reigned in the United States. The bloody conflict underway demonstrated the 'courage' of a 'free people who sacrificed everything to maintain the unity' of the country.[161]

Only when reconstructing the history of America in the colonial period did Laboulaye feel obliged to confront the issue of slavery. Although mitigated by reference to 'climate' (which rendered work intolerable for whites but not blacks), historical circumstances (at the time it was at its height, 'the slave trade was regarded as a pious undertaking'), and the particular characteristics of the people subjected to it (it involved a 'race of eternal minors'),[162] condemnation

---

158 Édouard Laboulaye, *De la Constitution américaine et de l'utilité de son étude*, Paris: Hennuyer, 1850, pp. 10–11.

159 Ibid., pp. 6, 9–10, 17.

160 Édouard Laboulaye, *L'état et ses limites suivi d'essais politiques*, Paris: Charpentier, 1863, p. 187.

161 Édouard Laboulaye, *Le parti libéral*, Paris: Charpentier, 1863, pp. viii–ix.

162 Édouard Laboulaye, *Histoire des États-Unis*, 3 vols, Paris: Charpentier, 1866, vol. 1, pp. 420–2.

of the institution was sharp. In the first volume, whose Preface is dated 1855, we read:

> In half of the United States there are two societies established on the same soil: the one powerful, active, united and prudent; the other weak, disunited, indifferent and exploited like cattle. And yet this despised herd is a constant threat to America ... The stain that soils this great society places it beneath Europe.[163]

Although sketching this realistic picture, the Preface continued to celebrate the United States indiscriminately as the privileged site of liberty, guaranteed and guarded by an 'admirable Constitution'.[164] However hard the lot of the blacks—silence persisted about the Indians—it was irrelevant when it came to formulating an overall judgement of the country under investigation. But there is more. Laboulaye acknowledged that slavery made its oppressive influence felt on the white master himself: he was denied the right to educate and eman-cipate his own slave, even if he or she was a child born from a relationship with a slave. He was required by law to inflict even the most drastic of punishments, including castration, on the guilty slave.[165] However, although criticized, these serious interferences with the individual freedom of white property-owners did not in the slightest darken the bright picture we already know.

In 1864 Laboulaye denounced the privilege granted by the 'three-fifths' con-stitutional provision to the 'particular, superior race' made up of the 'great lords' of the South who were the slave-owners (see above, Chapter 4, §1). But if things stood thus, if inequality marked relations within the elite itself, if even within the white community there was a privileged 'particular race', what was the meaning of the claim that the United States was characterized by 'the most absolute political equality'? Laboulaye felt no need to revise his positions. On the contrary, he did not hesitate to reiterate them in the Preface to the third volume, which continued to celebrate the American Revolution as the sole genuinely democratic one.

Like colonies in the strict sense, Ireland continued to be ignored. In the course of his journey to the British Isles, de Tocqueville visited the unhappy island and described its desperate situation unsparingly. It was not simply that 'the poverty is horrible'; denied here was liberal freedom itself, crushed by

---

163   Ibid., vol. 1, p. 431.
164   Ibid., vol. 1, p. vi.
165   Ibid., vol. 1, pp. 425–7, 430.

'military tribunals' and a 'large gendarmerie hated by the people'. At this point a comparison between England and Ireland occurred: 'The two aristocracies I have referred to have the same origin, the same customs and almost the same laws. Yet the one has for centuries given the English one of the best governments in the world, while the other has given the Irish one of the most detestable imaginable'.[166] This is an astonishing statement: not only are readers not informed that the aristocracy dominant in Ireland was itself British or of British origin, but they have the impression that they are dealing with two different countries, not two regions of a single state, subject to the authority of the same government and the same crown.

We can then understand de Tocqueville's admiring conclusion: 'I see the Englishman secure under the protection of his laws'.[167] Clearly, the Irish were not subsumed under the category of 'English', but such non-subsumption does not seem to be a problem, does not affect the laudatory judgement passed on the country visited and held up as a model of liberty.

14. The colonial question and the differential development of radicalism in France, England and the United States

Reference has sometimes been made to 'philosophic radicalism' in connection with Bentham and his school.[168] The theorist of utilitarianism adopted a debunking tone towards his country's political, legal and ideological tradition. He did hesitate to denounce the 'almost universal corruption' that raged in England and the ill-starred role of a 'corrupted and corrupting aristocracy'.[169] He did not even spare the Glorious Revolution, despite the religious aura habitually surrounding it: the *'original compact*—the compact between king and people—was a fabulous one—the *supervening* compact—the compact between King, Lords, and Commons, was but too real a one',[170] and sanctioned the domination of an oligarchy.

However, it is sufficient to look at the attitude Bentham took towards the liberal tradition's exclusion clauses to realize that we are very far removed from

---

166   Tocqueville, *Oeuvres complètes*, vol. 5, pt 2, pp. 94, 128, 133.

167   Ibid., vol. 5, pt 2, p. 91.

168   See Élie Halévy, *The Growth of Philosophic Radicalism*, trans. Mary Morris, London: Faber & Faber, 1972.

169   Jeremy Bentham, *The Works*, 11 vols, ed. John Bowring, Edinburgh: Tait, 1838–43, vol. 3, p. 442.

170   Ibid., vol. 4, p. 447.

radicalism in the sense specified here. Of the refuse and 'dross' and those confined in workhouses, we have already spoken. We must now concern ourselves with the condition of the blacks. Bentham included 'the still unabrogated sanction given to domestic slavery on account of difference of colour' among the 'imperfections of detail' to be found even in the 'matchlessly felicitous system' of the United States.[171] Starting from this rather euphemistic description of the institution of slavery, the English liberal stressed that a project of emancipation must proceed with extreme gradualism, and be implemented exclusively from above. In a text from 1822, we come across a significant declaration: 'The French have already discovered that the blackness of the skin is no reason why a human being should be abandoned without redress to the caprice of a tormentor.'[172] We are led to think of the abolition of slavery in the French colonies. But instead, as a note makes clear, the reference is to Louis XIV's *Code noir*!

As for gradualism, this was necessary for the purposes not only of respecting 'rights of property' (which must be compensated for the loss suffered), but also of educating slaves for liberty.[173] Bentham wanted an emancipation 'lottery' that might occur at the moment of hereditary transmission of this special property, and from which one-tenth of the slaves owned by the deceased could benefit. An appeal to masters to demonstrate flexibility was the counterpart of indignant condemnation of any initiative from below:

> The injustice and the calamity which have accompanied precipitate attempts, form the greatest objection against projects of emancipation.
>
> This operation need not be suddenly carried into effect by a violent revolution, which, by displeasing every body, destroying all property, and placing all persons in situations for which they were not fitted, might produce evils a thousand times greater than all the benefits that can be expected from it.[174]

Unquestionably, the prime site of the formation of radicalism, in the sense I have defined it, was France. It is easy to see why. The country was favourably disposed to accommodate it following defeat in the Seven Years' War and the loss of a large number of colonies. Subsequently, the controversy that developed either side of the Atlantic on the occasion of the English colonists' rebellion ended up discrediting both fractions of the liberal party. The American Revolution, with its development of relations of equality within the

---

171 Ibid., vol. 9, p. 63.
172 Ibid., vol. 1, p. 143.
173 Ibid., vol. 1, pp. 312–13.
174 Ibid., vol. 1, p. 346.

white community and clear demarcation from the world of feudal privilege, galvanized harsher criticism of the *ancien régime* in France and the crisis of the English model. Disenchantment with the non-abolition of slavery in America and the emergence of an unprecedented racial state also threw the American model into crisis. The roots of French radicalism lay in this dual crisis.

But what was its influence across the Channel and the Atlantic? The problem can be reformulated as follows. Liberal England, derived from the Glorious Revolution, and especially the American Revolution, made a powerful contribution to the ideological preparation of the French Revolution and subsequently, through the crisis of the two models, to the formation of radicalism. But why did the latter not seem to take deep root in the two classical countries of the liberal tradition? Obviously, the vexed course of the revolution and the explosion of the Terror immediately damaged France's powers of attraction. A far from negligible role in frustrating the diffusion of radicalism was also played by repression. In England in 1794 habeas corpus was suspended for eight years; a further suspension followed in 1817; while two years later there occurred what has passed into history as the Peterloo Massacre or (to put it in the indignant words of an English paper of the time) the 'slaughter of defenceless men, women and children, unprovoked and unnecessary'.[175] Suffering deportation to Australia and meeting with a horrible fate, sometimes dying under the lashes of merciless flogging, were members of workers' societies, clubs that were or more or less Jacobin in orientation, and Chartists engaged in the struggle to extend the suffrage, not to mention 'Irish dissidents' for whom 'Australia was the official Siberia ... at the turn of the century'. In total, 'between 1800 and 1850 ... about 1,800 were deported for political "crimes". Among them were representatives of nearly every protest movement known to the British Government'.[176] Obviously, the repression also struck circles that regarded violent revolution by black slaves as legitimate, or even invoked it.[177] In 1798 the Alien and Sedition Acts were passed in the United States, containing serious restrictions on constitutional liberties, granting the president a wide range of discretionary power and particularly hitting followers of ideas suspected of being influenced by the French Revolution. And we already know about the violence, predominantly from below, to which abolitionists were subject.

However, neither the Terror in France nor the repression in Britain and the United States suffice to explain the weakness of radicalism across the Channel

---

175   The text, taken from *Sherwin's Weekly Political Register*, 18 August 1819, is quoted in Paola Casana Testore and Narciso Nada, *L'età della Restaurazione*, Turin: Loescher, 1981, pp. 226–8.

176   Robert Hughes, *The Fatal Shore*, London: Collins Harvill, 1987, pp. 181, 195.

177   Blackburn, *Overthrow of Colonial Slavery*, pp. 325–6.

or the Atlantic. The analysis must be taken further. In England the outbreak of war made it possible for the dominant class to present as a patriotic duty the struggle against the revolutionary fanaticism raging in France, and which threatened to spread to Ireland, posing a mortal risk to the British Empire. As for the United States, it is interesting to observe the debate which, on the eve of the war against Britain that broke out in 1812, involved two prestigious representatives of the South. The first, Randolph, declared himself against the opening of hostilities. The situation was full of peril on the home front, where the 'infernal principles of French liberty' risked provoking a revolt by slaves; '[t]he French Revolution has polluted them.'[178] Calhoun, by contrast, did not share these concerns. Certainly, attention should be paid to the slaves' moods, but happily 'more than one-half of them never heard of the French revolution'.[179]

So radicalism, with its recognition of the right of black slaves or Irish semi-slaves to take up arms against their masters, posed a serious threat to the stability of the United States and the territorial integrity of the United Kingdom of Great Britain and Ireland. The lesser weight of the colonial question, or of populations of colonial origin, also helps explain the greater diffusion of radicalism in France. When the black revolution in San Domingo broke out, radical circles in Paris had no great difficulty recognizing and legitimating the fait accompli. Even if there was a risk of losing the remaining colonies, as anti-abolitionists never tired of warning, that would not be an irreparable tragedy.

The situation was different when it came to Britain and the United States. The black revolution in San Domingo provoked a wave of indignation in both countries. 'A Black State in the Western Archipelago', wrote *The Times*, 'is utterly incompatible with the system of all European colonisation.' And hence 'Europe will, of course, recover in that quarter the ascendancy and dominion which it justly claims from the superior wisdom and talents of its inhabitants'.[180] The United States not only refused to recognize the country born of a black revolution, but did everything it could to isolate, weaken and overthrow it.

Jefferson distinguished himself in this operation. At first sight he seems closest to radicalism. In January 1793, without allowing himself to be impressed by the charges against the Jacobins levelled by his former private secretary (referring to Paris, he spoke of 'streets … literally red with blood'), he continued passionately to defend the 'cause' of the French Revolution: 'rather than it

---

178   Randolph, quoted in Russell Kirk, *John Randolph of Roanoke*, Indianapolis: Liberty Press, 1978, pp. 167–8.

179   Calhoun, *Union and Liberty*, p. 293.

180   Geggus, 'British Opinion and the Emergence of Haiti', pp. 136–7.

should have failed, I would have seen half the earth desolated. Were there but an Adam & an Eve left in every country, & left free, it would be better than it now is.' Moreover, Jefferson positively contrasted France with the United States, where Anglophiles regarded the 1787 Constitution, with the very wide powers it conferred on the president and executive, as a first step towards the establishment of a monarchy.[181]

Yet the picture changed markedly following the black revolution in San Domingo. We know that Jefferson interpreted the principle of equality in radical fashion, but always within the ambit of the white community. He never believed in the possibility of whites and blacks coexisting on an equal basis: it would represent an unjustifiable challenge to 'the real distinctions which nature has made' and end in 'the extermination of the one or the other race'.[182] When the conflict between white owners and black slaves exploded on the Caribbean island, the North American statesman's sympathy immediately went to the former; his anxiety about 'the revolutionary storm now sweeping the globe' was profound. Hence his support for the invading army sent by Napoleon, which did not cease even in the face of recourse to revolting practices, such as the introduction of trained dogs to tear blacks to pieces and the organization around such events of mass spectacles, at once thrilling and educative.[183]

15. The liberal ebb of Christian radicalism

In the United States radicalism took shape on a Christian basis. Interpretation of the conflict in religious terms in fact involved serious limitations. Scarce attention was paid to the humiliation and oppression blacks also suffered in the North: this was a condition which did not take the immediately obvious form of slavery and sin. With the end of the Civil War, the abolitionist movement soon split, and thus was not in a position to offer theoretical, and still less practical, resistance to the regime of terroristic white supremacy that asserted itself in the South after the (anti-black) compromise of 1877 between the two sections of the white community. The weight of racial prejudice was too strong, and only the massive, prolonged presence of Union troops could have

---

181   Jefferson, *Writings*, p. 1004 (letter to William Short, 3 January 1793). On all this, see Stanley M. Elkins and Eric McKitrick, *The Age of Federalism*, New York: Oxford University Press, 1993, pp. 316–17.

182   Jefferson, *Writings*, p. 264.

183   Jefferson, quoted in Jordan, *White over Black*, p. 386; Zuckerman, *Almost Chosen People*, pp. 197, 210.

guaranteed blacks the enjoyment of political rights and full recognition of their civil rights. But all this would have involved too serious a violation of the liberal principle of self-government. Among the theorists of abolitionism, possibly the only one who was inclined to go the whole way on the road of imposing the principle of racial equality by force of arms was Wendell Phillips. But when in 1875 he sought to set out his reasons at an assembly in Boston, he was brusquely silenced. The previous year, a senator from the South had observed with satisfaction: '*Radicalism* is dissolving—going to pieces'.[184] With the withdrawal of federal troops from the South, local self-government was reasserted, but radical democracy disappeared and the Calvary of the blacks resumed.

Moreover, what prompted Anglo-American Christian abolitionism to condemnation of the sin of slavery was sympathy for a people largely converted to Christianity, who regarded Christianity as an instrument with which to overcome the condition of total de-humanization and achieve a minimum of recognition. Liberated from an obsession with sin and complicity in sin thanks to the abolition of slavery, Parker believed that there was no political solution to the persistent problem of the discrimination and injustice suffered by blacks: one could only place hope in the matrimonial fusion of the two races or the beneficent effects of the infusion of 'dreadful Anglo-saxon blood' in black veins. In a sense, this was a radical perspective, strongly counter to the dominant ideology. However, rather than on organizing the oppressed blacks, attention focused on overcoming the prejudices on the part of the oppressors that cemented barriers of race and caste. Radicalism thus tended to be reabsorbed by liberalism. Things were even worse for the Indians, regarded as savages and pagans. Parker had no hesitation in justifying the policy of 'continual aggression, invasion, and extermination' pursued by the indomitable people that were the Anglo-Saxons.[185] In fact, the end of the Civil War gave new impetus to the march into the Far West. The influence of the colonial question once again intervenes to explain the weakness of American radicalism.

16. Liberal socialism and radicalism

Much more so than Bentham, it was Kant who came close to radicalism. His clear adoption of a position favourable to revolutionary France is not so significant. More relevant is the fact that, intervening in 1795, a year after the abolition of slavery in the French colonies, with clear critical reference to

---

184   Eric Foner, *Reconstruction*, New York: Harper & Row, 1989, pp. 554, 528.
185   Slotkin, *Fatal Environment*, pp. 232, 230.

England, *Perpetual Peace* identified 'the sugar cane islands' as the 'site of the cruellest slavery that has ever been imagined'. There were two further decisive elements. Like the French radicals—we must not forget that the colonial question weighed even less heavily on Germany than France—Kant problematized the boundaries between civilization and barbarism: it was England that now represented the cause of 'slavery and barbarism'. Finally, quite unlike the liberals, he did not confine himself to criticizing Pitt, whom he said was rightly 'hated as an enemy of the human race'.[186] The German philosopher's radicalism did not escape his contemporaries: while Goethe regarded his attitude towards England as scarcely 'liberal', Wilhelm von Humboldt sharply distanced himself from the 'democratism' pervading *Perpetual Peace*.[187]

In England, rather than Bentham, it was John Stuart Mill who approximated to radicalism, when he identified slavery as 'the most flagrant of all possible violations' of liberal principles and branded those who defended it 'the powers of evil'.[188] In his *Autobiography*, along with 'the noble body of Abolitionists', Mill also celebrated John Brown, author of the failed attempt to get the slaves of the southern United States to rise up.[189] In a text of 1824 the English philosopher expressed his sympathy for the cause of the blacks of San Domingo–Haiti, whom the Napoleonic expedition vainly sought half to 'exterminate' and half to reduce to conditions of slavery once again.[190] Putting clear distance between himself and the overwhelming majority of his contemporaries, Mill did not seem to recoil in horror from the prospect of a revolution from below by black slaves. And yet, in another respect, he was the theorist of a new 'slavery', temporary and pedagogical in kind, for 'savages' (see below, Chapter 7, §3).

The English author asserted that the final stage of his development was characterized by gravitation towards 'socialism' and, at the same time, renewed distrust of 'democracy'. What caused and justified the latter was 'the ignorance and especially the selfishness and brutality of the mass'.[191] Already problematic in the metropolis, democracy proved decidedly dangerous and inadvisable when it came to the colonies and peoples of colonial origin (including Afro-Americans). Theorist of the planetary despotism of the West, Mill seems equally remote from radical, 'abolitionist democracy'.

---

186   Cf. Losurdo, *Autocensura e compromesso*, pp. 90–1.
187   Cf. ibid., pp. 91, 177, 184.
188   John Stuart Mill, *Collected Works*, 33 vols, ed. John M. Robson, Toronto and London: University of Toronto Press and Routledge and Kegan Paul, 1963–91, vol. 1, pp. 266–7.
189   Ibid., vol. 1, p. 266.
190   Ibid., vol. 1, pp. 304–5.
191   Ibid., vol. 1, p. 238.

Hence radicalism and socialism must not be confused. Socialist aspirations can readily be combined with colonialism. Followers of Fourier and Saint-Simon envisaged building communities of a more or less socialist type on land taken from the Arabs in Algeria.[192] Like 'democracy', 'socialism' can be envisaged restrictively for the 'master race' and at the expense of colonial peoples or peoples of colonial origin. At certain points in his evolution towards liberal socialism, Mill approached the threshold separating it from radicalism, but without crossing it.

With reference to Zionism, Arendt drew attention to the presence within it of what at first sight is a peculiar tendency. It was characterized, on the one hand, by support for 'chauvinist' objectives and, on the other, by commitment to pursuing collectivist experiments and a 'rigorous realization of social justice' within its own community. Thus crystallized 'a most paradoxical conglomerate of radical approach and revolutionary social reforms domestically, with outmoded and outright reactionary political lines in the field of foreign policy', and in the field of relations with colonial peoples.[193] In other words, 'master-race democracy' can also go further and take the form of 'master-race socialism', whereas what defines radicalism is precisely the argument against any claim by a particular ethnic or social group to pose as 'master race'.

When in 1860, during the Second Opium War, a Franco-British expedition destroyed the Summer Palace, it was Victor Hugo who proved to be the inheritor of radicalism with his denunciation of the barbarity committed by self-styled civilizers, while for Mill, as for the liberal culture of the time, there continued to be few doubts about the complete identity between the West and civilization (see below, Chapter 8, §3 and Chapter 9, §5).

---

192   Tocqueville mentions this critically in *Oeuvres complètes*, vol. 3, pt 1, pp. 250–1.

193   Hannah Arendt, 'Zionism Reconsidered', *The Menorah Review*, vol. 33, October 1945, pp. 171, 169, 175.

CHAPTER SIX

The Struggle for Recognition by the Instruments of Labour in the Metropolis and the Reaction of the Community of the Free

1. The excluded and the struggle for recognition

We have seen that the liberal tradition is shot through with two macroscopic exclusion clauses. In reality, there is a third—that directed at women, which in fact presents peculiar characteristics. When they belonged to the upper classes, they formed part, albeit in a subordinate role, of the community of the free; one thinks, in particular, of female slave-owners. The women's liberation movement was only able to acquire a mass social base later, when women previously confined to a position of slavery or restricted to the inferior levels of a caste society were able to participate in it. The development of liberalism in the eighteenth and nineteenth centuries is explained, in the first instance, by the struggle waged by the bipedal machines of the metropolis, on the one hand, and slaves and colonial populations or populations of colonial origin, on the other.

In both cases, even more than for the achievement of specific objectives, the excluded protested against the fact that the dignity of man was denied them. This was a struggle for recognition—in the sense specified by Hegel in a celebrated chapter of *The Phenomenology of Spirit*. The shackled black depicted by abolitionist propaganda demanded freedom, stressing (in the text attached to the image) that he too was a 'man'. In his turn, Toussaint L'Ouverture, the great protagonist of the San Domingo revolution, invoked 'the absolute adoption of the principle that no man, whether red, black or white, can be the property of his fellow being'.[1] Similar accents could be heard in Paris immediately

---

1   L'Ouverture, quoted in Florence Gauthier, *Triomphe et mort du droit naturel en Révolution*, Paris: Presses Universitaires de France, 1992, p. 282.

following the July Revolution, when popular periodicals accused 'bourgeois notables' of insisting on viewing workers not as 'men' but 'machines', nothing but 'machines' called upon to produce exclusively for the 'needs' of their masters. After the revolution of February 1848, the achievement by proletarians of political rights demonstrated in their view that they too were finally beginning to be raised to the 'rank of men'.[2] Condorcet emphatically recognized this status in black slaves, but denied it to their white masters. Similarly, Engels, referring to the English workers whom he was 'happy and proud' to have known and who suffered a 'slavery worse than that of the American negroes',[3] exclaimed: 'I have found you to be men, members of the great, universal family of humanity' who proclaimed 'the cause of humanity', trampled underfoot by capitalists engaged in an 'indirect trade in human flesh', in a barely disguised slave trade.[4]

Corresponding to the struggle of the excluded to be recognized in their dignity as men was the polemic against the Declaration of the Rights of Man on the other side. In the liberal camp the most celebrated intervention was Burke's. His condemnation of this subversive theory was absolute: it paved the way for the political and social demands of 'hair-dressers' and 'tallow-chandlers', 'to say nothing of a number of other more servile employments', for the demands of the 'swinish multitude', or at any rate people whose 'sordid mercenary occupation' entailed 'a mean contracted view of things'.[5]

Some decades later, in Bentham's view the 1789 Declaration of the Rights of Man was nothing but a pile of 'anarchical fallacies'. It sanctioned *égalité* between all men? The English liberal's comment was sarcastic:

> *All men* (i.e. all human creatures of both sexes) *remain equal in rights.* The apprentice, then, is equal in rights to his master; he has as much liberty with relation to the master, as the master has with relation to him; he has as much right to command and to punish him.

And hence the 'absurd principle of *égalité* can only please "fanatics" and the "ignorant multitude"'. The Declaration referred to law as an expression of the

---

2 Cf. Domenico Losurdo, *Democrazia o bonapartismo*, Turin: Bollati Boringhieri, 1993, ch. 1, §11.

3 Karl Marx and Friedrich Engels, *Werke*, 38 vols, Berlin: Dietz, 1955–89, vol. 2, pp. 229, 400.

4 Ibid., vol. 2, pp. 230–1.

5 Edmund Burke, *The Works: A New Edition*, 16 vols, London: Rivington, 1826, vol. 5, pp. 154, 105–6.

'general will'? But it is clear that therewith censitary restrictions of the vote could not be justified. The very theorization of property right contained in this solemn text was suspect to Bentham: the concrete object of such right was not clearly specified, and hence it involved a right which, once again, belonged 'to every individual, without any limit', even the propertyless person suffering from hunger:

> In other words, a universal property right is established—that is, everything is common to everyone. But because what belongs to everyone belongs to no one, what follows from it is that the effect of the Declaration is not to establish property but to destroy it. And that is how it was understood by Babeuf's supporters, those true interpreters of the Declaration of the Rights of Man, who can be criticized for nothing but being consistent in applying the most false and absurd of principles.[6]

Condemning these abstract 'general principles', for which Britain rightly displayed 'extreme repugnance' and which, when pronounced by 'famished mouths', could only result in catastrophe, Bentham referred to Malouet, one of the few in France to have attempted to dispel 'the cloud of confused ideas'.[7] In fact, it was the Anglomanes who sought to block the ratification of the Declaration of the Rights of Man. In appealing to 'general principles' and 'metaphysical' concepts, Malouet warned, people were playing with fire: they risked inciting the 'immense multitude of propertyless men', 'the unfortunate classes of society', 'the men placed by fate in a condition of dependency' and 'lacking enlightenment and means'. They must be taught 'just limits', rather than the 'extension of natural liberty'.[8]

It is significant that one of those to adopt a clear position against the category of rights of man was Malouet, who subsequently played a prominent part in the argument against abolitionism. It was this second aspect that played a central role in the United States, where within the white community the social question did not have the significance it possessed in France, but where the conflict over black slavery became increasingly impassioned. A particular target was the statement (contained in the Declaration of Independence) that

---

6   Jeremy Bentham, *Oeuvres*, 3 vols, ed. Étienne Dumont, Brussels: Société belge de librairie, 1840, vol. 1, pp. 509–21. The text quoted here was subsequently reprinted with alterations in Jeremy Bentham, *The Works*, 11 vols, ed. John Bowring, Edinburgh: Tait, 1838–43, vol. 2, pp. 491ff.

7   Bentham, *Oeuvres*, vol. 1, pp. 524–5.

8   Malouet, quoted in Antoine de Baecque, Wolfgang Schmale and Michel Vovelle, eds, *L'An des droits de l'homme*, Paris: CNRS Press, 1988, pp. 104–7.

'all men are created equal', with the right to enjoy 'certain unalienable Rights'. Present in it was the 'metaphysical folly' that subsequently found more concentrated expression in the French Revolution. This was the charge formulated by the 'American Burke'—namely, Randolph—who in this context explicitly appealed to the British liberal.[9] Born in the wake of the revolt against the alleged 'imprescriptible rights of the king' invoked by the British Crown, the United States now risked succumbing to the folly of the 'imprescriptible rights of black slaves'.[10] In similar fashion, Calhoun drew attention to the 'poisonous fruits' of that 'place in the declaration of our independence' which claimed to confer 'the same right to liberty and equality' on all men. This was the abolitionists' starting-point in the fanatical struggle they had unleashed against black slavery and 'Southern institutions' as 'outrageous on the rights of men'.[11]

In England, it was with his focus mainly on the colonies that Disraeli characterized the 'rights of man' as 'nonsense' in 1880.[12] The struggle for recognition waged by colonial populations or populations of colonial origin proved particularly long and complex. It would only achieve decisive results in the twentieth century. For now we must turn our attention to the struggle waged by the bipedal machines in the capitalist metropolis and within the white community.

2. The instrument of labour becomes a passive citizen

The social and political milieus which, on either side of the Atlantic, celebrated themselves as the community of the free understood by liberty not only the undisturbed enjoyment of the private sphere. Exclusion from representative bodies and political life was also perceived as an expression of despotism. On the other hand, denial of political rights to those with no title to be recognized as members of the community of the free seemed self-evidently proper. How could the 'horse' or 'beast of burden' to which Locke and Mandeville compared the wage-labourer, or the 'speaking instrument', 'bipedal instrument' or 'work machine' that Burke and Sieyès referred to, claim to form part of it?

---

9   Randolph, quoted in Russell Kirk, *John Randolph of Roanoke*, Indianapolis: Liberty Press, 1978, pp. 63–6.

10   Randolph, quoted in ibid., p. 177.

11   John C. Calhoun, *Union and Liberty*, ed. R. M. Lence, Indianapolis: Liberty Classics, 1992, pp. 568–9, 464.

12   Benjamin Disraeli, *Endymion*, 2 vols, New York and London: Walter Dunne, 1976, vol. 2, p. 80.

In other words, those who continued to be defined via the categories used by Aristotle to conceptualize the figure of the slave could not enjoy political citizenship. If they were men, they were members of a different, inferior people; they were barbarians (the quintessential slaves).

In the French case at least, the picture began to change significantly with the revolution. For some time Sieyès spoke nonchalantly of wage-labourers as the set of 'work machines' and 'bipedal machines', or of the 'always childlike multitude'.[13] But after 14 July 1789, while the Declaration of the Rights of Man was being discussed, he felt a new need—the need for greater 'clarity of language'. Hence a distinction between 'natural and civil rights', or 'passive rights', on the one hand, and 'political rights', or 'active rights', on the other. The first, which included the protection of the 'person', 'property' and 'liberty', applied to every man. The former bipedal machine now saw his dignity not only as a man but also as a citizen recognized, albeit a 'passive citizen' excluded from participation in political life, like 'women', 'children' and 'foreigners'.[14]

We are in the presence of a significant innovation. Just as 'free labour' had long been an oxymoron, because labour was in reality synonymous with *servitus*, so the category of 'passive citizen' had long sounded like an oxymoron. He who was subject to the necessity of labour, and hence to *servitus*, was by definition excluded from the group of freemen, who enjoyed liberty and citizenship to the full. For Locke it was meaningless to grant political rights to those who, as we have seen, were 'made slaves' by destitution, need, labour and the servitude implicit in this—and who did not form part of civil society, whose purpose was the defence of property. Blackstone argued in similar fashion: the right to vote could not be extended to 'persons of indigent fortunes', who by that token were 'under the immediate domination of others'.[15] Some decades later, Constant resorted to the same justification when he excluded the wage-labourer from the enjoyment of political rights: he lacked 'the necessary revenue to subsist independently of any external will' and 'property holders are the masters of his existence, since they may refuse him work.'[16] It is especially interesting to observe the development of the first major theorists of passive citizenship. In September 1789 Sieyès still did not hesitate to define as 'forced' the labour of

---

13   Emmanuel-Joseph Sieyès, *Écrits politiques*, ed. Roberto Zapperi, Paris: Éditions des archives contemporaines, 1985, p. 80.

14   Ibid., p. 199.

15   William Blackstone, *Commentaries on the Laws of England*, 4 vols, Chicago: University of Chicago Press, 1979, vol. 1, p. 165.

16   Benjamin Constant, *Political Writings*, ed. and trans. Biancamaria Fontana, Cambridge: Cambridge University Press, 1988, p. 216.

the 'uneducated multitude', which was therefore 'lacking freedom'.[17] It made no sense to pose the problem of conferring political liberty on someone destined to be deprived of liberty as such. On the contrary, it might be asked if it was not appropriate to transform the actually existing 'slavery of need' into a 'legally sanctioned slavery', in accordance with the model adopted in America for indentured white servants.[18]

The French Revolution challenged the configuration of the servant as a mere instrument of labour. The figure now emerged of the purely passive citizen, which in fact had a long gestation period behind it. A significant role was played by an exigency internal to the community of the free, interested in imparting credibility to its discourse and self-celebration. In the wake of the Glorious Revolution, Locke, Mandeville and Blackstone on the one hand recognized and, in order to avoid any misunderstandings, even highlighted the *servitus* to which the wage-labourer was—and must be—subject. On the other, they celebrated England as the land of the free, where there was no place for 'perfect slavery' (Locke), 'slavery in the strict sense' (Blackstone), or colonial slavery (Mandeveille). In the nineteenth century Burke observed that among the subaltern classes the 'common blessing' of liberty 'may be united with much abject toil, with great misery, with all the exterior of servitude'.[19] There is here an obvious concern to stress the liberty of the wage-labourer, who is called upon not to let himself be vexed and misled by the harshness of his material living conditions, but to identify with an order that, despite everything, guarantees him liberty.

The ideological dimension of this discourse clearly emerges from reading an eighteenth-century English author. Compared with legal coercion of the labourer–slave, Joseph Townsend regarded economic compulsion as more effective. It silently but unfailingly imposed obedience on servants, terrorized by the prospect of death from starvation. Taken for granted was the power exercised by 'the more delicate', who were excused work and 'left at liberty, without interruption', over those who, in one way or another, must be forced to perform 'the most servile, the most sordid, and the most ignoble offices'.[20] In the transition from one condition to the other, coercion had not disappeared, but become more imperious. This did not prevent the English liberal pastor from painting an edifying picture of his country: even the poorest was a

17   Sieyès, *Écrits politiques*, p. 236.

18   Ibid., p. 76.

19   Burke, *Works*, vol. 3, p. 54.

20   Joseph Townsend, *A Dissertation the Poor Laws by a Well-Wisher to Mankind*, Berkeley: University of California Press, 1971, p. 35.

'freeman', who supplied 'free service' on the basis of 'his own judgement and discretion', without the 'compulsion' to which the 'slave' was subjected.[21]

In the figure of the passive citizen there is something more. It is the expression of an exigency internal to the community of the free, but also and above all a response to the struggle for recognition waged by servants in the metropolis. At least potentially, the idea of universal citizenship, even if merely passive in a majority of cases, called into question the caste ordering of society with which Townsend continued to identify. Precisely on account of its novelty, the category of citizen did not impose itself at a stroke on Sieyès, who compared non-property-owners to 'foreigners' and 'children': the slave too was a foreigner—in fact, the foreigner par excellence, the barbarian. Or he was a child, and as such formed part of the master's extended family. In this sense, Constant was less shrewd than Sieyès, given that he continued to refer to non-property-owners excluded from political rights primarily as 'foreigners' and 'minors'.[22]

The category of 'passive citizenship' possessed the further advantage of answering Rousseau's objection, subsequently taken up by Robespierre. In a well-ordered state, the Genevan philosopher had stressed, no-one should be able to feel himself a 'stranger'.[23] Clearly distancing himself from absolute monarchy and aristocracy, where a single individual or a few individuals could say they had a 'homeland', while everyone else was stateless, it was a question of constructing a society, a 'democratic regime', the Jacobin leader later reiterated, where 'the state is genuinely the homeland of all individuals', all of them admitted on an equal footing 'to the rights of the citizen in full'.[24] Now, if not exactly in the strict sense of the term, the proletarian was likewise a citizen, a member of the 'nation' dear to Sieyès that Boulainvilliers and the nobility had wrongly wanted to divide into an aristocratic people, descended from the victorious Franks, and a plebeian people, descended from the vanquished Gallo-Romans.[25]

---

21   Ibid., p. 24. On Townsend, cf. Karl Marx, *Capital: Volume One*, trans. Ben Fowkes, Harmondsworth: Penguin, 1976, pp. 800–1.

22   Constant, *Political Writings*, p. 214.

23   Jean-Jacques Rousseau, 'Discours sur l'économie politique', in *Oeuvres complètes*, ed. Bernard Gagnebin and Marcel Raymond, Paris: Gallimard,1964, vol. 3, p. 255.

24   Maximilien de Robespierre, *Oeuvres*, 10 vols, Paris: Presses Universitaires de France, 1912–67, vol. 10, pp. 352–3.

25   Cf. Domenico Losurdo, *Nietzsche, il ribelle aristocratico*, Turin: Bollati Boringhieri, 2002, ch. 12, §8.

3. The invention of passive citizenship and negative liberty and the restriction of the political sphere

Compelled by the struggle waged by the excluded to grant them at least passive citizenship, the community of the free now found itself facing a new challenge to its exclusivism. Already in June 1790, Marat had a representative of the 'unlucky ones' to whom political citizenship was denied argue thus against the 'aristocracy of the rich': 'In your eyes we are still the rabble'.[26] And we have seen Robespierre compare non-property-owners excluded from political rights to slaves: the concession of passive citizenship did not end the struggle for recognition.

Constant sought to answer the objections of the most radical currents that had emerged during the French Revolution. No, the non-property-owner excluded from the enjoyment of political rights could not be confused with the slave.[27] Unlike the latter, the former, in common with all other citizens, was protected by laws and enjoyed full liberty within his private sphere. And this was what modern liberty consisted in. During the conflict with the monarchy, the community of the free in England and America had demanded a very different liberty, since it was in no way prepared to renounce administering public affairs. But it is clear that this platform could not survive the emergence of a struggle by the popular masses, which protested against exclusion from political rights and at the same time sought to change their labour relations and material living conditions. The dominant elite now developed a very different discourse: participation in political life was not an essential element of liberty; and, in the second place, labour relations and material living conditions pertained to an eminently private sphere, so that it was absurd and illegitimate to seek to change them through political action.

The new discourse did not impose itself at a stroke and wholly consistently. Constant let slip the admission that the provider of work was in fact 'master' of the worker's 'existence'. But even more significant is the oscillation we find in Macaulay. Fighting in 1831 for the political emancipation of Jews, the British liberal unhesitatingly rejected the thesis that a distinction should be made between civil rights and political rights, and that exclusion from the latter was not a factor of 'mortification' and discrimination. In reality, this was sophistry designed to justify 'a system full of absurdity and injustice'.[28] The

---

26   Henri Guillemin, *Benjamin Constant muscadin*, Paris: Gallimard, 1967, p. 13.

27   Constant, *Political Writings*, pp. 213–15.

28   Thomas Babington Macaulay, *Critical and Historical Essays*, 5 vols, Leipzig: Tauchnitz, 1850, vol. 1, pp. 291–2.

polemic was incisive and effective, but the liberal author was careful not to intervene on behalf of the British popular masses as well as of property-owners whose religion was Judaism!

A similar consideration applies to other exponents of the liberal tradition. In regarding the enjoyment of political rights as an essential element of liberty, the Jacobins argued no differently from the American revolutionaries. But in Burke the proposal of 'conciliation' of the rebel colonists, who with their demand for the right to representation had confirmed that they were worthy members of the community of the free, was followed by the proclamation of a crusade against a revolution led by the mob, which had demanded and wrested political rights. As to de Tocqueville, his notes on his travels in England were almost coeval with the publication of *Democracy in America*. But the warm appreciation of widespread political participation in the North American republic was certainly not matched by bitter denunciation of strict censitary discrimination in Britain, or the slightest support for the Chartist demand for an extension of the suffrage.

De Tocqueville's intervention was especially significant as regards the second point in the new liberal ideological platform, which drastically restricted the political sphere. In a text of 1842 he observed: 'Equality is everywhere extending its dominion, except in industry, which is daily organized in increasingly aristocratic form'. The wage-labourer found himself in a 'strict dependency' (*étroite dépendance*) on the provider of work. Despite the charming appearance of 'great French society' as a whole, 'industrial society' (*société industrielle*) in the strict sense continued to be characterized by a strict hierarchy, which left little room not only for equality, but also for the individual liberty of those placed on the lowest rungs of the hierarchy.[29] The harshness of the relations obtaining in factories was further confirmed by de Tocqueville's comparison between working conditions and prison conditions, even if it was made not to challenge the former but to reject naively philanthropic projects for reform of the latter:

> The majority of free workers, who in France painfully earn a living, have no rest but that taken at meal times, and cannot understand why criminals punished by society arouse so lively an interest that it gives way to tender-hearted exclamations and is on the verge of shedding tears at the idea of inflicting on them a deprivation suffered by all honest labourers.[30]

---

29 Alexis de Tocqueville, *Oeuvres complètes*, ed. Jacob-Peter Mayer, Paris: Gallimard, 1951–, vol. 3, pt 2, pp. 105–6.

30 Ibid., vol. 4, pt 1, p. 122.

Besides, we should not forget that the panopticon theorized by Bentham, a building designed to achieve surveillance from which there was no escape, could serve as prison, workhouse or even factory.[31]

We are put in mind of the 'immediate dominion' or 'forced labour' to which Blackstone and Sieyès, respectively, refer. However, this coercive relationship was no longer explicitly highlighted to justify censitary discrimination in political rights (whose enjoyment belonged only to freemen in the full sense of the term). Instead, the condition that subjected the worker to a 'strict dependency' (de Tocqueville), compelled him to work in prison-like institutions (Bentham and de Tocqueville), and to sell his labour power to buyers who were ultimately the 'masters of his existence' (Constant), was now recognized reluctantly, declared to be without political relevance and hence not corrosive of negative liberty, from which no one in the metropolis was excluded.

At this point we can read the notes written by de Tocqueville during his trips to England in 1833 and 1835. The picture that emerges is no less dramatic than the one Engels was to draw some years later. The industrial region of Manchester and the working-class districts appeared as an 'infected labyrinth', an 'inferno': the miserable little cottages were like

> the last asylum man can occupy between misery and death. Yet the unfortu-
> nate beings that inhabit such cubby-holes arouse the envy of their fellows.
> Under their wretched abodes one finds a row of cellars to which a semi-
> underground corridor leads. In each of these damp, repugnant places, ten or
> fifteen human creatures are massed higgledy-piggledy.

The appalling mass poverty formed a shocking contrast to the opulence of a few: 'the organized forces of a multitude produce for the benefit of a single one'. Such a spectacle elicited a significant exclamation: 'Here the slave, there the master; here the wealth of some, there the poverty of the greatest number'.[32] On another occasion, de Tocqueville even warned against the danger of 'slave wars',[33] thereby indirectly comparing modern proletarians with ancient slaves. We thus encounter the reality of unfreedom, and of unfreedom in its most drastic form. Yet this realistic analysis disappears as if by magic when it comes to drawing up an overall political balance sheet. We are dealing with the country that France was called upon to regard as a model, if it wished to save 'the future

---

31   Bentham, *Works*, vol. 4, p. 40.
32   Tocqueville, *Oeuvres complètes*, vol. 5, pt 2, pp. 80–2.
33   Ibid., vol. 3, pt 2, p. 727.

of free institutions'.[34] English liberal society realized liberty as such, regardless of the conditions of the kind of slavery de Tocqueville had had to register in the inferno of the industrial regions. The fact is that this inferno had nothing to do with the political sphere proper. And once poverty or even a condition of tangible slavery had been confined to a sphere lacking political relevance (for pertaining to private life), in a sphere where it was not legitimate or possible to intervene politically, the initially slimy and repugnant portrait of Manchester turned into its opposite:

> In the external appearance of the city, everything attests to the individual power of man and nothing to the regulatory power of society. At every step, liberty reveals its capricious, creative force there. Nowhere is the slow, continuous action of the government to be seen.[35]

4. 'Civil laws' and 'political laws'

The restriction of the political sphere is so radical as to seem paradoxical. Analysing the prison system in the United States, de Tocqueville drew attention to legislation that threw the poor into prison even for utterly insignificant debts. In Pennsylvania the number of individuals annually incarcerated for debt amounted to 7,000. If to this figure was added the number of those condemned for more serious crimes, it turned out that for every 144 inhabitants virtually one a year ended up in prison. But this was not the most important aspect. The French liberal was obliged to acknowledge the influence, direct as well as indirect, exercised by the wealthy over the administration of justice. The 'vagrant' or someone suspected of vagrancy was locked up in prison without having committed any offence. Worse, while awaiting legal proceedings, the poor witness or plaintiff lost his liberty, while the thief capable of standing bail retained his (see above, Chapter 4, §1). Clearly, the very principle of equality before the law ended up being travestied. But this was not de Tocqueville's conclusion: 'Of all modern peoples, it is the English who have instilled the greatest liberty in their political laws and made most frequent use of prison in their civil laws'. In their turn, although having largely altered the 'political laws', Americans had 'preserved most of the civil laws' of England.[36]

---

34 Ibid., vol. 5, pt 2, p. 84.
35 Ibid., vol. 5, pt 2, p. 80.
36 Ibid., vol. 4, pt 1, pp. 323–6.

With this distinction we have reached a key point. The liberal author formulated his judgement on the countries visited by him exclusively on the basis of their *lois politiques*, while the *lois civiles* were by definition politically irrelevant. Not by chance, there is little trace in *Democracy in America* of the data gathered in the course of the inquiry into the US prison system. It might be said that de Tocqueville's most interesting pages are those that did not make it into the work which sealed his fame. The almost triumphant conclusion then becomes explicable: in the transatlantic republic liberty had been comprehensively diffused, and did not constitute a privilege. Accustomed as he was to very different *lois civiles*, the traveller from France expressed his disappointment at legislation in the United States that seemed to him 'monstrous'. But 'the mass of [American] men of law' found no fault with it and did not regard it as contradicting the 'democratic constitution'.[37] This was precisely the standpoint de Tocqueville ended up adopting—though not without contradictions and embarrassment. We can glimpse the former if we give the French liberal the floor once again:

> It must be acknowledged that the American prison regime is severe. While US society affords the example of the most extensive liberty, this country's prisons offer a spectacle of utter despotism. The citizens subject to the law are protected by it; they cease to be free only when they become felons.[38]

In fact, by de Tocqueville's own admission, vagrants and poor witnesses also suffered 'severe' treatment in prisons, or workhouses similar to prisons.

And now let us observe the embarrassment. We have already encountered the protests of vagrants locked up in prison by a society that cannot solve the problem of unemployment in any other way. What was de Tocqueville's reaction? Just as it did not come within his 'tasks' to investigate possible remedies for unemployment, so it did not fall to him 'even to investigate to what extent the society is just that punishes the man who does not work and lacks work, and how it might furnish means of subsistence without putting him in prison'.[39] The sphere of politics and 'political laws' was so narrowly defined as to exclude not only material living conditions and relations of dependency in factories, but even the censitary discrimination that pervaded the administration of justice in the United States.

---

37   Ibid., vol. 4, pt 1, p. 325.
38   Ibid., vol. 4, pt 1, p. 196.
39   Ibid., vol. 4, pt 1, p. 51.

5. The de-politicization and naturalization of economic and social relations

Any expansion of the political was utterly intolerable to the liberal tradition, because it would involve relations that were not only private in character, but whose immutability was consecrated by nature or Providence. In Burke's view it was at once mad and blasphemous to believe that among 'the competence of government' was 'supply[ing] to the poor, those necessaries which it has pleased the Divine Providence for a while to with-hold from them'. Poverty was the result of 'Divine displeasure' and the latter could certainly not be placated by challenging 'the laws of commerce', which were 'the laws of nature, and consequently the laws of God'.[40] Some decades later, de Tocqueville argued no differently. On the eve of the 1848 Revolution, he noted with concern the behaviour of the 'working classes'. They seemed calm, no longer 'bedevilled by political passions'. Unfortunately, however, 'where once they had been political, their passions have become social'. Rather than the make-up of this or that ministry, they tended to question property relations themselves and hence the natural order of 'society', tearing 'to shreds the basis on which it rests'.[41] When the revolution broke out, the French liberal regarded it as socialist or infected with socialism as early as February, because prominent in it were 'the economic and political theories' which would have people 'believe that human miseries are the work of the laws and not of Providence, and that poverty can be abolished by changing the social order'.[42] Ranging beyond the political sphere, the 'threat of change in the social constitution' was configured as an attack on the 'ancient, holy laws of property and family on which Christian civilization is based'.[43]

Thus, on the one hand political economy was merged with theology, while on the other it tended to take its place, in the sense that 'science' was now called on to sanction and sanctify existing social relations. According to Malthus, it was wholly desirable that political economy be 'taught to the common people'. Thanks to it, the poor would understand that they must attribute the cause of their privations to Mother Nature or their own improvidence. Indeed, '[p]olitical economy is perhaps the only science of which it may be said that the

---

40 Burke, *Works*, vol. 7, p. 404.

41 Tocqueville, *Oeuvres complètes*, vol. 3, pt 2, p. 750 (speech in the Chamber of Deputies, 27 January 1848).

42 Ibid., vol. 12, pp. 92–4, 84.

43 Ibid., vol. 3, pt 3, pp. 221, 258.

ignorance of it is not merely a deprivation of good, but produces great evil.'[44]
But this was also the opinion of de Tocqueville, who believed it necessary

> to diffuse among the working classes ... some of the most elementary and
> certain notions of political economy, which would make them understand,
> for example, what is constant and necessary in the economic laws that govern
> the wage rate. Because such laws, being in some sense of divine law, in that
> they derive from the nature of man and the very structure of society, are
> situated beyond the reach of revolutions. [45]

While for Burke, 'Divine displeasure' explained the misery of the popular
masses, for Malthus it was the immorality of their behaviour, the sexual incon-
tinence that brought into the world beings whose subsistence people were not
in a position to ensure. Referring to 'Malthus's principle of population',[46] de
Tocqueville reprehended 'all the excesses of intemperance' widespread among
'the lower classes', their 'improvidence', or their tendency to live 'as if there
will be no tomorrow', and above all 'these early, imprudent marriages that
seem to have no other purpose than multiplying the number of unfortunates
on earth'.[47]

Notwithstanding the radical attitudes he liked to adopt, Bentham did not
reach very different conclusions: 'with respect to poverty, it is not the work
of the laws'; the poor man was like a 'savage' who had not succeeded in transcending the state of nature. Or, to put it in the words of a French disciple and
collaborator of the English philosopher, 'Poverty is not a result of the social
order. So why rebuke it? It is a legacy of the state of nature'.[48] Arguing against
natural law, the English philosopher waxed ironic about the recourse to nature
to ground rights that only made sense in society. But now nature popped up
again to remove responsibility for poverty from the politico-social order.

Given this elevation of existing social relations to the status of nature, and
to nature sanctioned by Providence, attempts to alter them could only be an
expression of madness. Burke expressed his utter 'horror' at revolutionaries or hasty reformists, who did not hesitate 'to hack that aged parent [their

---

44   Thomas Robert Malthus, *An Essay on the Principle of Population*, 2 vols, ed. Patricia Joyce,
Cambridge: Cambridge University Press and Royal Economic Society, 1989, vol. 2, p. 152 n. 10.

45   Tocqueville, *Oeuvres complètes*, vol. 16, p. 241 (speech to the Academy of Moral and
Political Science, 3 April 1852).

46   Ibid., vol. 7, p. 283 (letter to L. von Thun, 1835).

47   Ibid., vol. 16, p. 142.

48   Bentham, *Works*, vol. 1, p. 309; Étienne Dumont, Introduction to Bentham, *Oeuvres*, vol. 2,
p. 201.

country] in pieces, and put him into the kettle of magicians, in hopes that by their poisonous weeds, and wild incantations, they may regenerate the paternal constitution, and renovate their father's life'.[49] Similarly, for de Tocqueville the illusion that there was a political 'cure for this hereditary, incurable ill of poverty and work' provoked the incessant, ruinous *expérimentations* that characterized the French revolutionary cycle,[50] or 'the great social revolution' begun in 1789.[51]

6. Liberalism and radicalism: two different phenomenologies of power

In pronouncing his judgement on England and the United States, de Tocqueville ignored, in addition to colonial peoples or peoples of colonial origin, material living conditions, labour relations and even 'civil laws'. Extraneous to his research and analysis of democracy, he declared, was not only the oppression of blacks and Indians, but also the detention of white citizens ('vagrants' or poor people summoned to testify in a trial) who were not guilty of any offence. The cult of the '*holy* thing' that was liberty[52] ignored the fate of the excluded in their entirety, whether they lived in the colonies or the metropolis. And, once again, the divergence between liberalism and radicalism—of which Marx and Engels were the critical heirs—is already apparent at an epistemological level. In England, observed Engels, the 'aiding and abetting of the rich is explicitly recognized even in the law'.[53] Analysing the English 'civil laws' inherited by the United States, de Tocqueville arrived at the same conclusion. But this fact had political relevance only for Engels. And like the authors of the *Communist Manifesto*, the French liberal compared the worker of the time to the slave, forced to suffer a 'strict dependency' inside the factory and a degrading, oppressive poverty outside it. But de Tocqueville considered all this foreign to the political sphere proper.

It was precisely the drastic restriction of the political, and the consequent exclusion from it of the most profound dimension of the social totality, that prompted Marx's criticisms. From the standpoint of bourgeois society and

---

49 Burke, *Works*, vol. 5, pp. 183–4.
50 Tocqueville, *Oeuvres complètes*, vol. 16, p. 240 (speech to the Academy of Moral and Political Science, 3 April 1852).
51 Ibid., vol. 16, p. 256.
52 Ibid., vol. 5, pt 2, p. 91.
53 Marx and Engels, *Werke*, vol. 1, p. 590.

political theory, he observed in his early writings, social relations 'have only a private significance, not any political significance'.[54] In its most developed form, the bourgeois state limited itself 'to closing its eyes and declaring that certain *real* oppositions do not have a *political character*, that these do not bother it'. While regarded as lacking political relevance, bourgeois social relations and power relations in the factory and society could develop without inhibition or external impediment.[55]

Over and above poverty, the reality of the factory (stressed the *Communist Manifesto*) highlighted the 'despotism' that hung over workers, 'organised like soldiers' and '[a]s privates of the industrial army ... placed under the command of a perfect hierarchy of officers and sergeants'.[56] De Tocqueville's conclusion was scarcely milder. But now the despotism identified and denounced was not this reality, but attempts by political power to change or alleviate it. Against demands to put 'the prescience and wisdom of the state in the place of individual prescience and wisdom', the French liberal proclaimed that 'nothing authorizes the state to interfere in industry'.[57] This was the famous speech of 12 September 1848, made to persuade the Constituent Assembly to reject demands for the 'right to work' that had already been drowned in blood in the June Days. De Tocqueville went so far as to attribute to 'socialist doctrines' the regulation and reduction of working hours ('the twelve-hour day'), which therefore became an object of unequivocal condemnation.[58] Likewise dismissed as an expression of socialism and despotism was any legislative measure to alleviate the misery of the 'lower classes' through rent controls.[59]

The French liberal insisted on this intransigently. Immediately after the bloody June Days, he did not hesitate to accuse the Interior Minister of being inconsistent and soft: 'While Cavaignac and Lamorcière fought socialism in the streets, Sénard supported socialist doctrine as regards the twelve-hour day'.[60] Some months later, in his draft electoral circular of May 1849, de Tocqueville advertised as a badge of merit the fact that he had voted, *inter alia*, 'against the limit it was proposed to place on the working day, against progressive taxation, and finally against the abolition of military substitution'.[61] The last point was

---

54 Ibid., vol. 1, p. 284.

55 Ibid., vol. 1, pp. 101, 124.

56 Karl Marx and Frederick Engels, *Selected Works*, Moscow: Progress Publishers, 1969, vol. 1, p. 115.

57 Tocqueville, *Oeuvres complètes*, vol. 3, pt 3, pp. 179–80.

58 Ibid., vol. 8, pt 2, p. 38 (letter to Gustave de Beaumont, 3 November 1848).

59 Ibid., vol. 15, pt 2, p. 182 (letter to F. de Corcelle, 1 November 1856).

60 Ibid., vol. 8, pt 2, p. 38 (letter to Gustave de Beaumont, 3 September 1848).

61 Ibid., vol. 3, pt 3, p. 259.

no less significant than the others. In de Tocqueville's view, the option the rich man had of hiring a poor man to replace him when it came to performing the duty of military service did not involve an inequality, based on wealth and sanctioned by law, even in the face of the danger of death. Rather, it was a contract between individuals, which pertained to the private sphere and hence did not infringe the principle of legal equality.

Even in his capacity as a historian, when reconstructing the history of the collapse of the *ancien régime*, de Tocqueville stuck to this restriction of the political sphere and this peculiar phenomenology of power, which identified dominion and oppression exclusively with the intervention of political power in a private sphere that had been unduly expanded. He drew a terrible picture of the conditions of the popular classes. 'Beggars' and 'vagrants' were sometimes proceeded against 'in the most violent way', with the arrest and condemnation of thousands of people to forced labour without trial. Not much better was the treatment reserved for peasants. While, materially and socially, they lived in an 'abyss of misery and isolation', in terms of civil rights they were deprived of any protection: they 'were constantly arrested in connection with the levies of forced labour or the militia; for begging, for misdemeanours, and countless other minor offences'. In conclusion, the peasants were viewed rather like 'the Negroes in our colonies'.[62] Was the revolution therefore legitimate and necessary? Such was not de Tocqueville's opinion. France, which with the economists radically criticized and readied itself to overthrow the *ancien régime*, 'wanted not so much a recognition of the "rights of man" as reforms in the existing system'![63] An organ of the titled aristocracy and hence jointly responsible for the degradation of the peasants to 'negroes', the *parlements* were the body which, before unfortunately being dissolved by the revolution, embodied the whole cause of liberty. In the years preceding the fatal 1789, 'our judicial institutions were still those of a free people.'[64]

7. The new self-representation of the community of the free as a community of individuals

To the revolutionary demand for the rights of man and the equal dignity of every individual, which risked grinding society 'into the dust and powder of

---

62   Alexis de Tocqueville, *The Ancien Régime and the French Revolution*, trans. Stuart Gilbert, London: Fontana, 1966, pp. 155, 151.

63   Ibid., p. 185.

64   Ibid., p. 139.

individuality, and at length dispersed to all the winds of heaven', Burke opposed the sacredness of a community: 'a partnership not only between those who are living, but between those who are living, those who are dead, and those who are to be born', in 'the great primaeval contract of eternal society',[65] thanks to a 'relation in blood' that united and founded in an indivisible unity 'our state, our hearths, our sepulchers, and our altars'.[66] In other words, as against the individualism reprehended in the French revolutionaries, the British liberal vindicated an emphatic organicism. Not by chance, the partnership celebrated by him subsequently became in German culture the *Gemeinschaft* that played such an important role in nineteenth- and twentieth-century conservative and reactionary thinking.[67] Denunciation of the dissolvent charge contained in revolutionary individualism can also be found in de Tocqueville, who in 1843 observed: 'For some years, doubt and individualism have made us such progressives that the nation will soon no longer offer any foothold for resistance'.[68]

But already during the French Revolution a different attitude had begun to emerge. Barnave warned as follows against the demand for an extension of political rights to non-property-owners: 'Another step on the road of equality would mean the destruction of liberty.'[69] According to Constant, too, the diffusion among the popular masses of the demand for political rights and stress on their enjoyment risked making people lose sight of the centrality of 'private independence' or 'individual independence', leading to the subjection of individual existence to the collective body.[70] Albeit in a different idiom, Barnarve's argument was reintroduced: the generalization of political rights had a levelling, homogenizing effect at the expense of individual liberty. Later, Guizot declared that to fight for a society where everything revolved around 'order', 'well-being' and the 'equitable distribution ... of the means of life' meant forgetting 'the development of individual life, the development of the human mind and its faculties', and aspiring to an 'ant-hill or bee-hive'.[71]

This was a theme that enjoyed enormous success after 1848. The more the struggle for recognition developed as a struggle for the conquest of political

---

65   Burke, *Works*, vol. 5, pp. 183–4.

66   Ibid., vol. 5, pp. 79–80.

67   Cf. Domenico Losurdo, *Heidegger and the Ideology of War*, trans. Marella and Jon Morris, Amherst (NY): Humanity Books, 2001, ch. 3, §1; ch. 7, §6.

68   Tocqueville, *Oeuvres complètes*, vol. 3, pt 2, p. 117.

69   Barnarve, quoted in François Furet and Denis Richet, *La rivoluzione francese*, trans. Silvia Brilli Cattarini and Carla Patanè, Rome and Bari: Laterza, 1980, p. 168.

70   Constant, *Political Writings*, pp. 316–17, 318–19.

71   François Guizot, *General History of Civilisation in Europe*, Oxford and London: D. A. Talboys, 1837, pp. 13–15.

rights and of economic and social rights, the more the popular and socialist movement was accused of not understanding the autonomous dignity of the individual, and in fact of wanting to trample it underfoot. Rejecting the social demands that issued from the February Revolution, de Tocqueville gave full vent to his disgust at the emergence on the horizon of the spectre of a 'levelled society',[72] a 'society of bees and beavers', composed 'more of sapient animals than free, civilized men'.[73] And so in his turn did John Stuart Mill: 'At present individuals are lost in the crowd ... The only power deserving the name is that of masses, and of governments while they make themselves the organ of the tendencies and instincts of masses.'[74] Hence, in a reversal of positions compared with Burke, liberalism now rebuked the most radical currents not for their individualism, but for riding roughshod over the rights of the individual. De Tocqueville sought to provide this accusation with an epistemological foundation: conferring 'a separate existence on the species [*espèce*]', and expanding 'the notion of genus [*genre*]', radicalism and socialism were simply the application to politics of the 'doctrine of the realists' of scholastic fame. It entailed 'contempt for particular rights' and devaluation of the individual as such.[75] But what is the value of this theoretical construct? It is interesting to see how de Tocqueville rejects proposals for reforming the prison system promoted primarily by the radical and socialist movement:

> When philanthropy elicits our pity for an isolated unfortunate, we must not forget to reserve a little of our sympathy for a yet greater interest—that of the whole society. Let us distrust these narrow, ungenerous views that notice the individual but never the mass of men and let us eternally remember this thought of a great philosopher: pity for the wicked is a great cruelty to the good ... The social interest, which is nothing if not the interest of the honest mass, requires that the wicked be severely punished.[76]

Even the troubled diagnosis of massification was made with an eye to the fate of '[t]he nation, taken as a whole', which now risked turning out to be 'less brilliant, less glorious, and perhaps less strong'.[77] It was also in the name of

---

72 Tocqueville, *Oeuvres complètes*, vol. 12, p. 37.

73 Ibid., vol. 3, pt 3, p. 544.

74 John Stuart Mill, *Utilitarianism, Liberty, Representative Government*, ed. Harry B. Acton, London: Dent, 1972, p. 123.

75 Tocqueville, *Oeuvres complètes*, vol. 6, pt 1 (letter to H. Reeve, 3 February 1840).

76 Ibid., vol. 4, pt 1, p. 136.

77 Alexis de Tocqueville, *Democracy in America*, London: Everyman's Library, 1994, vol. 1, p. 10.

an emphatic (and chauvinist) idea of the nation that de Tocqueville invoked 'terror' against those who risked compromising the honour of France (see below, Chapter 8, §15).

At a concrete level, too, de Tocqueville was concerned to see what were for him the requirements of society prevail. In the years of the July Monarchy, faced with the spread of mass misery, he proposed nothing to prevent it except police measures gravely corrosive of the liberty of the individual (the poor individual): 'Could we not prevent the rapid movement of the population, so that men do not abandon the earth and move to industry, except to the extent that the latter can readily meet their needs?'[78] Restrictions on freedom of movement should also be imposed on 'vagrants'.[79]

Although committed to denouncing the expansion of the state—'the great evil of adding unnecessarily to its power'—Mill did not hesitate to assert: 'The laws which, in many countries on the Continent, forbid marriage unless the parties can show that they have the means of supporting a family, do not exceed the legitimate powers of the state'; they were 'not objectionable as violations of liberty'.[80] The view that any 'interference' in the procreation of human life was illegitimate was 'a superstition which will one day be regarded with as much contempt, as any of the idiotic notions and practices of savages'.[81] We can understand Proudhon's irony in connection with the liberal school:

> It, which in all circumstances and places professes *laissez-faire, laissez-passer*, which reprehends socialists for substituting their convictions for the laws of nature, which protests against any state intervention, and which demands liberty here, there and everywhere, nothing but liberty, does not hesitate when it comes to conjugal fertility to cry to the spouses: Stop there! What devil incites you![82]

In the conflict between liberalism and its critics, an inversion of positions has occurred as regards laissez-faire for the individual.

Disgusted by the radicalism of the 1848 revolution and Louis Bonaparte's coup d'état, de Tocqueville arrived at a bitter conclusion: 'The revolution

---

78   Tocqueville, *Oeuvres complètes*, vol. 16, p. 139.

79   Ibid., vol. 16, p. 160.

80   Mill, *Utilitarianism*, pp. 165, 163.

81   John Stuart Mill, *Collected Works*, 33 vols, ed. John M. Robson, Toronto and London: University of Toronto Press and Routledge and Kegan Paul, 1963–91, vol. 20, p. 350.

82   Pierre-Joseph Proudhon, *La giustizia nella rivoluzione e nella Chiesa*, ed. Mario Albertini, Turin: UTET, 1968, p. 408.

in England was made solely with a view to liberty, while that in France was made principally with a view to equality.'[83] The criticism also encompassed the Enlightenment culture that had prepared and promoted the collapse of the *ancien régime*: in it a sure 'zeal for equality' was matched by a rather 'tepid' 'desire for liberty'.[84] As we know, the first to counterpose liberty and equality and denounce the demand for political equality as an attack on liberty was Barnarve, who was nevertheless a defender of slavery. This institution continued to be alive and well in the United States when de Tocqueville held up the transatlantic republic, together with England, as the model country for love of liberty to a France devoured by the passion for equality. It was precisely here that slavery was justified and even celebrated by southern theorists as an instrument to ensure, along with their liberty, the equality of members of the white community. For confirmation of the problematic character of the opposition between liberty and equality, we might adduce the pre-1848 de Tocqueville, who criticized England for an erroneous conception of liberty in as much as it was based on 'privilege' (and inequality), and who attributed to the French Revolution the merit of having, in the name of equality, promoted the cause of the abolition of slavery and the freedom of the blacks (see above, Chapter 4, §9; below, Chapter 8, §7). At this time, far from being in opposition, liberty and equality were fully in accord.

The opposition was represented, in significantly different form, in the work of another important representative of the liberal tradition. In Bentham we read: 'When security and equality are in opposition, there should be no hesitation: equality should give way'.[85] In the very country held up by de Tocqueville as a model for its ability to understand the absolute priority of the value of liberty, we see that the reassertion of the subordinate value of equality occurs, in the first instance, in the name of the 'security' of society and the existing order.

8. Economic and social rights, the socialist 'ants' nest' and liberal 'individualism'

At this point it is appropriate to analyse nineteenth-century liberals' individualist profession of faith at greater length. Especially after 1848, in the midst

---

83 Tocqueville, *Oeuvres complètes*, vol. 2, pt 2, p. 334.
84 Tocqueville, *The Ancien Régime*, p. 185.
85 Bentham, quoted in Élie Halévy, *The Growth of Philosophic Radicalism*, trans. Mary Morris, London: Faber & Faber, 1972, p. 53.

of the struggle against the massification they reprehended in socialism, they sometimes seemed to consider individualism a pre-modern reality, which had, alas, faded in the course of subsequent historical developments. According to Mill, '[i]n ancient history, in the Middle Ages, and in a diminishing degree through the long transition from feudality to the present time, the individual was a power in himself'; he was not 'lost in the crowd' and the 'masses'.[86] De Tocqueville likewise paid homage to the 'individualism of the Middle Ages'.[87] Manifestly, he did not take into consideration the fate of serfs, just as he did not take account of the fate of slaves and blacks in general when he pointed to the United States as the country where '*every* individual' enjoyed unprecedented 'independence'. When he subsequently asserted that in colonized Algeria, 'the role of the individual is everywhere greater than in the motherland', de Tocqueville ignored the Arabs, who, by his own admission, were often equated with the occupying forces to 'evil beasts' (see above, Chapter 5, §13; below, Chapter 7, §6).

Thus emerges the somewhat problematic character of the pathos of the individual, which was the flag waved by liberalism in its conflict with radicalism and socialism. Who was more individualist? Toussaint L'Ouverture, the great protagonist of the slave revolution? Or Calhoun, the great US theorist of the slaveholding South? Who demonstrated respect for the dignity of the individual as such? The black Jacobin who, taking the Declaration of the Rights of Man seriously, considered that it was always inadmissible to reduce a man to an object of 'property' of one of 'his follow men'? Or Jefferson, who kept silent about his doubts about slavery out of a conviction of white superiority and his concern not to endanger the peace and stability of the South and the Union? Who expressed individualism better? Mill and his English and French followers, who considered the subjection and even slavery (albeit temporary) of colonial peoples beneficial and necessary? Or the French radicals who began to question colonial despotism as such ('Let the colonies perish if they are to cost honour, freedom'[88])?

The doubts are not dispelled even if we ignore the colonies and peoples of colonial origin. Prominent in the liberal tradition (for example, Laboulaye) is the polemic against the fanaticism of the French revolutionaries, who regarded access to the vote and representative office as a 'natural, absolute right' of

---

86   Mill, *Utilitarianism*, p. 123.

87   Tocqueville, *Oeuvres complètes*, vol. 5, pt 2, p. 49.

88   Pierre Dockès, 'Condorcet et l'esclavage des nègres', in Jean-Michel Servet, ed., *Les idées économiques sous la Révolution*, Lyon: Presses Universitaires de Lyon, 1989, p. 85 n. (this is an assertion which, with some variations, can be found in Dupont de Nemours as well as Robespierre).

every individual, rather than a 'political function' of society.[89] So which of the two positions better expressed individualism? On the other hand, if the generalization of political rights imperilled 'individual independence', as Constant seemed to believe, why direct such a reproof solely against French radicalism and not also against the American Revolution (which erupted in the wake of the demand for the colonists' right to political representation)?

Examined more closely, the cry of alarm at the danger of the disappearance of individuality, and the impeding 'ants' nest', expressed the disquiet of the restricted community of the free first at the extension of political rights and then, increasingly, at the extension of economic and social rights. Yet it was de Tocqueville himself who compared the hungry man to a slave—that is, a man or an individual deprived of liberty and recognition. Compared with the liberal tradition, Nietzsche proved much more lucid and consistent. Although inspired by an implacable hatred of socialism and the social state demanded by it, and in fact precisely because inspired by such hatred, the brilliant reactionary thinker understood that, with its 'individualistic agitation', socialism aimed to 'render many individuals possible', raising them above their condition as instruments of labour and their herd-like relationship to the masters. With its universalistic charge, socialism issued in the recognition of every individual, independently of wealth, sex or race, as a subject endowed at a moral level with equal human dignity and possessor, politically, of inalienable rights. That was why Nietzsche indignantly condemned individualism and socialism. Albeit with a converse value judgement, Oscar Wilde also connected the two terms: 'Individualism ... is what through Socialism we are to attain.'[90]

Confirming the ambiguous character of the liberal tradition's individualism, it is worth noting that, in criticizing the French Revolution and the danger of subversion represented by the working-class and socialist movement, it liked positively to oppose the countryside to the city. This is readily intelligible in the case of the theorist of organicist 'partnership', Burke, who with utter consistency celebrated the 'agricultural class' that 'of all others is the least inclined to sedition'.[91] With his attention still fixed on the French Revolution and the role in it played by Paris, Constant stressed the danger of '[a]rtisans, crowded into the towns'.[92] But the theme of distrust or hostility towards the city, which

---

89   Édouard Laboulaye, *Histoire des États-Unis*, 3 vols, Paris: Charpentier, 1866, vol. 3, p. 319.

90   Cf. Losurdo, *Nietzsche*, ch. 33, §1 (for Nietzsche); Alain Laurent, *Storia dell'individualismo*, Bologna: Il Mulino, 1994, p. 66 (for Wilde's *The Soul of Man under Socialism*).

91   Burke, *Works*, vol. 8, p. 400.

92   Constant, *Political Writings*, p. 218.

was the prime site for development of the individual, runs deep in the liberal tradition. In Mandeville's view, 'London is too big for the Country', and it was precisely there that disturbing phenomena of social insubordination were emerging. Much more reassuring were rural areas, where it was possible to count on 'the poor silly Country People', who in fact were conspicuous for their 'Innocence and Honesty' and who, 'from their very Infancy', could be educated into obedience to authority and respect for customs and tradition.[93]

A certain regret for this world can also be observed in de Tocqueville, when in 1834 he described the condition of the poor man in the *ancien régime*. Characterized by 'limited' desires and calm indifference to 'a future that did not belong to him', his lot 'was less to be felt sorry for than that of men of the people of our days'. Accustomed to their condition from time immemorial, the poor under the *ancien régime* 'enjoyed the kind of vegetative happiness whose attractiveness is so difficult for the civilized man to understand that he denies its existence'.[94]

With the resumption of revolution in France, against those who sought to 'stir up the working population of the city', Tocqueville called for reliance on 'the inhabitants of the countryside, [who] are full of good sense and, thus far, of balance'.[95] The first person to take this recommendation to heart was de Tocqueville himself, who described how he organized the elections in his native village as follows:

> We all had to go to vote together in the village of Saint-Pierre, a league from our hamlet. The morning of the election, all the electors (that is, the whole male population over the age of twenty) met in front of the church, and all these men formed a queue in twos in alphabetical order ... I reminded these good folk of the seriousness and importance of the act they were performing and recommended that they not allow themselves to be approached or led astray by those who, on our arrival in the village, might seek to mislead them, but instead proceed in a group and stay together, each in his place, until we had voted. 'Let no one—I said—go home either to eat something or to dry himself (it rained that day) before he has done his duty'. They shouted that they would do this and did it. All the votes were cast at the same time, and I have reason to believe that virtually all of them were given to the same candidate.[96]

---

93 Bernard de Mandeville, *The Fable of the Bees*, 2 vols, ed. Frederick B. Kaye, Indianapolis: Liberty Classics, 1988, vol. 1, pp. 269, 306–7.

94 Tocqueville, *Oeuvres complètes*, vol. 16, p. 121.

95 Ibid., vol. 15, pt 1, p. 242 (letter to F. de Corcelle, 3 April 1848).

96 Ibid., vol. 12, p. 114.

It is hard to regard as a manifestation of individualism the events narrated here by the French liberal, beneficiary of the plebiscitary vote of the village whose lord he remained.

Just as the dichotomy between English love of liberty and French egalitarianism proves unfounded, so the opposition between the individualism of the liberal tradition (whose favoured site was England) and the anti-individualism of radicalism (whose centre was in France) does not withstand critical analysis. To the French revolutionaries, who with their Declaration of the Rights of Man aimed simply 'to excite and keep up a spirit of resistance to all laws—a spirit of insurrection against all governments', Bentham opposed his principle of social utility: 'there is no right which, when the abolition of it is advantageous to society, should not be abolished'.[97] This was the view condemned by Marx, who indignantly reported the reasons with which the prime minister, Palmerston, had once justified his distrust or hostility towards the demand for emancipation advanced by Irish Catholics: 'because the legislature of a country has the right to impose such political disabilities upon any class of the community, as it may deem necessary for the safety and the welfare of the whole'.[98]

9. Criticism of liberalism as anti-modern reaction?

In fact, we encounter a paradoxical phenomenon. While, on the one hand, it cultivated pre-modern nostalgia, on the other, liberalism contested the movement engaged in the demand for political rights and economic and social rights, accusing it of a basic inability to understand and accept modernity. The first to set off in this direction was Constant. Clinging to the idea of unanimous participation in political life and hence to 'ancient liberty', the Jacobins forgot that the latter was based on slavery, the institution that made it possible for freemen to enjoy the *otium* required for them to be genuinely active citizens in every respect.[99] It was 1819 when the French liberal argued thus. At this time, in every country where modern liberty flourished, slavery continued in one form or another to be a living reality and, what is more, had assumed a harshness and naturalistic rigidity unknown in classical antiquity. Certainly,

---

97   Bentham, *Works*, vol. 2, p. 501.

98   Palmerston, quoted in Karl Marx, *Secret Diplomatic History of the Eighteenth Century and The Story of the Life of Lord Palmerston*, ed. Lester Hutchinson, London: Lawrence and Wishart, 1971, p. 171.

99   Constant, *Political Writings*, pp. 309–28.

although it had not ceased to play a significant role, the institution was mostly isolated and concealed in the colonies. But that was not the case in the United States. There slavery was not only highly visible but, according to the analysis of not a few southern theorists (who took up and developed a suggestion of Burke's), it encouraged the republican spirit of the free. In other words, 'ancient liberty' continued to survive in some sense in the United States, which was nevertheless pointed to by Constant as a 'great example' of the modern liberty dear to him.[100] On the other hand, in stressing the invigorating function that the presence of slaves had on the spirit of liberty of free citizens, Burke explicitly referred to the example of the 'ancient states' (above, chapter 5, §2). Hence Constant's theoretical construct is based on a colossal repression, which is all the more amazing if we bear in mind the bitter struggles over slavery that developed in France. Abolished by the Jacobins, it had been restored by Napoleon, who arrived in power with the support not only of Sieyès, but also (as we shall see) of Constant himself.

Rather than emulating a model from antiquity, the French Revolution and the most radical currents thrown up by it were sometimes accused of encouraging nostalgia for the Middle Ages. Spencer compared progressive taxation to a corvée (see below, Chapter 8, §4). This was a theme subsequently developed by him with the observation that 'national charity' (i.e. laws benefiting the poor) was merely a new version of the pre-modern 'established church'. And just as the old dissenter had fought for respect for the spontaneity of authentic religious sentiment, so the new 'dissenter from a poor law, maintains that charity will always be more extensive, and more beneficial, when it is voluntary'. While the old dissenter denied any authority the right to dictate laws to his religious conscience, the new 'dissenter from established charity, objects that no man has a right to step in between him and the *exercise* of his religion', and indignantly rejected 'the interference of the state, in the exercise of one of the most important precepts of [the] gospel'.[101] In the last analysis, the demand for economic and social rights, to be legally ratified in the name of moral and religious values such as compassion and human solidarity, were simply a claim to restore life to a state religion! And the prophets of this state religion likewise referred to a pre-modern world. From the French Revolution onwards, as we shall soon see, the liberal tradition was fond of equating trade unions with medieval corporations. Even at the end of the nineteenth century, Lecky reproved trade unions and the working-class movement for aspiring to

---

100 Ibid., p. 211.
101 Herbert Spencer, *The Man versus the State*, Indianapolis: Liberty Classics, 1981, pp. 197–9.

an 'industrial organization' similar to that of the Middle Ages and the Tudor period.[102] Trade unions, Pareto stressed some years later, claimed to enjoy (and did enjoy) a kind of 'Mediaeval immunity'.[103] In Lord Acton's view, even more so than the demand by unions for alleged economic and social rights, it was that for universal suffrage that amounted to a pre-modern, regressive phenomenon. It was 'absolutist and retrograde', since it favoured the expansion of the state and of despotism that had happily been transcended by liberalism.[104] In conclusion, rather than classical antiquity as for Constant, Jacobinism, socialism and sometimes democracy itself were now accused of cultivating nostalgia for the *ancien régime*, whether it was of the Middle Ages or absolute monarchy.

The latter theme found fullest expression in de Tocqueville, according to whom, with their statist pathos, radicalism, Jacobinism and socialism were in a line of continuity with the statism, 'administrative centralization' and 'paternal government' of the *ancien régime*.[105] However, this was an argument which, albeit with timely variations, proved especially dear to defenders of the *ancien régime* themselves! In Berlin the *Berliner politische Wochenblatt* never tired of repeating that revolution and absolutism were 'identical, when regarded from a higher viewpoint'. In citing Louis XIV's motto ('L'état c'est moi!'), the journal observed that 'revolutionary freedom … is reconciled with this centralization, this bureaucratic despotism, with this tutelage through ministerial assistants of the provinces and the community, with this Hobbesian governmental omnipotence'.[106] De Tocqueville stressed the revolutionary role played, even before 1789, by the figure of the 'intendant' and 'public administration', which had in fact already expelled the nobility.[107] The periodical cited above arrived at the same conclusion, identifying and branding in the figure of the 'civil servant' the author of the cancellation of 'local liberties' and all intermediate bodies liable to overshadow 'state power'.[108] According to de Tocqueville, 'those peoples who are so constituted as to have the utmost difficulty in getting rid of despotic government for any considerable period are the ones in which aristocracy has

---

102   William Lecky, *Democracy and Liberty*, 2 vols, Indianapolis: Liberty Classics, 1981, vol. 1, p. 218; vol. 2, p. 373.

103   Vilfredo Pareto, 'L'éclipse de la liberté', in *Mythes et ideologies*, ed. Giovanni Busino, Geneva: Droz, 1999, pp. 14, 24.

104   Lord Acton, *Selected Writings*, 3 vols, ed. J. Rufus Fears, Indianapolis: Liberty Classics, 1985–88, vol. 3, pp. 554–5.

105   Tocqueville, *Ancien Régime*, pp. 61, 70.

106   Wolfgang Scheel, *Das 'Berliner politische Wochenblatt' und die politische und soziale Revolution in Frankreich und England*, Göttingen: Musterschmidt, 1964, pp. 74, 80–1.

107   Tocqueville, *Ancien Régime*, pp. 214, 217, 220.

108   Scheel, *Das 'Berliner politische Wochenblatt'*, p. 78.

ceased to exist and can no longer exist'.[109] But this was precisely the guiding thread of the condemnation of the French Revolution pronounced by the organ of the Prussian nobility.

Immediately after the publication of *The Ancien Régime and the Revolution*, expressing his agreement and admiration, Lieber observed that the book as a whole was a historical running commentary on the analysis of 'Gallican' political tendencies he had already developed.[110] Obviously, a degree of boasting is not absent. Yet we should understand the German-American liberal's point of view. In 1849 he had underlined the continuity between Louis XIV and the 1789 revolution, and between it and Napoleon Bonaparte and the 1848 Revolution. It was a history utterly pervaded by the ideal of 'equality' and the 'concentration' and 'centralization of power', the 'organization' and generalized 'interference of public power', with a consequent inevitable sacrifice of freedom, 'individualism' and the principle of the 'limitation of government'. By contrast, the latter was at the heart of the concerns and aspirations of the 'Britannic race' or 'Anglican race'—i.e. England and the United States.[111] We are, I repeat, in 1849; and at this time de Tocqueville confined himself to an indictment of socialism. While 'on many points' it had a different orientation from the '*ancien régime*', it had inherited 'the opinion that the only wisdom lies in the state'. But the partial and limited continuity established here did not in any way include the French Revolution. In fact, in his anti-socialist polemic, de Tocqueville did not hesitate to refer to Robespierre:

Flee ... flee the old mania ... of wanting to govern excessively; allow individuals, allow families the right freely to do anything that does not harm others; allow the communes the right to manage their own affairs; in a word, restore to the liberty of individuals everything that has illegitimately been taken from them, everything that does not of necessity pertain to the public authority.[112]

At this time, far from formulating the thesis of continuity between the *ancien régime* and the Revolution, de Tocqueville was refuting it in advance. Someone who did support it was Lieber, who was in a sense justified in claiming priority. In fact, it must be added that, by his own explicit admission, he had derived the

---

109   Tocqueville, *Ancien Régime*, p. 29.

110   Francis Lieber, *Civil Liberty and Self-Government*, Philadelphia: Lippincott, 1859, p. 259 n.

111   Francis Lieber, 'Anglican and Gallican Liberty', *New Individualist Review*, vol. IV, no. 2, 1966, pp. 718–21.

112   Tocqueville, *Oeuvres complètes*, vol. 3, pt 3, p. 173; Robespierre *Oeuvres*, vol. 9, pp. 501–2.

thesis from Niebuhr, whose disciple he considered himself to be,[113] and, more generally, from the German culture he had absorbed before leaving Prussia at the age of twenty-seven. In the first instance, the thesis of continuity between the *ancien régime* and the Revolution met with great success in the country where the *ancien régime* proved most tenacious.

We are clearly dealing with a rhetorical strategy: the revolutionary movement that claimed to be constructing a new world was branded as antiquated. Yet the strains are obvious. If we analyse the arguments of the various exponents of the liberal tradition, we see that the French Revolution and Jacobinism are variously situated in a line of continuity with classical antiquity, the Middle Ages and monarchical absolutism. The past to which the new is returned and reduced can assume the most diverse forms. Thus, the revolution was criticized with arguments that are difficult to reconcile with one another, and which are even opposed. On the one hand, it was accused of having destroyed the intermediate bodies that predated the advent of the absolute state; on the other, of wanting to preserve or reintroduce bodies, such as trade unions, that pertained to feudal particularism and that tended to take the form of a state within the state.

In the light of subsequent historical experience, it is difficult to regard the demand for economic and social rights (in our day also ratified by the UN) as pre-modern and, contrariwise, the view, which was not foreign even to de Tocqueville, regarding mass poverty as a datum of nature pertaining to Providence, rather than determinate politico-social relations, as modern. And, still with reference to the French liberal, it is difficult to reconcile condemnation of Jacobinism and socialism as movements situated in the wake of the *ancien régime*, with alarmist and apocalyptic denunciation of the 'new race' of delirious ideologues and agitators,[114] who menaced 'European civilization', in fact civilization as such, with an unprecedented danger.[115]

---

113 Lieber, *Civil Liberty*, pp. 51, 326; on his relations with Berthold Georg Niebuhr, cf. Francis Lieber, *Erinnerungen aus meinem Zusammenleben mit Georg Berthold Niebuhr*, trans. Karl Thibaut, Heidelberg: Winter, 1837.

114 Tocqueville, *Oeuvres complètes*, vol. 13, pt 2, p. 337 (letter to L. de Kergolay, 16 May 1858).

115 Ibid., vol. 3, pt 3, p. 292.

10. 'Individualism' and the repression of working-class coalitions

In some instances, the individualist profession of faith played a manifestly repressive role. Together with the phenomenology of power and the restriction of the political sphere we are already familiar with, it operated to justify the proscription of working-class coalitions. At the beginning of the eighteenth century, Mandeville expressed his utter consternation at a new, disturbing phenomenon:

> I am credibly inform'd that a parcel of Footmen are arriv'd to that height of Insolence as to have enter'd into a Society together, and made Laws by which they oblige themselves not to serve for less than such a Sum, nor carry Burdens or any Bundle or Parcel above a certain Weight, not exceeding Two or Three Pounds, with other Regulations directly opposite to the Interest of those they Serve, and altogether destructive to the Use they were design'd for.[116]

What prompted the ban at this time was simply a refusal of recognition, as emerges from the contempt, in fact the disgust, provoked by the unheard of behaviour among servants. Organizing themselves autonomously, as if they were gentlemen, they pretended to raise themselves to the level of masters or even to usurp their rights (above, Chapter 3, §8). The absence of recognition continued to play a role in Burke. Certainly, in regarding only contracts drawn up outside any 'collusion or combination' as valid [117]—the allusion to and support for the Combination Acts, which banned and penalized working-class coalitions in these years, are transparent—he appealed to the principle of freedom of trade, which did not tolerate impediments of any kind. But it is clear that the wage labourer, unrecognized in his autonomous subjectivity and dignity and degraded to an *instrumentum vocale*, was to see himself denied the right of autonomous organization from below.

Smith's position was more tortured. He recognized that what led to the formation of workers' coalitions was the desperate attempt to counter the de facto coalition whereby suppliers of work lowered wages, and to escape the threat of death from starvation. However, these 'enlarged monopolies'[118] must

---

116   Mandeville, *Fable of the Bees*, vol. 1, pp. 305–6.

117   Burke, *Works*, vol. 7, p. 380.

118   Adam Smith, *An Inquiry into the Nature and Causes of the Wealth of Nations*, Indianapolis: Liberty Classics,1981, p. 79.

be prevented and repressed in order to assert the rights not only of the market, but also of the individual. It was necessary to 'allow ... every man to pursue his own interest in his own way, upon the liberal plan of equality, liberty, and justice';[119] in accordance with 'the system of natural liberty', every man must be able to contribute and bring into competition 'both his industry and his capital', without any obstacles whatsoever.[120] In no case could 'violations of natural liberty [and justice]' be tolerated.[121]

In its turn, the Le Chapelier law, which banned workers' coalitions in France in 1791, was also said to be aimed at defending individual freedom. In the name of 'alleged common interests', such coalitions violated the freedom to work possessed by every individual.[122] And de Tocqueville referred to this law when, after 1848, he condemned the working-class and socialist movement thus: while 'the revolution has swept away all the obstructions that impeded the liberty of the citizen, that is, corporations and craft associations [*les maîtrises, les jurandes*]', the socialists proposed to reintroduce this junk, albeit 'in a new form'.[123]

Perhaps Marx had in mind the liberalism of his time, as well as the French Revolution, when he criticized the Le Chapelier law for having banned 'working-class associations of any kind', on the pretext that they represented the 're-establishment of the mediaeval guilds'.[124] The theme, which stigmatized trade unions as a residue or reminiscence of the Middle Ages and the *ancien régime*, was widely diffused in the second half of the nineteenth century. In England, while Lecky condemned resumption of the 'guilds',[125] Spencer was even more vehement: acting as new tyrants and taking the place of monarchical despotism, trade unions suffocated individual autonomy and liberty in every way. It was true that they could also be consenting, but this did not alter the terms of the problem: 'If men use their liberty in such a way as to surrender their liberty, are they thereafter any the less slaves?'[126]

The picture was the same across the Atlantic. Lieber condemned unions in the name of economics and morality alike: they were guilty of encouraging

---

119   Ibid., p. 664.

120   Ibid., p. 687.

121   Ibid., p. 530.

122   The text of the Le Chapelier law is quoted in Jean-Pierre Potier, 'L'Assemblé constituante et la question de la liberté du travail', in Jean-Michel Servet, *Les idées économiques sous la Révolution*, Lyon: Presses Universitaires de Lyon, 1989, pp. 251–2.

123   Tocqueville, *Oeuvres complètes*, vol. 3, pt 3, p. 193.

124   Marx and Engels, *Werke*, vol. 31, p. 48.

125   Lecky, *Democracy and Liberty*, vol. 1, pp. 218–19.

126   Spencer, *The Man versus the State*, pp. 512–13, 25.

sloth and, ultimately, vice.[127] By contrast, Laboulaye demonstrated an attitude of cautious openness,[128] while Mill continued to be fundamentally hostile. He targeted the 'moral police, which occasionally becomes a physical one', exercised by the trade-union movement: 'the bad workmen who form the majority of the operatives in many branches of industry' tried to block 'piecework' and thus oppressed workers of 'superior skill or industry', who sought to earn more. In reality, the consequences of piecework had been described as follows by Smith some decades earlier: the workers subjected to it 'are very apt to over-work themselves, and to ruin their health and constitution in a few years'; if they listened to 'the dictates of reason and humanity', it would be the masters themselves who restricted this type of remuneration. But philanthropic inter-vention from above was one thing. Quite another was intervention from below by organizations that trampled over individual rights and arbitrarily interfered in what Mill too continued to regard as 'private concerns'.[129]

While they sought to impose intervention from above on bourgeois govern-ment itself, workers promoted an autonomous movement of transformation from below. However, in the sphere sovereignly declared by it to be 'private', the liberal bourgeoisie did not tolerate the intervention of political power, or even that deriving from civil society. Theoretically legalized in England in 1825, following a phase of persecution that even saw culprits condemned to deportation, trade unions continued to be attacked by the judiciary, in as much as they were defined as corporations hampering free enterprise. They acquired full legitimacy in 1871. However, 'what Gladstone's government gave with one hand it took away with another.' If not trade unions as such, it was individual workers who could be dragged before the courts on the basis of a new law: '"Watching and besetting", that is "picketing" workmen continuing at work during a strike, was made illegal even when done only by a single person.' This law was repealed by Disraeli in 1875.[130] In France, the Le Chapelier law was only repealed in 1887. What lay behind full recognition of the legitimacy of workers' coalitions and organizations was the gigantic struggles that culminated in the Paris Commune. Hence we are beyond 1870, the date that according to Hayek marks the beginning of 'the decline of the liberal movement'.[131] Expressing

---

127   Lieber, quoted in Frank Freidel, *Francis Lieber*, Gloucester (MA): Peter Smith, 1968, p. 194.

128   Édouard Laboulaye, *Le parti libéral*, Paris: Charpentier, 1863, pp. 25–6, 310.

129   Mill, *Utilitarianism*, p. 144; Smith, *Wealth of Nations*, p. 100.

130   George M. Trevelyan, *British History in the Nineteenth Century and After*, London: Longmans, Green and Co., 1937, p. 369.

131   Friedrich von Hayek, *New Studies in Philosophy, Politics, Economics and the History of Ideas*, London: Routledge and Kegan Paul, 1978, p. 128.

himself thus is an author who, not by chance, seems to want to call everything back into question. In his view, by destroying 'the competitive determination of the price' of labour power, and claiming to interfere in the 'game' of the market, trade unions undermined the liberal system at its roots; and it was 'the clear moral duty of government' to prevent this happening.[132]

The Paris Commune was a watershed in Europe, but not across the Atlantic. Passed in 1890, the Sherman Antitrust Act was 'applied first and most effectively to labour', which was guilty of combining in trade-union 'monopolies' that did not respect individual initiative and freedom. By contrast, so-called yellow-dog contracts were long considered perfectly respectful of the rules of the market and individual liberty: on the basis of them, when hired, workers and employees committed themselves (were forced to commit themselves) not to join any trade-union organization.[133]

11. The demand for economic and social rights and the transition from paternalistic liberalism to social-Darwinist liberalism

A social-Darwinist streak ran through liberal thought from the start. The arguments used by Joseph Townsend in England in the second half of the eighteenth century against any attempt to introduce legislation in favour of the poor are eloquent: it would only end up destroying the balance of nature, cancelling the 'peaceable, silent, unremitted pressure' that was hunger and encouraging the growth of an idle, redundant surplus population. Left to itself, without the artificial interference of law-makers moved by false compassion, nature would restore its own balance, just as occurred on an island inhabited solely by goats and dogs. The struggle for survival selected the strongest, most vital elements, condemning the rest to their fate.[134] From the outset, the tendency to naturalize social conflict, and to present the wealth and power of the dominant classes as the expression of an immutable natural law (in this sense Burke referred to a '*natural* aristocracy' consecrated by 'Nature'),[135] contained a social-Darwinist element *avant la lettre*. We are familiar with Franklin's criticisms of doctors

---

132   Ibid., p. 146; Hayek, *Law, Legislation and Liberty*, London: Routledge and Kegan Paul, 1982, p. 142.

133   Allan Nevins and Henry S. Commager, *America: Story of a Free People*, Oxford: Oxford University Press, 1943, p. 318; Valerie Jean Conner, *The National War Labor Board*, Chapel Hill: University of North Carolina Press, 1983, p. 10.

134   Townsend, *Dissertation on the Poor Laws*, pp. 23, 36–41.

135   Burke, *Works*, vol. 6, p. 218.

for their commitment to saving lives 'not worth saving'. The 'disease' such people suffered from was the manifestation of divine anger at 'Intemperance, Sloth, and other Vices'; and it was fitting that all this met with the 'punishment' provided for by nature and Providence.[136] God's higher design must not be hindered, especially if colonial populations were the target. This applied not only to the Indians. The terrible famine that decimated an Irish population already severely tried by the British colonizers' plundering and oppression in the mid-nineteenth century seemed to Sir Charles Edward Trevelyan— charged by the London government with following the situation—to be the expression of 'omniscient Providence', which thereby solved the problem of overpopulation.[137]

However, the social-Darwinist element was accentuated as the popular classes, shaking off their traditional subalternity, intervened directly on the political scene to assert their rights. In the United States, following the abolition of slavery, paternalism rapidly gave way to an explicitly violent attitude towards blacks, subject to the terror that threatened anyone who dared to challenge white supremacy. Something similar occurred in Europe. Large sections of the dominant class reacted to the new situation achieved by the struggle for recognition by brandishing the law of natural selection, which condemned the unfit to an early death.

The most conservative sections of the liberal movement responded to the demand for economic and social rights with a radical, uncompromising liberalism. The state must not in any way interfere with the kind of divine judgement, or struggle for existence, to which Spencer had referred before Darwin. The English political and economic liberal condemned any state interference in the economy with the argument that one should not frustrate that cosmic law which required the elimination of the unfit and life's failures: 'the whole effort of nature is to get rid of such—to clear the world of them, and make room for better'. All men were as if subject to a divine judgment: 'If they are sufficiently complete to live, they *do* live, and it is well they should live. If they are not sufficiently complete to live, they die, and it is best they should die.'[138] It was necessary to respect 'that universal law of Nature under which life has reached its present height—the law that a creature not energetic enough to maintain itself must die'.[139]

---

136   Benjamin Franklin, *Writings*, ed. J. A. Leo Lemay, New York: Library of America, 1987, p. 803 (letter to J. Fothergill, 1764).

137   Cf. Domenico Losurdo, *Il revisionismo storico*, Rome and Bari: Laterza, 1996, ch. 5, §10.

138   Herbert Spencer, *Social Statics*, New York: Appleton, 1877, pp. 414–15.

139   Spencer, *The Man versus the State*, pp. 32–3.

Distancing himself from attempts to improve the hygienic and sanitary conditions of the popular classes, Lecky observed that, in reality, 'in not a few cases', infant mortality was 'a blessing in disguise'. Indeed,

> Sanitary reform is not wholly a good thing when it enables the diseased and feeble members of the community, who in another stage of society would have died in infancy, to grow up and become parent stocks, transmitting a weakened type or the taint of hereditary disease.[140]

Arguing thus, Lecky aligned himself with eugenics, the new 'science' that had made its appearance in England and met with extraordinary success in the United States, where between 1907 and 1915 as many as thirteen states passed legislation for compulsory sterilization. According to the legislation of Indiana (the first state to move in this direction), subject to it were 'habitual delinquents, idiots, imbeciles and rapists'.[141] Like eugenics, Spencer celebrated his greatest triumph in the transatlantic republic.[142] Here William G. Sumner, often regarded as a kind of US Spencer, warned people not to forget the 'struggle for existence', as 'poets and sentimentalists' liked to.[143] Socialism's mistake primarily consisted in its claim 'to save individuals from any of the difficulties or hardships of the struggle for existence and the competition of life by the intervention of "the state"'.[144] Anti-statism and Social Darwinism went hand in hand.

In Germany Heinrich von Treitschke drew attention to the example of the United States:

> Let us examine the most delectable common people in the world, that of New York. It is a set of rejects who have merged from all over the whole earth. Yet left to themselves, these corrupted elements are compelled to control themselves. Do you think there is a Prussian police capable of keeping them at bay in the same way that they are held at bay by the harsh law of necessity? All are well aware: nobody takes any notice if someone dies of hunger.[145]

---

140   Lecky, *Democracy and Liberty*, vol. 1, p. 275.

141   Cf. Losurdo, *Nietzsche*, ch. 23, §2.

142   Richard Hofstadter, *Social Darwinism in American Thought*, Philadelphia: University of Pennsylvania Press, 1944, pp. 18–36.

143   William Graham Sumner, *On Liberty, Society and Politics*, ed. Robert C. Bannister, Indianapolis: Liberty Classics, 1992, pp. 187, 190–1.

144   Sumner, quoted in Hofstadter, *Social Darwinism*, p. 48.

145   Heinrich von Treitschke, *Politik*, 2 vols, ed. Max Cornicelius, Leipzig: Hirzel, 1897–98, vol. 2, p. 272.

Still in Germany, in August L. von Rochau's view the United States had the merit of applying the principle that every individual must, in the first instance, know how to help himself, unlike revolutionary, centralist France, which delegated care of individual well-being to the state, transforming the latter into a 'hospital' for 'sickly, deformed people' (*Schwächlinge und Krüppel*). The country across the Atlantic also asserted its 'entrepreneurial spirit' in its foreign policy, taking territory after territory from Mexico or the Indians, the latter a people now doomed to an 'unstoppable decline', and thus the equivalent on the international plane of the *Schwächlinge und Krüppel* who demanded state aid.[146]

It makes no sense to seek to exclude Treitschke and Rochau from the liberal tradition by looking forward to the Third Reich and presupposing a variety of infernal negative teleology at work in Germany. In reality, both authors, especially the first, viewed England and the United States with sympathy and admiration and, echoing a theme widely diffused in the liberal culture of the time, unstintingly denounced the statist and anti-individualist tradition that revolutionary, socialist and Bonapartist France had inherited from the *ancien régime*. In particular, the presence in Treitschke of the influence of Constant and de Tocqueville is immediately obvious. One thinks of his condemnation of the 'deification of the state' and the subsequent expansion of the political sphere. From 'semi-ancient concepts' and 'Rousseau's enthusiasm for the civic sense of the ancients' derived the 'omnipotent state power' constructed by the Jacobins, who were likewise oblivious of the cost of the unanimous participation of citizens in political life: 'the civic splendour of Athens rested on a vast foundation of slavery'.[147] This inability to understand modern liberty led to tragedy: from the *ancien régime* to the revolution, from Napoleon I to Napoleon III, 'under all the regimes, the state's excessive activity has remained the hereditary disease of France', whose ideal was 'the state's providential omnipotence'.[148]

We can understand why social Darwinism established itself above all in Britain, the United States and Germany. At the end of the nineteenth century, these were three countries on the crest of a wave of economic development and international influence and prestige. If the first two were able to boast powerful expansion overseas or continentally, the third was already engaged in a frenetic scramble for colonies. We shall see that all three regarded themselves

---

146 Augus Ludwig von Rochau, *Grundsätze der Realpolitik*, ed. Hans-Ulrich Wehler, Frankfurt am Main: Ullstein, 1972, pp. 150, 186, 212.

147 Heinrich von Treitschke, 'Die Freiheit', in *Historische und politische Aufsätze*, vol. 3, Leipzig: Hirzel, 1886, pp. 9–10.

148 Heinrich von Treitschke, 'Der Bonapartismus', *Preussische Jahrbücher*, vol. 16, 1865, p. 209.

as members of a single family or race which, setting out from Germany, had first crossed the Channel and then the Atlantic. And all three tended to regard Latins (not to mention colonial peoples) as failures, and to attribute their own success to the action of natural selection, which rewarded the best within any individual state, but especially at an international level.

CHAPTER SEVEN

The West and the Barbarians: A 'Master-Race Democracy' on a Planetary Scale

1. Self-government by white communities and deterioration in the conditions of colonial peoples

Asserting the principle of consent by the governed as a condition of the legitimacy of political power, liberalism galvanized national independence movements. This initially occurred with the American Revolution. And it immediately offered an example. Some years later, it was the French colonists of San Domingo, determined to defend their property in slaves against interference from central power, who entertained projects of independence or adhesion to the North American Union. However, the colonists' agitation had an utterly unanticipated consequence, in the emergence on the American continent of a new independent state ruled by blacks and which was the first to abolish the institution of slavery. But San Domingo—Haiti was the exception—and an exception that filled the liberal world in its entirety with horror and scandal.

The outcome of the war of independence against Spain also induced perplexity and unease. It was crowned with success thanks to the aid of the ex-slaves of San Domingo and, albeit amid bitter conflicts, witnessed the emergence of a new identity stamped by a restoration of pre-Columbian ancestry and a mixing of races. Giving vent to a widespread sentiment, at the start of the Latin American revolution a senator from South Carolina (Robert Y. Hayne) scornfully referred to its leaders as 'men of color', who were 'looking to Hayti ... with feelings of the strongest confraternity'.[1] They admired the island which, in Jefferson's view, could serve only as a dumping ground where blacks could

---

1   Hayne, quoted in Lester D. Langley, *The Americas in the Age of Revolution*, New Haven: Yale University Press, 1996, p. 141.

be deported and deposited. For the purposes of that operation—i.e. 'the definitive disappearance of the black race from our borders'—John O'Sullivan, the
theorist of 'manifest destiny', thought above all of the Latin American continent: 'The Spanish-Indian-American population of Mexico, Central America
and South America, afford the only receptacle capable of absorbing that race
... [They are] themselves already of mixed and confused blood'.[2] In the view
of Elam Lynds, 'father of the prison system' then in force and a prominent US
figure, 'whose practical talents are universally acknowledged' (the characterization is de Tocqueville's) 'the Spanish of South America' formed 'a race closer
to the ferocious beast and the savage than civilized man'.[3] The category traditionally employed to define Indians was now also applied to the populations
that had committed the error of mixing with them.

While white colonists in the British Commonwealth saw their right to self-
government recognized, the Latin American peoples, excluded from the white
community and the community of the free strictly defined, became part of the
colonial world. This explains the Monroe Doctrine. Reinterpreted and radicalized in 1904 by Theodore Roosevelt, it conferred an 'international police
power' on 'civilized society' in general, and the United States in particular, in
relation to Latin America.[4]

The white colonists of the British Empire encountered no serious difficulty achieving recognition. Having learnt the lesson implicit in the American
Revolution, the London government decided to pursue the policy of 'conciliation' formerly suggested by Burke in its relationship with peoples 'in whose
veins the blood of freedom circulates'. Thus, from the second half of the nineteenth century, Canada, New Zealand, Australia and South Africa first achieved
significant autonomy inside the Commonwealth and subsequently attained
complete independence. It was a well-founded principle (observed John Stuart
Mill in 1861) that, at least in domestic policy, the 'colonies of European race'
were fully entitled to self-government.[5]

As in the case of the United States, self-government by the colonists could
entail a drastic deterioration in the conditions of colonial peoples or peoples of
colonial origin, now subject to the exclusive, unhampered control of their direct

---

2   John O'Sullivan, 'Annexation', *United States Magazine and Democratic Review*, vol. 4, July
1845, p. 7.

3   Lynds, quoted in Alexis de Tocqueville, *Oeuvres complètes*, ed. Jacob-Peter Mayer, Paris:
Gallimard, 1951–, vol. 5, pt 1, pp. 63–4.

4   Roosevelt, quoted in Jean-Pierre Martin and Daniel Royot, *Histoire et civilisation des États-
Unis*, Paris: Nathan, 1989, p. 179.

5   John Stuart Mill, *Utilitarianism, Liberty, Representative Government*, ed. Harry B. Acton,
London: Dent, 1972, p. 378.

oppressors. We are familiar with Smith's observation about the catastrophic consequences that 'free' representative bodies monopolized or controlled by slave-owners could have for black slaves. Several decades later, in 1841, James Stephen, one of the actors in the struggle that had led to the abolition of slavery in British colonies, declared himself in favour of their firm control by the Crown: 'popular franchises in the hands of a great body of owners of slaves were the worst instruments of tyranny which were ever yet forged for the oppression of mankind'.[6]

The pertinence of this warning was tragically confirmed by subsequent developments. In 1864, referring to New Zealand, which for some years had been able to count on 'responsible government'—that is, ultimately, self-government by the white community—*The Times* observed:

> We have lost all imperial control in this portion of the Empire, and are reduced to the humble but useful function of finding men and money for a Colonial Assembly to dispose of in exterminating natives with whom we have no quarrel.[7]

In Australia the extermination of the Aborigines had already begun some time earlier. But in this case too it was the de facto self-government which the colonists succeeded in exercising that pressed on the accelerator, whereas expressing concern in 1830 about the 'indelible stain' being imprinted 'upon the character of the British Government' was the Colonial Secretary.[8] In this sense, according to the observation made at the start of the twentieth century by an English liberal whose position was highly anomalous—namely, John Hobson—what was occurring was a kind of 'private slaughter', carried out by colonists who had wrested self-government or substantial freedom of action.[9]

In the case of South Africa, once the government had defeated the Boer settlers and subjected them to the Empire, it reassured them: 'Your fate is in your own hands ... the good sense of the British people will never tolerate any intermeddling in the purely domestic concerns of the people to whom it has conceded the fullest liberties of government.'[10] Self-government by white

---

6   Stephen, quoted in Eric Williams, *From Columbus to Castro*, New York and Evanston: Harper & Row, 1970, p. 299.

7   Quoted in Henri Grimal, *De l'Empire britannique au Commonwealth*, Paris: Colin, 1999, p. 109.

8   Robert Hughes, *The Fatal Shore*, London: Collins Harvill, 1987, p. 420.

9   J. A. Hobson, *Imperialism*, London: Unwin Hyman, 1988, p. 252.

10   Chamberlain, quoted in Thomas J. Noer, *Briton, Boer and Yankee*, Kent (OH): Kent State University Press, 1978, p. 115.

settlers involved the emergence of a racial state, which segregated blacks in a semi-servile condition and remained in place for almost a century.

Significantly, this regime took the South of the United States as its model.[11] There, following a brief interlude (so-called Reconstruction) immediately after the Civil War, when African Americans were genuinely able to enjoy civil and political rights, the reconciliation between the former enemies in 1877 re-established in the southern states the self-government of whites, who subjected the recently emancipated slaves to a terroristic dictatorship based on the principle of white supremacy. As in South Africa with the compromise between the British and the Boers, in the United States the compromise between central government and the dominant class in the South, which re-acquired the right to self-government, paved the way for the reassertion of 'master-race democracy'.

2. The abolition of slavery and the development of servile labour

At this point a question suggests itself. The military defeat of the South was clear and irreversible, but had the principle of the racial delimitation of the community of the free really been overcome? Scorning abolitionism, Calhoun summarized the change that had occurred in Britain's colonies following the desired emancipation: blacks were 'forced to labor, not by the authority of the overseer, but by the bayonet of the soldiery and the rod of the civil magistrate'.[12] This statement dates from 1837. Laws against vagrancy forced the former slaves to work as 'apprentices'. In what conditions? A year prior to the intervention of the theorist of the slaveholding South, a representative of the British colonial administration, inspired by evangelical sentiments, had observed in a letter to the governor of the island of Mauritius:

> The design of the law might more accurately have been described as the substitution of some new coercion for that state of slavery which had been abolished; the effect of it, at least, is to establish a compulsory system scarcely less rigid, and in some material respects even less equitable than that of slavery itself.[13]

---

11   Ibid., pp. 106–7.

12   John C. Calhoun, *Union and Liberty*, ed. R. M. Lene, Indianapolis: Liberty Classics, 1992, p. 475.

13   Hugh Tinker, *A New System of Slavery*, London and New York: Oxford University Press, 1974, p. 17.

De Tocqueville would later observe that 'having nominally abolished slavery, the British have reintroduced it under the rubric of apprenticeship for a certain period of time'.[14]

Certainly, the apprenticeship only lasted a few years, even if much time had to pass before the ex-slaves could shake off the negative discriminations of every kind they continued to suffer. In any event, even before the abolition of slavery in its colonies, Britain was concerned to replace the blacks, importing indentured servants from Africa and Asia. Here we see at work Indian and Chinese coolies in particular. On their arrival in the British colonies, they were settled in the accommodation reserved for slaves. It is true that this involved indentured servants, but in fact many of them did not survive until the expiry of their contract. Even the sexual exploitation of women was not lacking. In the popular art of the time, the coolie was represented in chains, exactly like a slave. Obviously, there was no longer a hereditary transmission of the servile condition; in a sense, there was not even any need for it. British ships could continue to transport coolies from Asia in a voyage that resembled the classic slave trade. Conditions were harsh and the mortality rate high.[15] But the losses could rapidly be made up. A distinguished American historian of the institution of slavery has offered a summary of the golden age of liberalism that is worth quoting:

In 1860, as in 1760, non-European compulsory labor was still the labor of choice for rational capitalists who chose to cultivate the vast undeveloped parts of the tropics ... The 20 millions who left India alone, mostly as indentured servants, between the 1830s and the 1910s, amounted to twice the number of Africans forcibly landed in the Americas during the four centuries of the Atlantic slave trade.[16]

In Britain in 1840 a political figure of the first importance—Lord John Russell—expressed his unease at the advent of a 'new system of slavery'. Initially, it met with resistance from the abolitionist movement, which was still fairly strong. However, as a result of the already noted weakness of abolitionism inspired by Christianity, demands for the import from Africa and Asia of indentured servants, who in reality were a more or less compulsory labour force, soon got the upper hand.[17]

---

14   Tocqueville, *Oeuvres complètes*, vol. 3, pt 1, pp. 92, 97.
15   Tinker, *A New System of Slavery*, pp. 176–9.
16   Seymour Drescher, *From Slavery to Freedom*, London: Macmillan, 1999, p. 432.
17   Cf. Tinker, *A New System of Slavery*, p. vii; Drescher, *From Slavery to Freedom*, p. 421.

As well as in British colonies, this new servile labour force also made its appearance in the United States. Around 10,000 coolies imported from China were engaged in building inaccessible railroads, intended to consolidate the conquest of the Far West.[18] As Engels put it, this was an attempt to replace black slavery with the 'disguised slavery of Indian and Chinese coolies'.[19]

Was this confirmation of the thesis maintained by Calhoun of the inseparability of work and slavery? In North America, prior to being overshadowed and then definitively supplanted by more profitable black slavery, Indian slavery had long persisted here and there, even after the Glorious Revolution. In 1767 Sharp, the abolitionist we have already encountered, felt obliged to denounce it. In the case of Virginia it was only in 1808 that the Supreme Court definitively pronounced its illegality.[20] From the American Revolution onwards, the indentured servant or temporary white slave was completely replaced by the black slave, who in turn, after the end of the Civil War, gave way to the coolie from China or India—another temporary slave, even if the skin colour was now yellow. In 1834, the same year as the abolition of slavery in British colonies, the liberal Wakefield acknowledged that 'yellow slaves' were beginning to take the place of 'blacks', just as the latter had taken over from 'red' (Indian) slaves.[21] In reality, 'red' slavery or semi-slavery would have a new lease of life in the second half of the nineteenth century in Texas and California, taken from Mexico (see below, Chapter 9, §2).

Naturally, it can reasonably be objected to Calhoun that semi-slavery or slavery for a specified period of time is not the same thing as perpetual and hereditary slavery. But let us note the further development of the argument by the theorist of the slaveholding South. In any 'wealthy and civilized society', part of the population 'live[s] on the labor of the other'. This was a manifestly conflictual relationship: the best way of regulating it was achieved when 'the labor of the African race is, [as] among us, commanded by the European'.[22]

---

18   Allan Nevins and Henry S. Commager, *America: Story of a Free People*, Oxford: Oxford University Press, 1943, p. 246.

19   Karl Marx and Friedrich Engels, *Werke*, 38 vols, Berlin: Dietz, 1955–89, vol. 4, p. 132.

20   Almon Wheeler Lauber, *Indian Slavery in Colonial Times within the Present Limits of the United States*, Williamstown (MA): Corner House, 1979, pp. 306–7, 313.

21   Edward Gibbon Wakefield, *The Collected Works of Edward Gibbon Wakefield*, ed. M. F. Lloyd Prichard, London and Glasgow: Collins, 1968, pp. 473ff.

22   Calhoun, *Union and Liberty*, p. 474.

3. The expansion of Europe in the colonies and the diffusion of 'master-race democracy' in Europe

Not even Mill had any doubts about the dominion the 'European race' was called upon to exercise over the rest of the world. Certainly, he declared for recognition of the right of self-government by the 'colonies of European race'. But only for them. As for the rest,

> Despotism is a legitimate mode of government in dealing with barbarians, provided the end be their improvement, and the means justified by actually effecting that end. Liberty, as a principle, has no application to any state of things anterior to the time when mankind have become capable of being improved by free and equal discussion. Until then, there is nothing for them but implicit obedience to an Akbar or a Charlemagne, if they are so fortunate as to find one.

It is clear: freedom applied 'only to human beings in the maturity of their faculties' and could not be demanded by minors or 'those backward states of society in which the race itself may be considered as in its nonage'.[23] No different was the position of Lecky, who at the start of the twentieth century celebrated the glory of the United Kingdom thus:

> Nothing in the history of the world is more wonderful than that under the flag of these two little islands there should have grown up the greatest and most beneficent despotism in the world, comprising nearly two hundred and thirty millions of inhabitants under direct British rule, and more than fifty millions under British protectorates ...[24]

The 'despotism' theorized here was certainly synonymous with slavery from the standpoint of Locke and the protagonists of the American Revolution, all the more so in that it seemed to know no limits. In Mill's view, 'a ruler full of the spirit of improvement is warranted in the use of any expedients that will attain an end, perhaps otherwise unattainable'.[25] Political 'slavery' could not be equated with slavery in the strict sense. Yet Mill went further. He demanded the barbarians' 'obedience' for the purposes of their education for 'continuous

---

23   Mill, *Utilitarianism*, p. 73.
24   William Lecky, *Historical and Political Essays*, London: Longmans, Green and Co., 1910, p. 48.
25   Mill, *Utilitarianism*, p. 73.

labour', which was the foundation of civilization. And, in this context, he did not hesitate to theorize a transitional phase of 'slavery' for 'uncivilized races'.[26] The point was forcefully reiterated: there were 'savage tribes so averse from regular industry, that industrial life is scarcely able to introduce itself among them until they are ... conquered and made slaves of'.[27] On the other hand, the slave had no cause for complaint; he was 'one step in advance of a savage', and thanks to the conditions imposed on him had already achieved a certain progress. We are put in mind of Calhoun and the slaveholding South, all the more so when Mill refers to '*born* slaves' recalcitrant to work and discipline.[28] Certainly, despite his employment of the expression just noted, the English liberal envisaged a temporary slavery. This would in fact seem to hang over 'the great majority of the human race', which unfortunately was 'in a savage or semi-savage state'[29]—the condition dictating slavery. While, on the one hand, Mill sided decisively with the Union during the Civil War, on the other, he legitimized the practice of forced labour imposed by colonial powers on subject populations.

The other side of the coin of this opposition between civilized, adult England and savage races of minors was the process whereby the barrier separating servants from masters in the metropolis tended to lose its caste rigidity. The attitude adopted in the mid-nineteenth century by Disraeli, champion of the colonial expansion of 'superior' races and major theorist of race as the 'key to history' (see below, Chapter 8, §10), was significant. He denied that it was possible to speak of the existence in England of 'two nations'—'the rich and the poor'—as the Chartists claimed. On the basis of his assertion of the unity that now characterized the 'privileged, prosperous English people', Disraeli promoted the Second Reform Act, which extended political rights to significant sections of the popular masses.[30] Class differences within the white community remained, but were being reduced even at a social level. The exploitation of Chinese coolies and other more or less servile labour forces created the possibility of 'raising to the position of "independent gentlemen"', if not 'whole white populations of the West', as Hobson maintained,[31] then at least a significant proportion of them.

---

26   Ibid., p. 198.

27   John Stuart Mill, *Collected Works*, 33 vols, ed. John M. Robson, Toronto and London: University of Toronto Press and Routledge and Kegan Paul, 1963–91, vol. 2, p. 247.

28   Mill, *Utilitarianism*, p. 199.

29   Ibid., p. 215.

30   Cf. Domenico Losurdo, *Democrazia o bonapartismo*, Turin: Bollati Boringhieri, 1993, ch. 2, §5.

31   Hobson, *Imperialism*, p. 313.

The decisive barrier now lay elsewhere. The three 'castes' had become two—in the United States thanks to the abolition of slavery, and in Europe thanks to the reduction of differences within the white community, which was tending to develop more egalitarian internal relations than in the past, similar to those of the white community across the Atlantic. In this sense, 'master-race democracy' now characterized the overall relations between the West and the colonial world, whether internal or external.

Thus, Hobson could denounce the extreme expansion of 'the area of British despotism'. The London government resorted to 'distinctively autocratic methods' in its relations with an enormous number of human beings:

> Of the three hundred and sixty-seven millions of British subjects outside these isles, not more than eleven millions, or one in thirty-four, have any real self-government for purposes of legislation and administration.
>
> Political freedom, and civil freedom, so far as it rests upon the other, are simply non-existent for the overwhelming majority of British subjects.[32]

Essentially, this was the same analysis as Mill's (and Lecky's), with the difference that 'despotism' now had a negative connotation. Suffering it (stressed Hobson) were populations coerced into forced labour. And here too we have a convergence with Mill as regards factual analysis, but a sharp contrast when it comes to value judgement.

4. De Tocqueville, Western supremacy and the danger of 'miscegenation'

The model of 'master-race democracy' also had a clear influence on de Tocqueville. It is true that during the July Monarchy he stood for the abolition of slavery in French colonies. But how were the ex-slaves to be treated once they had been emancipated? It was necessary 'to prevent the negroes of our colonies imitating those of the English colonies and, like them, abandoning the major industries to retire to a piece of fertile soil, which has been bought cheaply or grabbed'. Hence emancipated slaves could be permitted to choose their 'master', but not to 'remain idle or to work exclusively for themselves'. That could not be tolerated:

---

32   Ibid., pp. 124, 114.

In temporarily banning negroes from owning land, what are we doing? We are artificially placing them in the position in which the European labourer naturally finds himself. This is certainly not tyranny and the man this obstacle is imposed on when he escapes slavery would not seem to have any right to complain.[33]

In fact, the measure suggested here was the one historically implemented in the colonies, making it possible to transform slavery proper into a semi-servile labour relationship. In any event, in addition to their political rights, notionally emancipated blacks were thus also deprived of civil rights, by its 'artificially' being made impossible for them to own a piece of land and freely choose their occupation. While he condemned legal regulation of working hours as 'despotism', de Tocqueville had nothing against the creation from above of a caste of wage-labour denied any possibility of social mobility. When he referred to workers from India or other parts of the world, called on by England to replace the emancipated black slaves, the French liberal also made indirect mention of the coolies.[34] Significantly, however, he ventured no critical remarks about a labour relationship construed even by influential representatives of the liberal world as a recreation of the institution of slavery in a different form. As in Mill, so in Tocqueville, the supremacy pertaining to Europeans was not only political, but also had direct consequences economically and socially. In any event, the gulf separating dominant and dominated was unbridgeable:

The European race has received from heaven, or acquired by its own efforts, such incontestable superiority over the other races which compose the great human family that the man placed by us, on account of his vices and ignorance, on the bottom rung of the social scale is still first among the savages.[35]

It was fitting that such colossally different races continued to remain clearly distinct. De Tocqueville referred with horror to the behaviour of some prisoners deported to Australia:

The condemned have fled in large numbers into the woods. There they have formed companies of looters; they have allied with the savages, married their children and partially adopted their customs. Out of this crossbreeding, a race of half-castes has been born that is more barbarous than the Europeans

---

33 Tocqueville, *Oeuvres complètes*, vol. 3, pt 1, pp. 103, 105.
34 Ibid., vol. 3, pt 1, p. 99.
35 Ibid., vol. 4, pt 1, p. 271.

but more civilized than the savages, and whose hostility has constantly disturbed the colony and sometimes caused it to run the greatest dangers. [36]

This denunciation of miscegenation, which imperilled European or white supremacy, is a theme that takes us back to the United States and, above all, to the ideology that continued to inspire the South even after the Civil War.

5. The 'empty cradle' and the 'destiny' of the Indians

While for some peoples it involved subjection to a form of servile labour, for others 'master-race democracy', which was now on the point of becoming established on a planetary scale, issued in decimation or destruction. Leading the Union's war against the secessionist states and promoting the abolition of slavery was a figure (Lincoln) who, like Jefferson before him, toyed with the idea of deporting the blacks to Africa or Latin America, and who was a veteran of the wars against the Indians, against 'men, women, and children ... mercilessly cut to pieces'.[37] In 1871 General Francis C. Walker, commissioner for Indian affairs, proposed to treat 'wild men' no differently from 'wild beasts'.[38] The comparison we have already encountered in Washington, and which presided over the substantial erasure of the Indians (and the natives of Australia and New Zealand) from the face of the earth, thus makes its reappearance.

A genealogical myth derived from the Old Testament was called upon to legitimize these genocidal practices. A major modern historian, Arnold Toynbee, observed:

> The 'Bible Christian' of European origin and race who has settled among peoples of non-European race overseas has inevitably identified himself with Israel obeying the will of Jehovah and doing the Lord's work by taking possession of the Promised Land, while he has identified the non-Europeans who have crossed his path with the Canaanites whom the Lord has delivered into the hand of his Chosen People to be destroyed or subjugated. Under this inspiration, the English-speaking Protestant settlers in the New World exterminated the North American Indian, as well as the bison, from coast to coast of the Continent ...[39]

---

36 Ibid., vol. 4, pt 1, pp. 271–2.

37 Nevins and Commager, *America*, p. 167.

38 Walker, quoted in Richard Slotkin, *The Fatal Environment*, New York: Harper Perennial, 1994, p. 314.

39 A. J. Toynbee, *A Study of History*, vol. 1, London and New York: Oxford University Press, 1962, pp. 211–12.

This genealogical myth, which presided over the expropriation, deportation and decimation of the Irish and the Indians, was explicitly present in Lieber: '[God] has given [this great country] to us, as much as He gave Palestine to the Jews'.[40] No mention was made of the Indians, even if they seem to be implicitly compared to the populations that occupied the Promised Land without authorization prior to the arrival of the chosen people.

Democracy in America seems to support this deadly genealogical myth. De Tocqueville underlined the religious fervour of New England's founders, who regarded themselves as descendants from 'Abraham's stock'. In the writings and documents left behind by them, one sensed 'the very savor of Gospel antiquity'.[41] It was an aroma that in a way ended up turning the head of the French liberal himself. He uncritically adopted and subscribed to the description Nathaniel Morton, one of the colony's founders and first leaders, gave of the Pilgrim Fathers' arrival in America:

> [W]hat could they see but a hideous and desolate wilderness, full of wilde beasts and wilde men? [A]nd what multitudes of them there were, they then knew not ... the whole country, full of woods and thickets, represented a wild and savage hew.[42]

In this text, as in the Old Testament description of the unauthorized inhabitants of Canaan, those destined to be subjugated or wiped out by the chosen people—or, as de Tocqueville characterized it, 'the germ of a great nation wafted by Providence to a predestined shore'—are completely confounded with nature.[43] This providential design is all the more clear because, ultimately, it involved a desert. It is a theme *Democracy in America* returns to repeatedly: the Indian 'has nothing to oppose to our perfection in the arts but the resources of the wilderness'.[44] One phrase is especially significant: 'the Indians were the sole inhabitants of the wilds whence they have since been expelled'.[45] The desert ceased to be such, becoming a place inhabited by humans, only with the entry of the Europeans and the flight or deportation of the indigenous population. As we know, Locke and Montesquieu preferred to speak of 'virgin

---

40 Lieber, quoted in Frank Freidel, *Francis Lieber*, Gloucester (MA): Peter Smith, 1968, p. 317.

41 Alexis de Tocqueville, *Democracy in America*, London: Everyman's Library, 1994, vol. 1, p. 33.

42 Ibid., vol. 1, p. 34.

43 Ibid., vol. 1, pp. 25, 33.

44 Ibid., vol. 1, p. 335.

45 Ibid., vol. 1, p. 337.

forests'. But even though the two metaphors are different, their meaning is identical: we are dealing with places where there is no human trace, an area that is (as Locke put it) 'vacant'.[46]

When subsequently forced to register the presence of the Indians, de Tocqueville hastened to stress that they had no right to the land occupied by them:

> Although the vast country that I have been describing was inhabited by many indigenous tribes, it may justly be said, at the time of its discovery by Europeans, to have formed one great desert. The Indians occupied without possessing it. It is by agricultural labor that man appropriates the soil, and the early inhabitants of North America lived by the produce of the chase.[47]

For Locke already, the sole possible foundation of property right was labour, of which a people dedicated exclusively to hunting were incapable. But an explicitly theological justification was added by de Tocqueville to seal the fate of the Indians:

> They seem to have been placed by Providence amid the riches of the New World only to enjoy them for a season; they were there merely to wait till others came. Those coasts, so admirably adapted for commerce and industry; those wide and deep rivers; that inexhaustible valley of the Mississippi; the whole continent, in short, seemed prepared to be the abode of a great nation yet unborn.[48]

In this way, de Tocqueville ended up legitimizing the policy of deportation implemented by Jackson, president of the transatlantic republic when the French liberal visited it. The argument of the 'empty cradle' was widespread in the US culture of the time. Oliver Wendell Holmes, a 'freethinker' aligned with the liberals and a writer and intellectual who enjoyed undisputed prestige in Boston,[49] had no doubts in interpreting God's will. Only pending the arrival of a superior stock had the Indians been placed on American soil. Thereafter

---

46 John Locke, *Two Treatises of Government*, ed. William S. Carpenter, London and New York: Everyman's Library, 1924, p. 134.

47 Tocqueville, *Democracy in America*, vol. 1, p. 25.

48 Ibid., vol. 1, p. 25.

49 Vernon L. Parrington, *Main Currents in American Thought*, 3 vols, New York: Harcourt, Brace and Company, 1930, vol. 2, pp. 454–5.

they were clearly marked out for 'destruction' or 'extermination'.[50] Franklin had not argued very differently, when he attributed to a providential design the devastating effect of alcohol on a population destined to be wiped off the face of the earth (see above, Chapter 1, §5).

De Tocqueville's attitude was more pained. He did not shut his eyes to the horrors that were occurring. Yet, however distressing, the tragedy of the Indians expressed both the progress of civilization and a providential design. In any event, it was ineluctable:

> Their implacable prejudices, their uncontrolled passions, their vices, and still more, perhaps, their savage virtues, consigned them to inevitable destruction. The ruin of these tribes began from the day when Europeans landed on their shores; it has proceeded ever since, and we are now witnessing its completion.[51]

True, de Tocqueville expressed unease at the 'cold egotism', 'utter insensitivity' and 'ruthless sentiment' with which the white population of the United States, so attached to its morality and Christianity, viewed the fate of the Indians. Yet the French liberal's description of the 'savages', more than ever recalcitrant to 'civilization', certainly did not conduce to the cause of their salvation:

> As a general rule, their mouth was disproportionately large and their facial expression ignoble and wicked ... Their physiognomy exhibited that deep depravity which can only derive from a long abuse of civilization, and yet they were still savages. Mixed with the vices they have adopted from us is something barbaric and uncivilized, making them a hundred times more repugnant ... Their movements were rapid and uncoordinated, their voice shrill and tuneless, their glance worried and savage. On first contact, one would be tempted to regard them as nothing but a beast of the forest on which education has been able to confer a semblance of humanity, but which has nevertheless remained an animal.

We can now understand the question de Tocqueville posed to his US interlocutors: 'Do the Indians have an idea that sooner or later their race will be destroyed by ours?'[52]

---

50   Thomas F. Gosset, *Race*, New York: Schocken Books, 1965, p. 243.

51   Tocqueville, *Democracy in America*, vol. 1, p. 25.

52   Tocqueville, *Oeuvres complètes*, vol. 5, pt 1, pp. 73–6, 223–5; cf. pp. 343–4.

The Indians' deportation and decimation made explicit the fact that the North American territory was an 'empty cradle', awaiting the white settler committed from the time of his arrival to 'struggl[ing] against the obstacles that nature opposes to him', against 'the wilderness and savage life'.[53] Once again, what ends up emerging is the process of de-humanization of the natives, reduced, even more than to barbarism, to inanimate nature.

6. De Tocqueville, Algeria and 'master-race democracy'

In de Tocqueville the American model asserted itself with particular clarity when he confronted the problem of Algeria. The letter sent to Francis Lieber on 22 July 1846 is revealing:

> At this time I am very concerned about our affairs in Africa, which assume greater importance with every passing day. For us *war* has become, and will remain, the secondary aspect as long we do not have quarrels in Europe. The principal aspect today is colonization, is how to attract a major *European* population of cultivators to Algeria and, above all, keep them there. We already have 100,000 *Christians* in Africa, not counting the army. But they have almost all settled in the towns, which are becoming large, beautiful cities, while the countryside remains a *desert*. It is impossible to consider colonization in Africa without thinking of the great examples furnished by the United States in this field. But how to study them? Have books or documents of any kind been published in the United States that can enlighten us on this point and tell us how things unfolded? Can this information be found in official or other kinds of reports? Anything you could provide in this connection would be received with great gratitude.[54]

I have highlighted four phrases in italics. Let us begin with the last of them. Like the lands inhabited or, rather, occupied without authorization by the Indians, Algeria was a desert prior to the arrival of the French or 'Christians'. A sort of Biblical aroma begins to make itself felt in connection with the landing in North Africa of a civilized people, who likewise seem invested with a providential mission. It was a people at once European and Christian: the colonial war tended to assume a religious character. Certainly, expelling the Algerians

---

53 Tocqueville, *Democracy in America*, vol. 1, p. 434.
54 Tocqueville, *Oeuvres complètes*, vol. 7, pp. 110–11 (letter to Francis Lieber, 22 July 1846).

from their 'desert' was an operation that met with fierce resistance, but de Tocqueville was careful in this instance not to speak of 'war'. That was a category which could only be applied to armed conflicts in Europe and between civilized peoples. It somehow implied recognition of the enemy, which was something denied Arabs and Indians alike.

Precisely because of this lack of recognition, the campaign of colonial conquest could resort to pitiless violence that did not spare the civilian population. On account of their brutal, indiscriminate character, the methods used to subjugate Algeria ended up eliciting reservations and disquiet in France. De Tocqueville was not among the 'excellent philanthropists' about whom Bugeaud, the general in charge of military operations,[55] ironized:

> I have often heard in France men whom I respect, but do not support, consider it reprehensible that crops are burned, silos emptied, and lastly that unarmed men, women and children are seized.
>
> For me, this is a regrettable necessity, but one to which any people that wants to make war on the Arabs will have to submit.[56]

According to de Tocqueville, the head of military operations in Algeria had the merit of having understood all this:

> He is the first who has known how to apply ubiquitously and simultaneously the kind of war which, in my view as in his, is the only kind of war that is feasible in Africa. He has pursued this system of war with incomparable energy and vigour.[57]

This was a 'new science' that must be taken to heart.[58] In order to starve them, and confront them with the clear alternative of capitulation or death from starvation, Arabs who insisted on resisting must be deprived not only of their harvest, but also of the possibility of trading with neighbours: 'They suffer greatly from being parked between our bayonets and the desert'.[59] And again we are explicitly referred to the American model; this is how 'the most barbaric Indian tribes' were disciplined: 'the tribe from which a robbery or

---

55   In an article published in the *Moniteur algérien*, 25 December 1843: ibid., vol. 3, pt 1, p. 227 (editorial note by André Jardin).

56   Ibid., vol. 3, pt 1, pp. 226–7.

57   Ibid., vol. 3, pt 1, p. 299.

58   Ibid., vol. 3, pt 1, p. 316.

59   Ibid., vol. 3, pt 1, p. 227.

murder has been committed' was subjected to collective punishment, which excluded it from the trade with Europeans absolutely vital to it.[60]

Finally, the rebel Arabs must by all means be prevented from the possibility of combining or settling anywhere:

> Despite the passionate taste they display for a nomadic existence, they need settlements. It is of the utmost importance to prevent them being able to establish a single one. All expeditions whose aim is to occupy or destroy existing towns and emerging towns seem to me useful.[61]

De Tocqueville had no hesitation in issuing a radical watchword:

> To destroy anything that resembles a permanent gathering of population or, in other words, a town: I believe it is of the utmost importance not to allow any town to survive, or arise, in the regions controlled by Abd el-Kader [the leader of the resistance].[62]

Thus the modality of the war. But what results was it intended to achieve? We know the model that inspired de Tocqueville. In May 1841, while visiting Philippeville, founded on land acquired at a derisory price from the indigenous inhabitants, he was pleased by the 'American aspect of the city', which was rapidly expanding.[63] Expropriation and colonization were proceeding apace. Once the process had been completed, what kind of society should be built? What relations might be developed between the Arabs and the French? De Tocqueville was in no doubt:

> The fusion of these two peoples is a chimera that can be dreamt of only when one has not been on the spot. Hence it is possible and necessary that there be two clearly distinct sets of laws in Africa, because we are faced with two clearly separate societies. When one is dealing with Europeans, *absolutely* nothing prevents us from treating them as if they were alone; the laws enacted for them must always be applied exclusively to them.[64]

---

60   Ibid., vol. 3, pt 1, p. 230 n.
61   Ibid., vol. 3, pt 1, p. 230.
62   Ibid., vol. 3, pt 1, p. 229.
63   Ibid., vol. 5, pt 2, p. 216.
64   Ibid., vol. 3, pt 1, p. 275.

Corresponding to scrupulous protection of the invaders' civil liberties was a terroristic law of suspects directed at the indigenous population. During his visit to Philippeville, the French liberal was invited to lunch by a colonel in the occupying army, who painted an eloquent picture of the situation:

> Sir, only force and terror work with these people … The other day, a murder was committed in the street. An Arab was brought before me who was a suspect. I interrogated him and then had him beheaded. You will see his head on the gate of Constantine.[65]

De Tocqueville seems to have betrayed no emotion. He repeated the idea of two sets of laws. As regards criminal trials of 'natives', 'if it is thought that our forms are too slow (which I do not think), war tribunals could be set up for them'. And even for 'civil trials', the 'emergency procedure' already in force could be retained.[66]

Arabs must also be discriminated against economically, as well as legally: 'Allow free entry into France of all produce from Algeria, especially that derived not from native industry but colonial industry'.[67] Only on these conditions would French settlers in North Africa genuinely be able to develop on the American model:

> It is no easy thing to instil in Europeans the desire to abandon their country, because they are happy there and enjoy certain rights and certain goods that are dear to them. It is even more difficult to attract them to a country where from the outset they encounter a torrid, unhealthy climate and a formidable enemy, who incessantly hangs around you to take your property or your life. To get inhabitants to come to such a country, it is first of all necessary to give them great opportunities to make their fortune; in the second place, they must find social conditions that conform to their habits and tastes.[68]

We have seen de Tocqueville celebrate the unprecedented zone of liberty enjoyed by the individual in the United States (see above, Chapter 5, §13). But now something similar is to be found in the African space conquered by France: 'The colonies of all the European peoples afford the same spectacle. Rather

---

65 Ibid., vol. 5, pt 2, p. 216.
66 Ibid., vol. 3, pt 1, p. 280.
67 Ibid., vol. 3, pt 1, p. 253.
68 Ibid., vol. 3, pt 1, p. 259.

than being smaller, the role of the individual is everywhere greater than in the mother country. His freedom of action is less restricted'.[69]

Naturally, the other side of the coin was a drastic deterioration in the condition of the Arabs. De Tocqueville did not hide the fact: 'We have decimated the population' and the survivors were being exterminated by the starvation caused by the methods of war we have noted; 'at this moment Abd el-Kader is *literally* dying of hunger'.[70] It had to be admitted that 'we have made Muslim society much more miserable, disorganised, ignorant and barbarous than it was before it knew us'.[71] So what was to be done? The French liberal distanced himself from the attitude of not a few officers and soldiers of the French army: in their view, 'the Arabs are like noxious beasts' and 'the death of each and every one of them seems a good thing'. No, 'it is not only cruel, but absurd and impracticable to want to snuff out or exterminate the natives'.[72] For a second, de Tocqueville lets slip an admission: 'At this time we are making war in much more barbarous fashion than the Arabs themselves. Currently, civilization is to be found on their side.'[73] Immediately afterwards, however, we find the declaration we have already noted: there was no room for humanitarian scruples in a colonial war that directly targeted the civilian populations, who were denied means of subsistence and the possibility of combining. Or: 'Once we have committed the major violence of the conquest, I believe we must not shrink from the minor forms of violence absolutely required to consolidate it.'[74]

Once the conquest had been completed, it was necessary to promote self-government by civil society (French and white). It was called on to free itself altogether of military control, which must continue to be deployed with the requisite firmness over the Arabs. The conflict across the Atlantic, which during the War of Independence against Britain and in subsequent decades saw local self-government reject any interference by central political power—be it in London or Washington—in the colonists' expansion or slave-owners' enjoyment of their legitimate property, also manifested itself in Algeria. On one side were the colonists, who demanded complete freedom of action and expropriation, and on the other the political and military authorities, called upon to administer a ruthless colonial conquest with a minimum of prudence. How

69   Ibid., vol. 3, pt 1, p. 252.

70   Ibid., vol. 15, pt 1, pp. 224–5 (letter to F. de Corcelle, 1 December 1846).

71   Ibid., vol. 3, pt 1, p. 323.

72   Ibid., vol. 15, pt 1, pp. 224–5 (letter to F. de Corcelle, 1 December 1846).

73   Ibid., vol. 3, pt 1, p. 226.

74   Tocqueville, quoted in André Jardin, *Alexis de Tocqueville*, Paris: Hachette, 1984, p. 304 (unpublished letter to C. L. L. J. de Lamorcière, 5 April 1846).

many colonists could Africa absorb and how far could the process of expropriation of the indigenous population be pushed? De Tocqueville criticized hesitations and doubts: 'It is not correct to say that the introduction of European farmers is a measure whose implementation is impractical', or feasible only to a limited extent. At issue was a territory over which 'the indigenous population is fairly scarce or fairly dispersed'. In any event, 'the common property of the tribe is not founded on any title'.[75]

The colonel encountered by de Tocqueville, who did not hesitate to have Arabs decapitated on the basis of mere suspicion, on the other hand expressed his contempt for the colonists, a 'mass of scoundrels' and 'thieves', for whom the army was nothing more than a tool for accumulating a 'fortune'.[76] The date is 30 May 1841. The previous year, Bugeaud had set out his policy to the Chamber of Deputies: 'Wherever there is clean water and fertile soil, it is necessary to settle colonists, without worrying about whom the land belongs to. It must be distributed to them so that it is enjoyed as rightful property'.[77] However, in the previously cited article published in the *Moniteur algérien* on 25 December 1843, he observed that, although conducting the merciless war dictated by circumstances, his army demonstrated generosity towards the Arab who finally decided to surrender: 'We return to him all his world and sometimes part of his herd'.[78]

This attitude seems to have prompted reservations in de Tocqueville, judging at any rate from his intervention in the Chamber in June 1846:

In some localities, rather than reserving the most fertile land, the best irrigated and most adapted for government property for Europeans, we have given it to the natives ... After betrayals and rebellions, the natives have often been received by us with singular magnanimity. There are some who, having indulged in soaking their hands in our blood, have had their goods, their honour and their power restored to them, thanks to our generosity. There is more. In many places where the civilized European population is mixed with the indigenous population, there are not unfounded complaints that in general it is the native who is better protected, while the European obtains justice with greater difficulty.[79]

---

75   Tocqueville, *Oeuvres complètes*, vol. 3, pt 1, pp. 380–2.

76   Ibid., vol. 5, pt 2, p. 216.

77   Bugeaud, quoted in Yves Lacoste, André Nouschi and André Prenant, *L'Algérie, passé et présent*, Paris: Éditions Sociales, 1960, p. 314.

78   Bugeaud, quoted in Tocqueville, *Oeuvres complètes*, vol. 3, pt 1, p. 227 (editorial note by André Jardin).

79   Ibid., vol. 3, pt 1, pp. 321–2.

In a letter from the same period, de Tocqueville even ended up ironizing about 'the tenderness towards the Arabs that came over Monsieur Bugeaud at the point when he saw in it a powerful means of blocking the development of civilized colonization'.[80]

We seem to hear once again the laments and protests of the American colonists against the London government, or of the southern planters of the United States against the threat of interference by federal government. And, in fact, de Tocqueville elaborated on his indictment of the political and military authorities. At issue was not only the assignment of land:

> We have lavished honorific distinctions on the Arab, which are intended to indicate the merit of our citizens ... One is led to conclude that our government in Africa is taking softness towards the vanquished so far as to forget its conquering position ... It is neither useful nor obligatory for us to permit exaggerated ideas of their own importance in our Muslim subjects, and not even to persuade them that we are obliged in any circumstances to treat them as if they were our co-citizens and equals. They know that we have a dominant position in Africa and they expect us to retain it.[81]

The idea of human equality could not be extended to embrace 'semi-civilized peoples' located outside the West: it was absolutely vital to avoid occasioning 'astonishment and confusion in their spirits, filling them with erroneous and dangerous ideas'.[82] In no case was it permissible to lose sight of the objective of building a society based on the legally sanctioned domination of French, Christian and European colonists. The attainment of this objective was now close at hand: 'The Arab element is ever more isolated and little by little is dissolving. The Muslim population is tending to decline relentlessly, while the Christian population is growing relentlessly'.[83] Indeed: 'Our weapons have decimated some tribes ... On the other hand, our cultivators willingly use native manpower. The European needs the Arab to make the most of his land; the Arab needs the European to obtain a high wage'.[84]

There is no doubt that de Tocqueville had not lost sight of the American model. The Algerians were part Indians, forced to suffer expropriation, and part blacks. In the latter guise, Arabs could not claim to enjoy the rights of

---

80   Ibid., vol. 15, pt 1, p. 220 (letter to F. de Corcelle, 11 October 1846).
81   Ibid., vol. 3, pt 1, pp. 321–2, 324.
82   Ibid., vol. 3, pt 1, p. 324.
83   Ibid., vol. 3, pt 1, p. 275.
84   Ibid., vol. 3, pt 1, p. 329.

citizenship either on a civil level or, still less, politically. Without being slaves, now deprived of land they could earn a living only by supplying 'manpower' to the new property-owners. The society hoped for here was not very different from the one that would be realized in the southern United States after the Civil War. In Algeria, French and Western supremacy took the place of 'white supremacy'. For the rest, there continued to exist two sets of laws, separated by a racial barrier, and the prejudice, on a more or less accentuated racial basis, called upon to justify these relations. Already at the beginning of the conquest, writing to de Tocqueville, Kergolay (his cousin and a life-long friend) had spoken of the Arabs as an 'infamous, despicable race', to be kept under constant control 'by force combined with simple, uncomplicated equity'.[85] The recipient of this letter seems not to have seen things very differently. After a notable interval of time, we find him using, in slightly different form, some of the expressions we have just noted: 'semi-civilized peoples' were only capable of understanding the discourse of 'correct but strict justice'; hence France should beware of indulging in 'magnanimity and leniency'—virtues that would be incomprehensible and, worse, might produce dangerous results.[86] On the other hand, writing precisely to Kergolay, de Tocqueville denounced the 'greed' and 'fanaticism' of the Arabs,[87] who, by his own admission, were suffering the systematic expropriation carried out by occupying forces inclined to regard their enemies as 'noxious beasts'.

To complete this picture, it is appropriate to mention a final detail. There was a moment in 1833 when the French liberal thought of settling as a colonist in Algeria.[88] Identification with the regime of white or Western supremacy, or 'master-race democracy', seems to have been total.

---

85 Ibid., vol. 13, pt 1, pp. 193, 199 (letters of 22 June and 8 July 1830).

86 Ibid., vol. 3, pt 1, p. 324.

87 Ibid., vol. 13, pt 2, p. 86 (letter to L. de Kergolay, 23 May 1841).

88 Cf. Jean-Jacques Chevallier and André Jardin, Introduction to Tocqueville, *Oeuvres complètes*, vol. 1, pp. 12–13.

CHAPTER EIGHT

Self-Consciousness, False Consciousness and Conflicts in the Community of the Free

1. Return to the question: What is liberalism? The well-born, the free and the liberals

Having briefly reconstructed periods in the history of liberalism and the concrete politico-social relationships developed in its name, we must now return to our opening question. Use of the term 'liberal' is usually dated to the political struggles that developed in Spain in the wake of the 1812 revolution and the opposition that emerged between 'liberals', engaged in defending the constitution, and their opponents, whom they branded 'servile'. Only now was the adjective transformed into a substantive. In fact, in revolutionary America the author of an article opposed to the institution of slavery had already signed himself 'A Liberal' (see Chapter 2, §10). But that is not the key point. When we come across a text from 1818 in which Constant sets out and supports the programme of the 'liberal party', it can be said that we are dealing with an adjective.[1] The political meaning of the term is clear; and implicit in it is the transition to the noun employed to define members of the party in question. On the other hand, there is not much difference between this stance in favour of the 'liberal party' and the stance in favour of the 'liberal political system' that we have seen make its appearance in a text by Washington as early as 1783. Hence the real problem is to identify the moment when, partly inheriting and partly transforming the meaning bequeathed by a long tradition, the term 'liberal' began to assume its modern political meaning. This was the precondition for the transition from the adjective to the substantive.

---

1 Benjamin Constant, *Recueil d'articles*, 2 vols, ed. Éphraim Harpaz, Geneva: Droz, 1972, vol. 1, p. 577.

It was a semantic event that cannot be uncoupled from the actual history of the liberal movement and liberal revolutions. We can start with the Glorious Revolution. Arguing against Robert Filmer, defender of the thesis that the Almighty had conferred exclusive ownership of, and dominion over, the earth to Adam, the first absolute monarch, Locke objected that God had bestowed his blessings 'with a liberal hand'. The hypothetical absolute property-owner or monarch who, rather than displaying 'liberal allowance', sought to exploit the needy situation of all other men in order to reduce them to 'hard service' or even the condition of a 'vassal', would be acting no differently from the bandit who threatened a man with death in order to reduce him to 'slavery'.[2] Clearly, 'liberal' is synonymous with generous here. However, God's liberal generosity is in contradiction with the political slavery that Filmer would like to impose on all men. The, as it were, constitutional and liberal God presupposed here refutes the claims of absolute monarchy. The vile, miserable condition of the 'vassal', of the individual subjected to 'hard service', of the servant or 'slave', was incompatible with the mode of being and feeling, in the first instance, of an Englishman and 'gentleman', who scornfully rejected the servile view that 'we are all born slaves'.[3]

In his turn, Hume on the one hand used the term 'liberal' synonymously with 'disinterested' and 'generous', and on the other criticized as 'illiberal' the popular agitation and plebeian riots that characterized the first English revolution.[4] Similarly, Smith distinguished in the moral field between the 'liberal' view peculiar to the well-off classes, restive at overly rigid bans on 'luxury' and the other pleasures of life, and the 'strict or austere' view peculiar to poorer classes, who by force of circumstance could not indulge in 'thoughtlessness and dissipation'.[5]

In the context of the 'liberal'/'servile' opposition that was crystallizing, the 'liberal' attitude was defined by antithesis either to the absolute power of the monarch or the servile or even merely plebeian condition. The liberal/illiberal dichotomy referred to a difference and conflict between two world-views, but also between two social conditions. In the course of the American Revolution, adopting a position in favour of conciliation of the rebel colonists, Burke deplored the restrictions on individual liberty introduced in Britain on account of the war, and regretted the fact that 'the liberal government of this

---

2   John Locke, *Two Treatises of Government*, ed. William S. Carpenter, London and New York: Everyman's Library, 1924, pp. 29–30.

3   Ibid., p. 4.

4   David Hume, *The History of England*, 6 vols, Indianapolis: Liberty Classics, 1983–85, vol. 6, p. 84; vol. 5, p. 372.

5   Adam Smith, *An Inquiry into the Nature and Causes of the Wealth of Nations*, Liberty Classics: Indianapolis, 1981, p. 794.

free nation is supported by the hireling sword of German boors and vassals'.[6] Once again the liberal profession of faith criticized the unwarranted expansion of the Crown's power, on the one hand, and distanced itself from the subaltern classes, subjected to work and hence servile, on the other. We can now understand the British Whig's scorn for those who, in the name of a so-called 'indiscriminate' freedom, wished to appeal to the servile hands of slaves or emancipated slaves to suppress the revolt of colonists who, precisely as slave-owners, nurtured with particular sincerity the love of liberty that must dwell in any non-servile soul. And we can also understand why as early as 1790, on account of the restructuring of the nobility's political influence, the 'liberty' of the French seemed to the British statesman to be contaminated with 'coarseness and vulgarity': it 'is not liberal'.[7] Opposed to anything vulgar and plebeian, 'liberal' tended to be synonymous with aristocratic. In fact, among Virginia's slave-owners the 'aristocratic spirit' was intimately bound up with 'a spirit of liberty' distinguished by its 'more noble and liberal' character.[8] While paying homage to the 'liberal government of this free nation', Burke declared himself a member of the 'aristocratick Party'—the party 'connected with the solid, permanent long possessed property of the Country'—and felt committed to fighting with all his energy for 'aristocratick principles, and the aristocratick Interests connected with them'.[9]

During the American Revolution, along with the celebration of the 'liberal political system' we have already noted, we find in Washington a celebration of patrons of the 'liberal arts', contrasted with 'mechanics', with immigrants of a modest social condition from Europe.[10] But particularly illuminating is the discourse of John Adams. For a well-ordered liberty to be achieved, it could not be 'mechanics' and the 'common people', 'without any knowledge in liberal arts or sciences', who exercised power. Instead, it must be those who had 'received a liberal education, an ordinary degree of erudition in liberal arts and sciences'; and they were the 'well-born and wealthy'.[11]

---

6   Edmund Burke, *The Works: A New Edition*, 16 vols, London: Rivington, 1826, vol. 3, p. 153.

7   Ibid., vol. 5, pp. 155–6.

8   Ibid., vol. 3, p. 54.

9   Edmund Burke, *Correspondence*, 10 vols, ed. Thomas W. Copeland and John A. Woods, Cambridge: Cambridge University Press, 1958–78, vol. 7, pp. 52–3 (letter to William Weddell, 31 January 1792).

10   George Washington, *A Collection*, ed. William B. Allen, Indianapolis: Liberty Classics, 1988, pp. 397 (letter to La Fayette, 28 May 1788), 455 (fragments of the discarded first inaugural address, April 1789)

11   Adams, quoted in Charles Edward Merriam, *A History of American Political Theories*, New York: Kelley, 1969, p. 132.

In France, too, the liberal party, which was in the process of being formed, defined itself during the polemic against the absolute monarchy but also, and possibly above all, against the popular masses and their vulgarity. Attention was turned to the Third Estate, to those circles where 'a sort of affluence allows men to receive a liberal education'.[12] Expressing himself thus was Sieyès, who subsequently played an important role on the occasion of the 18th Brumaire in 1799. Sealing the coup d'état was the 'proclamation of general-in-chief Bonaparte', who announced the 'disbandment of factions'—i.e. of popular and plebeian agitation—and the triumph of 'conservative, tutelary, liberal ideas' (*idées conservatrices, tutélaires, libérales*). This language was not the invention of a general, however brilliant: he enjoyed the support of the liberal circles of the time. The adjectival usage just noted refers to them. Constant, who later (as we know) declared himself a member of the 'liberal party', had already been recommended by Talleyrand to Napoleon in 1797 as a man 'passionate about liberty' and as an 'unshakeable, liberal republican'.[13] The following year, Constant had underlined the Directory's merit in having 'proclaimed its unshakeable attachment to the conservative system'.[14] Finally, shortly after the coup d'état, he paid homage to 'France's tutelary genius which, from 9 Thermidor, has rescued it from so many dangers'.[15] Synonymous with 'aristocratic' in Burke, 'liberal' was now synonymous with 'conservative' (and tutelary). For Constant (as for Madame de Staël), the cause of liberalism found expression in 'respectable people' (*honnêtes gens*),[16] or (as Necker made clear in a letter to his daughter) well-off, 'decent people' (*gens de bien*: see below, Chapter 10, §1).

As in England and America, so too in France it was the property-owning classes, proud of their non-servile condition and spirit, who tended to define themselves as liberals. This is further confirmed, even after the mid-nineteenth century, by de Tocqueville's stance. Those genuinely capable of defending the cause of liberty against Louis Bonaparte's 'illiberal' government were not 'the people strictly speaking, with their incomplete education', but the 'property-owners', the 'bourgeoisie', the 'men of culture'—'in a word, all those who have received a liberal education'.[17]

---

12   Emmanuel-Joseph Sieyès, *Écrits politiques*, ed. Roberto Zapperi, Paris: Éditions des archives contemporaines, 1985, p. 133.

13   Henri Guillemin, *Benjamin Constant muscadin*, Paris: Gallimard, 1958, p. 178.

14   Ibid., pp. 194–5.

15   Benjamin Constant, *De la force du gouvernement actuel de France et de la nécessité de s'y rallier*, ed. Philippe Raynaud, Paris: Flammarion, 1988, p. 46.

16   Constant, quoted in Guillemin, *Benjamin Constant*, pp. 60, 183, 271.

17   Alexis de Tocqueville, *Oeuvres complètes*, ed. Jacob-Peter Mayer, Paris: Gallimard, 1951–, vol. 7, pp. 144–5.

Under the spur also of popular struggles, the liberal/servile dichotomy gradually tended to lose its class connotation and came to refer exclusively to political ideologies. But at moments of acute struggle the original meaning re-emerged with all its discriminatory charge. For de Tocqueville, as we shall see, anyone who wanted to endow the ideal of liberty with a social content was 'made for serving'!

Bitter conflicts could, and did, develop within the property-owning classes. Debating with Burke, who suspected wealth not rooted in the mother country's land and soil of lacking in patriotism and even of subversive tendencies, Mackintosh declared that '[t]he commercial, or monied interest, has ... been less prejudiced, more liberal, and more intelligent, than the landed gentry.'[18] Similarly, in France, Sieyès saw 'liberal education' embodied in the Third Estate, and certainly not in an aristocracy used to pursuing 'the favour of servitude' at court.[19] Invitations not to discriminate, and create conflicts, between the different types of property were more frequent. In the view of the anti-Jacobin Jean-Joseph Mounier, in addition to the United States, the country that had diffused 'in the France the idea of liberty' was England, construed in fact as the country where 'a liberal education without genealogical tests confers the quality of gentleman'.[20]

It is clear that the term 'liberal' was generated by a proud self-consciousness, which had a simultaneously political, social and even ethnic connotation. We are dealing with a movement and party that intended to rally persons furnished with a 'liberal education' and genuinely free, or people who had the privilege of being free, the 'chosen race' (as Burke put it), the 'nation in whose veins the blood of liberty circulates'. All this is not surprising. As has been made clear by distinguished scholars of the Indo-European languages, 'freemen' is a 'collective notion'—a sign of distinction that applies to the 'well-born' and them alone. For this very reason, outside the community of the free and the well-born, not only was service or slavery not excluded, it was even presupposed. In Cicero's view, at the head of the *liberi populi* was Rome, which engaged in the mass enslavement of defeated peoples considered unworthy of freedom.[21] Similarly, in eighteenth-century liberal England what became a popular song ('Rule Britannia') lauded in these terms the empire that had just wrested the

---

18   James Mackintosh, *Vindiciae gallicae*, Oxford: Woodstock, 1989, pp. 136–7.

19   Sieyès, *Écrits politiques*, p. 171.

20   Jean-Joseph Mounier, *De l'influence attribuée aux philosophes, aux francs-maçons et aux illuminés sur la révolution de France*, Tübingen: Cotta, 1801, pp. 31, 36–7, 50.

21   Cf. Domenico Losurdo, *Nietzsche, il ribelle aristocratico*, Turin: Bollati Boringhieri, 2002, ch. 33, §2.

asiento, a monopoly on the slave trade, from Spain: 'This was the charter of the land, / And guardian angels sang this strain: / "Rule, Britannia! rule the waves: / Britons never will be slaves."'

2. The pyramid of peoples

This was a self-proclamation that was simultaneously an act of exclusion. It was not only colonial peoples who were affected by it. Even before the American Revolution, Franklin had established a hierarchy of nations on the basis of skin colour, which claimed to classify the whole human race: 'All *Africa* is black or tawny. *Asia* chiefly tawny.' The same applied to pre-Columbian America; it was 'wholly so'. The quantitative prevalence of peoples of colour was evident. In a way, their presence even made itself felt in Europe: 'the *Spaniards, Italians, French, Russians* and *Swedes*, are generally of what we call a swarthy Complexion'. The inhabitants of Germany did not come off much better. Representing the highest form of humanity were the English settled on both shores of the Atlantic, 'the Principal Body of White People', of 'purely white People',[22] and the only community to embody the cause of liberty. The classical seventeenth- and eighteenth-century theme of the great chain of Being[23] becomes here the great chain of Colour. And it excluded the non-European peoples from the sacred space of civilization, relegating much of the West to its margins.

If it rarely took such a naively naturalistic form, the pyramid dear to Franklin continued, in one shape or another, to be present in liberal culture. We find it again in Lieber. At its apex, obviously, was the 'Anglican race', which fully expressed authentic liberty, while forming the base were the colonial peoples (not only the blacks, but also the Chinese). In the middle we find jostling Spanish, Portuguese and Neapolitans, who had hitherto proved incapable of elevating themselves to the principle of self-government.[24]

John Stuart Mill employed a language that was scarcely different. The apex continued to be composed of the 'Anglo-Saxons' (to be precise, England and the United States), peerless champions of representative government and 'the general improvement of mankind', while at the base, in addition to more or

---

22   Benjamin Franklin, *Writings*, ed. J. A. Leo Lemay, New York: Library of America, 1987, p. 374.

23   Arthur O. Lovejoy, *The Great Chain of Being*, Cambridge (MA): Harvard University Press, 1957.

24   Francis Lieber, *Civil Liberty and Self-Government*, Philadelphia: Lippincott, 1859, pp. 21, 294–5.

less savage peoples,[25] we find the Chinese. It is true that the latter could boast a very ancient civilization. Yet 'they have become stationary—have remained so for thousands of years; and if they are ever to be farther improved, it must be by foreigners'.[26] Ireland could be assimilated to the other colonies or semi-colonies. '[H]alf civilized', in Bentham's view,[27] Ireland for Mill was not only incapable of self-government, but also in need of 'a good stout despotism', exactly like India.[28] Not much better was the situation of Greece: situated as it was at the confines of Europe, it was still 'too Oriental' in many respects to be able to govern itself.[29] Finally, at the centre of the pyramid we have the people of 'southern Europe', whose 'inactivity' and 'envy' prevented the development of industrial society, the establishment of a strong ruling group and the orderly functioning of institutions. By comparison with them, too, the Anglo-Saxons proved superior, free as they were of those characteristics ('submission', 'endurance', statism) typical of the French and 'continental nations', all of them rendered gangrenous by 'bureaucracy' and an envious craving for equality.[30]

Certainly, the 'continental nations' were not some homogenous whole. With its geographical location close to Africa and an Arabic past behind it, Spain came out of things badly. In the list Mill drew up of 'envy' of grandeur and 'inactivity', its inhabitants came immediately after 'Orientals'.[31] Visiting Spain in 1836, at a time when it was plunged in a civil war, Richard Cobden, rather than taking sides with one of the parties, reached a general conclusion about 'barbarians beyond the Bay of Biscay': Spain was 'a nation of bigots, beggars and cut-throats with a government of whores and rogues'.[32] The Spanish of Latin America were not worth speaking about because, from the standpoint of the dominant ideology in the United States at any rate, they formed part of the

---

25 John Stuart Mill, *Utilitarianism, Liberty, Representative Government*, ed. Harry B. Acton, London: Dent, 1972, pp. 213–15.

26 Ibid., p. 129.

27 Jeremy Bentham, *The Works*, 11 vols, ed. John Bowring, Edinburgh: Tait, 1838–43, vol. 1, p. 577.

28 John Stuart Mill, *Collected Works*, 33 vols, ed. John M. Robson, Toronto and London: University of Toronto Press and Routledge and Kegan Paul, 1963–91, vol. 12, p. 365 (letter to J. P. Nichol, 21 December 1837). On this see Eileen P. Sullivan, 'Liberalism and Imperialism: J. S. Mill's Defense of the British Empire', *Journal of the History of Ideas*, vol. 4, 1983, p. 606.

29 Pasquale Villari, *Dai cargeggi*, ed. Maria Luisa Cicalese, Rome: Istituto storico per l'età moderna e contemporanea, 1984, p. 151 (letter from Mill to Villari, 11 June 1862).

30 Mill, *Utilitarianism*, pp. 213–15.

31 Ibid., p. 213.

32 Cobden, quoted in Wendy Hinde, *Richard Cobden*, New Haven: Yale University Press, 1987, pp. 25–6.

colonial world. Finally, distinguishing themselves negatively in Senior's view were also the Neapolitans: 'I never saw so hateful a people; they look as wicked as they are squalid and unhealthy.' Moreover, no barrier separated the plebs from the upper classes.[33]

3. The community of the free and its dictatorship over peoples unworthy of liberty

Obviously, the charge of exclusion implicit in the self-proclamation of the community of the free displayed its full force in the relationship with colonial peoples. In most cases, far from being perceived as a contradiction, the theorization and practice of slavery at the expense of the excluded further strengthened the proud self-consciousness of the community of the free, who lauded themselves for their immunity from the servile spirit attributed to the barbarians subjugated by them. That was why Locke could set himself up as a champion of liberty and, at the same time, legitimize the absolute power the community of the free was called upon to exercise over black slaves. In 1809 Jefferson celebrated the United States as 'an empire for liberty', founded on a constitution that guaranteed 'self government'.[34] Expressing himself thus was a slave-owner, who exercised power over his slaves brutally, if need be selling the individual members of the family of his property as separate pieces or chattels. And he indulged in this celebration in a letter sent to another slave-owner, who had just taken his place in the US presidency. The Constitution held up as a model consecrated the birth of the first racial state, while the self-government extolled here guaranteed southern slave-owners legitimate enjoyment of their property without interference by the federal government.

The transition from hereditary slavery to semi-slavery, still at the expense of colonial peoples, did not radically change the overall picture. Albeit in different forms, the phenomenon we are already familiar with emerged. Thus, major authors such as Mill, de Tocqueville and Lecky passionately denounced monarchical or Jacobin absolutism, and at the same time enthusiastically saluted despotism at the expense of colonial peoples. This was a power relationship which, for a whole historical period, far from being fought or contained, was to be extended and generalized. Given that a 'vigorous despotism' was the only

---

33   Nassau William Senior, *Journals Kept in Italy and France from 1848 to 1852*, 2 vols, ed. M. C. M. Simpson, London: Henry S. King and Co., 1871, vol. 2, p. 7.

34   Thomas Jefferson, *The Republic of Letters*, 3 vols, ed. James Morton Smith, New York: Norton, 1995, vol. 3, pp. 1585–6 (letter to James Madison, 27 April 1809).

method capable of raising backward peoples or 'barbarians' to a higher level, the interests of civilization and peace were served by colonial conquests, which must therefore be expanded to embrace the entire globe. Already 'common', 'direct subjection' of 'backward populations' by 'the more advanced' was becoming 'universal'.[35]

So proud and self-confident was the self-consciousness of the community of the free that it could face down possible refutations from the history or empirical analysis of society without difficulty. In the years of the July Monarchy, unperturbed, de Tocqueville registered a disconcerting fact: in the Islamic world and 'the whole East', slavery presented itself in a 'milder' form than in the West. Tunisia was engaged in abolishing this institution, which by contrast continued to survive in the colonies of liberal France (and democratic America).[36] The balance-sheet drawn up by Mill on the morrow of the American Civil War was significant. In the United States a '[h]opeless slavery' that 'brutifies the intellect', and where 'it was a highly penal offence to teach a slave to read', had only just been abolished. Even worse, added the English liberal, was the situation at the time of the slave trade in 'our slave colonies', where slaves were in practice condemned to work themselves to death, to be rapidly replaced through the 'importation' of other unfortunates, who in their turn were soon doomed to be consumed. In the British colonies and the United States a form of slavery had prevailed with particularly repugnant characteristics, which was largely unknown 'in the ancient world and the East'.[37] Here the phenomenon of the twin birth of liberalism and racial chattel slavery seems to be perceived or intuited. And yet, like de Tocqueville, Mill had no doubts about the complete coincidence of the West and the cause of liberty, or about the West's right to exercise despotism over Islamic peoples.

The English liberal had no difficulty construing the Opium War as a crusade for free trade and for liberty as such: 'the prohibition of the importation of opium into China' violated 'the liberty ... of the buyer', rather than that of 'the producer or seller'.[38] The lesson taught to the Chinese 'barbarians' could only be salutary. This was not the time to split hairs over forms: 'appeals to humanity and Christianity in favour of ruffians, & to international law in favour of people who recognize *no* laws of war at all', were 'ridiculous'.[39] We are in 1857–58: even if we pass over the lot of the coolies in silence, in these years

---

35 Mill, *Utilitarianism*, p. 382.
36 Tocqueville, *Oeuvres complètes*, vol. 3, pt 1, p. 330.
37 Mill, *Collected Works*, vol. 2, pp. 245–7.
38 Mill, *Utilitarianism*, p. 151.
39 Mill, *Collected Works*, vol. 21, p. 528 (letter to Edwin Chadwick, 13 March 1857).

Britain had stained itself with the 'barbarism' referred to by de Tocqueville in connection with the repression of the sepoys' mutiny in India; in China it gave decisive support to the liquidation of the attempt by the Taiping to reverse the autocratic and decrepit Manchu dynasty; in Ireland a ferocious dominion continued to obtain ('in no country have I ever seen so many gendarmes', observed Engels);[40] finally, in the United States, Britain contributed to the wealth of the South, absorbing much of the cotton produced by the labour of black slaves. Yet Mill was in no doubt: his country promoted the cause of liberty in the world, imposing on China by force of arms the importation of opium produced in India on the initiative of the colonial power!

When the sepoys' revolt broke out in India, de Tocqueville did not conceal the fact that 'massacres by the [Indian] barbarians' were followed by 'the barbarism of the civilized'.[41] But this did not prevent him from arriving at a Manichaean conclusion: 'these Hindus are beasts who are as brutal as they are ferocious'; their victory would mean 'the restoration of barbarism', the victory of 'savages' and the defeat of the 'only surviving country of political liberty in Europe'.[42] The aspiration of the Chinese or Indians to maintain or recover their national independence, the desire to liberate themselves from colonial domination, were not even taken into consideration. Precisely because it assumed the position of exclusive representative of the cause of liberty, the community of the free interpreted the challenges it occasionally had to confront as attacks on liberty, as expressions of the servile spirit as well as barbarism.

Macaulay acknowledged that the English colonists in India behaved like Spartans confronting helots: we are dealing with 'a race of sovereigns' or a 'sovereign caste', wielding absolute power over its 'serfs'.[43] But this did not prompt any doubts about the right of free England to exercise dictatorship over the barbarians of the colonies. It was a dictatorship that could take the most ruthless forms. Macaulay powerfully describes how the governor of India, Warren Hastings, proceeded when, at a difficult moment for Britain, already engaged in the struggle against the American colonists and their French allies, he had to confront the colony's native population:

---

40   Karl Marx and Friedrich Engels, *Werke*, 38 vols, Berlin: Dietz, 1955–89, vol. 29, p. 26 (letter from Engels to Marx, 23 May 1856).

41   Tocqueville, *Oeuvres complètes*, vol. 8, pt 3, p. 496 (letter to Gustave de Beaumont, 17 August 1857).

42   Ibid., vol. 18, p. 424 (letter to A. de Circourt, 25 October 1857).

43   Thomas Babington Macaulay, *The History of England*, ed. Hugh Trevor-Roper, London: Penguin, 1986, pp. 301–3.

A reign of terror began, of terror heightened by mystery; for even that which was endured was less horrible than that which was anticipated. No man knew what was next to be expected from this strange tribunal ... It consisted of judges not one of whom was familiar with the usages of the millions over whom they claimed boundless authority. Its records were kept in unknown characters; its sentences were pronounced in unknown sounds. It had already collected round itself an army of the worst part of the native population ...

A wave of arrests without any charge was unleashed, not even sparing the elderly of 'the most venerable dignity'. There was an orgy of violence that did not respect sanctuaries and unchained the most bestial instincts. There were Indians who 'shed their blood in the doorway, while defending, sword in hand, the sacred apartments of their women'. In conclusion: 'All the injustice of former oppressors, Asiatic and European, appeared as a blessing when compared with the justice of the Supreme Court.' And yet, despite this horrifying description, Macaulay concluded that, for having saved England and civilization, Hastings deserved 'high admiration' and to rank among 'the most remarkable men in our history'.[44]

4. How to confront the barbarian threat in the metropolis in timely fashion

The challenge to the community of the free could arise in the metropolis as well as from the colonies. The status of the popular classes, whom the dominant elite often tended to assimilate to 'savages', long remained uncertain. The assimilation became a veritable identification on the occasion of rebellions and revolutions. And as in the case of external barbarism, the remedy for the internal variety was dictatorship. Montesquieu was in no doubt about the fact that 'the usage of the freest peoples that ever lived on earth makes me believe that there are cases where a veil has to be drawn, for a moment, over liberty, as one hides the statues of the gods'.[45] This is what occurred in a state of emergency: in facing it, it was necessary to take to heart the 'admirable institution' that

---

44　Thomas Babington Macaulay, *Critical and Historical Essays*, 5 vols, Leipzig: Tauchnitz, 1850, vol. 4, pp. 273–4, 266, 300–1.

45　Charles-Louis Montesquieu, *The Spirit of the Laws*, trans. and ed. Anne M. Cohler, Basia Carolyn Miller and Harold Samuel Stone, Cambridge: Cambridge University Press, 1989, p. 204.

was the Roman dictatorship.[46] However 'terrible', at the opportune moment it 'violently return[ed] the state to liberty'.[47]

People argued no differently across the Atlantic. The *Federalist* maintained that, with the onset of a state of emergency, the powers granted to the federal authorities 'ought to exist without limitation' and without 'constitutional shackles'. Hamilton pointed out that even the Roman republic did not hesitate 'to take refuge in the absolute power of a single man, under the formidable title of Dictator', when this was required to confront grave dangers and defend Rome against 'the seditions of whole classes of the community whose conduct threatened the existence of all government'.[48] The 'existence of all government' mentioned by Hamilton took the form of 'the public good' in Locke. When it was imperilled, 'prerogative' legitimately enabled the 'prince' to safeguard it through 'an arbitrary power', or 'discretion', which could be exercised 'without the prescription of the law and sometimes even against it'.[49] In favour of granting emergency powers to General Cavaignac, during the crisis of 1848, was de Tocqueville (see below, Chapter 10, §1).

It is particularly interesting to note that what prompted an energetic reaction from the community of the free was not necessarily an actual revolt. An indirect, potential threat was enough. For Locke the right to employ force already existed in the event of the imposition of a tax not authorized by those directly affected: 'the supreme power cannot take from any man any part of his property without his own consent'.[50] Even if mediated by the intervention of the legislative power, the intrusion of non-property-owners in the sphere of property was always an act of illegality and plunder, of violence, and hence one that could legitimately be countered with violence by the person under attack. There is more: paving the way for unlawful interventions in property, any alteration in the composition of the legislative power, with the restructuring, for example, of the House of Lords or abolition of the hereditary transmission of its seats, betokened 'the dissolution of government' and hence the unavoidability of a test of arms.[51]

Montesquieu was fairly explicit on the subject:

---

46   Ibid., p. 177.

47   Ibid., p. 16.

48   Alexander Hamilton, *Writings*, ed. Joanne B. Freeman, New York: Library of America, 2001, pp. 253, 373.

49   John Locke, *Two Treatises of Government*, ed. William S. Carpenter, London and New York: Everyman's Library, 1924, p. 223, 199.

50   Ibid., p. 187.

51   Ibid., pp. 224, 242.

In a state there are always some people who are distinguished by birth, wealth or honors; but if they were mixed among the people and if they had only one voice like the others, the common liberty would be their enslavement and they would have no interest in defending it, because most of the resolutions would be against them. Therefore, the part they have in legislation should be in proportion to the other advantages they have in the state, which will happen if they form a body that has the right to check the enterprises of the people, as the people have the right to check theirs ... The nobility should be hereditary.[52]

While Montesquieu denounced any interference that abolished the heredi-tary privileges of the nobility as illiberal and despotic, Constant regarded any challenge to a property-owners' monopoly on representative bodies as inad-missible. Since 'the necessary aim of those without property is to obtain some: all the means which you grant them are sure to be used for this purpose'; and political rights 'will inevitably serve to encroach upon property'. It was suffi-cient for non-property-owners to be admitted into 'representative assemblies' for '[t]he wisest of laws' to be 'suspected and consequently disobeyed'.[53] More explicitly, the Thermidorian Boissy d'Anglas, having warned against the 'fatal taxes' that would inevitably be imposed by the legislative power once it was at the mercy or under the influence of non-property-owners, added: 'A country governed by property-owners is in the social order; by contrast, one where non-property-owners govern is in the state of nature.'[54] And, in a situation without a legal order and legal norms, arms obviously came to the fore.

Constant's reasoning continued to resonate in de Tocqueville: 'For various reasons, all governments can be led to maintain the poor at state expense, but the democratic form of government is led by its very *nature* to act in this way.'[55] Encouraged by democracy more than by any other political regime, 'legal charity' (i.e. aid to the poor through the use of resources procured by the state through taxes on the wealthy) could only be synonymous with despoliation in the view of its victims: 'The rich man whom the law, without consultation, strips of part of his surplus regards the poor man as nothing but a grasping

---

52 Montesquieu, *Spirit of the Laws*, p. 160.

53 Benjamin Constant, *Political Writings*, ed. and trans. Biancamaria Fontana, Cambridge: Cambridge University Press, 1988, pp. 215–16.

54 Boissy d'Anglas, quoted in Georges Lefebvre, *La France sous le Directoire*, Paris: Éditions Sociales, 1984, p. 35.

55 Tocqueville, *Oeuvres complètes*, vol. 6, pt 2, p. 70 (letter to Nassau William Senior, 21 February 1835).

foreigner summoned by the legislator for the division of his goods'.[56] In effect, this was an expropriation: if prolonged, laws in favour of the poor would end up transforming 'proletarians' into effective beneficiaries of the land and 'property-owners' into their mere 'farm managers'.[57]

Mill fluctuated more. On the one hand, he reiterated positions we have already encountered: 'any power of voting' in the hands of those who did not pay taxes was 'a violation of the fundamental principle of free government'; to assign political rights, and hence participation in legislative power, to poor citizens, not subject to taxation, 'amounts to allowing them to put their hands into other people's pockets for any purpose which they think fit to call a public one'.[58] On the other hand, the English left-liberal expressed a more flexible position:

> The laws and conditions of the production of wealth partake of the character of physical truths. There is nothing optional or arbitrary in them ... It is not so with the Distribution of Wealth. That is a matter of human institution solely.[59]

This is a distinction that would seem to pave the way for a policy of income redistribution.

Any such prospect was violently opposed by the most conservative wing of liberalism. According to Spencer, taxation aimed at income redistribution ultimately introduced a sort of 'state *corvée*', which was no less iniquitous and slave-like than the medieval one just because it imposed payment of a determinate sum of money, rather than the provision of free services to the master.[60] In his turn, Lecky, having adopted the thesis already noted in Constant, according to which non-property-owners with political rights would inevitably be led to pursue 'predatory and anarchic purposes' and even 'break up society', defined the system that enabled non-property-owners to burden the well-off with taxes as 'a system of veiled confiscation'. In this way, the latter would in fact end up being 'completely disenfranchised'.[61] The unwarranted political

---

56 Ibid., vol. 16, p. 132.

57 Ibid. vol. 4, pt 1, p. 321.

58 Mill, *Utilitarianism*, p. 281.

59 Mill, *Collected Works*, vol. 2, p. 199.

60 Herbert Spencer, *The Principles of Ethics*, 2 vols, ed. Tibor R. Machan, Indianapolis: Liberty Classics, 1978, vol. 2, pp. 242–3.

61 William Lecky, *Democracy and Liberty*, 2 vols, Indianapolis: Liberty Classics, 1981, vol. 1, pp. 2, 21, 27.

emancipation of the popular classes involved the dis-emancipation of the only classes qualified to run the country.

5. The liberal tradition and its three theories of dictatorship

As well as averting the real or potential threat of the barbarians in the colonies or metropolis, dictatorship could also be useful and indispensable in confronting the most serious problems that the community of the freemen could not resolve by ordinary means. To abolish the institution of slavery, to which representative bodies hegemonized by slave-owners proved stubbornly attached, Smith looked to 'despotism', which effectively took shape during the Civil War and in the early post-war years. The attitude adopted in these circumstances by Lieber was significant. In publishing his principal work, he certainly foresaw the possibility of recourse to 'martial law' to confront a possible state of emergency, but was concerned to specify that it would not be the executive power which declared it. But with the outbreak of hostilities, he discarded his previous constitutional scruples: the suspension of habeas corpus must be implemented in any event and as extensively and radically as possible. In silencing his critics, Lincoln declared: 'Must I shoot a simple-minded soldier-boy who deserts, while I must not touch a hair of a wily agitator who induces him to desert?' Lieber was not only in full agreement, but as early as January 1862 was amazed and angry at the fact that no traitor or spy had as yet been hanged.[62]

A theory of temporary modernizing dictatorship can also be found in de Tocqueville. Reconstructing the catastrophe of the French Revolution, he arrived at a conclusion: given the irreversible crisis of the *ancien régime*, the radical transformation of society was inevitable, but it would have been better if, 'instead of being carried out by the masses on behalf of the sovereignty of the people, [it] had been the work of an enlightened autocrat'; indeed, '[a]n absolute monarch would have been a far less dangerous innovator.'[63] He would have been able to exercise against the most reactionary feudal aristocracy the temporary dictatorship over slave-owners invoked by Smith. Modernizing dictatorship was not evoked by de Tocqueville solely with a view to the past. The French liberal asked himself, and one of his English interlocutors, whether a 'temporary dictatorship, exercised in firm, enlightened fashion like that of

---

62   Frank Freidel, *Francis Lieber*, Gloucester (MA): Peter Smith, 1968, pp. 309–19 (for the quotation from Lincoln, see p. 312).

63   Alexis de Tocqueville, *The Ancien Régime and the French Revolution*, trans. Stuart Gilbert, London: Fontana, 1966, p. 187.

Bonaparte after 18 Brumaire, is not the only way of saving Ireland'.[64] The dictatorship hypothesized here is different from that theorized by Locke against 'papists', which was directly exercised by the British Protestant settlers, albeit with the support of central government. De Tocqueville seems to envisage a power imposed from London that would be above the parties (Catholic peasants and Anglo-Protestant property-owners), just as in Smith 'dictatorship' is called upon to situate itself above both property-owners and their slaves.

By contrast, the position taken by Mill was more general in character: 'I am far from condemning, in cases of extreme exigency, the assumption of absolute power in the form of a temporary dictatorship.' The dictator could, 'for a time strictly limited', 'employ … the whole power he assumes in removing obstacles which debar the nation from the enjoyment of freedom'.[65]

An integral part of the self-celebration of the community of the free (and the liberal tradition) was the opposition between intransigent, unconditional guardianship of the liberty it assigned itself and the inclination to despotism reprehended in opponents. In reality, we have seen three theories of dictatorship emerge: the dictatorship of civilized peoples over barbarians in the colonies; the dictatorship that suppresses popular subversion in the metropolis; and the dictatorship which, in a situation of stalemate, imposes the requisite reforms from above. A contrast with authors not within the liberal tradition, or even foreign to it, might prove useful. Mazzini invoked 'a highly centralized dictatorial Power', which proceeded to the 'suspension' of the bill of rights and finished its work only with the achievement of national independence and the final victory of the national revolution.[66] Marx applied this perspective to the social revolution as well as the national revolution. In both cases a dictatorship is envisaged that emerges in the wake of a popular revolution from below. But for de Tocqueville (and the liberal tradition as a whole), it was precisely 'revolutionary dictatorship' from below that was 'most hostile to liberty'.[67] Although not free of uncertainties, in Marx criticism of the pedagogical dictatorship that the community of the free claimed to exercise over barbarians was recurrent. In reality, it was precisely in the colonies that the 'profound hypocrisy and inherent barbarism of bourgeois civilization lies unveiled before our eyes'.[68]

---

64   Tocqueville, *Oeuvres complètes*, vol. 5, pt 2, p. 131.

65   Mill, *Utilitarianism*, p. 207.

66   Giuseppe Mazzini, *Note autobiografiche*, ed. Roberto Pertici, Milan: Rizzoli, 1986, p. 179.

67   Tocqueville, *Oeuvres complètes*, vol. 16, p. 234 n.

68   Karl Marx and Frederick Engels, *Selected Works*, Moscow: Progress Publishers, 1969, vol. 1, p. 498.

This also applied to Ireland: it groaned under 'police terrorism',[69] 'English terrorism',[70] a regime that kept the population under control 'solely by bayonets and by a state of siege sometimes open and sometimes disguised',[71] resorting to summary executions and the most drastic war measures.[72]

6. The ills of the community of the free: the psychopathology of French radicalism

In the central area of the pyramid of peoples, Mill also inserted the French. Likewise, along with the Spanish, Portuguese and Neopolitans despised by him, Lieber combined the people who more than any other embodied the spurious and wicked 'Gallic' or 'Gallican' freedom, which in reality was synonymous with extreme centralization and despotism.[73] The combination is surprising. According to Burke, at the point when the Estates General was summoned France was already in possession of a good legal order. Rid of the absolute monarchy, it had become a full member of the community of the free. What had occurred in the intervening years to provoke such a ruinous descent and consequent confinement to the grey border area between civilization and barbarism?

Unfortunately, Burke observed on 9 February 1790, with the transformation of the Estates General into a constituent National Assembly, and hence with the restructuring of the political influence of the nobility and clergy, the French had turned out to be infected with a 'disease'. Passing from despotism to anarchical subversionism, they had proved that they were 'a people, whose character knows no medium';[74] and (added the British Whig a year later) '[i]t is ordained in the eternal constitution of things, that men of intemperate minds cannot be free.' Lecky referred to this analysis some years later, repeating it: 'It was ... in the opinion of Burke a total mistake to suppose that political liberty of any kind can be, or ought to be, possessed by all nations'.[75]

---

69   Marx and Engels, *Werke*, vol. 18, p. 136.

70   Ibid., vol. 16, p. 449.

71   Karl Marx, *Capital: Volume One*, trans. Ben Fowkes, Harmondsworth: Penguin, 1976, p. 863.

72   Marx and Engels, *Werke*, vol. 11, p. 392 n.

73   Lieber, *Civil Liberty and Self-Government*, pp. 21, 294–5.

74   Burke, *Works*, vol. 5, p. 9.

75   Ibid., vol. 6, p. 64; William Lecky, *A History of England in the Eighteenth Century*, 8 vols, London: Longmans, Green and Co., 1883–88, vol. 5, p. 501.

The further radicalization of the revolution that had been sparked off in Paris confirmed this diagnosis. While the outbreak and manifestation of the disease could be variously dated, it was understood that the French lacked the 'practical good sense' that had enabled the Anglo-Americans and the United States in particular to avoid 'revolutionary times', the devastation and 'adventure' of civil war. This was a point tirelessly stressed by de Tocqueville and, in his wake, by Laboulaye and Guizot.[76]

Moreover, on inspection, it was not merely good sense and practical spirit that were wanting. In Anglo-Americans these qualities were a constitutive element in a more general mental disposition, whereby 'a man by following his own interest, rightly understood, will be led to do what is just and good'.[77] We know that, although de Tocqueville deplored it, the fate of Indians and blacks was irrelevant when it came to forming an overall judgement on the republic across the Atlantic. What promoted the undisturbed flourishing of liberty here was the mature personality of its inhabitants, who displayed manifest political and moral superiority to the French. De Tocqueville found the explanation suggested by his fellow countryman Victor Lanjuinais 'profound and original': 'socialism is our natural disease'. And socialism was synonymous with abstraction, but also with something worse. The French were 'afraid of isolation' and harboured a 'desire to be in the crowd'; they felt themselves members of a 'nation that marches to the same step in perfect alignment'; they regarded liberty as 'the least important of their possessions, and thus are always ready to offer it up with reason at moments of danger'. Hence a France irremediably 'revolutionary and servile'.[78]

Immediately after Louis Bonaparte's coup d'état, having stressed that it was 'contained in germ in the February revolution', when 'socialism had been seen to make its appearance', de Tocqueville offered a kind of epitaph on the French nation: 'It is incapable and, I say it certainly with regret, unworthy of being free'.[79] The oscillation between anarchical revolutionism and submission to despotism, and an inclination to surrender to passing impulses and moods, confronted one with a people whose 'basic characteristics are so constant that we can recognise the France we know in portraits made of it two or three

---

76   Tocqueville, *Oeuvres complètes*, vol. 7, pp. 177, 182 (letters to T. Sedgwick, 19 August and 14 October 1856); Édouard Laboulaye, *Histoire des États-Unis*, 3 vols, Paris: Charpentier, 1866, vol. 1, p. xviii; and on Guizot, cf. Marx and Engels, *Werke*, vol. 7, p. 210.

77   Alexis de Tocqueville, *Democracy in America*, London: Everyman's Library, 1994, vol. 1, p. 393.

78   Tocqueville, *Oeuvres complètes*, vol. 2, pt 2, pp. 331–3.

79   Tocqueville, quoted in André Jardin, *Alexis de Tocqueville*, Paris: Hachette, 1984, p. 437 (letter of 14 December 1851).

thousand years ago'.[80] The fact that the process begun in 1789 or 1787 had finally issued in the establishment of the Bonapartist dictatorship, dragging the country down to the level of the 'nations best made for servitude', clarified everything. In France, 'what at first seemed a genuine love of liberty proves to have been merely hatred of a tyrant. But what a nation with a real instinct for freedom cannot endure is the feeling of not being its own master.'[81]

The closing chapters of *The Ancien Régime and the French Revolution* are a bravura rhetorical performance. Rarely has the love of liberty been hymned in such impassioned terms. And the beauty and power of these passages prove all more the engaging if we bear in mind the polemic, allusive but transparent and courageous, against Napoleon III's despotism. However, read more coolly, this hymn to liberty proves problematic and even disturbing, with the opposition it sets up between 'peoples made to be free' and 'nations best made for servitude'. It was a divide reproduced within France at the level of social classes. The enlightened love of liberty, which had manifested itself at the start of the revolution, was rapidly overwhelmed by the blind passion for equality, from which the Terror and the equal enslavement of all to an unprecedented despotic power derived. How was this distortion to be explained? De Tocqueville had no doubts: it became 'less startling when we remember that the Revolution, though sponsored by the most civilized classes of the nation, was carried out by its least educated and most unruly elements'.[82]

A disdainful warning was issued to the latter, intent on pursuing 'material benefits' and incapable of appreciating liberty in and for itself: 'The man who asks of freedom anything other than itself is born to be a slave.' Once again we are presented with an opposition between those born for liberty and those born for servitude, between freemen and servants, between liberals and serviles. And for de Tocqueville it was futile to try to explain the presence or absence, or variable intensity, of the 'desire' for liberty by the level of historical development and material living conditions of particular peoples and social classes. It was ultimately of little use even to challenge the influence of erroneous theories; or rather, these referred to something more profound. The 'lofty aspiration' to liberty was a thing that some men are capable of feeling, while others are not: '[i]t is a privilege of noble minds which God has fitted to receive it, and it inspires them with a generous fervour.' The discourse has hitherto focused on a few noble souls: 'to meaner souls, untouched by the sacred flame,

---

80 Tocqueville, *Ancien Régime*, p. 227.
81 Ibid., p. 188.
82 Ibid., p. 224.

it may well seem incomprehensible'.[83] An original curse, which cannot be lifted, seems to hang over the men, classes or peoples who, on account of their vulgarity or coarseness, are excluded or expelled from the community of the free.

Moreover, in its sad destiny France was not alone. Some years earlier— in September 1848, to be precise—de Tocqueville had seen the spectre of socialism lurking across the Alps and had not hesitated to conclude that the Italians 'have likewise shown themselves unworthy of liberty'.[84] 'Likewise': which country is being alluded to? At this time, not yet invested by a coup d'état, France was still part of the community of the free. The reference is to Germany: as in much of Europe, there too the revolution continued to flare up and pursue radical objectives. The ambit of countries deserving of liberty thus risked being extremely restricted.

7. Interpretations of the interminable French Revolutionary cycle: from 'disease' to 'race'

It is not by chance that politico-social conflict came to be interpreted in a psychopathological register. Immediately after the February revolution, de Tocqueville was concerned to specify that '[i]t is not needs but ideas that have led to this great upheaval' and made the French 'so ill'.[85] It was madness that encouraged the socialist pretension to alter not only 'political laws', but even social and 'civil laws'—in particular, relations of property and production consecrated by nature and Providence. In the course of his journey in England, de Tocqueville compared workers to slaves and drew attention to the relations of 'strict dependency' that were being established within the factory. On the basis of this analysis, the struggle to overcome or alleviate the condition of slavery or 'strict dependency' could be construed as a struggle for freedom. But, as we know, this was not how the French liberal argued, as he denounced the 'despotism' of those who sought to regulate working hours and the servile spirit of those who contaminated the ideal of liberty with economic and social demands. The community of the free claimed the merit of pursuing the ideal of liberty in all its purity and in any circumstances for itself. Hence it interpreted not only challenges from the colonial and barbaric world, but also challenges

---

83   Ibid., pp. 188–9.

84   Tocqueville, *Oeuvres complètes*, vol. 8, pt 2, p. 44 (letter to Gustave de Beaumont, 14 September 1848).

85   Ibid., vol. 6, pt 2, p. 101 (letter to Nassau William Senior, 10 April 1848).

arising in the zone of civilization itself, as an attack on the ideal of liberty, which was lashed out at by those not in a position to appreciate its grandeur and beauty. Wholly understandable and, indeed, natural among savages, such deafness was construed as a pathological anomaly in a civilized people.

In this sense, the resort to explaining conflict in a psychopathological register was immanent in the liberal tradition. Burke spoke of French 'disease' in the very first stages of the revolution. And it should be added that for a time it was in fact the 'American inoculation', and hence a disease from across the Atlantic, which was held responsible for the contraction and contagious spread of ideas marked by abstract, insane extremism.[86] Denunciation of the disease and psychopathological diagnosis of the adversary could occur in the converse direction. As the abolitionist movement developed, it became a commonplace in the United States to condemn it as an expression of an illiberal spirit, fanaticism and madness. However, at the time of the British colonists' revolt in America, we find Josiah Tucker inviting the London government to accept and even encourage the secession, so as to avoid the 'contagion' of a '*mad, fanatical* liberty', which was sweeping through slaves or serfs, the contagion of a 'republicanism' that was indeed 'American', but which ultimately dated back to Locke and the 'Lockian Sect' and could count on the sympathy of Burke himself.[87]

After 1848, following the umpteenth return of revolution with yet more radical slogans, the tendency to warn against the disease raging in France dramatically intensified. Underlining the rootedness in the United States of the rule of law and liberal institutions, *Democracy in America* attributed much more weight to history and geography than *The Ancien Régime and the French Revolution*. Why had Napoleon Bonaparte's military dictatorship been imposed on France?

> War does not always give over democratic communities to military government, but it must invariably and immeasurably increase the powers of civil government ... If it does not lead to despotism by sudden violence, it prepares men for it more gently by their habits.[88]

---

86 François-Alphonse Aulard, *Histoire politique de la Révolution française*, Aalen: Scientia, 1977, p. 19 n. 1.

87 Josiah Tucker, *Collected Works*, London: Routledge and Thoemmes Press, 1993–96, vol. 4, pp. 65, 100, 140; vol. 5, p. 72.

88 Tocqueville, *Democracy in America*, vol. 2, pp. 268–9.

The situation across the Atlantic was very different: 'Fortune, which has conferred so many peculiar benefits upon the inhabitants of the United States, has placed them in the midst of a wilderness, where they have, so to speak, no neighbours; a few thousand soldiers are sufficient for their wants.'[89] While we once again encounter the dubious assimilation of the Indians (and even Mexico) to a 'wilderness', we are far removed from the explanation that peremptorily and definitively opposes a 'sublime desire' for freedom to vulgar indifference to it, 'noble souls' to 'mediocre souls'.

By way of confirming the anthropological drift that manifested itself with 1848, we can adduce the long letter (a small essay) sent by de Tocqueville twenty years earlier to his friend de Beaumont. The history of Europe was conceived here in such a unitary way that the terminology became interchangeable: mention was made of the 'Commons' in the case of France and the 'Third Estate' in the case of England. In the two countries the victory of the bourgeoisie had been achieved in different ways, which were in fact the 'forced result of the state of things'—that is, of the different configuration of power relations between the contending politico-social subjects.[90] Were statism and despotism the hereditary disease of the country where Jacobinism and Bonapartism had made their appearance? In truth, England had not only succeeded in constructing a strong state and military apparatus before France, but at the time of the Tudors had suffered an unlimited despotism: 'I know of no tyranny in history more complete than that of ... Henry VIII'; the Commons, 'which had denied the king's will a man's life', now ended up 'condemning without even giving a hearing'. A worse terror than the Jacobin version had manifested itself, as demonstrated by '"bills of attainder", a diabolical invention that not even the revolutionary Tribunal called into being'. Yet it was nonetheless a revolution that had played a positive role. It nurtured the 'first fruit of civilization' as a result of the fact that, albeit in its terrible absolutism, in England royal power attacked the 'vices of the feudal system' and subdued 'oligarchical liberty'. This was a general tendency, though in no country did 'despotism prove more terrible'. Was the island across the Channel, unlike France, characterized and blessed by a gradualism of historical evolution? The letter/essay we are examining explicitly argued against the thesis that the English Constitution had passed through 'successive, regular stages, before reaching the point it has arrived at today', so that it could be considered 'a fruit which has matured over

---

89   Ibid., vol. 2, p. 264.

90   Tocqueville, *Oeuvres complètes*, vol. 8, pt 1, pp. 57–8 (letter to Gustave de Beaumont, 5 October 1828).

successive centuries'. In truth, de Tocqueville observed, from Henry VIII onwards, 'I see the English people change religion four times according to the will of their master'.[91]

Naturally, one might try to devalue the letter/essay of 1828 as 'youthful'. However, even in subsequent years, if there was a contrast between France and England, it was often to the detriment of the latter, which continued to interpret liberty as a 'privilege' rather than a 'common right', as occurred in the country that was the protagonist of the 1789 revolution (see above, Chapter 4, §9). In 1843, having compared slave-masters in the colonies with the 'aristocracy' overthrown by the French Revolution, de Tocqueville celebrated 'the great principles' of the revolution, 'which was carried out entirely in the name of equality', in the name of the equality of the 'human race', and which had the further merit of being first to abolish slavery.[92] Starting from the 1848 revolution, under the impression made by the spectre of socialism, it was precisely the pathos of equality that defined the failure of the French Revolution and the disease of an entire people, who now prostrated themselves before Louis Napoleon.

The psychopathological interpretation of developments in the French situation had the advantage of dispelling possible anxieties in the community of the free, which absolved itself of any responsibility for the Bonapartist outcome of the 1848 revolution. De Tocqueville might have drawn up a critical balance-sheet of the conduct of the liberal party and himself. After the dictatorship's advent, with some exaggeration he denounced the limited resistance met with by Louis Napoleon in French society. Had the disappointment they experienced with the exclusion of three million Frenchmen from political rights contributed to the passivity of the popular masses? This was a measure the liberal bourgeoisie had been guilty of in 1850, thereby furnishing the dictator with the possibility of elevating himself into a champion of universal suffrage and the struggle against privilege and discrimination.[93] And what role in undermining the Second Republic had been played by intransigent liberalism à la de Tocqueville, who had branded the reduction of working hours and any intervention by political power in favour of the most deprived as intolerable 'despotism'? The Bonapartist regime had its stronghold in the countryside: had it not been primarily the liberal bourgeoisie, with de Tocqueville's active participation, which stirred it up against the city and mobilized it in the name

---

91   Ibid., vol. 8, pt 1, pp. 64, 67–9.
92   Ibid., vol. 3, pt 1, pp. 124–5, 109.
93   Cf. Domenico Losurdo, *Democraζia o bonapartismo*, Turin: Bollati Boringhieri, 1993, ch. 1, §9.

of the struggle against the terrible threat that hung over civilization, dictating extraordinary measures commensurate with the situation? And again: Had the discrediting of institutions and the rule of law been aided by the supreme contempt for the Constitution displayed by de Tocqueville, when in his capacity as foreign minister he demanded 'the right, in spite of our Constitution, to overthrow the Roman Republic'?[94]

Moreover, a basic contradiction ran through the French liberal's attitude. On the one hand, on an immediate political level, he vigorously condemned the Bonapartist regime; on the other, as an historian he regretted the fact that the requisite modernization of France had not been completed by an 'absolute prince' or 'despot', rather than a popular revolution (see above, Chapter 8, §5). But a modernizing 'absolute prince' or 'despot' is precisely what Napoleon I had wanted to be and what Napoleon III aspired to be! Rather than engage in an examination that was possibly too painful at a personal level, the author of *The Ancien Régime and the French Revolution* preferred to come to blows with a mythical, eternal France.

A not dissimilar evolution is found in Mill. In 1849 he vigorously defended the February Revolution of the previous year. Thereafter, he continued to make an important acknowledgement of 'the heroic and calumniated Provisional Government of France' for having promptly abolished slavery in the colonies, in an implicit contrast not only with the North American republic, but also with England, on whose history 'a lasting blot' was left by the support of 'the leading portion of our higher and middle classes' for the South's pro-slavery secession from the United States.[95] In his *Autobiography*, reminiscing about the debate that developed in Europe over the American Civil War, having denounced the 'furious' pro-Southern position of much of the English liberalism of the time, Mill added: 'None of the Continental Liberals committed the same frightful mistake.'[96] Yet in 1861 we have seen him inclined to exclude the French people and 'continental nations' in general from the community of the free in the strict sense. These were years when, not altogether in jest, people liked to say that 'negroes begin in Calais', just across the Channel.[97] In fact, if not skin colour alone, 'race' was now called on to explain the differential development of European countries. What must not be overlooked, observed Lieber, still pointing a finger at France, was 'the Celtic spirit of being

---

94 Tocqueville, *Oeuvres complètes*, vol. 15, pt 1, p. 342 (letter to F. de Corcelle, 30 July 1849).

95 Mill, *Collected Works*, vol. 20, pp. 319–63; and vol. 2, pp. 250–1.

96 Ibid., vol. 1, p. 267.

97 Jan Morris, *Pax Britannica*, London: Folio Society, 1992, vol. 2, p. 87.

swayed by masses' and hence surrendering to political, religious and literary 'centralization'. Absent there was 'the original Teutonic spirit of individual independence', which exhibited itself with particular vigour in the 'Anglican race'.[98]

8. 'Disease' as a symptom of racial degeneration

From 'disease' we have passed to 'race'. Were these two interpretations of politico-social conflict compatible? Burke, who denounced the outbreak of 'disease' across the Channel, celebrated the 'nation in whose veins the blood of freedom circulates', the 'chosen race of the sons of England'. It was a 'nation' and a 'race' possibly less vulnerable than others to the pathological manifestations raging in France. In other words, the question is whether the servile, herd spirit and inability to enjoy a regular, orderly liberty were a passing disturbance in the personality of a civilized people or possessed an ethnic origin that was yet to be identified.

In the United States, from the mid-nineteenth century the threat represented by the immigration of yellow skins—the coolies—was added to the traditional peril of miscegenation with blacks. The coastal region of the Pacific, warned Lieber, risked being 'mongolized' by Chinese, whose proliferation resembled that of 'mice'.[99] Spencer was even more drastic. Large-scale settlement by the Chinese (or Japanese) in America would result in catastrophe: 'they must either, if they remain unmixed, form a subject race in the position, if not of slaves, yet of a class approximating to slaves; or if they mix they must form a bad hybrid.' The upshot would be individuals with a 'chaotic constitution' internally, as was sadly demonstrated by 'the Eurasians in India, and the half-breeds in America'.[100]

Hitherto we have been dealing with populations of colonial or semi-colonial origin, and hence extraneous to the West. And Lieber and Spencer's agreement with legislation that prohibited non-whites from access to the land of liberty is not surprising. Although an enthusiastic expansionist, the former declared himself opposed to the annexation of any territory that involved a further incorporation of peoples of colour. But, as his biographer observes, he went further. He feared that an influx of immigrants from southern Europe

---

98   Lieber, *Civil Liberty*, p. 55 n. 1.

99   Lieber, quoted in Freidel, *Francis Lieber*, p. 393.

100   Herbert Spencer, *The Life and Letters of Herbert Spencer*, ed. David Duncan, London: Routledge and Thoemmes Press, 1996, pp. 322–3 (letter to Kentaro Keneko, 26 August 1892).

belonging to the 'Latin Race' might also cause a 'dilution of American blood'.[101] Later, likewise focusing on the United States, another distinguished representative of liberalism—Lecky—drew attention to the effect of 'the contamination of the immigrant vote', since immigrants were often 'revolutionary elements'.[102]

These are concerns that were powerfully echoed by de Tocqueville. As the storm clouds gathered over the North American republic that would shortly lead to the Civil War, the French liberal posed an anxious question: How was the fading of the 'practical good sense' that had hitherto spared the transatlantic republic the catastrophe of France and continental Europe to be explained? What had provoked the crisis was the 'rapid introduction into the United States of men alien to the English race', who for that very reason caused America to run 'the greatest danger'.[103] Its inhabitants were now no longer so 'united by ... common opinions' as to render a bloody division inconceivable, as *Democracy in America* had believed.[104] De Tocqueville warned his US friends and interlocutors that 'however great your capacity for assimilation, it is very difficult for so many foreign bodies to be digested' with such rapidity as to avoid their disturbing 'the economy and the health of your social body'.[105] The looming civil war was put down to the new immigrants from southern or eastern Europe: they were configured as a pathogenic element, attacking from without a social organism that was in itself healthy. In the face of such a danger, de Tocqueville tirelessly warned his transatlantic friends and interlocutors:

Alas, every day brings you so many foreign elements that you will soon no longer be yourselves: all the arguments that could be made about your nature become ever more uncertain. In fact, mixed as you are today with so many races, who could now say what your nature is?

And again: 'What frightens me is the prodigious number of foreigners that makes of you a new people'.[106]

The waves of migration condemned here obviously involved the North of the United States. Did they lead to the emergence of radical abolitionism? In that case, de Tocqueville's position would not be very different from that of

---

101   Freidel, *Francis Lieber*, pp. 393–6, 409.

102   Lecky, *Democracy and Liberty*, vol. 1, pp. 78, 80.

103   Tocqueville, *Oeuvres complètes*, vol. 8, pt 3, p. 229 (letter to Gustave de Beaumont, 6 August 1854).

104   Tocqueville, *Democracy in America*, p. 393.

105   Tocqueville, *Oeuvres complètes*, vol. 7, p. 159 (letter to T. Sedgwick, 14 August 1854).

106   Ibid., vol. 7, pp. 177, 182 (letters to T. Sedgwick, 29 August and 14 October 1856).

the theorists of the South. They branded as fundamentally alien to America, and ultimately reducible to radicalism of a European (and French and Jacobin) variety, the positions of those who, to abolish slavery, did not even shrink at the prospect of a bloody conflict. At all events, de Tocqueville's tendency in explaining the impending civil war is clear: he assigned responsibility for it to the growing presence of ethnic groups traditionally lacking in the political and moral qualities attributed to Anglo-Americans.

This type of explanation obviously proves impossible when dealing with an ethnically homogenous country. Or should we assume that such homogeneity is merely apparent? To this question de Gobineau replied decisively in the affirmative. But let us observe his starting-point. He fully shared the pitiless psychopathological diagnosis of the French people made by de Tocqueville. It was necessary to register the raging of an age-old disease in France that rendered the functioning of 'free institutions' impossible and which, in the name of 'public utility' or the 'monstrosity' that was alleged 'social right', constantly promoted 'the absorption of private rights into single state right'. We are dealing with 'a people for whom absolute centralization is the height of good government'.[107] As we can see, the same ideological themes and even the same language we have heard in de Tocqueville, Lieber and Mill recur.

But there was in fact something new. The disease now had a specific ethnic base. The carriers of it in France and the rest of the world were non-Aryans. Given the importance of such an innovation, it is an exaggeration to claim that de Gobineau was 'not so far removed from Alexis de Tocqueville, at one time his mentor and superior, as might be supposed'.[108] On the other hand, there is no doubt they moved in a cultural and political circle with not a few points of contact and commonality. On close epistolary and intellectual terms, de Tocqueville and Lieber were in full agreement in their diagnosis of the disease raging in France and which, as a result of waves of migration, also risked having a harmful impact on the United States. Advancing further down the road of interpreting history in an ethnic key, Lieber counterposed to the herd and servile spirit of the 'Celts' the jealous sense of individuality peculiar to the 'Teutons'. The latter were the vanguard of the West, or the 'western Caucasian portion of humanity'. Perhaps, concluded Lieber, for brevity's sake one could speak of 'cis-Caucasians', while the phrase 'Japhetics' had the drawback of being too broad.[109] As we can see, we are on the threshold of the Aryan mythol-

---

107   Ibid., vol. 9, pp. 272–4 (letter from Arthur de Gobineau, 29 November 1856).

108   Ernst Nolte, *Three Faces of Fascism*, trans. Leila Vennewitz, New York: Mentor, 1969, p. 635 n. 7.

109   Lieber, *Civil Liberty*, pp. 55 n. 1 and 22 n. 2.

ogy: 'Japhetics' were the descendants of Japheth, by contrast with the progeny of Sem ('Semites') and Ham ('Hamites'). And the American liberal expressed reservations about the category of Japhetics or Aryans solely because it referred to the mythical deeds of a people that had started out from India—in other words, a region foreign to the West. Hence the distance from de Gobineau was not great, even if the latter preferred to speak of Aryans, rather than employing what he regarded as the less rigorous categories of 'Japhetics, Caucasians and Indo-Germans'.[110]

9. De Gobineau, liberalism and the genealogical myths of the community of the free

From the outset, the self-proclamation of the community of the free felt the need to resort to genealogical myths that endowed this distinguishing gesture with a foundation. Montesquieu pointed to 'the forests' inhabited by 'the Germans' as the birthplace of free, representative government.[111] The origin was not accidental: if slavery was at home among 'the peoples of the south' (see above, Chapter 2, §4), by contrast 'the peoples of the north have and will always have a spirit of independence and liberty that the peoples of the south do not'.[112] Indeed, 'the peoples of the north', who had demonstrated 'remarkable wisdom against the Roman power' they ultimately destroyed, were also distinguished by 'good sense', courage, 'generous sentiment', and 'the strength of spirit necessary to guide one's own conduct'.[113] The 'northern nations' were referred to in England by Sidney and Hume, who celebrated as 'extremely free' the 'government of the Germans, and that of all the northern nations', which was established on the 'ruins of Rome' and its 'military despotism'.[114] Again, for the Mill of 1861, the French were excluded from the community of the free because they were 'essentially a southern people', stamped by 'the double education of despotism and Catholicism'.[115] Burke instead preferred to glory in descent from 'our Gothic ancestors', as well as in belonging to the English

---

110   Arthur de Gobineau, *Essai sur l'inégalité des races humaines*, 2 vols, Paris: Librairie de Paris, vol. 1, p. 372.

111   Charles-Louis Montesquieu, *The Spirit of the Laws*, trans. and ed. Anne M. Cohler, Basia Carolyn Miller and Harold Samuel Stone, Cambridge: Cambridge University Press, 1989, p. 166.

112   Ibid., p. 463.

113   Ibid., pp. 235, 234.

114   Algernon Sidney, *Discourses Concerning Government*, ed. Thomas G. West, Indianapolis: Liberty Classics, 1990, pp. 103, 167; Hume, *History of England*, vol. 1, p. 160.

115   Mill, *Utilitarianism*, p. 213.

'chosen race' of liberty, while Lieber worked 'Teutonic' ancestors into the coat of arms of the United States and the Anglican race.

At the end of the nineteenth century, the Teutonic genealogical myth met with great success. Notwithstanding the stabilization achieved with the Third Republic, the memory of the Paris Commune and of the interminable revolutionary cycle behind it influenced France's image. The scourge of brigandage in the south, and the geographical location (not properly Nordic) especially of its southern regions, affected the image of Italy. The Second Reich, by contrast, seemed to stand unproblematically alongside England and the United States in enjoying representative bodies, a liberal order and economic development. These were the three countries now celebrated as the vanguard of the community of the free, or as the peoples who best embodied the cause of liberty. In England, as early as 1860 Lord Robert Cecil—future Marquis of Salisbury and prime minister—contrasted 'the people of a southern climate' with those of 'Teutonic parentage';[116] and in 1889 Joseph Chamberlain (the colonial secretary) officially called on the United States and Germany to form a 'Teutonic' alliance with his country.[117] This was a position shared across the Atlantic by Alfred T. Mahan, the great theorist of geopolitics, who likewise declared for the unity of the 'Teutonic family', of peoples belonging to the same Germanic 'stock'. Mahan was on excellent terms with Theodore Roosevelt who, going still further in his celebration of 'German' and 'Teutonic' peoples, hymned the 'war-like prowess of the stalwart sons of Odin'.[118] This ideological climate prompted a reinterpretation of the category of Anglo-Saxons, which now tended to include Germany—the starting-point for the great adventure of the emigration of the descendants of liberty, praiseworthy for having rebelled against first Roman despotism and then Papal despotism.

10. Disraeli, de Gobineau and 'race' as the 'key of history'

The cultural and political universe to which de Gobineau belonged is becoming clear. With him, the approach chosen by de Tocqueville to explain the crisis

---

116   David Cannadine, 'The Context, Performance and Meaning of Ritual', in Eric Hobsbawm and Terence Ranger, eds, *The Invention of Tradition*, Cambridge: Cambridge University Press, 1983, p. 101.

117   Chamberlain, quoted in Henry Kissinger, *Diplomacy*, New York: Simon & Schuster, 1994, p. 186.

118   Alfred Thayer Mahan, *The Problem of Asia*, New Brunswick (NJ): Transaction Publishers, 2003, pp. 125–6; Thomas G. Dyer, *Theodore Roosevelt and the Idea of Race*, Baton Rouge: Louisiana State University Press, 1980, pp. 55–7, 48–50.

in the United States became a key to understanding universal history. Why did 'liberal institutions' in the North American republic exhibit a vitality unimaginable in Latin America? Because in the latter Europeans had mixed with the defeated natives. And as for Europe, why had France suffered a catastrophe unknown to England? Because the mixing of races had been much more radical in the former than the latter, 'that of all the countries of Europe where modifications of blood have been slowest and hitherto least varied'.[119] And why was an unprecedented crisis impending in the United States? De Gobineau's answer was substantially identical to de Tocqueville's: as a result of massive waves of migration that were heterogeneous in origin, the original Anglo-Saxon element was on the point of losing its identity.[120]

It is true that in de Gobineau the anthropological explanation underwent such a naturalistic rigidification as to prompt de Tocqueville to ironize about the decisive role of 'blood'.[121] Must we then regard the author of the *Essay on the Inequality of Human Races* as foreign to the liberal tradition? In reality, even if we ignore the South of the United States, where the theory and practice reigned whereby a single drop of black blood was enough to exclude a person from the community of the free (and the enjoyment of political and civil rights), in Europe itself and, what is more, in the other classic country of the liberal tradition, voices echoed that were not very different from that just heard. Declaring himself in favour of a legal ban on miscegenation, Spencer stressed: 'It is not at root a question of social philosophy. It is at root a question of biology. There is abundant proof, alike furnished by the inter-marriages of human races and by the inter-breeding of animals'.[122]

But in this context the figure of Disraeli assumes particular prominence. The positions he adopted were clear: race was 'the key of history'.[123] It made no sense to speak of 'progress' and 'reaction': in reality, '[a]ll is race';[124] '[a]ll is race; there is no other truth.'[125] Only thus could it be understood how, although fairly small in numbers, the Spanish conquistadores (or 'Goths', as Disraeli preferred to call them) had managed to triumph in America and the English in China.[126] And that was how the constant ravages devastating France

---

119   Gobineau, *Essai sur l'inégalité*, vol. 1, pp. 41ff.

120   Ibid., vol. 2, pp. 536–7.

121   Tocqueville, *Oeuvres complètes*, vol. 18, p. 110.

122   Spencer, *Life and Letters*, p. 322 (letter to Kentaro Kaneko, 26 August 1892).

123   Benjamin Disraeli, *Endymion*, 2 vols, New York and London: Walter Dunne, 1976, vol. 1, p. 359.

124   Benjamin Disraeli, *Lord George Bentinck*, London: Colburn, 1852, p. 331.

125   Benjamin Disraeli, *Tancred*, 2 vols, Leipzig: Tauchnitz, 1847, vol. 1, p. 169.

126   Disraeli, *Lord George Bentinck*, p. 495.

were to be explained: we were witnessing 'the great revolt of the Celts', or the ancient 'conquered races', against 'the northern and western races', who had assimilated 'the Semitic principle' (the Old and New Testaments) and embodied civilization.[127] The principal and primary aspect of these processes was not culture: the 'greatness' of a race 'results from its organisation'.[128] This was a physiological fact, and it was therefore necessary to 'study physiology',[129] so as to be able to orientate oneself correctly in the conflicts of the historical and political world: 'Language and religion do not make a race—there is only one thing which makes a race, and that is blood.'[130]

On the basis of this blood mythology, Disraeli too insisted on the superiority of the 'pure races of the Caucasus', to which the Jewish race belonged.[131] It was a purity to be jealously guarded: 'that pernicious doctrine of modern times, the natural equality of man', the doctrine of 'cosmopolitan fraternity' which led to mixing and contamination, was condemned out of hand; if really implemented, it 'would deteriorate the great races and destroy all the genius of the world'.[132]

Despite the partial difference of idiom, we are not removed from the ideological universe of de Gobineau. The latter, who celebrated the Aryans in the first instance for their liberal and individualistic 'traditions',[133] not by chance dedicated his book 'to His Majesty George V, King of Hanover'. Along with England, de Gobineau took the other classical country of the liberal tradition, the United States, as his model. It was an 'essentially practical land', as had been confirmed by the fact that, without allowing themselves to be fettered by the abstractions rampant in France, even the 'abolitionist papers had acknowledged the correctness' of the thesis of the natural inequality of races.[134] The celebration of racial purity was the celebration primarily of the 'Anglo-Saxons', the branch of the 'Aryan family' that more than any other had resisted the general bastardization.[135]

---

127 Ibid., pp. 508–9, 553.

128 Ibid., p. 495.

129 Benjamin Disraeli, *Coningsby*, ed. Sheila M. Smith, Oxford and New York: Oxford University Press, 1982, p. 221.

130 Disraeli, *Endymion*, vol. 1, p. 361.

131 Disraeli, *Coningsby*, pp. 221, 219.

132 Disraeli, *Lord George Bentinck*, p. 496.

133 Gobineau, *Essai sur l'inégalité*, vol. 2, p. 29.

134 Tocqueville, *Oeuvres complètes*, vol. 9, pp. 260–1 (letter from Arthur de Gobineau, 20 March 1856).

135 See Gobineau, *Essai sur l'inégalité*, vol. 2, pp. 520–30.

There is no reason to include Disraeli in the liberal tradition while excluding the author of the *Essay on the Inequality of Human Races*, all the less so given that the latter drew considerable inspiration from the English writer and statesman.[136] If de Gobineau ceased to be a liberal, it was when, now discouraged, he ended up accommodating, in de Tocqueville's harsh but accurate judgement, to the 'government of the sabre, and even of the baton'—that is, to the dictatorship of Napoleon III.[137] But it should not be forgotten that in these same years Disraeli believed the 'government of the sword' and the 'military camp' inevitable and legitimate, for France and continental Europe (see below, Chapter 10, §1). In any event, as a theorist of race, admirer and collaborator of de Tocqueville, and follower of Disraeli, the author, disgusted by the French revolutionary cycle and statism, and filled with admiration for the Anglo-Saxon world and the 'liberal traditions of the Aryans', fitted into the milieu of liberalism without difficulty.

The fact that the Aryan mythology was explicitly present in other exponents of this intellectual tradition should not be overlooked. Here is how Lecky came to the defence of Ireland, from which he originated: while they were Celts, the Irish were nevertheless part of 'the great Aryan race'.[138] Spencer reached the same conclusion in the course of his visit to the United States: 'descendants of the immigrant Irish lose their Celtic aspect, and become Americanised'; they had fused with the other 'varieties of the Aryan race' and, in this instance, the admixture had proved beneficial.[139] Things stood differently in the case of France. What explained its defeat in the war with Prussia and the raging of the Paris Commune was 'race', which seemed to have remained stubbornly Celtic (unlike Lecky, Spencer considered the Celts wholly alien to the Aryan race).[140] To the authors we have just cited might be added Renan, who also regarded himself as a liberal, was 'in regular contact' with de Gobineau,[141] and was a no less passionate cantor (as we shall see) of the excellence of the Aryan race and, more generally, the 'Aryan–Semitic races'. Finally, it should be noted that across the Atlantic the Aryan mythology was prominent, and in fact so widespread as to go beyond the circle of ideologies. In 1902 Arthur

---

136 Léon Poliakov, *The History of Anti-Semitism*, trans. Richard Howard, Natalie Gerardie and Mirian Kochan, London: Routledge and Kegan Paul, 1974–75, vol. 3, p. 336.

137 Tocqueville, *Oeuvres complètes*, vol. 9, p. 280 (letter from Arthur de Gobineau, 24 January 1857).

138 Lecky, *History of England*, vol. 2, p. 380.

139 Spencer, quoted in Thomas F. Gossett, *Race*, New York: Schocken Books, 1965, pp. 151–2.

140 Spencer, *Life and Letters*, pp. 154–5 (letter to E. Cazelles, 3 May 1871).

141 Tocqueville, *Oeuvres complètes*, vol. 9, p. 305 (letter of 21 March 1859).

MacArthur, military governor of the Philippines, demanded the United States' right to dominion on the grounds that it belonged to the 'magnificent Aryan people'.[142]

11. The repression of conflict, the search for the pathogenic element, and conspiracy theory

Even if he rejected the facile Aryan solution, this did not make de Tocqueville any less obsessed than de Gobineau with the problem of identifying the pathogenic element attacking a social organism that was healthy in itself. After 1848 there was no doubt: the carrier of the 'revolutionary disease', the 'permanent disease', the 'virus of a new and unknown kind', which raged incessantly in France, was a 'new race' (*race nouvelle*): 'we are always dealing with the same men, even if the circumstances vary'.[143] It is to be added that this 'virus' or 'race' was spreading alarmingly throughout the world. Having made their appearance in France, these '[r]evolutionaries of a hitherto unknown breed came on the scene … They were the first of a new race of men who subsequently prospered and proliferated in all parts of the civilized world, everywhere retaining the same characteristics.'[144]

What once again leaps to the eye is the transition from 'disease' or 'virus' to 'race'. Likewise in Constant, 'cold in their delirium', subversive intellectuals, those 'jugglers of sedition' (*jongleurs de sédition*), never tired of undermining not just a particular society, but 'the very foundations of the social order'. They were 'beings of an unknown species' (*êtres d'une espèce inconnue*) and in fact formed a 'new race' (*race nouvelle*), a 'detestable race' (*déstestable race*).[145] In a crescendo, an anthropological type of explanation tends to become a racial type of explanation—the transition from the category of *espèce* to that of *race* is symptomatic. At this point the idea of a radical solution emerges. One could only hope for the 'eradication' of this 'detestable race' composed of pathogenic agents:[146] such was the precondition for restoring the health and safety of society.

The term 'race' does not possess a genuinely ethnic connotation in either Constant or de Tocqueville. Yet its recurrence is a symptom of a tendency to

---

142   Cf. Losurdo, *Nietzsche*, ch. 20, §1.

143   Tocqueville, *Oeuvres complètes*, vol. 2, pt 2, pp. 348–9; vol. 13, pt 2, pp. 337–8.

144   Tocqueville, *Ancien Régime*, p. 178.

145   Guillemin, *Benjamin Constant*, pp. 13–14, 84, 194; Constant, *De la force du gouvernement actuel*, p. 44.

146   Guillemin, *Benjamin Constant*, pp. 13–14.

racialize the intellectuals who were carriers of the virus of subversion. Burke went significantly further. In addition to a clearly defined social stratum (non-property-owning intellectuals, who were not connected with the land and lacked roots), the ideological 'intoxication' of which radicalism was culpable[147] pertained to a social bloc that began to exhibit an ethnic dimension. What explained the catastrophe of the French Revolution was an alliance between two significantly different social strata: on the one hand, 'political men of letters' and, on the other, the 'new monied interest'. The reasons for this alliance, at first sight so strange, were readily understandable. To begin with, the two parties shared a hatred of Christianity: '[t]he literary cabal had some years ago formed something like a regular plan for the destruction of the Christian religion.'[148] But if the irreligiousness and atheism of intellectuals influenced by the Enlightenment were well-known, one should not lose sight of the fact that the 'Jews in Change-alley', already alien to Christianity for religious and ideological reasons, also had a material interest in undermining or destroying it: they were hoping for 'a mortgage on the revenues belonging to the see of Canterbury'.[149]

The attack on the Church was also an attack on 'the landed property of ecclesiastical corporations', on landed property as such. The revolutionaries' programme was sinister: 'Is the house of lords to be voted useless? Is episcopacy to be abolished? Are the church lands to be sold to Jews and jobbers[?]'[150] Intent on destroying a society whose pillars were Christianity and the landed aristocracy was an alliance between subversive intellectuals gathered in 'the revolution society' and 'the pulpit of the Old Jewry', or the 'gentlemen of the Old Jewry', engaged in distorting the real meaning of the Glorious Revolution and spreading 'the spurious revolution principles of the Old Jewry'.[151] As we can see, Burke did not tire of stressing the role of the Jews. These two components of the revolutionary bloc were linked by multiple affinities. Over and above hatred of the Church and the agrarian, Christian nobility, an important role was also played by their fundamental foreignness to the nation. The intellectual stratum was itself stateless, because intellectuals displayed 'attachment to their country' only to the extent that it conduced to their 'fleeting projects'.[152]

---

147 Burke, *Works*, vol. 7, p. 135.
148 Ibid., vol. 5, p. 207.
149 Ibid., vol. 5, p. 197.
150 Ibid., vol. 5, pp. 211, 113.
151 Ibid., vol. 5, pp. 75, 50–51.
152 Ibid., vol. 5, pp. 169–70.

But whence did subversion draw its shock force? To overthrow the existing order, intellectuals and usurers were insufficient. In reality, an integral, albeit subaltern, part of the subversive attack was 'the Tavern', the inebriated, blood-thirsty rabble. How was the unnatural union repeatedly denounced by Burke as the social bloc between 'Old Jewry' and 'the London Tavern' formed and sealed?[153] Who enrolled the most desperate in the retinue and service of the wealthiest, and in fact of the most parasitic, repugnant wealth—the wealth which, rather than being based on the land and love of the land, pertained exclusively to speculation and usury? It was the intellectuals—more precisely, rootless intellectuals of humble origin. It was 'feathered scoundrels' [*gueux plumées*],[154] wretches like the scoundrels of the Tavern whom they were con-stantly inciting. Wanting in religion, faith and genuine ideals, they called on the scoundrels, of whom they were an integral part, to rise up against wealth, but only against the most respectable wealth—landed wealth—while financial (and Jewish) wealth was spared. In France these intellectuals 'pretended to a great zeal for the poor … They became a sort of demagogues. They served as a link to unite, in favour of one object, obnoxious wealth to restless and desperate poverty.'[155] In their turn, the Jews were perfectly content to support the French rabble's attacks on monarchy and aristocracy, on the pillars of Christianity. The revolutionary atrocities seemed to Burke 'Theban and Thracian orgies, acted in France, and applauded only in the Old Jewry'.[156]

The contours of the subversive social bloc were now clear. Thanks to the work of plebeian, subversive intellectuals, here were the propertyless in the retinue of the usurers, the Tavern in the service of Old Jewry, or 'Jewish brokers contending with each other who could best remedy with fraudulent circulation and depreciated paper the wretchedness and ruin brought on their country by their degenerate councils'.[157] The Jews were ultimately at the head of the vari-egated social bloc of subversion. It was enough to observe the development of the revolution in France: 'The next generation of the nobility will resemble the artificers and clowns, and money-jobbers, usurers, and Jews, who will be always their fellows, sometimes their masters.'[158] Levelling and homogenizing every-thing, the French Revolution ended up making a single 'difference' prevail, that

---

153   Ibid., vol. 5, p. 232.
154   Ibid., vol. 9, p. 49.
155   Ibid., vol. 5, p. 210.
156   Ibid., vol. 5, p. 143.
157   Ibid., vol. 5, p. 102.
158   Ibid., vol. 5, p. 104.

constituted by 'money',[159] and hence sanctioning the predominance of finance (largely controlled by Jews). If remedial action was not promptly taken, a 'general earthquake' threatened to flatten the social order and civilization.[160]

Unquestionably, we are dealing with the first organic theory of revolution as a Jewish conspiracy. The *Reflections* and the denunciation of the infamous role of Old Jewry date from 1790. Only later did Abbé Barruel set himself to work. Exiled in England, he was received with honour by Burke, who warmly greeted him and the work that was taking shape: 'The whole of the wonderful narrative is supported by documents and proofs with almost juridical regularity and exactness.'[161]

In addition to chronological priority, another, more important characteristic highlights the novelty and perilousness of the conspiracy theory in Burke. While the *Reflections* also referred to the disturbing role of Enlightenment 'confederacies',[162] it was now no longer a question of pointing a finger at this or that sect or at freemasonry, as did Barruel, and exposing the role of Jews therein. Foremost among the charges against the latter was not hostility towards the dominant religion or throne and altar, as in the traditional Christian polemic. Burke, who was himself a mason,[163] aimed to explain a new politico-social conflict that was destined to last a long time. In the British Whig's view, we have on the one hand the countryside, as the site embodying the natural order of society and the values of attachment to the land, and a national community cemented (as we know) by a 'relation in blood'; on the other, the city as the site of rootlessness and stateless subversion, jointly promoted by Jewish finance, abstract, revolutionary intellectuals and the rabble. For the first time, the Jews were accused of simultaneously operating through rapacious, parasitic finance and a plebeian movement inspired by blind, destructive fury.

This motif reappeared in the liberal tradition after another major revolutionary upheaval. On the outbreak of the European revolutions of 1848, Disraeli immediately put them down to the 'manoeuvres' of 'secret associations', which were 'always vigilant and always prepared' to take 'society by surprise' and 'strik[e] at property and Christ'.[164] Some years later, the English statesman of Jewish origin drew up a more sophisticated, highly surprising balance-sheet. On

---

159 Ibid., vol. 7, pp. 18–19.

160 Ibid., vol. 5, p. 282.

161 Burke, quoted in Johannes Rogolla von Bieberstein, *Die These von der Verschwörung*, Bern and Frankfurt am Main: Lang, 1976, p. 111 n.

162 See Burke, *Works*, vol. 5, p. 282.

163 Cf. Rogolla von Bieberstein, *Die These*, p. 117.

164 Disraeli, quoted in George E. Buckle and William F. Monypenny, *The Life of Benjamin Disraeli Earl of Beaconsfield*, 6 vols, New York: Macmillan, 1914–20, vol. 3, p. 173.

account of 'their accumulated wealth', attachment to their religious tradition and proud racial self-consciousness, Jews tended to be hostile to 'the doctrine of the equality of man' and 'conservative'.[165] However, although shaking off oppression, they were not averse to the most unscrupulous operations and alliances: 'you find the once loyal Hebrew invariably arrayed in the same ranks as the leveller and the latitudinarian'.[166] There then spread the 'destructive principle' and 'insurrection ... against tradition and aristocracy, against religion and property'. Fuelling all of this was an unexpected ethnic and social group: the destruction of Christianity, 'the natural equality of man and the abrogation of property, are proclaimed by the secret societies who form provisional governments, and men of Jewish race are found at the head of every one of them'. There was no doubt: 'If the reader throws his eye over the provisional governments of Germany, and Italy, and even of France, formed at that period, he will recognise everywhere the Jewish element.' Thus, '[t]he people of God co-operate with atheists; the most skilful accumulators of property ally themselves with communists; the peculiar and chosen race touch the hand of all the scum and low castes of Europe!'[167]

It is not difficult to hear in this discourse an echo of the resentment of the Jew at humiliations and persecution suffered. But it remains the case that we are once again dealing with a new conspiracy theory destined to enjoy fatal success in the twentieth century. What encouraged such a theory was the tendency, widespread in the liberal culture of the time, to repress the objectivity of politico-social conflict. The picture Disraeli paints of the great revolutionary wave of 1848 is eloquent. Had it not been for the occult Jewish leadership, 'the uncalled for outbreak would not have ravaged Europe.' Not objective social needs, but 'the fiery energy and teeming resources of the children of Israel maintained for a long time the unnecessary and useless struggle'.[168]

Finally, still within the ambit of the liberal tradition, the cry of alarm at 'conspiracy' also resounded during another great revolutionary upheaval. When Napoleonic France's attempt to reintroduce slavery into San Domingo was defeated by the fierce resistance of the ex-slaves, Malouet warned against the 'universal plot of the blacks' who, with the complicity of the abolitionists, aspired to dominate and massacre the whites.[169] Obviously, this theme was

---

165   Disraeli, *Lord George Bentinck*, pp. 496–7.
166   Disraeli, *Coningsby*, p. 218.
167   Disraeli, *Lord George Bentinck*, pp. 497–8.
168   Ibid., p. 498.
169   Malouet, quoted in Yves Benot, *La démence coloniale sous Napoléon*, Paris: La Découverte, 1992, p. 190.

widely diffused in the South of the United States. Obsession with 'conspiracy' runs deep in the history of that country and both the contending alliances, in different forms, were constantly concerned to uncover and fight it. For example, in the years leading up to the Civil War, while the South denounced the North's 'abolitionist conspiracy', the latter endlessly warned against the plot that aimed to impose slaveholding power at a federal level. For this reason, reference has been made to a widespread 'paranoid style' in connection with the history of the North American republic.[170]

In this mythology of the conspiracy, one element was especially significant and pregnant with consequences. The actor in the black, abolitionist plot, the anti-slavery militant, tended to be delineated in accordance with the model generally used to stigmatize the Jew: 'Essentially weak and cowardly, he would pose no threat in a fair and open fight'; but this was where deception, intrigue and, precisely, conspiracy came in.[171]

12. The conflict of the two liberalisms, and mutual accusations of betrayal

In confronting the challenges represented by the struggle for recognition waged by the excluded, obviously the community of the free did not always react as one. On more than a few occasions, there were internal clashes and divisions. In broad terms, we can distinguish two tendencies. One fraction more or less stubbornly identified with the positions of the representatives of English proto-liberalism, who equated 'true liberty' with untrammelled control by the master over *his* family, as well as *his* servants and *his* goods. By contrast, another fraction sought to come to terms with the idea of liberty originally mobilized by servants, who refused to let themselves be assimilated to the master's belongings and pursued emancipation through intervention by political power on their behalf, be it existing political power or that formed in the wake of a revolution from below. The struggles waged by servants aggravated the sense of unease in some sections of the community of the free, who soon sought to acquire a good conscience by repressing slavery to the colonies and changing or masking the politico-social relations that most blatantly gave the lie to their proclaimed attachment to the cause of liberty.

The entanglement of, and clash between, these two different ideas of liberty,

---

170 David B. Davis, *The Slave Power Conspiracy and the Paranoid Style*, Baton Rouge: Louisiana State University Press, 1982, p. 38 and *passim*.

171 Ibid., p. 51.

and of the politico-social subjects who appealed to them, explains the especially complex and tortuous character of the first English revolution and the French Revolution as such. Not even the United States was spared this conflict. In fact, it flared up there in the most violent and bloody way during the Civil War, in a clash between, on the one hand, the idea of liberty understood as self-government by the dominant class and race and, on the other, the idea of liberty that experienced increasing disquiet because of the persistence of the institution of slavery. Defeated militarily, in slightly different form, as a regime of terroristic white supremacy, the idea of liberty dear to the South ended up achieving a political success in the United States that lasted beyond the midtwentieth century.

The two liberalisms we are referring to are to be construed in an ideal-typical sense: within the same author, it is possible to register fluctuation from one to the other. In condemning as contrary to liberty coalitions composed of 'desperate men', who sought to escape death from starvation, Smith clearly identified liberty with the self-government of civil society hegemonized by the very wealthy. On the other hand, in calling for a 'despotic government' to abolish slavery, he was embracing a different theoretical paradigm, which identified liberty with the abolition of oppressive relations existing within civil society itself. And the great economist adhered to this second paradigm when he observed that in eastern Europe 'serfdom' continued to exist in 'Bohemia, Hungary, and these countries where the sovereign is elective and consequently never could have great authority', and thus was not in a position to foil the resistance of feudal lords.[172]

This is an observation which, albeit to a lesser extent, also applies to de Tocqueville. When he condemned the reduction of the working day in factories to twelve hours as an expression of despotism, he clearly identified liberty with the self-government of civil society hegemonized by the bourgeoisie. But on other occasions the French liberal argued differently. In a letter of 1840 to an American correspondent, he observed:

> For me it is a rather melancholy reflection to think that your nation has incorporated slavery to such an extent that they expand together ... In practice, there are no precedents for an abolition of slavery on the master's initiative. It has only been abolished thanks to the power of a government that dominated master and slave alike. That is why, precisely because you are completely independent, slavery will last longer among you than anywhere else.[173]

---

172   Adam Smith, *Lectures on Jurisprudence*, Indianapolis: Liberty Classics, 1982, p. 455.
173   Tocqueville, *Oeuvres complètes*, vol. 7, p. 83 (letter to J. Sparks, 13 October 1840).

Rather than the locus of liberty, here self-government is the condition for the perpetuation of the evil of slavery. Only a strong government would be able to abolish it. More concerned about the stability of the United States than the freedom of blacks, de Tocqueville, unlike Smith, did not go so far as to come out in favour of a 'despotic government'. But in the case of Ireland, the same French liberal harboured the idea of a temporary dictatorship that would put an end to the terrible ills visited on the native population by the self-government of Anglo-Irish, Protestant property-owners.

Although convinced that 'public education is salutary, above all in free countries', Constant was firmly opposed to the introduction of compulsory schooling, since he considered unacceptable any form of 'restriction' that violated the 'rights of individuals', including 'those of fathers over their children'. True, poverty meant that in poor families children were taken out of school and put to work early. Yet it was necessary to renounce any restrictions and wait for poverty to fade away.[174] On the basis of this logic, in addition to rejecting compulsory schooling, Constant did not even entertain the hypothesis of state intervention against the scourge of child labour. Some decades later, by contrast, declaring himself in favour of compulsory schooling, Mill argued against the 'misplaced notions of liberty' of parents and added: 'The State ... is bound to maintain a vigilant control over his [the individual's] exercise of any power which it allows him to possess over others.'[175] In this different judgement, we see the transition from one theoretical paradigm to another; and the transition was also the result of the struggle of those who were excluded from liberty construed simply as self-government by civil society.

Reacting to the protests and challenge of the working-class movement, it was liberal England that regulated working hours and conditions in factories, abolishing or tempering the most odious aspects of what Marx and Engels branded as employers' 'despotism'. This aroused the protests of not a few liberal representatives and English capitalists themselves, who (observed *Capital*) 'denounced the factory inspector as a species of revolutionary commissioner reminiscent of the [Jacobin] Convention'.[176] Similarly, Bismarck made a profession of liberalism and thundered against the 'Royal Prussian Court Jacobin', who claimed to interfere in the relationship between masters and servants and hence to ride roughshod over the principle of self-government by civil society, hegemonized in this instance by feudal property and not an aristocratic-

---

174   Benjamin Constant, *Mélanges de littérature et de politique*, Louvain: Michel, 1830, vol. 2, pp. 8–9.

175   Mill, *Utilitarianism*, pp. 159–60, 163.

176   Marx, *Capital: Volume One*, p. 396.

bourgeois coalition, as in the British case. And it was precisely the Prussian–German statesman who distinguished between two types of liberalism in this connection. The first was characterized by 'repugnance at the power of bureaucracy', on the basis of 'liberal caste sentiments' widely diffused among the Junkers and nobility of pre-revolutionary Prussia; the second, utterly odious in Bismarck's view, was 'Rhineland–French liberalism', or the 'liberalism of civil servants' (*Geheimratsliberalismus*), inclined to incisive anti-feudal reforms from above, which inspired an oppressive, suffocating state bureaucracy with its 'tendency ... to levelling and centralization' and even 'bureaucratic omnipotence' (*geheimrätliche Allgewalt*).[177]

It is interesting to note that a similar distinction occurs in the young Marx. The *Rheinische Zeitung* edited by him defined itself as a 'liberal paper', but was careful to specify that its liberalism was not in any way to be confused with 'vulgar liberalism' (*gewöhnlicher Liberalismus*). While the latter saw 'all good on the part of representative bodies and all evil on the part of government', the *Rheinische Zeitung*, by contrast, was characterized by its attempt to analyse relations of domination and oppression in their concrete form, without hesitating in particular circumstances to underline 'the general wisdom of the government against the private egotism of representative bodies' (often monopolized by feudal strata and a narrow-minded, short-sighted big bourgeoisie). Contrary to 'vulgar liberalism', far from fighting 'bureaucracy one-sidedly', the *Rheinische Zeitung* had no difficulty acknowledging the merits of its struggle against the 'romantic' or 'romantic–feudal' current.[178] Despite the contrasting value judgements, in both Bismarck and Marx we witness a distinction between a liberalism inclined to consecrate the self-government of a civil society hegemonized by the feudal aristocracy or grand bourgeoisie, and a liberalism ready to intervene in the relations of domination and oppression that manifest themselves within civil society itself.

When they are located in this historical and theoretical context, we can understand two significant turns that occurred in the course of the liberal tradition. We know that, initially, the liberal/servile dichotomy had a strong social and ethnic connotation. This connotation tended to weaken as the struggle for recognition intensified and the concessions that the community of the free was forced to make became more significant. We can then understand the attempt

---

177 Otto von Bismarck, *Die großen Reden*, ed. Lothar Gall, Frankfurt am Main: Ullstein, 1984, p. 137; Bismarck, *Werke in Auswahl*, vol. 1, ed. Gustave Adolf Rein, Stuttgart: Kohlhammer, 1962, p. 354 (speeches in the Prussian Chamber of Deputies, 18 October 1849 and 14 February 1851).

178 Marx and Engels, *Werke*, vol. 1, p. 424.

by some sections of the liberal movement to differentiate between political liberalism and economic liberalism, and thus distance themselves from those (economic-liberal) sections which, crying scandal at any state intervention in the socio-economic sphere, refused to question the relations of domination and oppression present within civil society, within the 'private sphere'.

On the other hand, with every significant concession that the community of the free (or its most advanced sectors) found itself obliged to make to the excluded, engaged in the struggle for recognition, there were denunciations of 'betrayal' from the most intransigent sectors, with a consequent laceration and division of the liberal movement. Clearly distancing himself from those who refused to follow him in the crusade against the French Revolution, in 1791 Burke, in the name of loyalty to the 'Old Whigs', authors of the Glorious Revolution, broke with the 'new Whigs', guilty of having derived ideas and ideals 'from a French die, unknown to the impress of our fathers in the constitution'.[179] In this case, at the heart of the conflict was the idea of representation, which the French revolutionaries and their followers on British soil, in the name of the imaginary, 'pretended rights of man', interpreted in a merely quantitative sense, invoking the principle of calculating a majority by head, ignoring the special function of the aristocracy and trampling the healthy arrangement of society into estates underfoot.[180]

A century or so later, the struggle for recognition was continuing to develop in new, more advanced conditions. Over and above political citizenship, the 'multitude', previously branded 'swinish', demanded the right to health, education and a minimum of free time. It succeeded in wresting more or less sizeable concessions and enjoyed support from significant representatives of liberalism. In Britain this was true above all of T. H. Green, who theorized 'freedom in the positive sense' in controversy with the economic liberals of his time. They condemned state regulation of working hours in factories or of female and child labour, in the name of 'freedom of contract' and liberty understood exclusively as non-interference by political power in the private sphere of production and labour relations.[181] Once again, responding to the attempts at adaptation and reconciliation by some sectors of liberalism were cries of scandal from the movement's most intransigent sections. Spencer, Acton and Henry S. Maine were among the many to denounce the 'betrayal'.[182]

---

179   Burke, *Works*, vol. 6, p. 267.
180   See ibid., vol. 6, pp. 89, 248, 257, 220, 228.
181   Thomas Hill Green, 'Lecture on Liberal Legislation and Freedom of Contract', in *Works*, ed. Richard L. Nettleship, vol. 3, London: Longmans, Green and Co., 1973, p. 372.
182   George Howell, 'Liberty for Labour', in Herbert Spencer *et al.*, *A Plea for Liberty*,

Spencer particularly stood out. Those who, under the pretence of improving popular living conditions, banned the employment of children under the age of twelve, forced parents to send their children to school, subjected factory work (especially female labour) to a whole variety of regulations, and introduced compulsory insurance for illness and old age had ceased to be liberals: they had arrived at a 'New Toryism'. In effect, they were simply inflating the state, enlarging the zone of coercion and limiting that of freedom of contract and the autonomous development of the individual.[183] As in the case of Burke with the 'new Whigs', so Spencer branded the 'New Toryism': albeit in a different idiom, what was targeted was a spurious liberalism forgetful of its own noble past; a liberalism guilty of abandoning the cause of self-government by civil society (whether aristocratic or bourgeois) and of the spontaneity of the market, giving way to the blandishments of statism.

Celebration of the spontaneity of the market, as if its historically determinate form was not the result of political action, was philosophically ingenuous enough. For centuries the market of the liberal West had involved the presence of chattel slavery and the buying and selling of indentured white servants. Even the borderline that separated commodities on the one hand, and the figure of the buyer/seller on the other, was the result of political and even military intervention, abhorred for centuries as being synonymous with artificial, violent constructivism.

Let us ignore the peculiar 'commodities' long represented by slaves and indentured servants. When can the market be regarded as free of external disturbance, and hence such that the parties to any exchange find themselves in a position of liberty and equality? Locke regarded the truck-system, whereby workers were paid not in money but in commodities produced by the factory they worked in, as perfectly legitimate. In agreement with him was Frederick William III, who in 1832 silenced voices raised in protest against this system with the argument that the state did not have the right to intervene in a 'relationship of private right', trampling over 'civil liberty' or arbitrarily restricting it. For Smith, by contrast, 'the law which obliges the masters ... to pay their workmen in money and not in goods is quite just and equitable. It imposes no real hardship upon the masters.'[184] Unlike the liberal philosopher and the

---

Indianapolis: Liberty Classsics, 1981; Henry S. Maine, *Popular Government*, ed. George W. Carey, Indianapolis: Liberty Classics, 1976.

183 Herbert Spencer, *The Man versus the State*, Indianapolis: Liberty Classics, 1981, pp. 5–30.

184 Cf. Domenico Losurdo, *Hegel and the Freedom of the Moderns*, trans. Marella and Jon Morris, Durham (NC) and London: Duke University Press, 2004, ch. 3, §6.

Prussian monarch, the great economist was of the opinion that the truck-system violated the principle of equality between the contracting parties and therefore justified legal intervention that would have seemed intolerable to Locke.

Much later liberal authors like Lecky and others condemned state regulation of working hours as an inadmissible interference in the market sphere.[185] In our times, by contrast, Hayek believed that the promulgation by the state of 'general, equal, and known rules', of 'general conditions' which must be fulfilled by any contract, was not in itself a violation of the principle of liberty. But the Austro-American author, who distinguished himself by thundering against any form of statism and constructivism, would have seemed statist and constructivist to Lecky, whom Hayek regarded as a classic proponent of liberalism.[186]

Potentially a traitor in the eyes of economic liberals of the second half of the nineteenth century, Hayek elsewhere identified and denounced the betrayal of liberalism. Although in favour of the social state and hence aligning himself with Green, Hobhouse continued to profess himself a follower of that intellectual current. *Liberalism*, read the title of his book, which in fact, according to Hayek, would more accurately have been entitled *Socialism*.[187] Some years earlier, von Mises had reached the same conclusion: most British 'liberals' were 'so in name only. In fact, they are rather moderate socialists.'[188]

The charges of treason against the wing of liberalism disposed to make concessions to colonial peoples were even more violent. In France, immediately after Thermidor, anyone who resisted the turn intended to re-establish if not slavery, then the regime of white supremacy in the colonies, was branded 'African'.[189] In the United States of the 1820s, arguing against abolitionist tendencies, Randolph declared that the term 'liberal' now risked becoming synonymous with 'black alliance'.[190] The polemic against the 'black republicans' subsequently became the guiding thread of the struggle against the abolitionist tendencies that were coagulating in Lincoln's Republican Party, as emerges in particular from the debate which, a few years before the Civil War, pitted the

---

185 Lecky, *Democracy and Liberty*, vol. 2, pp. 321–2.

186 Friedrich von Hayek, *The Constitution of Liberty*, London: Routledge and Kegan Paul, 1960, pp. 230, 401.

187 Friedrich von Hayek, *The Fatal Conceit*, ed. William Warren Bartley III, London: Routledge, 1990, p. 110.

188 Ludwig von Mises, *Liberalism*, Indianapolis: Liberty Fund, 2005, p. xviii.

189 Florence Gauthier, *Triomphe et mort du droit naturel en Révolution*, Paris: Presses Universitaires de France, 1992, pp. 262–3.

190 Randolph, quoted in Russell Kirk, *John Randolph of Roanoke*, Indianapolis: Liberty Press, 1978, p. 63.

future president against Senator Stephen A. Douglas.[191] In subsequent years, Lecky was among those crying treason. The brief period of interracial and multi-ethnic democracy experienced by the South—Reconstruction—was, in his view, the triumph of the 'negro vote' and the disappearance of 'the influence of property and intelligence'; it was the advent, 'under the protection of the Northern bayonets', of 'a hideous orgie of anarchy, violence, unrestrained corruption, undisguised, ostentatious, insulting robbery, such as the world had scarcely ever seen'.[192]

13. The community of the free as a community of peace? Policing operations and colonial wars

We have hitherto concentrated on the challenges to the community of the free that might be mounted by the barbarians in the colonies or the metropolis, and on the acute crisis situations that could arise within an individual country. But what were the relations between the various countries into which the community of the free was divided? Precisely because it was inclined to repress the genesis of the conflict and situate it outside itself, it tended to present itself as the community of peace, deaf to the sirens of war and bellicose adventures, which were a pre-modern legacy, and as wholly absorbed in the production, exchange and peaceful enjoyment of the goods that constituted civilization. George Washington expressed the hope that the development of 'free commerce' and civilization, 'in such an enlightened, in such a liberal age', would put a stop to 'the devastations and horrors of war', uniting humanity 'like one great family in fraternal ties'.[193] Indeed, repeated Constant, in 'the age of commerce' even 'a successful war always costs more than it brings in': having become obsolete as a tool for acquiring wealth, war was destined to disappear; 'the uniform tendency is towards peace'.[194]

This ideal of perpetual peace, produced by freedom of industry and trade, was sometimes so deeply felt that it prompted harsh criticism of the realpolitik of war and conquest pursued, for example, by England. Thus authors like Cobden and Spencer, bitter critics of their country's foreign and military policy.

---

191   Cf. Abraham Lincoln, *Speeches and Writings*, 2 vols, ed. Don E. Fehrenbacher, New York: Library of America, 1989, vol. 1, pp. 498–504 and *passim*.

192   Lecky, *Democracy and Liberty*, vol. 1, p. 80.

193   George Washington, *A Collection*, ed. William B. Allen, Indianapolis: Liberty Classics, 1988, p. 326 (letter to La Fayette, 15 August 1786).

194   Constant, *Political Writings*, pp. 53–4.

In the mid-nineteenth century, the former exclaimed,

> We have been the most combative and aggressive community that has existed
> since the days of the Roman dominion. Since the Revolution of 1688 we have
> expended more than fifteen hundred millions of money upon wars, not one
> of which has been upon our own shores, or in defence of our hearths and
> homes ... this pugnacious propensity has been invariably recognized by those
> who have studied our national character.[195]

Yet the self-proclamation of the community of the free as a community of
peace could generate a different line of argument. However pitiless, the struggle against the 'savage beasts' represented (in Washington's view) by Indians
was not an act of war, but a policing operation. This applied to conflicts with
those peoples or, rather, those hordes that had not yet attained the stage of
civilization and peace. Against barbaric pirates it was necessary to organize
an expedition that 'would crush them into non-existence'; sooner or later, it
would be necessary to 'exterminate those nests of Miscreants'.[196]

De Tocqueville likewise tended to liken conflict with barbarians to a policing
operation. In September 1856 he expressed the fear that the clash between
North and South in the United States would end up provoking 'war in the
heart of a great continent whence it has been banished for more than a century'
(see above, Chapter 5, §9). Clearly, subsumed under the category of war were
neither the expeditions that had decimated and were decimating the Indians,
nor the armed conflict that had involved a significant amputation of Mexican
territory.

But the growing colonial expansion of Europe, and primarily of Britain,
which now also encompassed a country of ancient civilization like China, made
resort to the category of policing operation problematic. On the other side,
recognizing the reality of war might also play a positive role at the level of
domestic policy, might serve to overshadow the worsening social conflict, and
counter the vulgarly hedonistic ideology in whose wake radical and socialist
agitation had developed. The ideal tension that presided over war was thus positively contrasted with the pettiness of material demands advanced by popular
protest movements: 'The masses want tranquillity and earnings', and hence
peace, but the merit of war precisely lay in throwing this philistine view of life

---

195   Cobden, quoted in Daniel Pick, *War Machine*, New Haven and London: Yale University
Press, 1993, p. 21.

196   Washington, *A Collection*, p. 401 (letter to La Fayette, 19 June 1788).

into crisis, observed Burckhardt, who in this connection quoted Heraclitus' motto ('war is the father of all and the king of all').[197] For de Tocqueville war and 'great events' could form a useful antidote to 'our mediocre democratic and bourgeois soup', which was the breeding ground of sensualism and socialist hedonism.[198] *Democracy in America* forcefully asserted that 'I do not wish to speak ill of war: war almost always enlarges the mind of a people and elevates their character.'[199]

When it involved an advance by the West, and hence by the cause of liberty, war revealed its true nobility and beauty. De Tocqueville expressed himself in lyrical terms on the first Opium War (see below, Chapter 9, §6), in a letter whose addressee was the English liberal Reeve. He in turn, on the occasion of the Crimean War (which saw England allied with Bonapartist France), expressed himself no less magniloquently in the course of correspondence with the French liberal:

> We live at a time when it is necessary to know how to suffer and witness suffering. The sword of war cuts to the heart. But what a mighty influence this struggle has on the political and social body! What a unity of sentiment and endeavour it creates! What a reawakening of the forces which, after all, make up the greatness of a people. I willingly accept all the anguish and all the ills of war for what it brings morally even more than politically.[200]

14. The proud self-consciousness of the community of the free and the emergence of 'irritable patriotism'

War against barbarians in the colonies, or against countries situated on the margins of civilization, had hitherto been a subject for appreciation or celebration. At first sight, no cloud seemed to trouble the unity of the community of the free. However, after having desired the extension to the entire planet of the enlightened 'despotism' of civilized countries, Mill continued as follows: the gigantic 'federation', albeit 'unequal', that was the British Empire

---

197   Jacob Burckhardt, *Weltgeschichtliche Betrachtungen*, ed. Jacob Oeri, in *Gesammelte Werke*, vol. 4, Basel: Schwabe, 1978, pp. 150, 118–19.

198   Tocqueville, *Oeuvres complètes*, vol. 8, pt 1, p. 421 (letter to Gustave de Beaumont, 9 August 1840).

199   Tocqueville, *Democracy in America*, vol. 2, p. 268.

200   Reeve, quoted in de Tocqueville, *Oeuvres complètes*, vol. 6, pt 1, p. 150.

has the advantage, especially valuable at the present time, of adding to the moral influence, and weight in the councils of the world, of the Power which, of all in existence, best understands liberty—and whatever may have been its errors in the past, has attained to more of conscience and moral principle in its dealings with foreigners than any other great nation seems either to conceive as possible or recognise as desirable.

Backward populations had an interest in becoming part of the British Empire, in order to avoid 'being absorbed into a foreign state, and becoming a source of additional aggressive strength to some rival power'.[201]

In the years of the July Monarchy, de Tocqueville had responded prematurely and indirectly to Mill's claim to raise the British Empire to the status of unique, privileged representative of a universal cause. The English were characterized by

their constant commitment to seek to demonstrate that they are acting in the interests of a principle, or for the good of the natives, or even for the benefit of the sovereigns whom they subjugate; honest is their indignation at those who put up resistance; these are the procedures with which they always cover up violence.[202]

With the disappearance of the semblance of complete unity, rivalry emerged between the different countries that made up the community of the free— rivalry that became all the more intense as the liquidation of despotism and, more generally, the construction of a new political regime deemed more advanced reinforced the self-consciousness of the individual protagonists. This was soil wherein was rooted the celebration, dear to Burke, of the 'nation in whose veins the blood of freedom circulates'. The most lucid exponents of liberalism were perfectly well aware of this. While it also made itself felt in the works of authors such as Constant and, above all, Spencer, in this intellectual tradition the illusion that the collapse of the *ancien régime* betokened the advent of perpetual peace did not play the role it had in the French Revolution and radicalism. A source of possible conflicts between the various countries, observed Hamilton, was not only the diversity of political orders and interests:

---

201   Mill, *Utilitarianism*, p. 380.
202   Tocqueville, *Oeuvres complètes*, vol. 3, pt 1, p. 505.

Are there not aversions, predilections, rivalships, and desires of unjust acquisitions, that affect nations as well as kings? Are not popular assemblies frequently subject to the impulses of rage, resentment, jealousy, avarice, and of other irregular and violent propensities? ... Has commerce hitherto done anything more than change the object of war?[203]

The advent of the representative regime and the transfer of power from absolute monarchy to the nation were not in themselves an antidote to war. Holland and England, the first two nations to have equipped themselves with liberal orders, had turned out to be 'frequently engaged in war'.[204] Hamilton felt great admiration for Britain: 'I believe the British government forms the best model the world ever produced.'[205] Yet on the level of international policy, Britain remained an enemy to be defeated. The American statesman rebuked Europe, which wanted 'to plume herself as the Mistress of the World' and tended 'to consider the rest of mankind as created for her benefit'. This was a pretence that must be countered with force: 'It belongs to us to vindicate the honour of the human race, and to teach that assuming brother, moderation.' Sooner or later, the new Union would be the one 'able to dictate the terms of the connection between the old and the new world!'[206] Even if the enemy was generically identified as Europe and the Old World, the particular reference was to Britain which at this time (1787), following France's defeat in the Seven Years' War, was the only great imperial power. Jefferson was more explicit. The 'empire for liberty' desired by him presupposed Britain's defeat: not only was it called upon to be the most grand and glorious 'since the creation', and hence to outclass the British Empire, but it also presupposed the annexation of Canada (in addition to Cuba), 'which would be of course in the first war'.[207]

For de Tocqueville, too, shared membership of the community of the free by certain countries did not guarantee permanent relations of friendship and peace between them. In defining its foreign policy, France must not exclusively assert its 'interest in developing the principles of liberty in the world'. Only the naive could believe that their spread meant the simultaneous disappearance of the threat of war:

---

203 Hamilton, *Writings*, p. 179.
204 Ibid., p. 180.
205 Hamilton, quoted in Samuel E. Morison, ed., *Sources and Documents Illustrating the American Revolution*, Oxford: Clarendon Press, 1953, p. 259.
206 Hamilton, *Writings*, p. 208.
207 Jefferson, *The Republic of Letters*, vol. 3, p. 1586 (letter to Madison, 27 April 1809).

Will anyone go so far as to claim that two peoples must necessarily live in peace with one another just because they have similar political institutions? That all the causes of ambition, rivalry, jealousy, all the bad memories have been abolished? Free institutions render these feelings even more vital.[208]

In its turn, *Democracy in America* stressed that '[a]ll free nations are vainglorious'; the 'restless and insatiable vanity of a democratic people' was self-evident. This was confirmed, in particular, by the transatlantic republic: 'The Americans, in their intercourse with strangers, appear impatient of the smallest censure and insatiable of praise ... Their vanity is not only greedy, but restless and jealous'.[209] We are dealing with an excessive 'national pride', an 'irritable patriotism' (*patriotisme irritable*), which did not tolerate criticism of any kind.[210] This was a demand for primacy that sought utter exclusivity. If a foreigner admired the 'freedom' enjoyed by Americans, they would react by accepting the compliment, but immediately rendering it more emphatic and more exclusive: 'few nations are worthy of it'. If a foreigner admired their 'purity of morals', the American interlocutor would react by denouncing 'the corruption that prevails in other nations'.[211]

When he turned to the international rivalry between the countries making up the community of the free and the West, de Tocqueville did not hesitate to speak harshly of the United States. Writing to an American interlocutor, and referring to attempts to expand southwards also made by 'private' adventurers (he was thinking of William Walker), the French liberal wrote:

> Not without concern, I have seen this spirit of conquest, even of rapine, exhibited among you for some years. It is not a sign of good health in a people that already has more territory than it can fill. I confess that I could not but be sad if I came to learn that the [American] nation had embarked on an operation against Cuba or—even worse—entrusted it to its lost sons.[212]

The American interlocutor might easily have retorted by recalling de Tocqueville's enthusiastic support for France's policy of 'conquest' and 'rapine' in Algeria. But the key point is different. Far from damping it down, the common waving of the flag of liberty further fuelled international rivalry. After

208   Tocqueville, *Oeuvres complètes*, vol. 3, pt 3, p. 249.
209   Tocqueville, *Democracy in America*, vol. 2, pp. 225–6.
210   Ibid., vol. 1, p. 244.
211   Ibid., vol. 2, p. 225.
212   Tocqueville, *Oeuvres complètes*, vol. 7, p. 147 (letter to T. Sedgwick, 4 December 1852).

the February Revolution, de Tocqueville declared that 'starting from 1789' France once again donned the 'role' of 'saviour' 'of peoples whose liberty is in danger'.[213] An 'empire for liberty' was thus evoked whose capital was Paris, and which tended to come into conflict with the 'empire for liberty' cherished by Jefferson.

15. De Tocqueville's 'irritable patriotism'

The realism with which the most lucid representatives of the liberal tradition analysed the persistence of national rivalries, despite their shared reference to the ideal of liberty, had another aspect to it: the candid, avowed chauvinism presiding over the international policy programme. This applies to de Tocqueville in particular. The principle of consent by the governed as a criterion for legitimizing political power gave impetus to national movements in Europe as well. Prima facie, it would seem that the liberal world as a whole should have felt unequivocal sympathy for them. In this case, we are dealing not with colonial peoples, but with peoples regarded as more or less civilized, who primarily came into conflict with the Habsburg Empire—that is, a power which had remained foreign to liberal development. Yet de Tocqueville proved cool, or frankly hostile. A partial explanation of this attitude can be found in the social demands that contaminated such movements and imperilled the traditional liberal delimitation of the political sphere. The Mazzinian republic established in Rome was 'the red republic' and against it, and 'the anarchical party in Rome and the rest of the world', no blows should be spared. Ideological fury impelled the French liberal to speak of his political opponents in Italy as 'a whole category of political criminals'.[214] De Tocqueville proved harsh and even cynical about one of the protagonists of the Hungarian national revolution: rather than agitating to save 'Kossuth's skin', it might happily be made into a 'drum'.[215]

Over and above rejection of radicalism, what motivated this attitude was 'irritable patriotism', concerns of a chauvinistic kind, as emerges in particular from de Tocqueville's furious polemic against 'our imbecile agents' in Germany, who were guilty of not countering the prospect of that country's 'political unification' more firmly and effectively. Certainly, 'the population's passion for this idea seems sincere and profound'; but 'nothing would be more

---

213   Ibid., vol. 3, pt 3, p. 249.
214   Ibid., vol. 15, pt 1, pp. 249, 277, 399 (letters to F. de Corcelle, 10 and 20 June and 12 September 1849).
215   Ibid., vol. 15, pt 2, p. 92 (letter to F. de Corcelle, 30 January 1854).

frightful for us'.[216] But did this not ride roughshod over the liberal principle of self-government and consent by the governed as a criterion of the legitimacy of any government? That was a problem de Tocqueville did not pose. He hoped for 'the victory of the princes' and the Prussian army to put paid to 'excessive decentralization' that encouraged the swarming of 'revolutionary breeding grounds'.[217]

In relation to Italy, chauvinistic concerns should have played a more modest role. Yet in September 1848, in his capacity as Foreign Minister, de Tocqueville summarized his position as follows: 'preservation of the old territories ... and real, significant changes in institutions'.[218] As we can see, there was no place for demands for national unity. And the principle of consent by the governed? Having invited the organization of 'a *Roman demonstration*' in favour of restoring the Pope's temporal power, de Tocqueville continued as follows:

> In my opinion, this is *indispensable*. And, in order to achieve this result, if we do not also have the reality, it is *absolutely* necessary to produce at least the semblance. This is the only way to connect the expedition with one of the main objectives we have always assigned it and on which the National Assembly has always wished to stand firm—coming to the aid of the real will and hidden desires of the people of Rome.[219]

In this passage the roles of appearance and reality are reversed rapidly and inadvertently. The 'semblance' of a demonstration to be organized at all costs expressed the 'hidden' but nevertheless 'real' will of the Roman population, whose interpreter was the government of the occupying power. At this point it was also possible to resort to radical measures with a clear conscience:

> I cannot really understand why, in the twenty-four hours following the city's capture, we did not, with utmost rapidity and energy, close the clubs, tear down the flag of the Republic, disarm the citizens and soldiers, arrest all those who, in their attitude, indicated that they disapproved of our presence [*tous ceux qui faisaient mine de trouver mauvais notre présence*]—in a word, strike our enemies with terror in order to conquer the terror that had gripped our friends.[220]

---

216 Ibid., vol. 8, pt 2, pp. 29, 38 (letters to Gustave de Beaumont, 27 August and 3 September 1848).

217 Ibid., vol. 8, pt 2, pp. 133–4 (letter to Gustave de Beaumont, 18 May 1849).

218 Ibid., vol. 8, pt 2, p. 44 (letter to Gustave de Beaumont, 14 September 1848).

219 Ibid., vol. 15, pt 1, p. 276 (letter to F. de Corcelle, 20 June 1849).

220 Ibid., vol. 15, pt 1, p. 323 (letter to F. de Corcelle, 18 July 1849).

So here we have an invitation to make arrests even on the basis of mere suspicion. Not by chance, reference is made to terror. It is a term that recurs frequently; it amounts to a veritable watchword: 'strike the demagogic party with terror and lift the liberal party'.[221] But another watchword was immediately added: 'negate the rigours of the past, although leaving terror to waft over the future'.[222] Indeed, European public opinion, which already felt 'deep repulsion' at France's conduct, must not be unduly ruffled. Yet it was a question of 'advancing and advancing with the most extreme rigour'; all the more so because the country's honour was at stake. It found itself faced with a 'terrible alternative'—a Hobson's choice:

> Either to deliver Rome over to all the horrors of war or to retreat shamefully, beaten by the same men who for eighteen months fled all the battlefields of Italy. The first would be a great misfortune, but the second would be a fearful disaster and, as far as I am concerned, I have no hesitation.[223]

Once again, chauvinism took priority over any other concern.

16. The conflict of ideas of mission from the American Revolution to the First World War

So we can understand the recurrent divisions that opened up in the community of the free. The one that occurred in the two decades preceding the foundation of the United States is illuminating. The Seven Years' War was also experienced and fought by the English colonists in America, and in fact primarily by them, not only as a war for the defence of English liberty, but also (as the sermons of Protestant ministers never tired of repeating) as a holy war in which it was God himself who guided and saved England–Israel from the threat represented by France. The victory achieved over the enemies of Israel was proof of the 'favourable providential presence of God with his people'.[224] A few years later, it was England's turn to form the core of the alliance of the 'enemies of God', while the rebel American colonists continued to be 'true Christians, good

---

221 Ibid., vol. 15, pt 1, p. 323 (letter to F. de Corcelle, 18 July 1849).

222 Ibid., vol. 15, pt 1, p. 294 (letter to F. de Corcelle, 2 July 1849).

223 Ibid., vol. 15, pt 1, p. 293 (letter to F. de Corcelle, 1 July 1849).

224 Ellis Sandoz, ed., *Political Sermons of the American Founding Era*, Indianapolis: Liberty Press, 1991, pp. 216–19.

soldiers of Jesus Christ', called upon to cultivate 'a martial spirit' and 'the art of war', so as to accomplish 'the work of the Lord'.[225]

This was the first major conflict to convulse the community of the free, and it spans the period that extends from the American Revolution to the war of 1812–15. As the latter was coming to an end, Jefferson expressed the opinion that Great Britain was no less despotic than Napoleon. Moreover, while the latter would take 'his tyrannies' to the grave with him, a whole 'nation' was seeking to impose its absolute domination over the seas; and it was an 'insult to the human understanding'.[226] Such was his ideological fury that the American statesman ended up declaring: 'Our enemy has indeed the consolation of Satan on removing our first parents from Paradise: from a peaceable and agricultural nation, he makes us a military and manufacturing one.'[227] Having heard the news of the end of hostilities, Jefferson wrote that it was 'an armistice only'. So radical was the antagonism not only of interests, but also of principles, that the two countries were in fact engaged in an 'eternal war', which would terminate or was destined to end with the 'extermination of the one or the other party'.[228]

The second major conflict was the one that exploded with the American Civil War. The dialectic we have already encountered was on display once again. The fact that for decades the antagonists had regarded themselves as members of the chosen people of liberty, far from reducing the bitterness of the clash, accentuated it. Both sides were convinced that they were fighting a holy war; they appealed to Holy Scripture and half of their propaganda texts were written by ecclesiastics.[229]

The first major conflict survived the second, which was eclipsed at the end of the nineteenth century by the rising tide of chauvinism that invested the United States as a whole, without significant distinctions between North and South. In 1889 Kipling noted with disappointment that the 4 July celebrations in San Francisco were the occasion for official speeches against what the Americans defined as 'our natural enemy', represented by Great Britain 'with her chain of fortresses across the world'.[230] In reality, this antagonism too was

---

225   Ibid., pp. 623–4.

226   Thomas Jefferson, *Writings*, ed. Merrill D. Peterson, New York: Library of America, 1984, pp. 1272–3 (letter to Madame de Staël, 24 May 1813).

227   Ibid., p. 1357 (letter to William Short, 28 November 1814).

228   Ibid., p. 1366 (letter to La Fayette, 14 February 1815).

229   Eugene D. Genovese, 'Religion in the Collapse of the American Union', in Randall M. Miller, Harry S. Stout and Charles Reagan Wilson, eds, *Religion and the American Civil War*, Oxford and New York: Oxford University Press, 1998, pp. 74–5.

230   Kipling, quoted in Gosset, *Race*, p. 322.

being damped down, because a completely new international situation was maturing. More than ever engaged in colonial expansion, and increasingly taken in by the idea of the freedom mission they assigned themselves in competition with one another, between the nineteenth and twentieth centuries the various national centres of the community of the free turned out to be on a collision course. This is the context in which we can situate the third major conflict in the history of liberalism. Starting with the First World War, in particular it saw ranged against one another Britain (and the United States) and Germany—the most recent and ambitious recruit to the community of the free, which at the end of the nineteenth century had likewise begun to cherish the idea of an empire for liberty, putting itself at the head of a crusade for the abolition of slavery in the colonies.[231]

The interpretation of the third major conflict suggested here might occasion astonishment. What obstructs an understanding of this event is the negative teleology that tends to interpret German history in its entirety as a series of stages leading inexorably to the horror of the Third Reich. In reality, on the eve of the First World War Germany was not obviously less 'democratic' than the United States, where racial oppression raged, or than Great Britain, which completely disregarded universal male suffrage (on which elections to the Reichstag were based), and exercised imperial domination on a global scale and even in Europe itself, at the expense of Ireland. Above all, it must not be forgotten that, at the turn of the nineteenth century, even in England and America, Germany was regarded as a full member of the exclusive club of free peoples.

So the by now familiar dialectic emerges once again. Confronting one another in a total war, which required the mobilization of culture as well as armies, were antagonists who had previously congratulated one another on being members, or even especially influential members, of the community of the free—in this case, of the great Teutonic or Aryan family, united by a jealous custodianship of individual autonomy and love of self-government and liberty.

---

231   Cf. Losurdo, *Nietzsche*, ch. 17, §3.

CHAPTER NINE

Sacred Space and Profane Space in the History of Liberalism

1. Historiography and hagiography

Our history of liberalism ends with the outbreak of the First World War, when (according to Weber) even in countries with the most stable liberal tradition the state was assigned '"legitimate" power over the life, death and liberty' of individuals, and 'unlimited disposition over all the economic goods accessible to it'.[1] Indeed, as Furet puts it, 'in virtually all of Europe, the canons of August 1914 literally and metaphorically buried liberty in the name of country'.[2] It is appropriate to take a look back from this watershed.

Following the prelude of the revolt against Philip II's absolutism by the Netherlands, liberalism asserted itself in two counties so positioned that they were sheltered from the threats to which continental European states were exposed. It should be added that, not by chance, the Glorious Revolution succeeded England's victory first over Spain and then over France, while the American colonists' revolt only began with the defeat of France in the Seven Years' War. Thus, the two liberal revolutions both presupposed a clear improvement in the geopolitical situation.

As regards continental Europe, we can distinguish two phases: after the defeat of Turkey at the gates of Vienna in 1683 and the fading of the Ottoman threat, criticism of absolutism became widespread. The second phase was the so-called hundred years' peace, which extended from the end of the Napoleonic

---

1 Max Weber, 'Der Sinn der "Wertfreiheit" der soziologischen und ökonomischen Wissenschaften', in *Methodologische Schriften*, ed. Johannes Winckelann, Frankfurt am Main: Fischer, 1968, p. 276.

2 François Furet, *Il passato di un'illusione*, ed. Marina Valensise, Milan: Mondadori, 1995, p. 98.

Wars to the outbreak of the First World War. This was the period when liberalism also asserted itself at a concrete political level. And just as the institutions that emerged from the 1789 revolution did not survive the war which engulfed revolutionary France, from 1914 the liberal institutions that had flourished in continental Europe during the hundred years' peace experienced a dramatic crisis. Taken as a whole, as well as enjoying a more or less high degree of peace and geopolitical security, the liberal countries had another characteristic in common: in the period under investigation here, they had marked possibilities of defusing politico-social conflict in the metropolis through colonial expansion, whether continentally or overseas.

With the epochal rupture of 1914 there erupted in all its horror the second Thirty Years' War, as the two global conflicts in the first half of the twentieth century, separated by a fragile armistice, have often been defined. What is the relationship between all this and the preceding historical period? Or are we to believe that there is no relationship and that the *belle époque* came to an unanticipated end, brought about exclusively by circumstances altogether foreign to the liberal West? This is the conclusion that seems to be suggested by an eminent English historian of the modern world, A. J. P. Taylor:

> Until August 1914 a sensible, law-abiding Englishman could pass through life and hardly notice the existence of the state, beyond the post office and the policeman. He could live where he liked and as he liked. He had no official number or identity card. He could travel abroad or leave his country forever without a passport or any sort of official permission. He could exchange his money for any other currency without restriction or limit ... Unlike the countries of the European continent, the state did not require its citizens to perform military service ... It left the adult citizen alone.[3]

Citing this picture, already problematic enough in itself, a contemporary British liberal scholar elevates it into 'the historical paradigm of a liberal civilization'.[4] In reality, a couple of pages later, Taylor himself observes that '[s]ome 50 million Africans and 250 million Indians were involved, without consultation, in a war of which they understood nothing'.[5] But let us ignore the colonies, and even Ireland, which formed part of the United Kingdom and experienced such political and military oppression from the London government that it was (again in Taylor's words) the protagonist of 'the only national rebellion in any

---

3   A. J. P. Taylor, *English History 1914–1945*, Oxford: Oxford University Press, 1992, p. 1.
4   John Gray, *Liberalism*, Milton Keynes: Open University Press, 1986, p. 26.
5   Taylor, *English History*, p. 3.

European country during the First World War—an ironical comment on the British claim to be fighting for freedom' and to represent the cause of liberty.[6]

As for England specifically, I do not know if Cobden 'noticed' the state that inspected his mail, but it was certainly on its guard against a citizen who was unquestionably 'sensible and law-abiding', but whose fault was to be suspected of Chartist sympathies.[7] And the state even more readily 'noticed' the Chartism and the working-class movement in general, which faced repeated suspension of habeas corpus and recourse to the use of *agents provocateurs* who elicited horror not only in the liberal Constant, but also in a 'statist' like Hegel.[8] In the England of the time, 'a whole subclass of informers, police narks and thief-takers' was at work.[9] Even the contrast with the continent as regards military conscription is mistaken: this had already made its appearance some years earlier in the United States during the Civil War and, in order to impose it, Lincoln, putting down violent resistance, had no hesitation in having an army corps march on New York.[10] Military conscription was not a practice imposed on the liberal world from without, from the continent!

Historiography tends to shade into hagiography. I use this term in a technical sense: it involves a discourse completely focused on what, for the community of the free, was the restricted sacred space. It is enough, however briefly, to introduce the profane space (slaves in the colonies and servants in the metropolis) into the analysis, to realize the inadequate, misleading character of the categories (absolute pre-eminence of individual liberty, anti-statism, individualism) generally used to trace the history of the liberal West. Was eighteenth- and nineteenth-century Britain the land of religious freedom? Referring to Ireland, the liberal de Beaumont, who was de Tocqueville's companion during his trip to America, spoke of 'unimaginable religious oppression'. We are dealing with a people not only deprived of its 'religious freedom', but also forced, notwithstanding its poverty, to subsidize the wealthy Anglican Church that oppressed it with tithes. The vexations, humiliations and suffering inflicted by British 'tyranny' on this 'slave people' proved that 'a degree of egotism and madness is present in human institutions whose limits cannot be defined'.[11]

---

6   Ibid., p. 56.

7   Wendy Hinde, *Richard Cobden*, New Haven: Yale University Press, 1987, p. 111.

8   Cf. Domenico Losurdo, *Heidegger and the Ideology of War*, trans. Marella and Jon Morris, Amherst (NY): Humanity Books, 2001, ch. 5, §8.

9   Robert Hughes, *The Fatal Shore*, London: Collins, Harvill, 1987, p. 27.

10   Cf. Domenico Losurdo, *Il revisionismo storico*, Rome and Bari: Laterza, 1996, ch. 2, §5.

11   Gustave de Beaumont, *L'Irlande sociale, politique et religieuse*, 2 vols, ed. Goderlaine Charpentier, Villeneuve d'Ascq: CERIUL-Université Charles-de-Gaulle Lille III, 1990, vol. 1, p. 331; vol. 2, pp. 306, 201.

But let us concentrate on the metropolis. Celebrating the individualism and anti-statism attributed to the liberal tradition, Hayek pays homage to Mandeville, for whom the 'arbitrary exertions of government power would be minimized'.[12] In truth, the author elevated into a model here was not only completely undisturbed by the spectacle of hundreds or thousands of wretches 'daily hanged for trifles', but invoked summary trials and an acceleration in death sentences—and demanded state intervention even in the private life of these poor people, on whom the observance of Sunday worship should be imposed from infancy (see above, Chapter 3, §8). It is clear that what held Hayek's attention was neither the colonies nor metropolitan servants.

Things do not fall out right even if such neglect is regarded as innocuous. The experience of the British colonies in America that subsequently became the United States is particularly revealing. Servile, semi-servile and free labour-power came from across the Atlantic in ways and in accordance with rules fixed by the political authorities, which also played a decisive role in delimiting the area opened up to colonization from time to time. The slavery or marginalization and degradation imposed on blacks ended up impinging on the 'modern liberty' of the whites themselves—and so seriously that the wrong choice of sexual or marriage partner risked transforming the culprit into a 'felon', a traitor to his own country and race! The white population as a whole, and slave-owners themselves, were subject to a whole series of laws that gravely interfered in even the most intimate aspect of private life. The political authorities exercised comprehensive surveillance so that miscegenation and, above all, the potential fruit of such noxious mixing did not lead to emancipation and did not threaten the purity of the community of the free with its false presence. It was a crime to give or even merely furnish writing materials to slaves. The postal administration prevented the circulation of materials vaguely critical of the institution of slavery. In the South a climate of terror reigned over citizens suspected of harbouring abolitionist ideas.

It was not only the race issue and the dark cloud it suspended over the civil rights of the white community itself. We can take a key state in the history of the North American revolution and republic: 'Pennsylvania was ... renowned in the nineteenth century for its stringent laws against blasphemy, profanity, and desecrating the sabbath'.[13] Independently of the prohibition of miscegenation, which remained in force beyond the mid-twentieth century, sexual

---

12   Nathan Rosenberg, quoted in Friedrich von Hayek, *New Studies in Philosophy, Politics, Economics and the History of Ideas*, London: Routledge and Kegan Paul, 1978, p. 259.

13   Eric Foner, *The Story of American Freedom*, London: Picador, 1999, pp. 53–4.

freedom in the United States was restricted in ways that were largely foreign to the despised, 'statist' continental Europe. Here is the picture drawn in 2003 by a distinguished US newspaper:

> All 50 states had laws banning sodomy until 1961 ... The number had dwindled to 24 states by 1968 and stands at 13 today ... Most of the remaining states with anti-sodomy laws forbid anal or oral sex among consenting adults no matter their sex or relationship.[14]

To this we must add the constitutional amendment of 1919 that sought to prevent the production and consumption of 'intoxicating liquors'—a further intervention in the private life of citizens with few parallels in other Western countries.

Overall, the history of the English colonies in America and then of the United States—both classical countries of the liberal tradition are thus involved to differing degrees—is better explained by the complexity of the process of constructing and protecting the sacred space, than by the categories of anti-statism and individualism.

2. The liberal revolution as a tangle of emancipation and dis-emancipation

Once the field of hagiography has been evacuated, in reconstructing the history of liberalism it is better to start with the slogan advanced by the rebel American colonists: 'We won't be their Negroes!' On the one hand, the rebellion began by demanding equality, while on the other it reasserted inequality and further deepened it. The two demands were indissolubly linked: precisely because they established a marked superiority over blacks and Indians, the colonists felt themselves completely equal to gentlemen and property-owners residing in London, and demanded that such equality be recognized and consecrated at every level. The dialectic that issued in the Glorious Revolution was not very different. We have seen an exponent of English proto-liberalism demanding, in the face of interference by monarchical power, peaceful enjoyment of his own possessions and servants. Far from questioning it, 'true liberty' consecrated the existing relations of service (and, in the colonies, slavery) as belonging to

---

14 Joel Brinkley, 'US Court Strikes Down Sodomy Ban', *International Herald Tribune*, 27 June 2003.

an inviolable private sphere. The equality property-owners demanded with the sovereign, who could now be nothing but *primus inter pares*, went hand in hand with the reification of servants, who tended to be likened to other objects of property. That is why liberalism and racial chattel slavery emerged together in a twin birth.

At this point we should analyse as a whole the three revolutions from which we started out. Of the first, which occurred in Holland, Huizinga observed that 'the revolt against the Spanish government was a conservative revolution and could not have been otherwise'.[15] The same conclusion has been reached by other eminent historians. Philip II was concerned to 'require that bishops be technically skilled (that is, theologians rather than sons of great lords)' and was opposed to the nobility's attempt to transform the Council of State into 'an exclusively aristocratic executive body'. We can then understand that 'large parts of the "Netherlands" nobility were suddenly afraid that the prince was not their *agent*, that his policies would in the short and medium run threaten their interests significantly'.[16] So, on the one hand, we have Philip II, who surrounded himself with 'secretaries who were generally from modest origins, passive instruments of his will'; on the other, 'an oligarchic princely republic of communal cities and feudal lordships', a 'grand aristocracy', a 'feudal oligarchy' engaged in defending 'privileges and customs' that consecrated its power and prestige.[17] It is as if the nobles of the Netherlands, like large English property-owners and the English colonists in America subsequently, declared: 'We don't want to be treated as your servants!' In its initial stages, the revolt against Philip II was not very different from the contemporaneous agitation of the Fronde in France.[18] In both cases, what ignited the powder was the clash between the high nobility's autonomist and in some sense liberal aspirations and the Crown's centralizing tendencies—except that, in the second case, the influence of the struggle for national independence and the intervention of the popular masses in it profoundly altered the initial picture.

We have already seen the impetus given by the Glorious Revolution to the slave trade and the development of racial slavery in the colonies. The aspect of dis-emancipation also emerges with clarity in Ireland. Systematic expropriation

---

15   Huizinga, quoted in Hans-Christoph Schröder, *Die Revolutionen Englands im 17. Jahrundert*, Frankfurt am Main: Suhrkamp, 1986, p. 51.

16   Immanuel Wallerstein, *The Modern World System*, 3 vols, New York: Academic Press, 1974–89, vol. 1, pp. 203–4.

17   Giorgio Spini, *Storia dell'età moderna*, Turin: Einaudi, 1982, pp. 272, 276–7.

18   Charles Tilly, *European Revolutions, 1492–1992*, Oxford and Cambridge (MA): Blackwell, 1993, p. 160.

of the natives intensified; in 1688 Catholics still owned 22 per cent of Irish land, but the figure fell to '14 per cent in 1703 and a mere 5 per cent in 1778'.[19] And that is not all: 'Catholics—the overwhelming majority of the Irish population—were excluded from all public offices and from the legal profession.'[20] In England itself, the Glorious Revolution swept away the obstacles that still stood in the way of enclosures. As Marx put it, having attained full control of power, land-owners and capitalists 'inaugurated the new era by practising on a colossal scale the thefts of state lands which had hitherto been managed more modestly'.[21] To the extent that rural labourers had found an ear more or less attentive to their lamentations, it was from the Stuart monarchy.[22] Up to 1688, by dint of the control over them exercised from above, Justices of the Peace had some autonomy from the landed aristocracy. They subsequently lost it, becoming 'virtual dictators of local government' and answering only to the members of their own class who sat in parliament.[23] Finally, we must not lose sight of the incredible increase in the number of crimes against property that carried the death penalty, with the establishment of a regime of terror over the popular masses.

The dimension of dis-emancipation is even more obvious in the American Revolution. The terms in which Theodore Roosevelt celebrated it at the start of the twentieth century are revealing:

The chief factor in producing the Revolution, and later in producing the War of 1812, was the inability of the motherland country to understand that the freemen who went forth to conquer a continent should be encouraged in that work … The spread of the hardy, venturesome backwoodsmen was to most of the statesmen of London a matter of anxiety rather than of pride, and the famous Quebec Act of 1774 was in part designed with the purpose of keeping the English-speaking settlements permanently east of the Alleghanies, and preserving the mighty and beautiful valley of the Ohio as a hunting-ground for savages …[24]

---

19   Ibid., p. 115.

20   Christopher Hill, *The Century of Revolution*, New York: Norton, 1961, p. 258.

21   Karl Marx, *Capital: Volume One*, trans. Ben Fowkes, Harmondsworth: Penguin, 1976, p. 884.

22   Barrington Moore Jr, *The Social Origins of Dictatorship and Democracy*, Boston: Beacon Press, 1966, pp. 12–13.

23   Hill, *Century of Revolution*, p. 3.

24   Theodore Roosevelt, *The Strenuous Life*, New York: Century, 1901, pp. 246–7.

Unquestionably, the tragedy of the Indians was dramatically hastened by the foundation of the United States.[25] Great Britain's interests in its transatlantic possessions were commercial rather than territorial; and, as we know, it was loyalists who had taken refuge in Canada who accused the insurgents of a systematic policy of genocide.

If Indians gained nothing from the American Revolution, what about blacks? The foundation of the United States involved the advent of a racial state and an unprecedented consolidation of racial chattel slavery. It is true that, in line with the watchword of the struggle against (political) slavery advanced during the revolt against Britain, the Northern states abolished slavery in the strict sense. But blacks did not thereby acquire freedom, confined as they were to a 'caste' different from that of freemen. In any event, there is a fact that provides food for thought: Britain abolished slavery in its colonies in 1834, while it survived in the United States for another three decades. Even the condition of free blacks was worse there, for example, than in Canada. In that British colony between 1850 and 1860, 20,000 blacks found refuge who had abandoned the United States, where they feared that laws on the return of fugitive slaves to their legitimate owners might furnish pretexts for the enslavement even of free blacks. But already, some decades earlier, more than a thousand black slaves had sought refuge in Canada after their delegation had been benevolently received by the local authorities with a stinging polemic against the United States: 'Tell the Republicans on your side of the line that we royalists do not know men by their colour. Should you come to us you will be entitled to all the privileges of the rest of His Majesty's subjects.'[26] Obviously, this declaration was not free from an ideological, self-serving element. But it remains the case that blacks in the US looked to Canada as the promised land of liberty.[27]

The most significant steps in the expansion of the United States simultaneously sealed the extension of the democracy and domination, in its harshest forms, of the 'master race'.[28] In 1803 Napoleon sold Louisiana. Although already in force, slavery had not yet assumed a clearly racial form. There were

---

25   Colin G. Calloway, *The American Revolution in Indian Country*, Cambridge: Cambridge University Press, 1995.

26   Leon F. Litwack, *North of Slavery*, Chicago: University of Chicago Press, 1961, pp. 249, 73.

27   Reginald C. Stuart, *United States Expansionism and British North America*, Chapel Hill: University of South Carolina Press, 1988, pp. 167ff.

28   Ronald Creagh, *Nos cousins d'Amérique*, Paris: Payot, 1988, pp. 248–9; Joseph Zitomersky, 'Culture, classe ou État?', in Marcel Dorigny and Marie-Jeanne Rossignol, eds, *La France et les Amériques au temps de Jefferson and de Miranda*, Paris: Société des études robespierristes, 2001, pp. 77–84.

Sacred and Profane Spaces

20,000 half-castes, who to all intents and purposes were free and sometimes engaged in the liberal professions. They might even be very wealthy, and thus form part of the dominant elite. Transfer to the United States involved the consecration of local self-government and the power, in the final analysis, of white property-owners (French and Anglo-American). The result was a deterioration in the conditions not only of slaves—emancipation became increasingly difficult—but, above all, of freemen of colour. Their numbers diminished in absolute terms, and even more appreciably in percentage terms (their immigration was discouraged, while that of whites was encouraged). Hit by a series of discriminatory measures, freemen of colour now began to form an intermediate caste closer to slaves than freemen proper. In Louisiana, annexed to the United States, the twin birth of free representative bodies and racial chattel slavery was also seen in due course.

A new, considerable expansion of US territory occurred some decades later with the drastic amputation of Mexico. We already know about the introduction of slavery into Texas. But even more significant was the tragedy that struck the Indians in both Texas and California. Subjected to forced labour and a thinly disguised slavery, their children in effect became *res nullius*. Particularly desirable were young girls because, as a local paper put it, they served the dual purpose of 'work and lust'.[29] But this was only one chapter in a horrific story: 'The destruction and degradation of the California Indians is one of the sorriest blotches on the honor and intelligence of a nation. It was less a matter of war than of "sport".'[30]

3. The *longue durée* and comparativism

Viewed comparatively and from the perspective of the *longue durée*, the American Revolution appears as the start of a long series of attempts by white colonists to rid themselves of the obstacle represented by central power, whether ecclesiastical or monarchical. In 1537 Pope Paul III declared that the sacraments must be forbidden to colonists who, denying the humanity of Indians, reduced them to slavery. 'Moralistic interference' was also carried out by the Spanish and Portuguese crowns. Thus, a 'continuing tension between slavery and Christian ideals' made itself felt. But the colonists, for whom forced labour was an

---

29   David E. Stannard, *American Holocaust*, New York and Oxford: Oxford University Press, 1992, pp. 142–3.

30   Wilcomb E. Washburn, *The Indian in America*, New York: Harper & Row, 1975, p. 196.

305

unavoidable necessity, responded by expelling the Jesuits from Brazil or provoking veritable 'colonial insurrections'.[31] On the other side, the first rebellions by black slaves tended to appeal to the Crown and to look to central government for a counter-weight to the despotism of local masters.[32]

As for British America, the revolt that developed in Virginia a century before the American Revolution, and which was led by Nathaniel Bacon, must be borne in mind. While on the one hand targeting the privileges of the governing faction, on the other the rebels 'demanded land, without regard to the rights or needs of the border Indians', who in fact were exterminated in some instances.[33] The conflicts that subsequently emerged in the American Revolution are present here *in nuce*: on the one hand, the polemic against central government arrogance and interference; on the other, the demand for complete freedom vis-à-vis 'savages'. And in fact, when we read in Bacon's manifesto his denunciation of the collusion, in the course of the struggle against the champions of liberty, between the governor of Virginia and the 'barbarous', bloodthirsty Indians,[34] we are reminded of the Declaration of Independence.

We know that the French and English colonists also waved the flag of self-government, independence and imitation of the US model against the policy of emancipating slaves, for which they criticized the central political power. But events in Southern Africa are especially significant. Here, too, whether the colonies were controlled by the Dutch or British, the development of self-government by civil society went hand in hand with the emergence and consolidation of racial slavery. At the end of the eighteenth century, revolts erupted which, in the name of liberty and the struggle against despotism, denounced interference by central government and its claim to limit the right of masters to punish their slaves.[35] The civil society referred to was, obviously, the white community. The natives were descendants of Ham, condemned to perpetual slavery by the Old Testament, or were assimilated to the inhabitants of Canaan, doomed to destruction by the chosen people, the Boer settlers who embodied the cause of liberty and self-government.[36]

---

31   David B. Davis, *The Problem of Slavery in Western Culture*, Ithaca and New York: Cornell University Press, 1966, pp. 165, 170–1.

32   Eugene D. Genovese, *From Rebellion to Revolution*, Baton Rouge: Louisiana State University Press, 1979, pp. 84–5.

33   Bernard Bailyn *et al.*, *The Great Republic*, Lexington (MA): D. C. Heath, 1977, p. 149.

34   Bacon, quoted in Richard Hofstadter, ed., *Great Issues in American History*, 3 vols, New York: Vintage Books, 1958–82, vol. 1, pp. 105–6.

35   George M. Frederickson, *White Supremacy*, New York: Oxford University Press, 1982, pp. 40–6, 146–7.

36   Ibid., pp. 170–1.

The crucial question posed by eminent US historians in connection with the English colonists' revolt in America is thus wholly understandable: Was the 'movement of political emancipation by a section of the white settlers against control from England'[37] really a revolution? Or are we dealing with 'a reactionary slaveholders' rebellion'? In the case of the South at least, this was the principal aspect: 'With the threat of British interference removed and a relatively weak central government to contend with, the road to regional power lay open before the slaveholders, who constituted the only class capable of treading it.'[38] A not dissimilar conclusion has been reached on the basis of an analysis of the relationship the Union as a whole had with the Indians: the American Revolution 'had some of the character of a white settlers' revolt against imperial policy', which afforded relative protection to the natives.[39]

At this point we can draw a comparison between the role played by the 'redskin question' in the colonists' rebellion that issued in the American Revolution and the part the 'negro question' played in the sparking off the Civil War:

[T]he British authorities prior to 1776, by promulgating regulations restricting the colonists' geographic expansion beyond the Appalachians, also alienated wealthy planters and merchants with speculative investments in western territory, as well as less affluent farmers who hoped for a new and inexpensive start on fresh lands ... In 1860–61, when a newly elected Republican administration promised to prohibit the further westward expansion of slavery, the response from most white Southerners was another revolution for political autonomy.[40]

If this is the case, the history of the United States is characterized by two reactionary secessions (or secessions with more or less strong reactionary components), the one victorious, the other defeated. And, although defeated, the second would be situated in a line of substantial continuity with the first.

The triumphal rise of the United States created an ideological climate in which, when reconstructing the American Revolution, historians tended to identify directly and naively with the rebel colonists' arguments. But today it is

---

37 Pierre L. Van den Berghe, *Race and Racism*, New York: Wiley, 1967, p. 77.
38 Eugene D. Genovese, *The World the Slaveholders Made*, London: Allen Lane, 1970, p. 99.
39 Frederickson, *White Supremacy*, p. 44.
40 Shearer David Bowman, *Masters and Lords*, New York: Oxford University Press, 1993, p. 141.

inadmissible to continue to ignore the voices of their opponents, in particular those (for example, Samuel Johnson and Josiah Tucker) who from the outset highlighted the significance of the black and Indian questions in the divisions that occurred between the two shores of the Atlantic. When the subsequent clash between the two sections of the Union loomed, claiming the legacy of the American Revolution were also, and perhaps primarily, the theorists of the South. Calhoun referred to Washington the 'slave-owner'. An utterly instrumental attitude? It was in fact endorsed by the most radical currents in abolitionism, which had no hesitation in publicly burning a Constitution branded as intrinsically pro-slavery and hence, ultimately, satanic. In their interpretation of the American Revolution, Calhoun and Garrison in a way vindicated Johnson and Tucker. Just as the Declaration of Independence accused George III of seeking to incite black slaves against the colonists, so the Confederacy accused Lincoln of wanting to provoke a slave war in the South. In both cases the rebels criticized central political power for misunderstanding the self-government that was due to free, civilized men and for attempting to erase the boundary line between civilization and barbarism. Not by chance, the attempted secession could count on passionate support from prominent representatives of the liberal world and culture even in England. One thinks, in particular, of Lord Acton, who to the end believed he was supporting an authentic, great liberal revolution, just as the leaders of the secessionist, slaveholding South thought they were promoting an authentic, great liberal revolution (see above, Chapter 5, §9).

Further developing a comparative perspective and the optic of the *longue durée*, it might be observed that in the twentieth century the process of decolonization was itself accompanied by secessionist movements, initiated by colonists who sought to maintain control over the natives and colonial populations in general, waving the flag of self-government and continuing to be inspired by the model of 'master-race democracy'—one thinks, in particular, of South Africa and Rhodesia.

However, it is precisely the optic of the *longue durée* and a comparative perspective that expose the reductive, misleading character of the view which conceives the American Revolution as a mere 'reactionary rebellion'. To begin with, we are dealing with a more general problem. We find Marx defining the Glorious Revolution as a 'parliamentary coup d'état', thanks to which the English landed aristocracy succeeded in consolidating its domination over the unfortunate Irish (the Indians and blacks of the situation) and giving impetus to the enclosure of common land and the expulsion of the peasantry. Moreover, we must not lose sight of the other side of the coin. The conquest of self-government by civil society had a genuine revolutionary significance. Liberated

308

from an arbitrary power, the members of the class that had assumed power granted one another liberty and respect for the rules, with the construction of the constitutional state and the advent of the liberal rule of law. The first to achieve this novel phenomenon were precisely the Glorious Revolution and the American Revolution, which therefore cannot be put on the same level as subsequent historical movements inspired by them. In other words, the tangle of emancipation and dis-emancipation that characterized the Glorious Revolution and the American Revolution subsequently saw the second aspect prevail ever more markedly.

4. Realization of the rule of law within the sacred space and the widening of the gulf with the profane space

At its inception, liberalism expressed the self-consciousness of a class of owners of slaves or servants that was being formed as the capitalist system began to emerge and establish itself, thanks in part to those ruthless practices of expropriation and oppression implemented in the metropolis, and especially the colonies, which Marx described as 'original capitalist accumulation'.[41] Against monarchical despotism and central power, this class demanded self-government and peaceful enjoyment of its property (including that in slaves and servants), under the sign of the rule of law. We can then say that this liberalism was the intellectual tradition which most rigorously circumscribed a restricted sacred space wherein the rules of the limitation of power obtained. It was an intellectual tradition characterized more by celebration of the community of free individuals that defined the sacred space than by celebration of liberty or the individual.

Not by accident, the classical countries of the liberal tradition were those where, through Puritanism, the Old Testament had the deepest impact. This already applies to the Dutch Revolution or, at least, to the Boers of Dutch origin, who identified themselves with the 'chosen people'.[42] And it applies a fortiori to England. Especially from the Reformation, the English regarded themselves as the new Israel, 'the people chosen by the Almighty for a special and at the same time a universal mission'.[43] This ideology and missionary consciousness were diffused, in accentuated form, across the Atlantic. It is

---

41   Marx, *Capital: Volume One*, pp. 873ff.

42   Thomas J. Noer, *Briton, Boer and Yankee*, Kent (OH): Kent State University Press, 1978, p. 21.

43   Léon Poliakov, *The Aryan Myth*, trans. Edmund Howard, London: Sussex University Press and Heinemann Educational Books, 1974, p. 42.

enough to think of Jefferson, who suggested that the US coat of arms should represent the children of Israel guided by a ray of light.[44] Once again the distinction between sacred space and profane space is seen in all its radicalism.

In the Old Testament beloved of the dominant elite, which liked to identify with the chosen people that conquered Canaan and destroyed its inhabitants, or which recruited its slaves from gentiles, two strict, drastic delimitations are operative. Anthropocentrism sharply separates from circumambient nature the human world, wherein an absolutely privileged and unique role is reserved for the 'chosen people'. The sacred space, the tiny sacred island, is thus delimited with the utmost clarity from the infinite profane space. We might say that outside the chosen people everything tended to be reduced to deconsecrated nature, within whose orbit also came the populations condemned by Jehovah to be wiped off the face of the earth. The destruction fell upon 'both man and woman, young and old, and ox, and sheep, and ass'; or, in more pregnant terms, 'all the souls', 'all that breathed', 'all the inhabitants of the cities, and that which grew upon the ground'.[45] Within the specifically profane space, the distinction between man and nature does not seem to emerge, or does not play a prominent role.

But the exclusive restriction of the sacred space also performs an enormously positive function. Among the chosen people specific rules are in force, so that there is room for servitude but not for slavery in the strict sense. Thousands of years later, this was the viewpoint of Locke who, explicitly appealing to the Old Testament, distinguished between the servitude of wage-labourers (in the metropolis) and slavery in the colonies. And the continuity turns out to be even more striking when we bear in mind that destined for slavery were blacks, whom the theology and ideology of the time regarded as the descendants of Ham and Canaan, condemned in perpetuity by Noah, according to Genesis, to wear chains.

We thus arrive at a paradoxical result, at least with respect to the dominant ideology. The West is at once the culture which most rigorously and effectively theorizes and practises the limitation of power, and which, with the greatest success and on the largest scale, is engaged in the development of chattel slavery—an institution that involves the full deployment of the master's power over slaves reduced to chattels and 'nature'. And this paradox is exhibited in especially striking fashion precisely in the countries with the most established liberal tradition.

---

44   Cf. Domenico Losurdo, *Democrazia o bonapartismo*, Turin: Bollati Boringhieri, 1993, ch. 3, §9.
45   Joshua 6, 25; 10, 35 and 40; Genesis 19, 25.

Certainly, already within Judaism the exclusivist pathos of the sacred space tended to take the form of a universalism that relied sometimes on the sub-jugation (or destruction) of the profane, and sometimes on its co-option. As becomes apparent above all in post-exile Judaism, the absolute transcendence of Jehovah prompted a process of de-naturalization of the sacred space/profane space dichotomy. The mobility of borders, and hence the possibility of effect-ing co-options within the sacred space and civilization, applies a fortiori to the Puritans and the liberal tradition, which inherited Judaism filtered through Christianity. On the other hand, the albeit partial amplification of the sacred space was a necessary response to the struggles waged by the excluded, who often derived different motifs from the Old Testament opposed to those dear to the dominant elite. They were inspired by the story of the people reduced to slavery in a foreign land who finally managed to free themselves from the Pharaoh's domination. This was the ideology that inspired the slave revolt which broke out in 1800 in Virginia, whose leader posed as a new Moses.[46] The slaves' ability to derive justifications for rebellion from the dominant culture itself led property-owners to regard even religious education with suspicion.

5. Delimitation of the sacred space and theorization of a planetary dictatorship

By rigorously delimiting the sacred space, liberalism radically widened the gulf separating it from the profane space. The element of regression in this is clear. A comparison will suffice to account for it.

In the most exalted texts of its culture, Europe long strove to maintain a lucid and self-critical view of itself, refusing to allow itself to be intoxicated and carried away by euphoria on account of the irresistible march begun with the discovery–conquest of America. And this approach continued to display its vitality in the Enlightenment and the culture that became part of the inherit-ance of French radicalism. Let us read Raynal and Diderot: 'The conquistadores' first steps were marked by rivers of blood ... In the inebriation of their success, they took the decision to exterminate those they had robbed. Countless people vanished from the face of the earth on the arrival of these barbarians', who took to 'treating the brothers they had just discovered without remorse, as they treated the wild beasts of the old hemisphere'.[47] Denunciation of the

---

46   Winthrop D. Jordan, *White over Black*, New York: Norton, 1977, p. 393.

47   Guillaume-Thomas Raynal, *Histoire philosophique et politique des Deux Indes*, ed. Yves Benot, Paris: Maspero, 1981, p. 143.

extermination of the Indians was rounded off with condemnation of the trade in slaves called upon to replace them as labour.[48] In any event, it was not only in the New World that the 'European barbarians' stained themselves with genocide;[49] the 'unhappy Hottentots' likewise suffered a 'pitiless' massacre.[50] In addition to the colonial conquest, Louis-Sébastien Mercier drew attention to further dark pages in Europe's history in the second half of the French eighteenth century. His utopian novel imagined a 'singular monument' in which 'the nations represented ... asked humanity's pardon' for the cruelty shown by them. Along with the genocide of the Indians, the expiatory monument recalled forced labour, or 'the slow torture of so many unfortunates condemned to the mines', and the subsequent black slave trade symbolized by 'numerous mutilated slaves'. Incontestably responsible for all this were 'the Europeans', also charged with 'the atrocity of the crusades', 'the horrible Saint Bartholomew's night' and the wars of religion.[51]

By contrast, let us now observe the way Edgar Quinet argues. In 1845, sketching in broad outline the history of the West, the French liberal historian came to the Spanish conquest of America. He could not ignore the extermination of the indigenous populations, but hit upon an explanation that was simultaneously ingenuous and reassuring. True, it had been carried out by Spain, a country that was an integral part of the West. But at the time Spain had experienced a decisive influx of the culture and religion of Islam, which was thus the actual, if indirect, executioner of the Indians.[52] The same line of argument was adopted for other black pages in the West's history. Had not the Inquisition had its centre in a Spain widely influenced by barbarians? And as to the crusade that destroyed the Albigensian heretics, without distinction of age and sex, was it not perhaps prepared by the prayers of the Spaniard San Domenico di Guzmán?[53] Via Spain, all signs pointed to Islam, at whose door could be laid even the Crusades, which precisely had as their stated target the Muslim 'infidels'. Quinet passed judgement: 'In the Crusades the Catholic Church enacted the principle of Islamism: extermination.'[54]

---

48   Ibid., p. 257.

49   Ibid., p. 49.

50   Ibid., pp. 54–5.

51   Louis-Sébastien Mercier, *L'An deux mille quatre cent quarante*, ed. Raymond Trousson, Bordeaux: Ducros, 1971, pp. 201–6.

52   Edgar Quinet, *Le Christianisme et la Révolution française*, Paris: Fayard, 1984, p. 146.

53   Ibid., p. 159.

54   Ibid., p. 137 (Quinet had already expressed himself to this effect in the subtitles to the eighth lecture).

But not only Islam was stigmatized as synonymous with barbarism. European high culture had long regarded China with curiosity and interest. Where were the wars of religion that had covered Europe with blood? They were prevented by a religion that shunned mystery and dogma, resolving itself into an ethics.[55] For the *philosophes* it was easier to recognize themselves in the mandarins than the Catholic clergy or Protestant ministers. The importance of the role played by a layer of secular intellectuals in the great Asiatic country was confirmed by the fact that the highest administrative public offices were often allocated through public competition, rather than being the monopoly (as in France) of a titled aristocracy, allied and intertwined with the clergy. In any event, in China the secular, modern principle of merit prevailed over the obscurantist principle of privilege based on birth and blood. The Enlightenment's sympathetic attention to non-European cultures, employed as a critical mirror of Europe, became a charge in the indictment drawn up by de Tocqueville: the *philosophes* had turned for a 'model' to China, '[t]hat unenlightened, barbarian government which lets itself be manipulated at will by a handful of Europeans'.[56]

The feudal aristocracy's prevalence in Europe was also the prevalence of bellicose values, while China (observed Leibniz, an author already completely infused with the pathos of Enlightenment) was distinguished by its aversion to anything that 'creates or nourishes ferocity in men',[57] thereby constituting a reference point for *philosophes* engaged in criticizing the *ancien régime*'s privy wars. Thus the *History of the Two Indias* applauded the pacific spirit exhibited by Chinese culture.[58] All this became off-key at the moment of the triumph of colonial expansionism. And so in de Tocqueville, corresponding to the celebration of war as an expression of the nation's grandeur and an antidote to the socialist movement's vulgar hedonism, we find an intensification of the indictment against China, also reproved for its unwarlike character. The French liberal displayed his contempt for a country whose army enjoyed 'peacefully scraping a living', overwhelmed as it was by the 'general softness of ideas and desires'.[59] Fortunately, all this facilitated the conquest of China: 'It would be

---

55   Voltaire, *Essai sur les moeurs et l'esprit des nations*, 2 vols, ed. René Pomeau, Paris: Garnier, 1963, vol. 1, pp. 69, 219.

56   Alexis de Tocqueville, *The Ancien Régime and the French Revolution*, trans. Stuart Gilbert, London: Fontana, 1966, p. 184.

57   Leibniz, quoted in Jonathan D. Spence, *The Chan's Great Continent*, Norton: New York, 1998, p. 84.

58   Raynal, *Histoire*, pp. 19, 32.

59   Alexis de Tocqueville, *Oeuvres complètes*, ed. Jacob-Peter Mayer, Paris: Gallimard, 1951–, vol. 15, pt 2, p. 54 (letter to F. de Corcelle, 13 May 1852).

difficult for me to console myself if, before dying, I did not see China opened and the eye of Europe penetrate there with its arms'.[60]

Now there was nothing to be learnt from non-European civilizations. In 1835 Macaulay declared that 'a single shelf of a good European library [is] worth the whole native literature of India and Arabia'.[61] Accordingly, we can understand the indifference with which the destruction of the Summer Palace, in all its incomparable beauty, by English and French troops during the second Opium War was viewed. Expressing his indignation was Victor Hugo: 'We Europeans are the civilized ones and for us the Chinese are barbarians. And here is what civilization has done to barbarism. In history's eyes, one bandit will be called France, the other will be called England'.[62] Some years later, on the occasion of the Commune, the good liberal Bagehot expressed his contempt for the behaviour of the rebels, whom he criticized for having wanted to destroy everything worth seeing and admiring in Paris, any testament to 'culture' and civilization.[63] Thus was credited the rumour, which subsequently proved unfounded, that the communards had destroyed the Louvre. But no mention was made here of the destruction of the Summer Palace in Peking, which actually occurred roughly ten years earlier, with the decisive participation of the country that for Bagehot was the privileged embodiment of the cause of liberty and civilization.

Authors like Las Casas and Montaigne had problematized the boundaries between civilization and barbarism and made them fluid. In this perspective civilization advanced through exchanges between different cultures. Developing their thinking in the years when missionaries from Christian Europe were received with respect and benevolence in China, while in France Louis XIV revoked the Edict of Nantes and resumed persecution of the Huguenots, Bayle and Leibniz reached a radical conclusion. It was a pity that the relationship between China and European was marked by its one-sidedness; the presence of Chinese missionaries in Europe would definitely be beneficial![64] Later, Raynal and Diderot's *History* assigned a black Spartacus the task of advancing the cause of freedom, breaking the chains of slavery and putting an end to the barbarism of which Europeans were the agents. But this attempt to cast a glance at

60   Ibid., vol. 6, pt 2, p. 199 (letter to Nassau William Senior, 8 March 1857).

61   Quoted in Ramsay Muir, ed., *The Making of British India 1756–1858*, Lahore: Oxford University Press, 1969, p. 299.

62   Hugo, quoted in Nora Wang, Xin Ye and Lou Wang, *Victor Hugo et le sac du Palais d'été*, Paris: Indes savantes, 2003, pp. 9–10 (letter to Captain Butler, 25 November 1861).

63   Walter Bagehot, 'The Destruction in Paris of What the World Goes to See in Paris', in *Collected Works*, ed. Norman St John-Stevas, vol. 8, London: The Economist, 1974, p. 197.

64   Cf. Giorgio Borsa, *La nascita del mondo modern in Asia orientale*, Milan: Rizzoli, 1977, pp. 84, 89; Spence, *The Chan's Great Continent*, p. 85.

Europe, as it were, from without, recognizing the contributions of different cultures to the cause of advancing civilization, did not survive the irresistible march of colonial expansionism. Having triumphed on a planetary scale, the liberal West saw fit to identify itself permanently with the cause of civilization and liberty. On the basis of this absolute and immutable pre-eminence, we see an exclusive elite—the restricted community of the free—explicitly formulate the claim, hitherto unknown and unheard of, to exercise a planetary dictatorship over the rest of humanity.

6. The triumph of colonial expansionism: liberalism as an ideology of war

The celebration of civilization and liberty now took the form of an ideology of war. It was an ideology refuted by Raynal and Diderot who, addressing the 'monsters' or European conquistadores, expressed themselves as follows:

> You are proud of your *lumières*, but what use are they to you, and what use would they be to the Hottentot? ... If, disembarking on his shores, you proposed to lead him towards a more civilized life, to customs that seem to you preferable to his, you might be excused. But you have landed in his country to take it from him. You have approached his hut to expel him, to replace him, if you can, by an animal that works under the farmer's lash.[65]

This criticism is all the more apt if we bear in mind Washington's characterization of the Indians as an 'unenlightened race' (see above, Chapter 1, §5).

So exalted was the self-consciousness of the liberal West in the nineteenth century that sometimes it did not even feel the need to confer ideological legitimacy on its wars. Unlike John Stuart Mill, de Tocqueville did not present the Opium War as a crusade for free trade and liberty as such. For the French liberal the main cause for celebration was the West's overwhelming power, and this power was also configured as a war machine ideologically:

> Here finally we have Europe's mobility at grips with Chinese immobility! It is a great event, above all if one believes that it is merely the sequel, the latest step in a multiplicity of events of the same kind that are gradually impelling the European race beyond its borders and successively subjecting all the

---

65   Raynal, *Histoire*, pp. 53–4.

other races to its empire and influence. It is the enslavement of four-fifths of the world by the other fifth. Hence it is best not to be unduly despairing about our century and ourselves; the men are petty, but the events are great.[66]

De Tocqueville's attitude left de Gobineau puzzled. The first ridiculed the mythology of blood entertained by the second. There was in fact another side to the coin. Once adopted as the key to explaining universal history, racial contamination cast its fatal shadow over the West itself, which was likewise condemned to decadence. Hence for de Gobineau there was no insurmountable barrier between conquerors and colonial peoples. As for the economy, the latter would sooner or later manage to develop the textile industry (the key industry of the period) and defeat British and European competition in general.[67] Morally, there was no reason to idealize the conquerors: in Persia and the Middle East 'their immorality and rapacity' were manifest. If the natives 'are rogues', 'in some respects they can be considered our cousins'; 'this is how we will be tomorrow'.[68] De Tocqueville's criticism focused precisely on this point: 'You say that one day we shall resemble the rabble you see before you: maybe. But before this happens, we shall have been its masters.' As we can see, from the 'rogues' they were in de Gobineau, the peoples of the Middle East have now been transformed into a 'rabble', with this fully legitimizing the domination exercised over them by European 'masters'. It is with reference to the latter that de Tocqueville employs the more indulgent term 'rogues': 'If, as I agree, they are often great rogues, at least they are rogues to whom God has given strength and power and whom He has manifestly placed, for a certain period, at the head of the human race'. Faced with this, de Gobineau's reservations about the 'immorality' and 'rapacity' of the conquerors, and the thesis of their basic kinship with subject peoples, seemed to lose any significance. De Tocqueville continued:

You are in the heart of the Asiatic and Muslim world: I would be curious to know to what you attribute the rapid and seemingly unstoppable decadence of all the races you have seen passing through ... Some millions of men who, a few centuries back, lived virtually without shelter, in the forests and marshes, will in less than one hundred years be the transformers of the globe they inhabit and the dominators of their whole species. Nothing is more

66 Tocqueville, *Oeuvres complètes*, vol. 6, pt 1, p. 58 (letter to Henry Reeve, 12 April 1840).
67 Ibid., vol. 9, pp. 254–6 (letter of 15 January 1856).
68 Ibid., vol. 9, p. 232.

clearly preordained in the sight of Providence ... Nothing will resist them on the surface of the earth. I have no doubt of it. I fear that all this might sound to you like a philosophical heresy. But if you have theory on your side, I am confident that I have the facts on mine—a not unimportant detail.[69]

De Gobineau, who regarded himself as a 'citizen of the world', refused to give in: 'I take an extraordinary interest in my daily conversations with the natives, and am very far from having the bad opinion of them people are pleased to entertain in Europe'.[70] This was not a viewpoint de Tocqueville could share. We already know his opinion that the 'last' member of the 'European race' was always 'first next to the savages'—that is, in the last analysis, next to 'all the other races'. Of his daughter, de Gobineau remarked: 'She has made herself a true Turkoman, save for her colour, which is that of an Abyssinian'.[71] De Tocqueville did not respond to this observation, but it should not be forgotten that for him it was precisely 'half-breeds' who represented the most serious threat to the West's supremacy and civilization as such (see above, Chapter 7, §4).

There is no doubt about the greater intellectual and political subtlety of de Tocqueville who, criticizing the blood myth, distanced himself from the ideology increasingly prevalent in the South of the United States, where de Gobineau's views about the natural and eternal inequality of races met with understandable success. Yet it is to be noted that, much more so than the latter, it was the former who created an unbridgeable gulf between the West and colonial peoples. How are we to explain this fact?

Straddling the American Revolution, '[r]acism became an essential, an unacknowledged, ingredient of the republican ideology'—that is, of the ideology which presided over the construction of 'master-race democracy'.[72] In the mid-nineteenth century this regime tended to characterize the relationship between the West as a whole and colonial peoples. Certainly, in order to impart credibility to its self-proclamation, the community of the free was ever more inclined in this period to abolish slavery in the strict sense—hereditary slavery—which was in fact replaced by other forms of forced labour. But the model of a 'master-race democracy' remained unchanged. The gradual abolition of censitary discrimination in the metropolis gave further impetus

---

69   Ibid., vol. 9, pp. 243–4.
70   Ibid., vol. 9, p. 241.
71   Ibid., vol. 9, p. 231 (letter of 7 July 1851).
72   Edmund S. Morgan, *American Slavery, American Freedom*, New York: Norton, 1995, p. 386.

to colonial expansion, which now in fact enjoyed the consent of the popular classes in the metropolis. These, like the poor whites in the North American republic, aspired to be co-opted into the bloc of 'masters'. And once again what explained and legitimized the barrier dividing masters and servants was a more or less marked, and more or less crude racial ideology, which was now pervasive. This was a trend that also made its influence felt on de Tocqueville.

Having been asserted in countries (Holland, England and the United States) more involved than any others in the slave trade and colonial expansion (overseas in the case of the first two, continentally in that of the third), liberalism spread in the West at a time when it seemed destined by Providence itself to dominate the whole world and wipe out all other cultures. In these circumstances, the self-critical thinking and awareness of limits that had characterized the pre-eminent voices of European and Western culture tended to disappear. The inheritors of that tradition were French radicalism, and then Marx. The latter waxed ironic about the 'civilizing wars' of the colonial powers. In reality, during the Opium War, while China, 'the semi-barbarian[,] remained faithful to the principles of the moral law', the 'civilized' opposed to it the principle of free trade,[73] the principle so eloquently defended by Mill. But especially significant are the pages of *Capital* devoted to original capitalist accumulation and denunciation of 'the extirpation, enslavement and entombment in mines of the indigenous population', and the transformation of Africa into 'a preserve for the commercial hunting of blackskins'.[74] This was a chapter of history that was extended in the subsequent colonial expansion.

7. Oscillations and limitations of the Marxian model

Clearly distancing himself from the apologetics more dominant than ever today, Marx drew attention to the 'conservative character of the English revolution'. While, on the one hand, it marked 'the transition from absolute monarchy to constitutional monarchy', and promoted the development of industry and the bourgeoisie,[75] on the other, it gave impetus to a gigantic, ruthlessly implemented expropriation of peasants. Examined closely, the Glorious Revolution emerged as 'a parliamentary coup d'état for [the] transformation of [communal

---

73 Karl Marx and Friedrich Engels, *Werke*, 38 vols, Berlin: Dietz, 1955–89, vol. 13, p. 516; vol. 12, p. 552.

74 Marx, *Capital: Volume One*, p. 915.

75 Marx and Engels, *Werke*, vol. 7, pp. 209–10.

property] into private property'.[76] We thus encounter a formula that in a way evokes the tangle of emancipation and dis-emancipation I have stressed: the mention, albeit vague, of parliament's decisive role in this event draws attention to the disappearance of the absolute monarchy, while making clear reference to the tragedy of the peasantry. Someone who distinguished himself in the ideological legitimation of the colossal expropriation and ruthless repression that struck its victims was Locke. This 'most particular supporter of the lash for vagrants and paupers'[77] was in fact, at the same time, the 'father' of 'free-thinking',[78] the protagonist of the great ideological battle that deconsecrated absolute monarchy and stripped it of its Christian and Biblical cover. And once again, as in the Glorious Revolution, so in the liberal philosopher in whom it found theoretical expression, the tangle of emancipation and dis-emancipation reveals itself. Finally, Marx recalled that corresponding to the advent of constitutional monarchy in England was a further intensification of the dictatorship exercised by English property-owners over Ireland.

Over and above any particular country, what should especially be borne in mind are the general considerations offered by *The Holy Family*. With the disappearance of the *ancien régime*, corresponding to the dissolution of the 'political existence' of property was its 'more potent existence', which could now unfold 'the full scale of its own existence'.[79] Or, as *On the Jewish Question* put it: 'The shaking-off of the political yoke was at the same time the shaking-off of the bonds which had held in check the egoistic spirit of civil society. Political emancipation was at the same time the emancipation of civil society from politics, from even the *appearance* of a universal content.'[80]

Marx brought out the entanglement of emancipation and dis-emancipation. The 'more potent existence' injected into property was also the autonomization of property in human cattle from the controls, albeit vague, of the Church and Crown, with the consequent crystallization of racial chattel slavery. And it was also the disappearance of the restrictions placed by the Crown on the expansion of the colonists, who could now proceed unhindered, without being in any way concerned with the terrible human costs inflicted on the Indians. In England, enclosure of common land was followed by the new law of 1834 which, abolishing any other form of assistance, confronted the poor with a brutal alternative: death from starvation or internment in a total institution.

76　Marx, *Capital: Volume One*, p. 886.
77　Marx and Engels, *Werke*, vol. 3, pp. 510–11.
78　Ibid., vol. 7, p. 209.
79　Ibid., vol. 2, p. 124.
80　Karl Marx, *Early Writings*, Harmondsworth: Penguin, 1975, p. 233.

However, we must not lose sight of the fact that we are not dealing with an autonomization of property as such. What corresponded to the 'more potent existence' of the colonists' property was the death-agony of another form of property. It was a gigantic process of expropriation (justified and theorized by Locke and de Tocqueville alike), which unfolded at the expense not only of colonial peoples—in America or Ireland—but also of English peasants. The same reasons that led me to regard the category of 'proprietorial individualism' as inadequate and misleading now prompt me to seek to clarify Marx's analysis. The process we are examining was the autonomization of the property of those who already enjoyed recognition, of those who aspired to form themselves into the community or caste of freemen. Liberated from the fetters of control by Crown and Church was not only bourgeois property, but also traditional noble property. In the England that emerged from the Glorious Revolution, the landed aristocracy consolidated its enjoyment of certain privileges (hunting, for example) and consecrated its political power in representative bodies—in the first instance, the House of Lords.

With Marx we can say that '[t]he political revolution is the revolution of civil society.'[81] But it should be added that civil society can be hegemonized by the bourgeoisie or the landed aristocracy, or can be characterized by a compromise between these two classes. And the liberal revolution consists in this political revolution. Up to this point we can only subscribe to Marx's analysis and admire it for its acuteness. But he continues by opposing the 'political revolution' to the 'social revolution', or 'political emancipation', which is the objective of the first, to 'social emancipation' (the end of class domination), which is the objective of the second. The limitation of this conceptual couplet is that it does not take account of the fact that for some social or ethnic groups the liberal revolution did not involve any kind of emancipation, but in fact meant the reverse. Is it really correct to define the United States of 1844 (the year *On the Jewish Question* was published) as 'the country of complete political emancipation'?[82] Certainly, the reference is to the rapid disappearance of censitary discrimination, which continued to be marked in France under the July Monarchy, and in Britain. However, what induced this differential development in the case of the North American republic was the availability of land (taken from the Indians) and the confinement of a large part of the 'dangerous classes' in slavery. In other words, the property barrier proved much weaker because the race barrier was much more rigid. Differently put, in the United

---

81   Ibid., p. 232.
82   Marx and Engels, *Werke*, vol. 1, p. 352.

States democracy emerged first because it emerged as a *Herrenvolk* democracy, as a 'master-race democracy', and this specific form proved so tenacious that it survived the Civil War by many decades. It is highly problematic to regard *Herrenvolk* democracy as complete political emancipation.

Even if we restrict the comparison to New World countries, some questions are indicated: Was political emancipation more advanced in the North American republic, which saw slavery flourish in these years and which a little earlier had extended that institution to the Texas taken from Mexico? Or was political emancipation more advanced precisely in Mexico and those Latin American countries that had abolished the institution of slavery some decades before? In these years US leaders and ideologues liked positively to contrast the ban on miscegenation imposed by them with the cross-breeding that was spreading in Latin America: Where was political emancipation more advanced?

We cannot even unreservedly endorse Marx's thesis that '[p]olitical emancipation is certainly a big step forward.'[83] We already know that the most tragic chapter in the history of the Indians began with the American Revolution, and that the period between the Glorious Revolution and the American Revolution witnessed the emergence of a racial chattel slavery of unprecedented harshness. In the case of Britain, it was Marx himself who drew attention to the far from positive consequences of the 'coup d'état' of 1688–89 for English peasants and the Irish population.

Even more debatable is the subsequent identification of political revolution with bourgeois revolution. The latter category is at once too narrow and too broad. As regards the first aspect, it is difficult to subsume under the category of bourgeois revolution the Glorious Revolution and the parliamentary revolt that preceded the upheavals that began in France in 1789, not to mention the struggles against monarchical absolutism, explicitly led by the liberal nobility, which developed in Switzerland and other countries. On the other hand, the category of bourgeois revolution is too broad: it subsumes both the American Revolution that sealed the advent of a racial state and the French Revolution and the San Domingo Revolution, which involved complete emancipation of black slaves.

The model proposed here is different. It equates 'political revolution' qua 'revolution of civil society', referred to by Marx, with the liberal revolution in the strict sense. Certainly, in order to be able to promote its emancipation from absolute power, civil society had to have achieved a certain level of development. Analysed in their initial phases, the revolutions that occurred in

---

83   Marx, *Early Writings*, p. 221.

the Netherlands, England, America, France and Latin America were not very different from one another: they were all liberal revolutions. What clearly differentiated them were three factors: the varying configurations of civil society; the social, political and ideological conflicts that developed within it (one thinks in the French case of the struggle between nobility and bourgeoisie); and the irruption in the struggle of servants and slaves. With the emergence of the last factor, the struggle for the emancipation of civil society waged by the property-owning classes became entangled with the struggle waged against them by those who did not want to be regarded as objects of property and who sought to secure recognition.

The secessionist revolt of the slaveholding South also presented itself as a liberal revolution: it was a new struggle for self-government by civil society, like the one that had sanctioned the independence of the United States. Was the Confederacy a liberal country? If we regard the country born from the War of Independence against England and long led by slave-owners as liberal, it is hard to see why such recognition should be denied to the Confederacy. Yet, rather than at a conceptual level, the solution to the problem is to be sought at a historical level. At the point when the principle of the 'uselessness of slavery among ourselves' was imposed in the liberal world, an author like Fletcher, who also recommended slavery for white vagrants, ceased to be a liberal. Almost a century after its first turn, the liberal world underwent a second: now condemnation of hereditary slavery as such was dictated as a constitutive element in its identity.

After the end of the Civil War and the abolition of slavery, the racial state largely survived. And once again the question arises: Was the United States, where discrimination and oppression raged against blacks and genocidal practices against Indians, a liberal country? The principle of racial equality became a constitutive element in liberal identity only from the mid-twentieth century onwards. The racial state continued to exist for some decades in South Africa. However, although historically inspired by Britain in the area of self-government and representative bodies, and by the southern United States in that of race relations, it was henceforth regarded as alien to the liberal world.

CHAPTER TEN

Liberalism and the Catastrophe of the Twentieth Century

1. The struggle for recognition and coups d'état: the conflict in the metropolis

The catastrophic crisis that struck Europe and the whole planet with the outbreak of the First World War was already maturing within the liberal world. To account for it, we must take stock of the situation on the eve of 1914. Let us deal with the metropolis first. There is no doubt that the struggle for recognition had achieved important successes. True, we are still a long way from the universal assertion of the principle 'one person, one vote'—and not only because women continued to be excluded from the enjoyment of political rights. More or less conspicuous traces of censitary discrimination still survived. But the fact remains that the vote was no longer the exclusive privilege of wealth. Also largely defeated was the attempt to reintroduce through the back window the censitary discrimination that had been shown the door, in the shape of plural votes to be granted to the more 'intelligent' (this was a solution entertained above all by John Stuart Mill!). Here and there the first elements of a social state began to emerge; and if this involved fairly modest results, we should bear in mind the legalization of workers' coalitions and trade unions, determined to wrest much more substantial concessions. Even in this milieu, the long road travelled by the former instruments of labour leaps to the eye![1]

However, it must immediately be added that this was quite the reverse of a pacific development. Each of its stages was marked not only by intense struggles, but also by profound divisions in the liberal alliance. While one

---

1   On all this, cf. Domenico Losurdo, *Democrazia o bonapartismo*, Turin: Bollati Boringhieri, 1993, ch. 1, §7 (on the plural vote) and *passim*.

wing of it was open to concessions, the other proved intransigent and sought confrontation. Thus, we witness a succession of coups d'état which, prior to issuing in the establishment of an open dictatorship at any rate, could count on the support or sympathy of distinguished representatives of the liberal world. Availing itself of Sieyès' active participation, Napoleon's 18th Brumaire elicited the 'enthusiasm' of Madame de Staël, as emerges from the letter her father sent her a few days later: 'You paint for me in lively colours the part you take in the power and glory of your hero'.[2] Constant too viewed the turn with confidence. Thirty years later, he recalled having on its eve been in daily contact with Sieyès, 'the true author of the 18th Brumaire', or the 'main motor' of the novelty that was already foreshadowed.[3] As early as 1795, Constant had made it clear that it was necessary to go beyond Thermidor: the taxation that continued to weigh on property for the benefit of the poor, who were now turning into 'a privileged caste',[4] was excessive. In fact, according to various pieces of evidence (including Madame de Staël's), the combined effect of famine and inflation was reducing 'the last class of society to the most wretched condition', visiting 'unheard of ills'[5] on it, up to and including 'starvation'.[6] However, for the liberalism of the time there was no doubt: the risks run by property legitimized the coup d'état. After the homage already noted to 'conservative, liberal, tutelary ideas', in the days immediately afterwards the new government hastened to abolish any trace of progressive taxation. On 24 December 1799, the same day Bonaparte became First Consul, Constant entered the Tribunate. But Madame de Staël harboured the idea of an even more ambitious political career for him, in the shadow of the one who (wrote Necker to his daughter at the end of 1800) promised to be 'the protector of all respectable' and well-off folk, finally liberated—such was Constant and Madame de Staël's sigh of relief—from the threat of the 'riffraff' (*populace*).[7] The significance of the initial hopes and subsequent disappointment in liberal circles was clarified by Guizot in 1869. Acquitting the task of 'putting an end to anarchy', Napoleon's 'dictatorship' was 'natural, urgent'—in fact, 'beneficial and glorious'. However, contrary

---

2   Necker, quoted in Henri Guillemin, *Madame de Staël, Benjamin Constant et Napoléon*, Paris: Plon, 1959, p. 7.

3   Constant, quoted in Henri Guillemin, *Benjamin Constant muscadin*, Paris: Gallimard, 1958 ibid., p. 249.

4   Constant, quoted in ibid., pp. 76–7.

5   Germaine de Staël-Holstein, *Considérations sur la Révolution française*, ed. Jacques Godechot, Paris: Tallandier, 1983, p. 347.

6   According to the testimony of J. Mallet du Pan, quoted in Guillemin, *Benjamin Constant*, p. 37.

7   Guillemin, *Madame de Staël*, pp. 8–19 and *Benjamin Constant*, pp. 29, 63n.

to expectations, 'this accidental, temporary regime' transformed itself into 'a dogmatic and permanent system of government'.[8]

A not dissimilar dialectic emerged after Louis Bonaparte's coup d'état, greeted with 'indecent haste' (the phrase is Marx's) by liberal England.[9] This was not opportunism: once the beneficent 'traditional influences' had disappeared, wrote Disraeli in 1851, what checked anarchy and dissolution was 'the government of the sword'. Indeed, 'the state quits the senate and takes refuge in the camp'; only thus was it possible to avoid the catastrophe of the domination of 'secret societies' and a 'convention' of the Jacobin variety.[10]

In the case of France, setting aside a figure like Granier de Cassagnac, who declared himself a 'liberal' and openly sided with Louis Napoleon,[11] it is worth dwelling on de Tocqueville's participation in the various stages of the ideological and political reaction that ended up de-legitimizing and then overthrowing the Second Republic. In the French liberal's view, it was the product of a revolution—that of February 1848—which had developed in a socialist and hence despotic spirit, and which had unfolded throughout continental Europe. In Germany and Italy, de Tocqueville desired and promoted 'the victory of the princes' (see above, Chapter 8, §15). But was his attitude towards France very different? As early as March, even before the working-class revolt of June, de Tocqueville thundered against 'this ultra-democratic revolution, which has extended the right to vote beyond all the limits known even in America'.[12] While the clouds that presaged the June storm were gathering, the French liberal expressed his opinion that 'the National Guard and the army will be without pity this time'. In order to achieve the objective of maintaining or restoring order and destroying the 'anarchical party', one should not hesitate to recruit into the police unscrupulous types and rabble—'outlaws', 'thieves', 'scoundrels' and all the 'rejects of society'.[13] Evoked with precision here is the politico-social formula that subsequently presided over Louis Bonaparte's coup d'état, which was successful thanks to the support not only of the property-owning classes and traditional state apparatuses, but also of a sub-proletariat happy to perform the function of gang intimidation entrusted to it.

---

8 François Guizot, *Mélanges politiques et historiques*, Paris: Lévy, 1869, pp. iii–iv.

9 Karl Marx and Friedrich Engels, *Werke*, 38 vols, Berlin: Dietz, 1955–89, vol. 17, p. 278.

10 Benjamin Disraeli, *Lord George Bentinck*, London: Colburn, 1852, pp. 554–6.

11 Cf. Losurdo, *Democrazia o bonapartismo*, ch. 2, §1; ch. 3, §1.

12 Alexis de Tocqueville, *Oeuvres complètes*, ed. Jacob-Peter Mayer, Paris: Gallimard, (1951–), vol. 6, pt 2, p. 108 (letter to Nassau William Senior, 8 March 1849).

13 This emerges from a conversation of 25 May 1848 reported by Nassau William Senior: cf. ibid., vol. 6, pt 2, pp. 242–3.

After the outbreak of the workers' revolt, de Tocqueville was not only in favour of conferring emergency powers on Cavaignac, but recommended shooting on sight anyone caught 'in a posture of defence'.[14] The bloody repression of the June Days was not enough to assuage anxiety; and so we have the invocation of an 'energetic and definitive reaction on behalf of order',[15] required to put an end to revolutionary and anarchic chaos not only in France, but in Europe as a whole. In any event, 'France is among those who will restore order'[16] and terminate the 'follies of 1848'.[17] More than a year after the desperate working-class revolt, when pitiless repression seemed to have averted the Jacobin and socialist peril for good, the French liberal believed that an iron fist was still required: it was necessary to proceed 'as far as reaction'; 'palliatives' would not do; to sweep away not only the Mountain, but also 'all the surrounding hills', it was necessary 'courageously to take the lead of all those who want to re-establish order, whatever their complexion'. There should be no hesitation even over 'a heroic ... remedy'.[18] What is indirectly suggested is the need for emergency measures with the suspension of constitutional liberties. If as a historian he tirelessly condemned the Jacobin Terror, as a politician de Tocqueville had no hesitation invoking 'terror' for the purposes of suppressing 'the demagogic party' (see above, Chapter 8, §15).

In these years, every so often a shudder ran through the liberal self-consciousness: perhaps there was a risk of the ruthless methods used to subjugate barbarians in the colonies spreading in Europe. Although warmly applauding the pitiless energy with which the conquest of Algeria was conducted, de Tocqueville let slip a sort of exclamation: 'God spare us ever seeing France led by an officer of the army of Africa'.[19] In fact, Cavaignac, having implemented the 'new science' called on to liquidate Arab resistance at any cost, was subsequently the author of the bloody, ruthless repression that struck the barbarians of the metropolis, the Parisian workers who rose up demanding the right to work and life. Notwithstanding the preceding admonition, however, de Tocqueville offered him constant, unwavering support.

Later, starting with the Paris Commune, there spread throughout the liberal West a tendency to challenge not only the democratic concessions wrested by the popular masses, but also the rule of law itself. In the United States

---

14 Ibid., vol. 12, p. 176.

15 Ibid., vol. 8, pt 2, p. 52 (letter to Gustave de Beaumont, 24 September 1848).

16 Ibid., vol. 8, pt 2, p. 31 (letter to Gustave de Beaumont, 27 August 1848).

17 Ibid., vol. 7, p. 143 (letter to Francis Lieber, 4 August 1852).

18 Ibid., vol. 8, pt 2, p. 53 (letter to Gustave de Beaumont, 24 September 1848).

19 Ibid., vol. 3, pt 1, p. 236.

Theodore Roosevelt stated an expeditious method for putting down strikes and social conflicts: 'The sentiment now animating a large proportion of our people can only be suppressed ... by taking ten or a dozen of their leaders out, standing ... them against a wall, and shooting them dead.'[20]

These tendencies underwent further radicalization after the October Revolution. We can now fully understand the fascist coup d'état in Italy in 1922. Numerous figures who professed themselves liberals, and who in fact claimed to be restoring genuine liberalism, supported it for a more or less extended period of time. This was true of Luigi Einaudi, who saluted the return of 'classical liberalism'. For a while Croce likewise viewed the attempt to return to 'pure liberalism', not to be confused with insensate 'democratic liberalism', with sympathy. Even in 1929, implicitly endorsing Mussolini's condemnation of any 'demo-liberal regime', Antonio Salandra defined himself as an 'old liberal of the right (without the *demo*)'.[21]

As we can see, a benevolent attitude towards the fascist coup d'état is not explicable solely by the severe social and political crisis of the time. Instead, at issue was cancelling, or more or less drastically reducing, the democratic concessions won from liberal society by the popular movement. While the *belle époque* still persisted, in 1909 Einaudi had branded progressive taxation a kind of 'organized brigandage to steal money from others through the state'.[22] Mussolini hastened to put an end to such 'brigandage', thereby eliciting applause from not a few liberals. In the preceding decades Pareto had, as a liberal, developed a sharp polemic against the 'myth' of the social state, had agreed with the positions of Spencer and Maine, and had adhered, still as a liberal, to the Liberty and Property Defence League.[23] In 1922–23 he breathed a sigh of relief at the coup d'état that finally averted threats, if not to liberty, in any event to property.

On the other hand, von Mises seemed to be referring exclusively to the state of emergency when, in 1927, he pointed to fascist *squadrismo* as 'an emergency makeshift' adequate to the task of saving 'European civilization'.[24] In fact, five

---

20   Richard Hofstadter, *The American Political Tradition and the Men Who Made It*, New York: Knopf, 1951, p. 216.

21   Cf. Domenico Losurdo, *La Seconda Repubblica*, Turin: Bollati Boringhieri, 1994, ch. 2, §1.

22   Einaudi, quoted in Paolo Favilli, *Riformismo e sindicalismo*, Milan: Franco Angeli, 1984, pp. 106–7.

23   See, especially, Vilfedo Pareto, 'L'éclipse de la liberté', in *Mythes et idéologies*, ed. Giovanni Busino, Geneva: Droz, 1966, pp. 224–5; Thomas Mackay, Introduction to George Howell, 'Liberty for Labour', in Herbert Spencer *et al.*, *A Plea for Liberty*, Indianapolis: Liberty Classics, 1981, pp. vii, xii (on Pareto's adhesion to the League).

24   Ludwig von Mises, *Liberalism*, Indianapolis: Liberty Fund, 2005, p. 30.

years earlier, having distanced himself from the democratic and even socialist contaminations liberalism had undergone in England, he had thundered against the 'destructionism', the 'destructionist policy' and 'terrorism' of the trade unions with their strikes.[25] Thanks to Mussolini, all this had ceased in Italy. The fact remains that, in a book whose very title is devoted to the celebration of liberalism, we can read an emphatic eulogy of the coup d'état which, albeit with rough and ready methods, had saved civilization: 'The merit that Fascism has thereby won for itself will live on eternally in history.'[26]

2. The struggle for recognition by colonial peoples and threats of secession

While the struggle for recognition waged by the servants in the metropolis was constantly countered by the threat or implementation of a coup d'état, the more intransigent sectors of the liberal and bourgeois world reacted to the struggle for recognition waged by colonial peoples or peoples of colonial origin with the threat or implementation of secession. This is a dialectic we have already analysed in relation to San Domingo in the late eighteenth century and the British West Indies in the early decades of the nineteenth century. During the July Monarchy, de Tocqueville observed that the colonists, in rejecting any abolitionist project, were denying the French parliament and government 'the right to take this great work in hand and carry it through'.[27]

Obviously, in this context the most striking case was the secession of the South of the United States, which effected advancing liberal slogans in defence of the natural right to self-government and the peaceful enjoyment of property. The North's military victory did not terminate the conflict. Supporters of white supremacy immediately reacted to the fleeting advent of multiracial democracy not only with the lynchings and anti-black terrorism unleashed by the Ku Klux Klan, but by resorting to guerrilla warfare and armed violence. In 1874 an appeal circulated in the South to found a White League to foil by any means attempts by Congress to make black emancipation effective: 'our war [will be] interminable and merciless'.[28] In conclusion, '[a]s surely as the struggle between 1861 and 1865 was civil war, so was the conflict from 1865 to 1877, with all the more bitterness and hatred, but less bloodshed.'[29]

---

25 Ludwig von Mises, *Die Gemeinwirtschaft*, Jena: Fischer, 1922, pp. 469ff.

26 Mises, *Liberalism*, p. 30.

27 Tocqueville, *Oeuvres complètes*, vol. 3, pt 1, p. 116.

28 Richard Hofstadter, ed., *Great Issues in American History*, New York: Vintage Books, 1958–82, vol. 3, p. 43–4.

29 John Hope Franklin, *From Slavery to Freedom*, New York: Alfred A. Knopf, 1967, p. 328.

This second stage in the Civil War ended in a substantial victory for the South. While slavery in the strict sense was not reintroduced, a regime of terroristic white supremacy was imposed. Although formally emancipated, the Afro-Americans now embarked on one of the most tragic phases in their history. It might even be said that their condition touched a 'nadir'.[30] By contrast, racist 'dogmas' and 'racial fundamentalism' reached their zenith.[31]

A sequence of events with notable similarities to the American Civil War unfolded in Great Britain. Here what was at stake was the emancipation not of the blacks but of the Irish. The dominant class in Ulster reacted to the London government's decision to introduce Home Rule for the island as had the southern US to the challenge of central power, even when democratically elected. It threatened and prepared secession, arming a militia tens of thousands strong. While the planters across the Atlantic could not tolerate the loss of the domination guaranteed to them by the possession of human cattle, the Protestant property-owners in Ireland rejected with horror the prospect of being governed at a local level by Catholic ragamuffins. In both cases the self-government demanded was the self-government that the descendants of the settlers were summoned to enjoy, and which sanctioned white supremacy or Anglo-Protestant supremacy. In both cases the secessionists proclaimed that they were the true inheritors of the American Revolution and the Glorious Revolution, respectively. And only the outbreak of the First World War blocked an impending war of secession in Britain: in Northern Ireland thousands of men armed to the hilt and organized militarily were ready to go into action.[32]

3. The de-humanization of colonial peoples and 'social cannibalism'

On the eve of the First World War, unlike that waged by the servants in the metropolis, the struggle for recognition by colonial servants or servants of colonial origin could boast very few successes. In fact, the advances made by the former on the road of emancipation were often used to widen still further the gulf that separated the dominant 'European race' from the rest. In the late nineteenth century, while a sign was displayed at the entrance to some public parks in the southern United States reading 'No Dogs and Niggers Allowed',[33]

---

30 Rayford W. Logan, *The Betrayal of the Negro*, New York: Da Capo Press, 1997, p. xxi.
31 Stanley M. Elkins, *Slavery*, Chicago: University of Chicago Press, 1959, pp. 13, 16.
32 Cf. Jan Morris, *Pax Brittanica*, London: Folio Society, 1992, vol. 3, pp. 179–85.
33 Leon F. Litwack, *Trouble in Mind*, New York: Knopf, 1998, p. 467.

in Shanghai the French concession defended its purity by clearly drawing attention to the notice 'No Entry for Dogs and Chinese'.[34] What made the comparison between colonial populations and domestic animals more credible was certain collective punishments, like that provided for by the British government in India in 1919:

> [T]he most degrading measure was a 'crawling order' imposed on all Indians who passed a narrow lane in the city where a medical missionary, Miss Sherwood, had been assaulted during the disturbances. The humiliation of crawling on all fours to and from one's home, for many lived in this lane, was not to be forgotten or forgiven by those who were subjected to this indignity, or indeed, by any sensitive Indian.[35]

It was only in 1920, after the First World War and the October Revolution, that the chapter of history involving the coolies was definitively concluded, in the wake of a movement of anti-colonial struggle which no longer intended to tolerate 'the blot of indentured labour' imprinted by that institution on the whole Indian race.[36] It is true that, having played a central role in black enslavement and the black slave trade, and then in the promotion of the semi-slavery of the coolies, the liberal West presented itself as the champion of the struggle against slavery. It was precisely with this watchword that it promoted colonial expansion. But this is how a missionary described the work the indigenous population was forced to perform in the rubber plantations of the Belgian Congo:

> Each town and district is forced to bring in a certain quantity to the headquarters of the *Commissaire* every Sunday. It is collected by force; the soldiers drive the people into the bush. If they will not go, they are shot down, and their left hands cut off and taken as trophies to the *Commissaire* ... these hands, the hands of men, women and children [are] placed in rows before the *Commissaire*.[37]

The imposition of forced labour was sometimes bound up with genocidal practices, while on other occasions it gave way to them. In the late nineteenth century Theodore Roosevelt issued a general warning to 'inferior races':

---

34   Office d'Information, *Les droits de l'homme en Chine*, Beijing, 1991, p. 3.

35   Michael Brecher, *Nehru*, London: Oxford University Press, 1959, p. 63.

36   Hugh Tinker, *A New System of Slavery*, London and New York: Oxford University Press, 1974, p. 364.

37   Colm Tóibín, 'The Tragedy of Roger Casement', *New York Review of Books*, 27 May 2004, p. 53.

should one of them attack the 'superior' race, the latter would be entitled to react with 'a war of extermination', destined 'to put to death man, woman and child, exactly as if they were crusaders'.[38]

In truth, there were races whose disappearance was desired regardless of their actual behaviour. Franklin greeted as a providential design the slaughter that the rum diffused by the conquerors was wreaking among the Indians. However, according to the charge formulated by loyalists who had taken refuge in Canada, the rebel colonists proceeded directly to the annihilation of entire ethnic groups (see above, Chapter 1, §5). In 1851, while the hunt for individual Indians was raging, the governor of California pronounced judgement:

> That a war of extermination will continue to be waged between the two races until the Indian race becomes extinct, must be expected; while we cannot anticipate this result with but painful regret, the inevitable destiny of the race is beyond the power and wisdom of man to avert.[39]

The programme set out by General Sherman was unambiguous: 'We must act with vindictive earnestness against the Sioux, even to their extermination, men, women and children. Nothing else will reach the root of the case.' In the course of his two expeditions against the Cheyenne and the Arapaho, a colonel ordered that even the new-born should be killed and scalped: 'Nits make lice!'[40] All this would not seem to have particularly disturbed Theodore Roosevelt: 'I don't go so far as to think that the only good Indians are the dead Indians. But I believe nine out of every ten are, and I shouldn't like to inquire too closely into the case of the tenth.'[41]

It should not be thought that this sinister ideology, in its variations and different gradations, caught on exclusively in the United States, where, for obvious historical reasons, the racial question was more acutely felt. Let us take a look at Europe. Lord Acton coldly observed: 'The Red Indian is gradually retreating before the pioneer, and will perish before many generations, or dwindle away in the desert.'[42] There were races, Disraeli in turn believed, which

38   Theodore Roosevelt, *Letters*, ed. Elting E. Morison and John M. Blum, 8 vols, Cambridge (MA): Harvard University Press, 1951–54, vol. 1, p. 377 (letter to Charles Henry Pearson, 11 May 1894).

39   Reginald Horsman, *Race and Manifest Destiny*, Cambridge (MA): Harvard University Press, 1981, p. 279.

40   Dee Brown, *Bury My Heart at Wounded Knee*, London: Barrie and Jenkins, 1970, p. 90.

41   Roosevelt, quoted in Hofstadter, *The American Political Tradition*, p. 208.

42   Lord Acton, *Selected Writings*, 3 vols, ed. J. Rufus Fears, Indianapolis: Liberty Classics, 1985–88, vol. 1, p. 261.

experienced 'exterminat[ion] without persecution, by that irresistible law of Nature which is fatal to curs'.[43] In fact, this was not a completely spontaneous process, as Disraeli ended up acknowledging, when he mentioned the tragic end of the 'Aztecs', 'overthrown by Cortez and a handful of Goths', in accordance with 'the inexorable law of nature' that sanctioned the complete victory of 'a superior race' and the irrevocable defeat of 'an inferior'.[44] More explicit was Burckhardt, for whom the 'erasure or enslavement of the weakest races' seemed to pertain to the 'great economy of world history'.[45] Renan, an author who liked to situate himself among the 'enlightened liberals'[46] (and who was appreciated by Hayek for his 'important' contribution to this intellectual tradition),[47] reached the same conclusion: the 'semi-savage races' were destined to be subjugated or exterminated by the 'great Aryan-Semitic family'.[48]

Not even the greatest figures in the liberal tradition succeeded in mounting effective resistance to this view. This applies to de Tocqueville who, while he drew a decidedly repugnant picture of the Aborigines, was a passionate cantor of the motif of the 'empty cradle'—that is, of the deadly genealogical myth dear to colonists. And, to a lesser extent, it applies to Mill. His discourse could hardly arouse a strongly sympathetic interest in the victims. The Indians seemed to belong to the 'community' whose state, 'in point of culture and development, ranges downwards to a condition very little above the highest of the beasts'. In any event, '[n]othing but foreign force would induce a tribe of North American Indians to submit to the restraints of a regular and civilised government.'[49] No mention is made here of the fated disappearance, still less of the destruction, of the Indians; instead, a temporary pedagogical dictatorship is theorized. However, as emerges from the stance of another distinguished exponent of English liberalism, on the occasion of bitter conflicts the dictatorship over barbarians, having been pedagogical, risked turning exterminatory. After the rebellion that challenged the British Empire in India, Macaulay wrote:

43   Benjamin Disraeli, *Coningsby*, ed. Sheila M. Smith, Oxford and New York: Oxford University Press, 1982, p. 221.

44   Disraeli, *Lord George Bentinck*, p. 495.

45   Jacob Burckhardt, *Weltgeschichtliche Betrachtungen*, ed. Jacob Oeri, in *Gesammelte Werke*, vol. 4, Basel: Schwabe, 1978, p. 190.

46   Ernest Renan, *Oeuvres complètes*, ed. Henriette Psichari, Paris: Calmann-Lévy, 1947–, vol. 1, p. 443.

47   Friedrich von Hayek, *The Constitution of Liberty*, London: Routledge and Kegan Paul, 1960, p. 435 n. 32.

48   Renan, *Oeuvres complètes*, vol. 8, p. 585.

49   John Stuart Mill, *Utilitarianism, Liberty, Representative Government*, ed. Harry B. Acton, London: Dent, 1972, pp. 197, 178.

The cruelties of the Sepoy natives have inflamed the Nation to a degree unprecedented within my memory. Peace Societies, Aborigines Protection Societies, and societies for the reformation of criminals are silent. There is one terrible cry to revenge ... The almost universal feeling is that not a single Sepoy within the walls of Delhi should be spared, and I own that is a feeling with which I cannot help sympathizing.[50]

Expressing genuine dissent were unexpected representatives of the liberal tradition or figures who moved on its margins. While he interpreted the social conflict in the metropolis in a social-Darwinist register, Spencer protested against 'the barbarous maxim' that the strongest 'have a lawful right to whatever territories they can conquer'. What followed the expropriation of the defeated was in fact their 'extermination'. Paying the price were not only the 'North American Indians' and the 'natives of Australia'; in India 'whole regiments of [natives] have been put to death, for daring to disobey the tyrannical commands of their oppressors'.[51] Unfortunately, 'we have entered upon an era of social cannibalism in which the strong nations are devouring the weaker'; it could now indeed be said that 'the white savages of Europe are overrunning the dark savages everywhere'.[52] Certainly, Spencer pointed an accusing finger at the state 'system of colonisation',[53] at the statism that was now expanding at every level—as if this statism had not accompanied the history of the liberal West from the outset, and as if the terrible practices denounced by Spencer had not often actually been promoted in the name of the self-government and free disposal of property, and had not taken the form (to use Hobson's phrase) of 'private slaughter'! (See above, Chapter 7, §1).

4. The 'final and complete solution' of the Indian and black questions

It was precisely Hobson (an author close to the liberal circles branded 'socialist' by von Mises and Hayek) who effectively summed up the attitude to barbarians adopted by the West, and in the first instance the liberal West, which was in

---

50 Macaulay, quoted in Eric Williams, *British Historians and the West Indies*, New York: Africana Publishing Corporation, 1972, p. 152.

51 Herbert Spencer, *The Man versus the State*, Indianapolis: Liberty Classics, 1981, p. 224.

52 Herbert Spencer, *The Life and Letters of Herbert Spencer*, ed. David Duncan, London: Routledge and Thoemmes Press, 1996, p. 410 (letter to Moncure D. Conway, 17 July 1898).

53 Spencer, *The Man versus the State*, p. 224.

the forefront of colonial expansion in the Far West and overseas. The populations that were susceptible to 'profitable exploitation by the superior white settlers' survived, while the rest 'tend[ed] to disappear' or be destroyed.[54] In fact, from the late nineteenth century the theme of the inevitable disappearance of savages and peoples who could not be used as forced labour became an obsession. Articulating it were often authors who at the same time saluted the triumph of liberal institutions and ideas in the civilized world. In 1885 a book by a Protestant minister, Josiah Strong, enjoyed extraordinary success. His celebration of 'liberty', of 'self-government', of 'the right of the individual to himself', was passionate.[55] He frequently appealed to Burke, de Tocqueville, Guizot, Macaulay and Spencer. Strong and emphatic was his assertion of the primacy of the Anglo-Saxon world, which had the merit of quintessentially embodying both 'love of liberty' and a 'genius for colonizing'[56] that expanded the zone of freedom. But this expansion also entailed the inexorable 'extinction of inferior races'.[57] Albert J. Beveridge, a Republican senator and prominent US political figure, argued in similar fashion at the start of the twentieth century. The homage paid to the 'gospel of liberty',[58] the sons of liberty and, in particular, the United States as the country and people that were 'leading the world to liberty' went hand in hand with the assertion that 'a part of the Almighty's infinite plan [was] the disappearance of debased civilisations and decaying races before the higher civilisation of the nobler and more virile types of man'.[59]

A watchword even emerged that was to assume an unambiguously genocidal meaning in the twentieth century and know tragic success. While Strong invoked 'God's final and complete solution of the dark problem of heathenism among many inferior peoples',[60] in 1913 a book published in Boston evoked the 'ultimate solution' of the 'negro problem' in its title. Even in this instance, it did not involve an author foreign to the liberal world, and not only because he lived and worked in the United States, advancing ideas diffused and echoed even by influential political figures of the time. Far from regretting the 'abhorrent practice' of slavery, he identified with the 'comparatively few liberal and enlightened men' or 'liberal intellects' who had wanted to abolish it when deliberating the 'splendid instrument' that was the Constitution of the

---

54   J.A. Hobson, *Imperialism*, London: Unwin Hyman, 1988, p. 253.

55   Josiah Strong, *Our Country*, Cambridge (MA): Belknap Press, 1963, p. 200.

56   Ibid., pp. 200, 212.

57   Ibid., p. 215.

58   Albert J. Beveridge, *The Meaning of the Times*, Freeport (NY): Books for Libraries Press, 1968, pp. 50, 288.

59   Ibid., p. 42.

60   Strong, *Our Country*, p. 216.

United States, 'the guiding star of the greatest temporal power in history'.[61] Nevertheless, in the land of liberty there was no room for races intellectually incapable of participating in the superior 'Caucasic civilization and culture'.[62] In reaching this conclusion, the author knew that he was situated in the wake of Franklin and Jefferson. Happily, nature and the law of the 'survival of the fittest' were already acting on their behalf: Afro-Americans were being wiped out by tuberculosis, pneumonia, venereal disease and other illnesses that confirmed the natural inferiority of this people. '[F]ew Negro children are born without scrofulous tendencies, rickets, blindness, or other transmitted evidence of ancestral infection'. The 'ultimate solution' of the 'Negro problem' was in sight, and it would be a happy repeat of the already accomplished final solution of the Amerindian question.[63] In the words of a southern senator who was on the same wavelength, 'God's law of evolution, the survival of the fittest, and the extinction of the unfit is operating', and would bring about 'a gradual whitening of the South' and the United States as a whole[64]—the touch of white already dreamt of by Franklin.

In fact, the Indians had largely been wiped off the face of the earth. In 1876, to celebrate its centenary as an independent country, the United States organized an exhibition in Philadelphia that drew the world's attention to its extraordinary development. Along with marvels of industry and technology, sideshows exhibited 'wild children from Borneo, a five-legged horse, and wax figures of famous Indian chiefs'.[65] In summer 1911, in a remote part of California, an Indian was discovered who could not communicate in English or Spanish. Ethnological experts subsequently verified that he was a survivor of the Yahi tribe, largely exterminated over the course of a generation. The unknown, who refused to give his name or recount the history of his destroyed family, was put in a museum, where he became an object of much amused curiosity on the part of adults and children, all the more so in that the local press drew attention to the 'last aborigine', the 'wild man of California', a 'genuine survivor of Stone Age barbarism'. After his death, his brain was conveniently preserved for further study.[66] A great philosopher, Edmund Husserl, who was certainly liberal and democratic in orientation, observed twenty

---

61   Edward Eggleston, *The Ultimate Solution of the American Negro Problem*, New York: AMS Press, 1973, pp. 133–5, 141–3.

62   Ibid., p. 62.

63   Ibid., pp. 183–5, 224.

64   John Sharp Williams, quoted in George M. Frederickson, *The Black Image in the White Mind*, Hanover (NH): Wesleyan University Press, 1987, pp. 257–8.

65   Richard Slotkin, *The Fatal Environment*, New York: Harper Perennial, 1994, p. 4.

66   Clifford Geertz, 'Morality Tale', *New York Review of Books*, 7 October 2004, p. 4.

years later, alas without any critical accent, that totally foreign to Europe and the West, the Indians (or rather the surviving ones) 'are exhibited in fairground booths'.[67]

5. From the nineteenth to the twentieth century

In the years leading up to the outbreak of the second Thirty Years' War, we witness the accumulation of a mass of explosive material. At the end of the nineteenth century, corresponding to the formation of the Liberty and Property Defence League in England was the formation of the White Leagues (and the Ku Klux Klan) in the United States. At stake was halting or reversing the two struggles for recognition with which we are familiar. Across the Atlantic the restoration of white supremacy registered its triumph as early as 1877; in Europe the Liberty and Property Defence League would have to wait until 1922 to record its first victory, in Italy. The persistent unrest of servants or ex-servants in the metropolis, and of slaves or ex-slaves in the colonies or of colonial origin, and the increasing aggressiveness of the social and political circles that felt threatened by these two agitations, were compounded by contradictions within the community of the free and of Teutonic stock (previously celebrated in its entirety as the chosen people or race of liberty), which now tended to assume an antagonistic form. Moreover, these multiple conflicts were further exacerbated by an ideological climate marked by the assertion of trends—social Darwinism, a racial interpretation of history and conspiracy theory—present from the outset in the liberal tradition, but which now met with ever weaker resistance, rendering a rational understanding and limitation of the conflict impossible. Not by chance have we heard two deadly slogans echo: the first declared that 'race is everything'; the second invoked the 'ultimate solution', or the 'final and complete solution', of the racial question!

The degree of continuity between the nineteenth and twentieth centuries has not escaped a whole series of scholars who cannot be suspected of preconceived hostility to the liberal world. While she generously overlooked the North American republic (which had had the merit of offering her refuge), Hannah Arendt explained the genesis of twentieth-century totalitarianism commencing with the colonies of the British Empire. It was here that 'a new form of government', 'a more dangerous form of governing than despotism and

---

67   Cf. Domenico Losurdo, *Heidegger and the Ideology of War*, trans. Marella and Jon Morris, Amherst (NY): Humanity Books, 2001, ch. 3, §8.

arbitrariness' saw the light of day,[68] and where the temptation of 'administrative massacres' as an instrument for maintaining domination began to emerge.[69] But especially interesting in this context is the fact that not a few US scholars, in order to explain the history of their country, have turned to the category of 'master-race democracy' or '*Herrenvolk* democracy', in an eloquent linguistic admixture of English and German, and a German that in several respects refers to the history of the Third Reich.

Not only the concentration-camp universe as a whole, but also the individual total institutions of the twentieth century, began to take shape well before the end of the supposed *belle époque*. We may begin with deportation. The successive bloody deportations of Indians, starting with the one implemented by Jackson's America (held up as a model of democracy by de Tocqueville), recall the 'horrors created by the Nazi handling of subject peoples'.[70] The Indians were not the only victims of this practice. The slave trade represented 'the largest involuntary movement of human beings in all history'.[71] The deportees were subsequently forced to work in a slave plantation that bore some similarities to the concentration camp.[72] The comparison does not seem exaggerated. Precisely in this context the process of de-humanization reached levels that were difficult to match. In Jamaica, in the liberal British Empire of the mid-eighteenth century, we find a type of punishment at work that speaks volumes: 'a slave was forced to defecate into the offending slave's mouth, which was then wired shut for four or five hours'.[73] Even his completely innocent fellow slaves were forced to participate in the de-humanization of the victim and, with him, of the ethnic group. Should all this not seem sufficiently cruel, at the end of the nineteenth century and the beginning of the twentieth, white supremacy was imposed in the United States:

> Notices of lynchings were printed in local papers, and extra cars added to trains for spectators from miles around, sometimes thousands of them. Schoolchildren might get a day off school to attend the lynching.

---

68 Hannah Arendt, *The Origins of Totalitarianism*, New York: Harcourt, Brace and World, 1966, pp. 186, 212–13.

69 Ibid., pp. 131, 133–4, 216.

70 Thus William T. Hagan, quoted in agreement by Laurence M. Hauptman, *Between Two Fires*, New York: Free Press, 1995, p. 5.

71 Davis, quoted in Gordon S. Wood, 'What Slavery Was Really Like', *New York Review of Books*, 18 November 2004, p. 43.

72 Elkins, *Slavery*.

73 Wood, 'What Slavery Was Really Like', p. 43.

The spectacle could include castration, skinning, roasting, hanging, and shooting. Souvenirs for purchasers might include fingers, toes, teeth and bones, even genitals of the victim, as well as picture postcards of the event.[74]

Once again we encounter a process of de-humanization difficult to emulate.

First in the North and then, after the Civil War, in the South, notionally 'free' blacks suffered humiliation and persecution of every kind. In fact, stresses a historian in language that once again demands our attention, they became the target of veritable 'pogroms'.[75] Carrying them out were gangs already active in the North in the 1820s and 1830s and which later, in the South, achieved consummate form in the Ku Klux Klan, an organization that seems to anticipate the 'Blackshirts' of Italian fascism and the 'Brownshirts' of German Nazism.[76] No less brutal than extra-legal violence was official justice: in the South blacks continued to be subject to a prison system so sadistic that it calls to mind 'the prison camps of Nazi Germany'.[77]

In any event, the two situations were united by the violence of racist ideology. Theodore Roosevelt can calmly be approximated to Hitler.[78] Over and above individual figures, we must not lose sight of the general picture: 'The effort to guarantee "race purity" in the American South anticipated aspects of the official Nazi persecution of the Jews in the 1930s.' If we bear in mind the rule whereby a single drop of impure blood was enough for someone to be excluded from the white community in the South of the United States, a conclusion dictates itself: 'the Nazi definition of a Jew was never as stringent as "the one-drop rule" that prevailed in the categorization of Negroes in the race-purity laws of the American South.'[79]

Again, two US scholars have recently referred to the 'Nazi Connection', or the 'American legacy' present in Nazism, to explain the parabola of eugenics,

---

74   C. Vann Woodward, 'Dangerous Liaison', *New York Review of Books*, 19 February 1998, p. 16.

75   Richard Maxwell Brown, *Strain of Violence*, New York: Oxford University Press, 1975, p. 30.

76   Nancy MacLean, *Behind the Mask of Chivalry*, New York: Oxford University Press, 1994, p. 184.

77   Fletcher M. Green, quoted in C. Vann Woodward, *Origins of the New South 1877–1913*, Louisiana State University Press and Littlefield Fund for Southern History, University of Texas, 1951, p. 215.

78   Pierre L. Van den Berghe, *Race and Racism*, New York: Wiley, 1967, p. 13; Thomas G. Dyer, *Theodore Roosevelt and the Idea of Race*, Baton Rouge: Louisiana State University Press, 1980, p. xiii.

79   George M. Frederickson, *Racism*, Princeton: Princeton University Press, 2002, pp. 2, 124.

the 'science' born in liberal England and massively diffused in the other classic country of that intellectual tradition, which experienced its greatest triumphs in the Third Reich![80] In this connection we in fact encounter a paradox. Having disappeared together with Hitler's Germany, eugenic measures continued to survive for some time in the United States. Let us observe the situation in 1952: 'At the present time some thirty states in the Union legally forbid "interracial marriage." In almost all these states miscegenation is a felony; in many a crime.' Regarded as elements of contamination were not only 'Negroes' but also, in this or that state, 'Mulattoes', 'Indians', 'Mongolians', Koreans, 'members of the Malay race', Chinese, or '[any] person of negro or Indian descent to the third generation inclusive', or even anyone 'having one-eighth or more negro, Japanese or Chinese blood', or even someone with 'one-fourth or more' 'Kanak [Hawaiian] blood'.[81] Reporting these facts is a US scholar who feels obliged to draw a bitter conclusion in respect of 'racism' (and Nazism): 'The monster that has been let loose upon the world is to a large extent of our own making, and whether we are willing to face the fact or not we are, all of us, individually and collectively, responsible for the ghastly form which he has assumed.'[82]

Finally, genocide. An eminent scholar, Tzvetan Todorov, has defined the destruction of the Indians, whose final chapter was written in the English colonies in America and then in the United States, as 'the greatest genocide in human history'.[83] As for the tragedy of the natives in America, Australia or the British colonies in general, other authors have referred, respectively, to the 'American holocaust' (or the 'final solution' of the Amerindian question), the 'Australian holocaust' and 'late Victorian holocausts'.[84] Not to mention the 'black holocaust'—the deportation and enslavement of the survivors, who numbered one in three or four—that Afro-Americans seek to draw attention to, and whose main protagonist was the liberal world. Finally, branded as the author of a tragedy to be regarded as the prototype of twentieth-century geno-

80   Stefan Kühl, *The Nazi Connection*, New York: Oxford University Press, 1994; Edwin Black, *War against the Weak*, New York: Four Walls Eight Windows, 2003, pp. 385–409.

81   Ashley Montagu, *Man's Most Dangerous Myth*, New York: Harper and Brothers, 1966, pp. 302ff.

82   Ibid., p. 265.

83   Tzvetan Todorov, *The Conquest of America*, trans. Richard Howard, London: Harper Perennial, 1992, p. 5.

84   David E. Stannard, *American Holocaust*, New York and Oxford: Oxford University Press, 1992; Philippe Jacquin, *Storia degli indiani d'America*, trans. Franco Moccia, Milan: Mondadori, 1976; Thomas Schmid, 'Australiens Holocaust', *Die Zeit*, 31 May 2000; Mike Davis, *Late Victorian Holocausts*, London and New York: Verso, 2001.

cides, the principal official (Sir Charles Edward Trevelyan) of the British policy that led to the death from starvation of hundreds of thousands of Irish in the mid-nineteenth century has sometimes been defined as the 'proto-Eichmann'.[85]

This is not the place to proceed to a comparative history of massacres, decimations and genocides, or to discuss the pertinence of the categories employed to describe them. But one point seems to me to be settled: it is banally ideological to characterize the catastrophe of the twentieth century as a kind of new barbarian invasion that unexpectedly attacked and overwhelmed a healthy, happy society. The horror of the twentieth century casts a shadow over the liberal world even if we ignore the fate reserved for peoples of colonial origin. 'Totalitarian society': thus has been defined the one that swallowed up deportees from Britain in Australia.[86] And, with particular reference to the 'development of industrial capitalism' in England, it has been claimed that 'the gulag is not a twentieth-century invention'.[87] The usual hagiography proves unfounded even when, in reconstructing the liberal world, we restrict ourselves to analysing the metropolis and the white community.

Let us take an author celebrated by de Tocqueville as the apex of the liberal tradition. Jefferson raised the spectre of genocide in three very different contexts. He referred to 'extermination' in connection with the Indians as a process that was underway in the United States, could not be stopped, and was in fact to be attributed exclusively to the British. He pointed to the 'extermination' of the blacks as the inevitable outcome of the utopia of constructing a multiracial society. Finally, he experienced the clash with Britain as a total war, destined to issue in the 'extermination' of one of the contending parties (see above, Chapter 1, §5; Chapter 5, §14; and Chapter 8, §16). As we can see, even a conflict completely internal to the community of the free provoked an ideological violence that might well bring to mind the twentieth century.

6. After the catastrophe and beyond hagiography: the enduring legacy of liberalism

The horror of the twentieth century was not something that burst into a world of peaceful coexistence suddenly and from without. At the same time, being dissatisfied with the edifying picture of the habitual hagiography and situating oneself on the firm ground of reality, with its contradictions and conflicts, does

---

85   Domenico Losurdo, *Antonio Gramsci dal liberalism al 'comunismo critico'*, Rome: Gamberetti, 1997, ch. 5, §§10, 13; Stannard, *American Holocaust*, pp. 317–18 n. 9.

86   Robert Hughes, *The Fatal Shore*, London: Collins Harvill, 1987, p. 383.

87   Robert Castel, *Les métamorphoses de la question sociale*, Paris: Fayard, 1995, p. 157.

not in any way mean denying the merits and strong points of the intellectual tradition under examination. But we certainly must bid farewell once and for all to the myth of the gradual, peaceful transition, on the basis of purely internal motivations and impulses, from liberalism to democracy, or from general enjoyment of negative liberty to an ever wider recognition of political rights.

Meanwhile, the presupposition of that discourse turns out to be wholly imaginary: the community of the free asserted itself demanding both negative and positive liberty, while excluding populations of colonial origin and metropolitan semi-slaves and servants from both. In addition, I would like to adduce a series of reasons, which I shall set out in ascending order of importance.

In the first place, it should not be forgotten that not only did the classics of the liberal tradition refer to democracy with coldness, hostility and sometimes frank contempt, but regarded its advent as an unlawful, intolerable rupture of the social contract and hence as a legitimate cause for the 'appeal to Heaven' (in Locke's words) or to arms.

Secondly, it must be borne in mind that the exclusion clauses were not overcome painlessly, but through violent upheavals of a sometimes quite unprecedented violence. The abolition of slavery in the wake of the Civil War cost the United States more victims than both world wars combined. As for censitary discrimination, a decisive contribution was made to its abolition by the French revolutionary cycle. Finally, in major countries like Russia, Germany and the United States the accession of women to political rights had behind it the war and revolutionary upheavals of the early twentieth century.

Thirdly, in addition to not being painless, the historical process that resulted in the advent of democracy was quite the reverse of unilinear. Emancipation—that is, the acquisition of rights previously not recognized or enjoyed—might well be followed by dis-emancipation—that is, deprivation of the rights whose recognition and enjoyment the excluded had won. Asserted in France in the wake of the February 1848 revolution, universal (male) suffrage was abolished two years later by the liberal bourgeoisie and was shortly afterwards reintroduced not as a result of the maturation of liberalism, but by the coup d'état of Louis Napoleon, who used it to stage the ritual of plebiscitary acclamation. In this context the most striking example is provided by the United States. The end of the Civil War inaugurated the happiest phase in the history of Afro-Americans, who now won civil and political rights and began to participate in representative bodies. But this was a kind of brief interlude in the tragedy. The 1877 compromise between the whites of the North and South involved the loss of political and, often, civil rights for blacks, as is attested by the regime of racial segregation and the savage violence of pogroms and lynching. This phase of dis-emancipation, which developed in a society that continued to define itself as liberal, lasted almost a century.

There is then a fourth reason. The process of emancipation very often had a spur completely external to the liberal world. The abolition of slavery in British colonies cannot be understood without the black revolution in San Domingo, which was viewed with horror, and often combated, by the liberal world as a whole. Around thirty years afterwards, the institution of slavery had been abolished even in the United States. But we know that the most ardent abolitionists were accused by their opponents of being influenced or infected by French and Jacobin ideas. The brief experience of multiracial democracy was followed a long phase of dis-emancipation marked by a terroristic white supremacy. When was the turning point? In December 1952 the US Justice Secretary sent the Supreme Court, which was engaged in deliberating on the issue of integration in public schools, an eloquent letter: 'Racial discrimination furnishes grist for the Communist propaganda mills, and it raises doubt even among friendly nations as to the intensity of our devotion to the democratic faith.' Washington, observes the American historian who has reconstructed this story, ran the risk of alienating the 'colored races' not only in the East and the Third World, but in the very heart of the United States. Even there communist propaganda met with considerable success in its attempt to win blacks to the 'revolutionary cause', making them lose 'faith in American institutions'.[88] On close examination, first slavery and then the terrorist regime of white supremacy were thrown into crisis by the San Domingo revolt and the October Revolution, respectively. The implementation of an essential principle, if not of liberalism then of liberal democracy (in the usual sense of the term), is inconceivable without the decisive contribution of two of the chapters of history most hated by the liberal culture of the time.

The fifth and final reason is the most important. I refer to the tangle of emancipation and dis-emancipation that distinguishes the individual stages in the process of overcoming the exclusion clauses characteristic of the liberal tradition. In the United States the disappearance of censitary discrimination, and affirmation of the principle of political equality, were aided by the quantitative containment and political and social neutralization of the 'dangerous classes', thanks to the expropriation and deportation of Indians—which for a long time made it possible to enlarge the class of landowners—and the enslavement of blacks. In Europe extension of the suffrage in the nineteenth

---

88   C. Vann Woodward, *The Strange Career of Jim Crow*, New York: Oxford University Press, 1966, pp. 131–4.

century proceeded in tandem with colonial expansion and the imposition of forced labour on peoples or 'races' deemed barbarous or childlike. This tangle sometimes presented itself in a decidedly tragic form. Subject to humiliation, discrimination and persecution of every kind in the South, Afro-Americans sought to win recognition by participating in the front line in the Union's wars. And so in some circles homage began to be paid to the courage displayed by soldiers of colour in the Battle of Wounded Knee.[89] Thus, blacks' hopes for emancipation took the form—were obliged to take the form—of their active participation in destroying Indians!

However, it is precisely from such historical reconstruction, remote from any apologetic, edifying tones, that the genuine merits and real strong points of liberalism emerge. Demonstrating an extraordinary flexibility, it constantly sought to react and rise to the challenges of the time. It is true that, far from being spontaneous and painless, such transformation was largely imposed from without, by political and social movements with which liberalism has repeatedly and fiercely clashed. But precisely in this resides its flexibility. Liberalism has proved capable of learning from its antagonist (the tradition of thinking that, starting with 'radicalism' and passing through Marx, issued in the revolutions which variously invoked him) to a far greater extent than its antagonist has proved capable of learning from it. Above all, the antagonist has proved incapable of learning what constitutes the second major strong point of liberalism. Certainly, liberalism's learning process was quite the reverse of smooth, at least for those who wanted to overcome the exclusion clauses that run deep in this intellectual tradition. None has been as committed as it to thinking through the decisive problem of the limitation of power. However, historically, this limitation of power went hand in hand with the delimitation of a restricted sacred space: nurturing a proud, exclusivist self-consciousness, the community of the freemen inhabiting it was led to regard enslavement, or more or less explicit subjection, imposed on the great mass dispersed throughout the profane space, as legitimate. Sometimes they even arrived at decimation or annihilation. Has this dialectic on the basis of which liberalism was transformed into an ideology of domination, and even an ideology of war, wholly disappeared?

In economics, clearly distancing itself from an insipid ideology of social harmony miraculously lacking any element of contradiction, conflict and tension, liberal thought has vigorously insisted on the need for competition between individuals in the market, in order to develop social wealth and the productive forces. This is a further, major historical merit to be acknowledged.

---

89   Litwack, *Trouble in Mind*, p. 463.

However, at this level, too, there emerged the awful exclusion clauses we are already familiar with. Far from being a site where all individuals freely meet as sellers and buyers of commodities, for centuries the liberal market was a site of exclusion, de-humanization and even terror. In the past the ancestors of today's black citizens were commodities, not autonomous buyers and sellers. And for centuries the market functioned as an instrument of terror: even more than the lash, what imposed total obedience on the slave was the threat of being sold, like a commodity exchanged on the market, separately from other family members.[90] For a long time indentured white servants were also bought and sold on the market, and thus condemned to a fate not very different from that of black slaves. And in the name of the market, workers' coalitions were repressed and economic and social rights ignored and denied, with a consequent commodification of essential aspects of the human personality and human dignity (health, education, and so on). In extreme cases the superstitious cult of the Market sealed huge tragedies, like the one which in 1847 saw Britain condemn an enormous mass of actual (Irish) individuals to death from starvation. Is all this a definitively concluded chapter of history? Moreover, has liberalism definitively left behind it the dialectic of emancipation and dis-emancipation, with the dangers of regression and restoration implicit in it? Or is this dialectic still alive and well, thanks to the malleability peculiar to this current of thought?

Yet however difficult such an operation might be for those committed to overcoming liberalism's exclusion clauses, to take up the legacy of this intellectual tradition is an absolutely unavoidable task. On the other hand, liberalism's merits are too significant and too evident for it to be necessary to credit it with other, completely imaginary ones. Among the latter is the alleged spontaneous capacity for self-correction often attributed to it. If one starts out from such a presupposition, the tragedy of peoples subjected to slavery or semi-slavery, or deported, decimated and destroyed, becomes utterly inexplicable. This was a tragedy which, far from being impeded or prevented by the liberal world, developed in close connection with it. Unfounded on a historiographical level, the habitual hagiography is also an insult to the memory of the victims. Only in opposition to the pervasive repressions and transfigurations is the book now ending presented as a 'counter-history': bidding farewell to hagiography is the precondition for landing on the firm ground of history.

---

90   Walter Johnson, *Soul by Soul*, Cambridge (MA): Harvard University Press, 1999, pp. 19, 22–3.

References

Acton, John E. E. Dalberg, *Selected Writings*, 3 vols, ed. J. Rufus Fears, Indianapolis: Liberty Classics, 1985–88.

Arblaster, Anthony, *The Rise and Decline of Western Liberalism*, Oxford: Blackwell, 1987 [1984].

Arendt, Hannah, 'Zionism Reconsidered', *The Menorah Review*, vol. 33, October, 1945.

——*On Revolution*, London: Faber & Faber, 1963.

——*The Origins of Totalitarianism*, new edn, New York: Harcourt, Brace & World, 1966 [1951].

Aulard, François-Alphonse, *Histoire politique de la Révolution française*, Aalen: Scientia, 1977 [1926].

Babeuf, François-Noël, *Écrits*, ed. Claude Mazauric, Paris: Messidor, 1988.

Baecque, Antoine de, Wolfgang Schmale, and Michel Vovelle, eds, *L'An des droits de l'homme*, Paris: CNRS Press, 1988.

Bagehot, Walter, 'The Destruction in Paris of What the World Goes to See at Paris', in *Collected Works*, ed. Norman St John-Stevas, vol. 8, London: The Economist, 1974 [1871].

Bailyn, Bernard, et al., *The Great Republic: A History of the American People*, Lexington, MA: D.C. Heath, 1977.

Barnave, Antoine-P.-J.-M., *Introduction à la révolution française*, ed. Fernand Rude, Paris: Colin, 1960 [1792].

Barret-Ducrocq, Françoise, *Pauvreté, charité et morale à Londres au XIX siècle. Une sainte violence*, Paris: Presses Universitaires de France, 1991.

Baudry des Lozières, Louis-Narcisse, *Les égarements du nigrophilisme*, Paris: Migneret, 1802.

Beaumont, Gustave de, *Marie, ou L'esclavage aux États Unis. Tableau des moeurs américains*, 4th edn, Paris: Gosselin, 1840.

——*L'Irlande sociale, politique et religieuse*, 2 vols, ed. Goderlaine Charpentier, Villeneuve d'Ascq: CERIUL-Université Charles-de-Gaulle Lille III, 1990 [1839].

Benot, Yves, *La révolution française et la fin des colonies*, Paris: La Découverte, 1988.

——*La démence coloniale sous Napoléon. Essai*, Paris: La Découverte, 1992.

Bentham, Jeremy, *The Works*, 11 vols, ed. John Bowring, Edinburgh: Tait, 1838–43.

———*Oeuvres*, 3 vols, ed. Étienne Dumont, 3rd edn, Brussels: Société belge de librairie, 1840.

Berlin, Isaiah, *Four Essays on Liberty*, Oxford: OUP, 1969.

Beveridge, Albert J., *The Meaning of the Times, and Other Speeches*, Freeport, NY: Books for Libraries Press, 1968 [1908].

Biondi, Carminella, *Mon frère, tu es mon esclave. Teorie schiavistiche e dibattiti antropologico-razziali nel Settecento francese*, Pisa: Libreria Goliardica, 1973.

Biondi, Jean-Pierre, and François Zuccarelli, *16 pluviôse an II. Les colonies de la Révolution*, Paris: Denoël, 1989.

Bismarck, Otto von, *Gedanken und Erinnerungen*, Stuttgart-Berlin: Cotta, 1928 [1898].

———*Werke in Auswahl*, vol. 1, ed. Gustave Adolf Rein, Stuttgart: Kohlhammer, 1962.

———*Die großen Reden*, ed. Lothar Gall, Frankfurt am Main: Ullstein, 1984.

Black, Edwin, *War against the Weak: Eugenics and America's Campaign to Create a Master Race*, New York: Four Walls Eight Windows, 2003.

Blackburn, Robin, *The Overthrow of Colonial Slavery*, 1776–1848, London and New York: Verso, 1990 [1988].

———*The Making of New World Slavery: From the Baroque to the Modern, 1492–1800*, London and New York: Verso, 1997.

Blackstone, William, *Commentaries on the Laws of England*, 4 vols, Chicago: University of Chicago Press, 1979 [1765–1848].

Bodin, Jean, *I sei libri dello Stato*, transl. Margherita Isnardi Parente, 2nd edn, Turin: UTET, 1988 [1576].

———n.d., *Six Books of the Commonwealth*, abridged and transl. M. J. Tooley, Oxford: Basil Blackwell.

Bolívar, Simón, n.d., *Obras completas*, 3 vols, ed. Vicente Lecuna, Caracas: Ministerio de Educación nacional de los Estados Unidos de Venezuela.

Bonno, Gabriel, *La Constitution britannique devant l'opinion française de Montesquieu à Bonaparte*, Paris: Champion, 1931.

Borsa, Giorgio, *La nascita del mondo moderno in Asia orientale. La penetrazione europea e la crisi delle società tradizionali in India, Cina e Giappone*, Milan: Rizzoli, 1977.

Bourne, Henry R. Fox, *The Life of John Locke*, 2 vols, Aalen: Scientia, 1969 [1876].

Bowman, Shearer Davis, *Masters and Lords: Mid-19th Century Planters and Prussian Junkers*, New York: OUP, 1993.

Brecher, Michael, *Nehru: A Political Biography*, London: OUP, 1959.

Brinkley, Joel, 'US Court Strikes Down Sodomy Ban', *International Herald Tribune*, 27 June, 2003.

Brogan, Hugh, Introduction to Alexis de Tocqueville, *Oeuvres completes*, ed. Jacob-Peter Mayer, Paris: Gallimard, 1951–, vol. 7, pt 2.

Brown, Dee, *Bury My Heart at Wounded Knee: An Indian History of the American West*, London: Barrie & Jenkins, 1970.

Brown, Richard Maxwell, *Strain of Violence: Historical Studies of American Violence and Vigilantism*, New York: OUP, 1975.

Buckle, George E., and William F. Monypenny, *The Life of Benjamin Disraeli Earl of Beaconsfield*, 6 vols, New York: Macmillan, 1914–20.

Burckhardt, Jacob, *Weltgeschichtliche Betrachtungen*, ed. Jacob Oeri, in *Gesammelte Werke*, vol. 4, Basel: Schwabe, 1978.

Burke, Edmund, *The Works: A New Edition*, 16 vols, London: Rivington, 1826.

——*Correspondence*, 10 vols, ed. Thomas W. Copeland and John A. Woods, Cambridge: CUP, 1958–78.

Calhoun, John C., *Union and Liberty: The Political Philosophy*, ed. R. M. Lence, Indianapolis: Liberty Classics, 1992.

Calloway, Colin G., *The American Revolution in Indian Country: Crisis and Diversity in Native American Communities*, Cambridge: CUP, 1995.

Cannadine, David, 'The Context, Performance and Meaning of Ritual: the British Monarchy and the "Invention of Tradition", c. 1820–1977', in Eric Hobsbawm and Terence Ranger, eds, *The Invention of Tradition*, Cambridge: CUP, 1983.

——*The Decline and Fall of the British Aristocracy*, New Haven and London: Yale University Press, 1990.

Cannon, John, *Aristocratic Century: The Peerage of Eighteenth-Century England*, Cambridge: CUP, 1984.

Carlyle, Thomas, *Latter-Day Pamphlets*, ed. Michael K. Goldberg and Jules P. Seigel, Ottawa: Canadian Federation for the Humanities and Social Sciences, 1983 [1850].

Casana Testore, Paola, and Narciso Nada, *L'età della Restaurazione. Reazione e rivoluzione in Europa*, 1814–1830, Turin: Loescher, 1981.

Casas, Bartolomé de las, *La leggenda nera. Storia proibita degli spagnoli nel Nuovo Mondo*, transl. Alberto Pincherle, Milan: Feltrinelli, 1981 [1906].

Castel, Robert, *Les métamorphoses de la question sociale. Une chronique du salariat*, Paris: Fayard, 1995.

Chevallier, Jean-Jacques, and André Jardin, *Introduction to Tocqueville*, *Oeuvres Complètes*, vol. 3, pt 1, 1962.

Clavière, Étienne, and Jacques-Pierre Brissot de Warville, *De la France et des États-Unis*, Preface by Marcel Dorigny, Paris: Éditions du CTHS, 1996 [1787].

Colley, Linda, *Captives: Britain, Empire and the World, 1600–1850*, London: Random House, 2002

Commager, Henry S., ed., *Documents of American History*, 2 vols, 7th edn, New York: Appleton-Century-Crofts, 1963 [1934].

——*Theodore Parker*, Gloucester, MA: Peter Smith, 1978 [1947].

Condorcet, Marie-Jean-Antoine, *Oeuvres*, 12 vols, ed. Arthur Condorcet O'Connor and François Arago, Stuttgart and Bad Cannstatt: Frommann-Holzboog, 1968 [1847–49].

Conner, Valerie Jean, *The National War Labor Board*, Chapel Hill: University of North Carolina Press, 1983.

Constant, Benjamin, *Mélanges de littérature et de politique*, 2 vols, Louvain: Michel, 1830.

——*Oeuvres*, ed. Alfred Roulin, Paris: Gallimard, 1957.

——*Recueil d'articles. 'Le Mercure', 'La Minerve', et 'La Renommée'*, 2 vols, ed. Éphraim Harpaz, Geneva: Droz, 1972.

——*Political Writings*, ed. and transl. Biancamaria Fontana, Cambridge: CUP, 1988.

——*De la force du gouvernement actuel de la France et de la nécessité de s'y rallier*, ed. Philippe Raynaud, Paris: Flammarion, 1988 [1796].

Costa, Emília Viotti da, *Crowns of Glory, Tears of Blood: The Demerara Slave Rebellion of 1823*, New York: OUP, 1994.

Cranston, Maurice, *John Locke: A Biography*, 2nd edn, London: Longman, 1959 [1957].

Creagh, Ronald, *Nos cousins d'Amérique. Histoire des Français aux États Unis*, Paris: Payot, 1988.

Davis, David B., *The Problem of Slavery in Western Culture*, Ithaca and New York: Cornell University Press, 1966.

——*The Problem of Slavery in the Age of Revolution, 1770–1823*, Ithaca: Cornell University Press, 1975.

——*The Slave Power Conspiracy and the Paranoid Style*, Baton Rouge: Louisiana State University Press, 1982 [1969].

——*Slavery and Human Progress*, Oxford and New York: OUP, 1986 [1984].

—— 'White Wives and Slave Mothers', *New York Review of Books*, 20 February, 1997.

—— 'A Big Business', *New York Review of Books*, 11 January, 1998.

Davis, Mike, *Late Victorian Holocausts: El Niño Famines and the Making of the Third World*, London and New York: Verso, 2001.

Defoe, Daniel, *Giving Alms No Charity, And Employing the Poor a Grievance to the Nation*, London, 1704.

Delanoë, Nelcya, and Joëlle Rostowski, *Les Indiens dans l'histoire américaine*, Nancy, Presses Universitaires de Nancy, 1991.

Diderot, Denis, *Oeuvres politiques*, ed. Paul Vernière, Paris: Garnier, 1963.

——*Saggio sui regni di Claudio e di Nerone e sui costume e gli scritti di Seneca*, transl. Secondo Carpanetto and Luciano Guerci, Palermo: Sellerio, 1987 [1782].

——*Réfutation suivie de l'ouvrage d'Helvétius intitulé 'L'homme'*, in *Oeuvres*, ed. Laurent Versini, vol. 1, Paris: Laffont, 1994.

Disraeli, Benjamin, *Tancred; or, The New Crusade*, 2 vols, Leipzig: Tauchniz, 1847.

——*Lord George Bentinck: A Political Biography*, 2nd edn, London: Colburn, 1852 [1851].

——*Endymion*, 2 vols, New York and London: Walter Dunne, 1976 [1880].

——*Coningsby; or, The New Generation*, ed. Sheila M. Smith, Oxford and New York: OUP, 1982 [1844].

Dockès, Pierre, 'Condorcet et l'esclavage des nègres', in Jean-Michel Servet, ed., *Les idées économiques sous la Révolution, 1789–1794*, Lyon: Presses Universitaires de Lyon, 1989.

Douglass, Frederick, 'What to the Slave is the Fourth of July', in Alice Moore Dunbar, ed., *Masterpieces of Negro Eloquence, 1818–1913*, Mineola, NY: Dover Publications, 2000 [1852].

Drescher, Seymour, *Capitalism and Antislavery: British Mobilization in Comparative Perspective*, Oxford and New York: OUP, 1987.

——*From Slavery to Freedom: Comparative Studies in the Rise and Fall of Atlantic Slavery*, London: Macmillan, 1999.

Du Bois, Willaim E. B., *Black Reconstruction in America: 1860–1880*, ed. David L. Lewis, New York: Atheneum, 1992 [1935].

Dumont, Étienne, Introduction, in Bentham *Oeuvres*, vol. 2, 1840.

Dunn, Richard S., 'The Glorious Revolution and America', in Nicholas Canny ed., *The Origins of Empire: British Overseas Enterprise to the Close of the Seventeenth Century*, Oxford and New York: OUP, 1998.

Dyer, Thomas G., *Theodore Roosevelt and the Idea of Race*, Baton Rouge: Louisiana State University Press, 1980.

Eggleston, Edward, *The Ultimate Solution of the American Negro Problem*, New York: AMS Press, 1973 [1913].

Elkins, Stanley M., *Slavery: A Problem in American Institutional and Intellectual Life*, Chicago: University of Chicago Press, 1959.

——and Eric McKitrick, *The Age of Federalism: The Early American Republic, 1788–1800*, New York: Oxford University Press, 1993.

Farrand, Max, ed., *The Records of the Federal Convention of 1787*, 4 vols, New Haven: Yale University Press, 1966 [1911–37].

Favilli, Paolo, *Riformismo e sindicalismo. Una teoria economica del movimento operaio: tra Turati e Graziadei*, Milan: Franco Angeli, 1984.

Faÿ, Bernard, *L'esprit révolutionnaire en France et aux États-Unis à la fin du XVIII siècle*, Paris: Champion, 1925.

Finkelman, Paul, *An Imperfect Union: Slavery, Federalism, and Comity*, 3rd edn, University of North Carolina Press, Chapel Hill, 1985 [1981].

——*Slavery and the Founders: Race and Liberty in the Age of Jefferson*, Armonk, NY: Sharpe, 1996.

Fitzhugh, George, *Sociology for the South; or, The Failure of Free Society*, Richmond: Morris, 1854.

Fogel, Robert William, *Without Consent or Contract: The Rise and Fall of American Slavery*, New York: Norton, 1991 [1989].

Foner, Eric, *Reconstruction: America's Unfinished Revolution*, 1863–1877, New York: Harper & Row, 1989 [1988].

——*The Story of American Freedom*, London: Picador, 1999.

Franklin, Benjamin, *Writings*, ed. J. A. Leo Lemay, New York: Library of America, 1987.

Franklin, John Hope, *From Slavery to Freedom: A History of Negro Americans*, 3rd edn, New York: Alfred A. Knopf, 1967 [1947].

Fredrickson, George M., *White Supremacy: A Comparative Study in American and South African History*, New York: OUP, 1982 [1981].

——*The Black Image in the White Mind: The Debate on Afro-American Character and Destiny*, 1817–1914, Hanover, NH: Wesleyan University Press, 1987 [1971].

——*Racism: A Short History*, Princeton: Princeton University Press, 2002.

—— 'America's Original Sin', *New York Review of Books*, 25 March, 2004.

Freidel, Frank, *Francis Lieber, Nineteenth-Century Liberal*, Gloucester, MA: Peter Smith, 1968 [1947].

Furet, François, *Il passato di un'illusione. L'idea comunista nel XX secolo*, ed. Marina Valensise, Milan: Mondadori, 1995.

——and Denis Richet, *La rivoluzione francese*, transl. Silvia Brilli Cattarini and Carla Patanè, Rome and Bari: Laterza, 1980 [1973].

Gauthier, Florence, *Triomphe et mort du droit naturel en Révolution*, Paris: Presses Universitaires de France, 1992.

Geertz, Clifford, 'Morality Tale', *New York Review of Books*, 7 October, 2004.

Geggus, David, 'British Opinion and the Emergence of Haiti, 1791–1805', in James Walvin ed., *Slavery and British Society, 1776–1846*, London: Macmillan, 1982.

Genovese, Eugene D., *The World the Slaveholders Made: Two Essays in Interpretation*, London: Allen Lane, 1970.

——*From Rebellion to Revolution: Afro-American Slave Revolts in the Making of the Modern World*, Baton Rouge: Louisiana State University Press, 1979.

——*A Consuming Fire: The Fall of the Confederacy in the Mind of the White Christian South*, Athens: University of Georgia Press, 1998.

—— 'Religion in the Collapse of the American Union', in Randall M. Miller, Harry S. Stout and Charles Reagan Wilson, eds, *Religion and the American Civil War*, Oxford and New York: OUP, 1998.

Gobineau, Arthur de, *Essai sur l'inégalité des races humaines*, 2 vols, 4th edn, Paris: Librairie de Paris, 1900 [1853–55].

Gossett, Thomas F., *Race: The History of an Idea in America*, New York: Schocken Books, 1965 [1963].

Gray, John, *Liberalism*, Milton Keynes: Open University Press, 1986.

Green, Thomas Hill, 'Lecture on Liberal Legislation and Freedom of Contract', in *Works*, ed. Richard L. Nettleship, vol. 3, 3rd edn, London: Longmans, Green & Co, 1973 [1881].

Grégoire, Henri, *De la noblesse de la peau, ou Du préjugé des blancs contre la couleur des Africains et celle de leurs descendants noirs et sang-mêlé*, Grenoble: Jérôme Millon, 1996 [1826].

——*An Enquiry Concerning the Intellectual and Moral Faculties, and Literature of Negroes*, transl. David Bailie Warden, Armonk, NY: Sharpe, 1997 [1809].

Grimal, Henri, *De l'Empire britannique au Commonwealth*, Paris: Colin, 1999 [1971].

Grimsted, David, *American Mobbing, 1828–1861: Toward Civil War*, New York: OUP, 1998.

Grotius, Hugo, *On the Truth of Christianity*, transl. J. Spencer Madan, London: Dodsby, 1782 [1639].

——*The Rights of War and Peace*, 3 vols, ed. Richard Tuck, Indianapolis: Liberty Fund, 2005 [1646].

Guillemin, Henri, *Benjamin Constant muscadin*, 1795–1799, 6th edn, Paris: Gallimard, 1958.

——*Madame de Staël, Benjamin Constant et Napoléon*, Paris: Plon, 1959.

——*La première résurrection de la République*, Paris: Gallimard, 1967.

Guizot, François, *General History of Civilisation in Europe*, Oxford and London: D. A. Talboys, 1837.

—— 'Discours sur l'histoire de la révolution d'Angleterre', in *Histoire de la révolution d'Angleterre*, Brussels: Société Typographique Belge, 1850 [1826].

——*Mélanges politiques et historiques*, Paris: Lévy, 1869.

Halévy, Élie, *The Growth of Philosophic Radicalism*, transl. Mary Morris, London: Faber & Faber, 1972 [1901–04].

Hamilton, Alexander, *Writings*, ed. Joanne B. Freeman, New York: Library of America, 2001.

Hanke, Lewis, *Aristotle and the American Indians: A Study in Race Prejudice in the Modern World*, London: Hollis & Carter, 1959.

Harris, Ronald W., *England in the Eighteenth Century, 1689–1793*, London: Blandford Press, 1963.

Hauptman, Laurence M., *Between Two Fires: American Indians in the Civil War*, New York: Free Press, 1995.

Hayek, Friedrich A., *The Constitution of Liberty*, London: Routledge & Kegan Paul, 1960.

——*New Studies in Philosophy, Politics, Economics and the History of Ideas*, London: Routledge & Kegan Paul, 1978.

——*Law, Legislation and Liberty: A New Statement of the Liberal Principles of Justice and Political Economy*, London: Routledge & Kegan Paul, 1982 [1973–79].

——*The Fatal Conceit: The Errors of Socialism*, ed. William Warren Bartley III, London: Routledge, 1990 [1988].

Hegel, Georg W. F., *Werke*, 20 vols, ed. Eva Moldenhauer and Karl Markus Michel, Frankfurt am Main: Suhrkamp, 1969–79.

Helvétius, Claude-Adrien, *De l'homme*, in *Ouevres complètes*, vols 7–12, Hildesheim: Olms, 1967–69 [1773].

Hill, Christopher, *The Century of Revolution: 1603–1714*, New York: Norton, 1961.

——*Reformation to Industrial Revolution*, Harmondsworth: Penguin, 1969 [1967].

Himmelfarb, Gertrude, *The Idea of Poverty: England in the Early Industrial Age*, New York: Vintage Books, 1985 [1983].

Hinde, Wendy, *Richard Cobden: A Victorian Outsider*, New Haven: Yale University Press, 1987.

Hobhouse, Leonard Trelawney, *Liberalism*, introd. Alan P. Grimes, London and New York: OUP, 1977 [1911].

Hobson, J. A., *Imperialism: A Study*, 3rd edn, London: Unwin Hyman, 1988 [1902].

Hocquellet, Richard, 'Crise de la monarchie hispanique et question coloniale (1793–

1814)', in Yves Benot and Marcel Dorigny, eds, *1802, Rétablissement de l'esclavage dans les colonies françaises*, Paris: Maisonneuve et Larose, 2003.

Hofstadter, Richard, *Social Darwinism in American Thought*, Philadelphia: University of Pennsylvania Press, 1944.

———*The American Political Tradition and the Men Who Made It*, New York: Knopf, 1951.

———ed., *Great Issues in American History*, 3 vols, New York: Vintage Books (vol. 1 in collaboration with Clarence L. Ver Steeg; vol. 3 in collaboration with Beatrice K. Hofstadter), 1958–82.

Horsman, Reginald, *Race and Manifest Destiny: The Origins of American Racial Anglo-Saxonism*, Cambridge, MA: Harvard University Press, 1981.

Howell, George, 'Liberty for Labour', in Herbert Spencer *et al.*, *A Plea for Liberty: An Argument against Socialism and Socialistic Legislation*, Indianapolis: Liberty Classics, 1981 [1891].

Hughes, Robert, *The Fatal Shore: A History of the Transportation of Convicts to Australia, 1787–1868*, London: Collins Harvill, 1987 [1986].

Hume, David, The History of England, 6 vols, Indianapolis: Liberty Classics, 1983–85 [1778].

———*Essays, Moral, Political, and Literary*, 2nd edn, Indianapolis: Liberty Classics, 1987 [1772].

Jacquin, Philippe, *Storia degli indiani d'America*, transl. Franco Moccia, Milan: Mondadori, 1977 [1976].

Jaffe, Hosea, Sudafrica. *Storia politica: dal razzismo legale al razzismo illegale*, new edn, transl. Alda Carrer and Davide Danti, Milan: Jaca Book, 1997 [1980].

Jardin, André, *Alexis de Tocqueville, 1805–1859*, Paris: Hachette, 1984.

Jefferson, Thomas, *Writings*, ed. Merrill D. Peterson, New York: Library of America, 1984.

———*The Republic of Letters: The Correspondence between Thomas Jefferson and James Madison, 1776–1826*, 3 vols, ed. James Morton Smith, New York: Norton, 1995.

Jennings, Francis, *The Creation of America: Through Revolution to Empire*, Cambridge and New York: CUP, 2000.

Jernegan, Marcus W., *Laboring and Dependent Classes in Colonial America: 1607–1783*, Westport, CT: Greenwood Press, 1980 [1931].

Johnson, Walter, *Soul by Soul: Life inside the Antebellum Slave Market*, Cambridge, MA: Harvard University Press, 1999.

Jordan, Winthrop D., *White over Black: American Attitudes towards the Negro, 1550–1812*, New York: Norton, 1977 [1968].

Kirk, Russell, *John Randolph of Roanoke: A Study in American Politics*, Indianapolis: Liberty Press, 1978.

Kissinger, Henry, *Diplomacy*, New York: Simon & Schuster, 1994.

Klein, Herbert S., *Slavery in the Americas: A Comparative Study of Virginia and Cuba*, Chicago: Dee, 1989 [1967].

Kraditor, Aileen S., *Means and Ends in American Abolitionism: Garrison and His Critics on Strategy and Tactics, 1834–1850*, Chicago: Dee, 1989 [1967].

Kühl, Stefan, *The Nazi Connection: Eugenics, American Racism, and German National Socialism*, New York: OUP, 1994.

Laboulaye, Édouard, *De la Constitution américaine et de l'utilité de son étude*, Paris: Hennuyer, 1850.

——*Le parti libéral. Son programme et son avenir*, Paris: Charpentier, 1863.

——*L'état et ses limites suivi d'essais politiques*, Paris: Charpentier, 1863.

——*Histoire des États-Unis, depuis les premiers essais de colonisation jusqu'à l'adoption de la Constitution fédérale, 1620–1789*, 3 vols, Paris: Charpentier, 1866.

Lacoste, Yves, André Nouschi, and André Prenant, *L'Algérie, passé et présent. Le cadre et les étapes de la constitution de l'Algérie actuelle*, Paris: Éditions Sociales, 1960.

Langley, Lester D., *The Americas in the Age of Revolution: 1750–1850*, New Haven: Yale University Press, 1996.

Lauber, Almon Wheeler, *Indian Slavery in Colonial Times within the Present Limits of the United States*, Williamstown, MA: Corner House, 1979 [1913].

Laurent, Alain, *Storia dell'individualismo*, transl. Maria Cristiana Marinelli, Bologna: Il Mulino, 1994 [1993].

Lecky, William E. H., *A History of England in the Eighteenth Century*, 8 vols, 3rd edn, London: Longmans, Green & Co., 1883–88.

——*Historical and Political Essays*, London: Longmans, Green & Co., 1910 [1896].

——*Democracy and Liberty*, 2 vols, Indianapolis: Liberty Classics, 1981 [1896].

Lefebvre, Georges, *La France sous le Directoire, 1795–1799*, Paris: Éditions Sociales, 1984 [1942–43].

Lence, Ross M., Foreword to Calhoun, *Union and Liberty*.

Lieber, Francis, *Erinnerungen aus meinem Zusammenleben mit Georg Berthold Niebuhr, dem Geschichtsschreiber Roms*, transl. Karl Thibaut, Heidelberg: Winter, 1837.

——*Civil Liberty and Self-Government*, 2nd edn, Philadelphia: Lippincott, 1859.

—— 'Anglican and Gallican Liberty', *New Individualist Review*, vol. IV, no. 2, 1966 [1848].

Lincoln, Abraham, *Speeches and Writings*, 2 vols, ed. Don E. Fehrenbacher, New York: Library of America, 1989.

Litwack, Leon F., *North of Slavery: The Negro in the Free States, 1790–1860*, Chicago: University of Chicago Press, 1961.

——*Trouble in Mind: Black Southerners in the Age of Jim Crow*, New York: Knopf, 1998.

Locke, John, *The Conduct of the Understanding*, Edinburgh: William & Robert Chambers, 1839 [1706].

——*Two Treatises of Government*, ed. William S. Carpenter, London and New York: Everyman's Library, 1924 [1690].

——*Two Tracts on Government*, ed. Philip Abrams, Cambridge: CUP, 1967 [1660].

——*An Essay Concerning Human Understanding*, ed. Peter H. Nidditch, Oxford: OUP, 1975.

——*The Correspondence*, 8 vols, ed. Esmond S. De Beer, Oxford: Clarendon Press, 1976–89.

——*Political Writings*, ed. David Wootton, London and New York: Penguin, 1993.

Logan, Rayford W., *The Betrayal of the Negro: From Rutherford B. Hayes to Woodrow Wilson*, New York: Da Capo Press, 1997 [1954].

Lorimer, Douglas A., *Colour, Class and the Victorians: English Attitudes to the Negro in the Mid-Eighteenth Century*, Leicester: Leicester University Press, 1978.

Losurdo, Domenico, *Autocensura e compromesso nel pensiero politico di Kant*, Naples: Bibliopolis, 1983.

——*Democrazia o bonapartismo. Trionfo e decadenza del suffragio universale*, Turin: Bollati Boringhieri, 1993.

——*La Seconda Repubblica. Liberalismo, federalismo, postfascismo*, Turin: Bollati Boringhieri, 1994.

——*Il revisionismo storico. Problemi e miti*, Rome and Bari: Laterza, 1996.

——*Antonio Gramsci dal liberalismo al 'comunismo critico'*, Rome: Gamberetti, 1997.

——*Heidegger and the Ideology of War: Community, Death and the West*, transl. Marella and Jon Morris, Amherst, NY: Humanity Books, 2001 [1991].

——*Nietzsche, il ribelle aristocratico. Biografia intellettuale e bilancio critico*, Turin: Bollati Boringhieri, 2002.

——*Hegel and the Freedom of the Moderns*, transl. Marella and Jon Morris, Durham (NC) and London: Duke University Press, 2004 [1992].

Lovejoy, Arthur O., *The Great Chain of Being: A Study of the History of an Idea*, Cambridge, MA: Harvard University Press, 1957.

Macaulay, Thomas Babington, *Critical and Historical Essays, contributed to the 'Edinburgh Review'*, 5 vols, Leipzig: Tauchnitz, 1850.

——*The History of England*, ed. Hugh Trevor-Roper, abridged edn, London: Penguin, 1986 [1848–61].

Mackay, Thomas, Introduction to Howell, 1981.

Mackintosh, James, *Vindiciae gallicae: Defence of the French Revolution*, Oxford: Woodstock, 1989 [1791].

MacLean, Nancy, *Behind the Mask of Chivalry: The Making of the Second Ku Klux Klan*, New York: OUP, 1994.

Macpherson, C. B., *The Political Theory of Possessive Individualism*, Oxford: OUP, 1962.

Mahan, Alfred Thayer, *The Problem of Asia*, New Brunswick, NJ: Transaction Publishers, 2003 [1900].

Maine, Henry S., *Popular Government*, ed. George W. Carey, Indianapolis: Liberty Classics, 1976 [1885].

Malouet, Pierre-Victor, *Mémoire sur l'esclavage des nègres*, Neufchâtel, 1788.

Malthus, Thomas Robert, *An Essay on the Principle of Population*, 2 vols, ed. Patricia Joyce, Cambridge: CUP and Royal Economic Society, 1989 [1798].

Mandeville, Bernard de, *The Fable of the Bees*, 2 vols, ed. Frederick B. Kaye, Indianapolis: Liberty Classics, 1988 [1705].

Marshall, T. H., *Citizenship and Social Class and Other Essays*, Cambridge: CUP, 1950.

Martin, Jean-Pierre, and Daniel Royot, *Histoire et civilisation des États-Unis. Textes et documents commentés du XVIIe siècle à nos jours*, Paris: Nathan, 1989.

Marx, Karl, *Manuskripte über die polnische Frage (1864–1864)*, ed. Werner Conze and Dieter Hertz-Eichenrode, The Hague: Mouton, 1961.

——*Secret Diplomatic History of the Eighteenth Century and The Story of the Life of Lord Palmerston*, ed. Lester Hutchinson, London: Lawrence & Wishart, 1971.

——*Early Writings*, Harmondsworth: Penguin, 1975.

——*Capital: Volume One*, transl. Ben Fowkes, Harmondsworth: Penguin, 1976 [1867].

——and Frederick Engels, *Werke*, 38 vols, Berlin: Dietz, 1955–89.

——and Frederick Engels, *Selected Works*, vol. 1, Moscow: Progress Publishers, 1969.

Mazzini, Giuseppe, *Note autobiografiche*, ed. Roberto Pertici, Milan: Rizzoli, 1986 [1861–66].

Mercier, Louis-Sébastien, *L'An deux mille quatre cent quarante. Rêve s'il en fût jamais*, ed. Raymond Trousson, Bordeaux: Ducros, 1971 [1771].

Merriam, Charles Edward, *A History of American Political Theories*, New York: Kelley, 1969 [1903].

Mill, John Stuart, *Collected Works*, 33 vols, ed. John M. Robson, Toronto and London: University of Toronto Press and Routledge & Kegan Paul, 1963–91.

——*Utilitarianism, Liberty, Representative Government*, ed. Harry B. Acton, London: Dent, 1972.

Millar, John, *The Origin of the Distinction of Ranks*, reprint of 4th edn, Aalen: Scientia, 1986 [1771].

Mises, Ludwig von, *Die Gemeinwirtschaft. Untersuchungen über den Sozialismus*, Jena: Fischer, 1922.

——*Liberalism: The Classical Tradition*, Indianapolis: Liberty Fund, 2005 [1927].

Mohl, Robert von, 'Gwerbe- und Fabrikwesen', in Lothar Gall and Rainer Koch, eds, *Der europäische Liberalismus im 19. Jahrhundert*, vol. 4, Frankfurt am Main: Ullstein, 1981 [1838].

Montagu, Ashley, *Man's Most Dangerous Myth: The Fallacy of Race*, 3rd edn, New York: Harper & Bros, 1952 [1942].

Montaigne, Michel de, *The Complete Essays*, ed. and transl. M. A. Screech, London: Penguin, 2003 [1580–88].

Montesquieu, Charles-Louis, *Oeuvres complètes*, 2 vols, ed. Roger Caillois, Paris: Gallimard, 1949–51.

——*The Spirit of the Laws*, transl. and ed. Anne M. Cohler, Basia Carolyn Miller and Harold Samuel Stone, Cambridge: CUP, 1989 [1748].

Moore Jr., Barrington, *The Social Origins of Dictatorship and Democracy: Lord and Peasant in the Making of the Modern World*, Boston: Beacon Press, 1966.

Morgan, Edmund S., 'Slavery and Freedom: The American Paradox', *The Journal of American History*, vol. LIX, no. 1, 1972.

——*American Slavery, American Freedom: The Ordeal of Colonial Virginia*, New York: Norton, 1995 [1975].

Morison, Samuel E., ed., *Sources and Documents Illustrating the American Revolution, 1764–1788, and the Formation of the Federal Constitution*, 2nd edn, Oxford: Clarendon Press, 1953 [1923].

Morris, Jan, *Pax Britannica*, 3 vols, London: Folio Society, 1992.

Mounier, Jean-Joseph, *De l'influence attribuée aux philosophes, aux francs-maçons et aux illuminés sur la révolution de France*, Tübingen: Cotta, 1801.

Muir, Ramsay, ed., *The Making of British India 1756–1858*, Lahore: OUP, 1969 [1915].

Nevins, Allan, and Henry S. Commager, *America: Story of a Free People*, Oxford: OUP, 1943.

Noer, Thomas J., *Briton, Boer and Yankee: The United States and South Africa, 1870–1914*, Kent, OH: Kent State University Press, 1978.

Nolte, Ernst, *Three Faces of Fascism*, transl. Leila Vennewitz, New York: Mentor, 1969 [1963].

Office d'Information, *Les droits de l'homme en Chine*, Beijing: Office d'information du Conseil des affaires d'État de la République Populaire Chinoise, 1991.

O'Sullivan, John, 'Annexation', *United States Magazine and Democratic Review*, vol. 4, July, 1845.

Pagden, Anthony, 'The Struggle for Legitimacy and the Image of Empire in the Atlantic to c. 1700', in Nicholas Canny, ed., *The Origins of Empire: British Overseas Enterprise to the Close of the Seventeenth Century*, Oxford and New York: OUP, 1998.

Paine, Thomas, *Collected Writings*, ed. Eric Foner, New York: Library of America, 1995.

Pakenham, Thomas, *The Year of Liberty: The Story of the Great Irish Rebellion of 1798*, New York: Random House, 1969.

Palmer, Robert R., *The Age of Democratic Revolution: A Political History of Europe and America, 1760–1800*, 2 vols, Princeton: Princeton University Press, 1959–64.

Pareto, Vilfredo, 'L'éclipse de la liberté', in Mythes et idéologies, ed. Giovanni Busino, Geneva: Droz, 1966 [1903].

——*Trasformazione della democrazia*, ed. Emanuela Susca, introd. Domenico Losurdo, Rome: Editori Riuniti, 1999 [1920].

Parrington, Vernon L., *Main Currents in American Thought: An Interpretation of American Literature from the Beginning to 1920*, 3 vols, New York: Harcourt, Brace & Co., 1930.

Perrot, Michelle, Introduction to Tocqueville, *Oeuvres Complètes* vol. 4, pt 1.

Pick, Daniel, *War Machine: The Rationalisation of Slaughter in the Modern Age*, New Haven and London: Yale University Press, 1993.

Pocock, J. G. A., *The Machiavellian Moment: Florentine Political Thought and the Atlantic Republican Tradition*, Princeton: Princeton University Press, 1975.

——*Virtue, Commerce, and History*, Cambridge: CUP, 1988 [1985].

Poliakov, Léon, *The Aryan Myth: A History of Racist and Nationalist Ideas in Europe*, transl. Edmund Howard, London: Sussex University Press and Heinemann Educational Books, 1974 [1971].

——*The History of Anti-Semitism*, transl. Richard Howard, Natalie Gerardie and Miriam Kochan, London: Routledge & Kegan Paul, 1974–75 [1955–68].

Post, C. Gordon, Introduction to John C. Calhoun, *A Disquisition on Government*, New York: Liberal Arts Press, 1953.

Potier, Jean-Pierre, 'L'Assemblé Constituante et la question de la liberté du travail', in Jean-Michel Servet, ed., *Les idées économiques sous la révolution, 1789–1794*, Lyon: Presses Universitaires de Lyon, 1989.

Potter-Mackinnon, Janice, *The Liberty We Seek: Loyalist Ideology in Colonial New York and Massachusetts*, Cambridge, MA: Harvard University Press, 1983.

Proudhon, Pierre-Joseph, *La giustizia nella rivoluzione e nella Chiesa*, ed. Mario Albertini, Turin: UTET, 1968 [1858].

Quinet, Edgar, *Le Christianisme et la Révolution française*, Paris: Fayard, 1984 [1845].

Raynal, Guillaume-Thomas, *Histoire philosophique et politique des Deux Indes*, ed. Yves Benot, Paris: Maspero 1981 [1781] (the 3rd edn of 1781 contains an expansion of Diderot's contribution).

Renan, Ernest, *Oeuvre complètes*, ed. Henriette Psichari, Paris: Calmann-Lévy, 1947–.

Rice, C. Duncan, 'The Missionary Context of the British Anti-Slavery Movement', in James Walvin, ed., *Slavery and British Society, 1776–1846*, London: Macmillan, 1982.

Robespierre, Maximilien de, *Oeuvres*, 10 vols, Paris: Presses Universitaires de France, 1912–67.

Rochau, August Ludwig von, *Grundsätze der Realpolitik*, ed. Hans-Ulrich Wehler, Frankfurt am Main: Ullstein, 1972 [1853–69].

Rogalla von Bieberstein, Johannes, *Die These von der Verschwörung, 1776–1945*, Bern and Frankfurt am Main: Lang, 1976.

Roosevelt, Theodore, *The Strenuous Life: Essays and Addresses*, New York: Century, 1901.

——*Letters*, ed. Elting E. Morison and John M. Blum, 8 vols, Cambridge, MA: Harvard University Press, 1951–54.

Rousseau, Jean-Jacques, 'Discours sur l'économie politique', in *Oeuvres complètes*, ed. Bernard Gagnebin and Marcel Raymond, vol. 3, Paris: Gallimard, 1964 [1755].

Ryerson, Egerton, *The Loyalists of America and Their Times: From 1620 to 1816*, 2 vols, New York: Haskell House, 1970 [1880].

Sala-Molins, Louis, *Le Code noir, ou Le calvaire de Canaan*, 2nd edn, Paris: Presses Universitaires de France, 1988 [1987].

Salbstein, Michael C. N., *The Emancipation of the Jews in Britain: The Question of the Admission of the Jews to Parliament, 1820–1860*, London and Toronto: Associated University Presses, 1982.

Salvadori, Massimo L., *Potere e libertà nel mondo moderno. John C. Calhoun: un genio imbarazzante*, Rome and Bari: Laterza, 1996.

Sandoz, Ellis, ed., *Political Sermons of the American Founding Era: 1730–1805*, Indianapolis: Liberty Press, 1991.

Sartori, Giovanni, *Democrazia e definizioni*, 4th edn, Bologna: Il Mulino, 1976.

——*The Theory of Democracy Revisited*, Chatham, NJ: Chatham House Publishers, 1976.

Scheel, Wolfgang, *Das 'Berliner politische Wochenblatt' und die politische und soziale Revolution in Frankreich und England*, Göttingen: Musterschmidt, 1964.

Schlesinger Jr, Arthur M., ed., *History of US Political Parties*, New York and London: Chelsea House & Bawker, 1973.

Schmid, Thomas, 'Australiens Holocaust', *Die Zeit*, 31 May 2000.

Schoelcher, Victor, *Esclavage et colonisation*, ed. Émile Tersen, Paris: Presses Universitaires de France, 1948.

——*Des colonies françaises. Abolition immédiate de l'esclavage*, Paris: Éditions du CTHS, 1998 [1842].

Schröder, Hans-Christoph, *Die Revolutionen Englands im 17. Jahrundert*, Frankfurt am Main: Suhrkamp, 1986.

Senior, Nassau William, *Journals Kept in France and Italy from 1848 to 1852*, 2 vols, ed. M. C. M. Simpson, London: Henry S. King & Co., 1871.

——*Three Lectures on the Rate of Wages*, 2nd edn, New York: Kelley, 1966 [1831].

Shain, Barry Alan, *The Myth of American Individualism: The Protestant Origins of American Political Thought*, Princeton: Princeton University Press, 1994.

Sidney, Algernon, *Discourses Concerning Government*, ed. Thomas G. West, Indianapolis: Liberty Classics, 1990 [1698].

Sieyès, Emmanuel-Joseph, *Écrits politiques*, ed. Roberto Zapperi, Paris: Éditions des archives contemporaines, 1985.

Skinner, Quentin, *Liberty Before Liberalism*, Cambridge: CUP, 1998.

Slotkin, Richard, *The Fatal Environment: The Myth of the Frontier in the Age of Industrialization, 1800–1890*, New York: Harper Perennial, 1994 [1985].

Smith, Adam, *An Inquiry into the Nature and Causes of the Wealth of Nations*, Indianapolis: Liberty Classics, 1981 [1776] (reprint of 3rd edn of 1783).

——*Lectures on Jurisprudence*, Indianapolis: Liberty Classics, 1982.

——*Correspondence*, ed. Ernest Campbell Mossner and Ian Simpson Ross, Indianapolis: Liberty Classics, 1987.

Sombart, Werner, *Der moderne Kapitalismus*, 3 vols, Munich: DTV, 1987 (reprint of 2nd edn of 1916–27).

Spence, Jonathan D., *The Chan's Great Continent: China in Western Minds*, New York: Norton, 1998.

Spencer, Herbert, *Social Statics*, New York: Appleton, 1877 [1850].

——*The Principles of Ethics*, 2 vols, ed. Tibor R. Machan, Indianapolis: Liberty Classics, 1978 [1879–93].

——*The Man versus the State: With Six Essays on Government*, Society, and Freedom, Indianapolis: Liberty Classics, 1981 [1843–84].

——*The Life and Letters of Herbert Spencer*, ed. David Duncan, London: Routledge and Thoemmes Press, 1996 [1908].

Spini, Giorgio, *Storia dell'età moderna*, 6th edn, Turin: Einaudi, 1982 [1965].

Staël-Holstein, Germaine de, *Considérations sur la Révolution française*, ed. Jacques Godechot, Paris: Tallandier, 1983 [1818].

Stannard, David E., *American Holocaust: Columbus and the Conquest of the New World*, New York and Oxford: OUP, 1992.

Stevenson, Brenda, *Life in Black and White: Family and Community in the Slave South*, New York: OUP, 1996.

Strong, Josiah, *Our Country*, Cambridge, MA: Belknap Press of Harvard University Press, 1963 [1885].

Stuart, Reginald C., *United States Expansionism and British North America: 1775–1871*, Chapel Hill: University of South Carolina Press, 1988.

Sullivan, Eileen P., 'Liberalism and Imperialism: J. S. Mill's Defense of the British Empire', *Journal of the History of Ideas*, vol. 4, 1983.

Sumner, William Graham, *On Liberty, Society, and Politics*, ed. Robert C. Bannister, Indianapolis: Liberty Classics, 1992.

Tawney, Richard H., *Religion and the Rise of Capitalism: A Historical Study*, West Drayton: Pelican, 1948 [1926].

Taylor, A. J. P., *English History 1914–1945*, Oxford: OUP, 1992 [1965].

Thomas, Hugh, *The Slave Trade: The Story of the Atlantic Slave Trade, 1440–1870*, New York: Simon & Schuster, 1997.

Thompson, E. P., *Whigs and Hunters: The Origin of the Black Act*, Harmondsworth: Penguin, 1977 [1975].

——*The Making of the English Working Class*, London and New York: Penguin, 1988 [1963].

Tilly, Charles, *European Revolutions, 1492–1992*, Oxford and Cambridge, MA: Blackwell, 1993.

Tinker, Hugh, *A New System of Slavery: The Export of Indian Labour Overseas, 1830–1920*, London and New York: OUP, 1974.

Tocqueville, Alexis de, *Oeuvres complètes*, ed. Jacob-Peter Mayer, Paris: Gallimard, 1951–.

——*The Ancien Régime and the French Revolution*, transl. Stuart Gilbert, introd. Hugh Brogan, London: Fontana, 1966 [1856].

——*Democracy in America*, introd. Alan Ryan, London: Everyman's Library, 1994 [1835–40].

Todorov, Tzvetan, *The Conquest of America: The Question of the Other*, transl. Richard Howard, London: Harper Perennial, 1992 [1982].

Tóibín, Colm, 'The Tragedy of Roger Casement', *New York Review of Books*, 27 May, 2004.

Townsend, Joseph, *A Dissertation on the Poor Laws by a Well-Wisher to Mankind*, Berkeley: University of California Press, 1971 [1786].

Toynbee, A. J., *A Study of History*, vol. 1, London and New York: OUP, 1962 [1934–54].

Treitschke, Heinrich von, 'Der Bonapartismus', *Preussische Jahrbücher*, vol. 16, 1865.

—— 'Die Freiheit', in *Historische und politische Aufsätze*, vol. 3, Leipzig: Hirzel, 1886 [1861].

——*Politik.Vorlesungen gehalten an der Universität zu Berlin*, 2 vols, ed. Max Cornicelius, Leipzig: Hirzel, 1897–98.

Trevelyan, George M., *British History in the Nineteenth Century and After (1782–1919)*, London: Longmans, Green & Co., 1937 [1922].

——*History of England*, London: Longmans, Green & Co., 1945.

Tucker, Josiah, *Collected Works*, London: Routledge and Thoemmes Press, 1993–96 [1775–82].

Tudesq, André-Jean, *Les grands notables en France (1840–1849)*, Paris: Presses Universitaires de France, 1964.

Turner, Frederick Jackson, 'The Significance of the Frontier in American History', in *The Significance of the Frontier in American History and Other Essays*, ed. John Mack Faragher, New York: Holt, 1994 [1893].

Van den Berghe, Pierre L., *Race and Racism: A Comparative Perspective*, New York: Wiley, 1967.

Venturi, Franco, *Settecento riformatore*, 5 vols, Turin: Einaudi, 1969–90.

Villari, Pasquale, *Dai carteggi*, ed. Maria Luisa Cicalese, Rome: Istituto storico per l'età moderna e contemporanea, 1984.

Voltaire, *Essai sur les moeurs et l'esprit des nations*, 2 vols, ed. René Pomeau, Paris: Garnier, 1963 [1751].

——*Candide and Other Stories*, transl. and introd. Roger Pearson, London: Everyman's Library, 1992 [1759].

——*Philosophical Letters*, transl. Ernest Dilworth, Mineola, NY: Dover Publications, 2003 [1734].

Wakefield, Edward Gibbon, *The Collected Works of Edward Gibbon Wakefield*, ed. M. F. Lloyd Prichard, London and Glasgow: Collins, 1968.

Wallerstein, Immanuel, *The Modern World System*, 3 vols, New York: Academic Press, 1974–89.

Wallon, Henri-Alexandre, Introduction to *Histoire de l'esclavage dans l'antiquité*, vol. 1, Aalen: Scientia, 1974 [1879].

Wang, Nora, Xin Ye, and Lou Wang, *Victor Hugo et le sac du Palais d'été*, Paris: Indes savants, 2003.

Washburn, Wilcomb E., *The Indian in America*, New York: Harper & Row, 1975.

Washington, George, *A Collection*, ed. William B. Allen, Indianapolis: Liberty Classics, 1988.

Weber, Max, 'Der Sinn der "Wertfreiheit" der soziologischen und ökonomischen Wissenschaften', in *Methodologische Schriften. Studiensausgabe*, ed. Johannes Winckelmann, Frankfurt am Main: Fischer, 1968 [1917].

Wiener, Joel H., *Great Britain: The Lion at Home—A Documentary History of Domestic Policy, 1689–1973*, New York: Chelsea House, 1983.

Wilberforce, Robert Isaac, *The Life of William Wilberforce, by His Sons*, 5 vols, London: Murray, 1838.

Williams, Eric E., *From Columbus to Castro: The History of the Caribbean, 1492–1969*, New York and Evanston: Harper & Row, 1970.

——*British Historians and the West Indies*, New York: Africana Publishing Corporation, 1972 [1964].

——*Capitalism and Slavery*, London: Deutsch, 1990 [1942].

Williamson, Joel, *New People: Miscegenation and Mulattos in the United States*, New York: Free Press, 1980.

Wills, Garry, *'Negro President': Jefferson and the Slave Power*, Boston: Houghton Mifflin, 2003.

Wolf, Eric R., *Europe and the Peoples without History*, Berkeley: University of California Press, 1982.

Wood, Forrest G., *Black Scare: The Racist Response to Emancipation and Reconstruction*, Berkeley: University of California Press, 1968.

Wood, Gordon S., 'What Slavery Was Really Like', *New York Review of Books*, 18 November, 2004.

Woodward, C. Vann, *Origins of the New South 1877–1913*, Louisiana State University Press and Littlefield Fund for Southern History, University of Texas, 1951.

——*The Strange Career of Jim Crow*, 2nd edn, New York: OUP, 1966 [1955].

—— 'Dangerous Liaison', *New York Review of Books*, 19 February, 1998.

Zilversmit, Arthur, *The First Emancipation: The Abolition of Slavery in the North*, 3rd edn, Chicago: University of Chicago Press, 1969 [1967].

Zimmer, Anne Y., *Jonathan Boucher, Loyalist in Exile*, Detroit: Wayne State University Press, 1978.

Zitomersky, Joseph, 'Culture, classe ou État? Comment interpréter les relations raciales dans la Grande Louisiane française avant et après 1803?', in Marcel Dorigny and Marie-Jeanne Rossignol, eds, *La France et les Amériques au temps de Jefferson et de Miranda*, Paris: Société des études robespierristes, 2001.

Zuckerman, Michael, *Almost Chosen People: Oblique Biographies in the American Grain*, Berkeley: University of California Press, 1993.

Index